Human Competence and Business Development
Emerging Patterns in European Companies

Springer
London
Berlin
Heidelberg
New York
Barcelona
Budapest
Hong Kong
Milan
Paris
Santa Clara
Singapore
Tokyo

Peter Docherty and Barry Nyhan (Eds)

Human Competence and Business Development
Emerging Patterns in European Companies

Springer

Peter Docherty, PhD, Dsc
Associate Professor,
Institute for Management of Innovation and Technology,
Stockholm School of Economics, Box 6501, S-113 83 Stockholm, Sweden

Barry Nyhan, B Phil, M Ed
Senior Researcher,
European Centre for Work and Society,
35 Rue des Deux Eglises, B-1040 Brussels, Belgium

ISBN-13: 978-3-540-19972-4   e-ISBN-13: 978-1-4471-0915-0
DOI: 10.1007/978-1-4471-0915-0

British Library Cataloguing in Publication Data
Human competence and business development : emerging patterns in European companies
1. Employees – Training of – European Union countries 2. Organisational learning – European Union countries
I. Docherty, Peter II. Nyhan, Barry
658.3'124'094
ISBN 3540199721

Library of Congress Cataloging-in-Publication Data
A catalog record for this book is available from the Library of Congress

Apart from any fair dealing for the purposes of research or private study, or criticism or review, as permitted under the Copyright, Designs and Patents Act 1988, this publication may only be reproduced, stored or transmitted, in any form or by any means, with the prior permission in writing of the publishers, or in the case of reprographic reproduction in accordance with the terms of licences issued by the Copyright Licensing Agency. Enquiries concerning reproduction outside those terms should be sent to the publishers.

© Springer-Verlag London Limited 1997
Softcover reprint of the hardcover 1st edition 1997

The use of registered names, trademarks etc. in this publication does not imply, even in the absence of a specific statement, that such names are exempt from the relevant laws and regulations and therefore free for general use.

The publisher makes no representation, express or implied, with regard to the accuracy of the information contained in this book and cannot accept any legal responsibility or liability for any errors or omissions that may be made.

Typesetting: camera ready by editors

34/3830-543210 Printed on acid-free paper

Foreword

European competitiveness in a global perspective is a major issue on the agenda of the European Union and European industry. The question of competitiveness is often related to continual technological change and changing work structures to create more flexible and adaptive work places. But these changes are in themselves insufficient to meet the demands of a turbulent business environment, if they are not brought about in close relationship with and anchored to the development of the human resource potential. Technological innovation and modern post-Tayloristic work structures place new demands on workers. Workers' abilities and competencies must be raised in virtually every sphere – in what are termed the new key/core competencies related to knowledge and cognitive skills, social skills, general and work related personality characteristics together with a high level of technological ability. At the same time, to make optimal use of the human potential, the way in which work is organised and accordingly the way in which people are managed, must allow workers to develop and use the required competencies. An integrated Human Resource Development approach is needed in which workers abilities and competencies take a central place. European competitiveness, from this perspective, implies a strategic choice by European companies and policy makers to invest in people and their (potential) abilities.

This publication addresses the question whether a new European organisational paradigm is emerging in which competitiveness is reached through learning and competence development. In answering this question, case studies were carried out across European manufacturing industry. Although the manufacturing sector throughout Europe is declining in terms of jobs, it still accounts for some 28% of the total employment volume. The high level of technological innovation and the changing service orientation within the sector and the subsequent necessity for new competencies provide us with excellent examples of fundamental organisational change in order to increase competitiveness. The cases in the book can also be regarded as descriptions of stages in a development process, leading to a new paradigm in work organisations. Putting it differently, they can be viewed as descriptions of phases in the development towards an organisational culture incorporating learning and competence development as natural cornerstones.

The seeds of the ideas and concepts developed in this book can be traced to the launch in 1988 of the Work and Learning Programme[1] by the European Centre for Work and Society (ECWS). This dealt with the growing need for the integration of work and learning and examined some of the risks involved in the implementation of such an approach. It recognised, very much ahead of its time, the dramatic and revolutionary developments of the workplace, driven by the rapidly evolving technologies and marked the realisation in the more enlightened firms that human resources were an appreciable asset through which high levels of return on investment could be generated, and the long term future of the firm better secured.

The publication in 1991, "A European Perspective on Self-Learning Competency and Technological Change", was the sequel to the Work and Learning Study[2]. This publication was followed by the development of the concept of "The Learning Organisation"[3], as a European model on which to build the training systems and the enterprises of the future. In a learning organisation the whole system is involved; strategy, structure and culture are no longer separate entities, but integral elements of an organisation in which learning is embedded in the culture and the day-to-day work of a company.

The present volume, "Human Competence and Business Development" is in direct continuity with these earlier publications. Analogous to the ongoing learning processes, it accompanies two other publications of the European Centre for Work and Society, published in 1996 and in which other aspects of organisational change and learning are highlighted. The first concerns the application of new learning principles and competence development skills[4], and the second publication[5] deals with changing roles of trainers as a consequence of and a prerequisite for organisations turning into learning organisations.

The present book is the result of a project conducted as a joint venture between researchers at the European Centre for Work and Society, Brussels, and the Institute for Management of Innovation and Technology (IMIT), Stockholm. The project managers from two organisations are the editors. In this respect their editing work can be regarded as a typical example of the expanding international scientific cooperation between different European organisations in the field of Research and Development.

Jack Horgan
Director
European Centre for Work and Society
Brussels, January 1996

Notes

1 Grootings, P. (ed.), *Work and Learning. Maastricht: European Centre for Work and Society*, Presses Interuniversitaires Europeennes, 1988.
2 Nyhan, B., *Developing, People's Ability to Learn: A European Perspective on Self-Learning Competency and Technological Change,* Brussels: European Interuniversity Press, 1991 (EUROTECNET study).
3 Stahl, T., Nyhan, B. and D' Aloja, P., *The Learning Organisation: A Vision for Human Resource Development.* Brussels: European Interuniversity Press, 1992 (EUROTECNET study).
4 Skell, W., *Psychological Regulation of Activity and Vocationally Oriented Learning,* Brussels: European Centre for Work and Society, 1996 (in press).
5 D' Aloja, P. and Osterricth, S., *New Roles in the field of Training within Self-Learning Organisations,* Brussels: European Centre for Work and Society, 1996 (in press).

Contents

Foreword
Jack Horgan v

Contributors ix

Acknowledgements
Peter Docherty and Barry Nyhan xiii

1. **Understanding Industry in Transition**
   Peter Docherty and Barry Nyhan 1

2. **Understanding Changing Competence Demands**
   Peter Docherty and Christer Marking 19

3. **Meeting the New Challenges**
   Peter Docherty and Barry Nyhan 43

4. **A New Plant Designed as a Learning Organisation: Aluminium Dunkerque**
   Olivier du Roy 66

5. **From Workers to Business Partners: A Response to Crisis in Bord na Mona**
   Sean Mistéil and Michael Lawlor 78

6. **Manducher: A Capability-based Strategy in the Plastics Industry**
   Peter Docherty 96

7. **Improving Performance through Entrepreneurship at Sara Lee/Douwe Egberts**
   Wim Heine 109

8. **Developing Unique Production and Work Structuring Principles through a Creative Search and Learning Process: The Volvo Uddevalla Final Assembly Plant**
   Thomas Engström, Lars Medbo, Dan Jönsson, Lennart Nilsson and Kajsa Ellegård 130

9. **Semi-Autonomous Work Groups at Audi-Volkswagen**
   Karlheinz Sonntag and Michael Freiboth 149

10. **The Impact of TQM Strategy on Worker Roles and Competence at Cadbury**
    Michael Kelleher 171

11. **Many Small Companies under One Roof: The Production Island Principle at Felten & Guilleaume**
    Ludger Deitmer and Uwe Köster 191

12. **The Development of 'Collective Intelligence' at Autoplastique**
    Mari-Claire Villeval 227

13. **A Learning Opportunity on the Shopfloor at AB Bygg och Transportekonomi**
    Christer Marking 245

14. **The Evolution of Management Thinking on Production Systems at Clark-Hurth**
    Franz Ghyssaert 265

15. **A Human Centred Framework of Learning as Social and Organisational Innovation**
    Karamjit S. Gill 275

Contributors

Ludger Deitmer
Ludger Deitmer is a research fellow at the Institute of Technology and Education at the University of Bremen and a member of the executive secretariat of the regional "Arbeit und Technik" programme. The latter body initiates and co-ordinates several co-operative project networks in SMEs and craft trade companies to promote social modernisation in specific innovative fields. He has degrees in electrical engineering and education.

Peter Docherty
Peter Docherty is director of the research programme on "Information Technology and Management" at the Institute for Management of Innovation and Technology and associate professor in Business Administration at the Stockholm School of Economics. He is also co-ordinating researcher in the programme for Learning Organisations, organised and financed by the Swedish Work Environment Fund. His research interests are the interdependencies in development and change processes between new technology, organisation and people's values, needs and abilities.

Kaijsa Ellergård
Kaijsa Ellergård is associate professor in Human and Economic Geography at the School of Economics and Legal Science at the University of Gothenburg. She was one of the main researchers in the study of the development of the Uddevalla plant in the Volvo car company. She is an advisor to the Swedish Confederation of Staff Unions on training issues.

Thomas Engström
Thomas Engström is associate professor and head of the Materials Handling research group at the Department of Transportation and Logistics at Chalmers University of Technology in Gothenburg. His research concerns such issues as the development of new materials feeding techniques, layouts, material flow structures, work structuring principles for long-cycle assembly work. He has worked with such companies as SAAB-Scania, Volvo and SKF. He was actively involved in the development of the Uddevalla plant.

Michael Freiboth
Michael Freiboth is a researcher at the Institut für Arbeitswissenschaft at the University of Kassel, GhK. He has been involved in several national and EU projects on organisational development and qualification. His special field of interest is forms of work organisation in the German car industry, in particular the impact of group work on productivity and organisation. He has a degree in education and electronic engineering.

Karamjit S. Gill
Karamjit S. Gillis director of the SEAKE (Social and Educational Applications of Knowledge Engineering) Centre at University of Brighton and is Honorary Professor in Human Centred Systems at University of Urbino. He is also editor of "AI & Society", the Journal of Human-Centred Systems and Machine Intelligence and of the Springer Verlag scientific book series in the same field. His own research focuses on the interaction of human values, culture and organisation and new information technology.

Frans Ghyssaert
Frans Ghyssaert whose background is in mechanical engineering, is a training advisor in the Flemish Employment and Vocational Training Agency (VDAB) in new technologies (CNC and CAD/CAM). He has been involved as a technical expert in the European vocational training programmes Eurotecnet, Euroform and Euroqualifications. He has

considerable industrial experience as a maintenance, production and process engineer in electronics, heavy electrical and mechanical engineering companies.

Wim Heine
Wim Heine is the training and development manager at Sara Lee/Douwe Egberts where he has had major responsibility for productivity improvement programmes, strengthening the corporation's core competencies, compensation systems and company mergers. He has degrees in law and civil engineering and has previously worked in the building industry and as a consultant for professional engineering bodies.

Dan Jönsson
Dan Jönsson is associate professor at the Department of Sociology at Gothenburg University. He has recently being conducting research on the interdependence and integration of technical and social aspects of production system design for extended work cycle assembly. This work aims at elaborating principles and methods for holistic design and analysis of innovative production systems. He was actively involved in the development of the Uddevalla factory.

Michael Kelleher
Michael Kelleher is a research fellow at the Centre for Research and Educational Development, Gwent, Wales. He was previously European research officer at the Welsh Joint Education Committee and before that a researcher in sociology at the University of Bath, studying the relationship between skill shortages and the reorganisation of work in manufacturing industries. He worked for over ten years as an un- / semiskilled worker and shop steward in the Post Office before being awarded scholarships to read a degree in sociology with industrial relations. He has a Ph.D. from Bath University.

Uwe Köster
Uwe Köster is a consultant at the Institute for Science Transfer and Human Resource Management (IWP) in Bremen. Previously he worked for five years as an educational staff specialist at Felten & Guilleaume. He completed his apprenticeship and worked several years in industry as a toolmaker before taking a degree in education.

Michael Lawler
Michael Lawler is a senior consultant in employee involvement and participation issues at the Irish Productivity Centre and has conducted assignments in major organisations in both the private and public sector. He was previously Community Secretary to the Brewery Council, the formal joint council on participation questions at Guinness and was nominated to the Advisory Committee on Worker Participation.

Christer Marking
Christer Marking is a researcher at the Swedish Metalworkers' Union working with conditions of work, especially work organisation, new technology and competence and learning issues. He was recently chief secretary in the Swedish Commission on the Development of Competence and Skills in Working Life. He was previously a researcher in production systems at the Swedish Institute for Work Life Studies and at the Institute of Industrial Economics at the Royal Institute of Technology. He has an M.Sc. in mechanical engineering.

Lars Medbo
Lars Medbo is a researcher in the Materials Handling research group at the Department of Transportation and Logistics at Chalmers University of Technology in Gothenburg. His research concerns such issues as the development of new layouts and work structuring principles for long-cycle assembly work. He was actively involved in the development of the Uddevalla plant.

Sean Mistéil
Sean Mistéil is a specialist on organisation development and training with Bord na Mona, specialising in the management of change, communications and team development. In the eighties he was a development and training officer with the Civil Service Training Centre and Telecom Eireann. Prior to that he was an executive officer in the civil service. He has a M.Mgt.Sc. in Organisational Behaviour.

Lennart Nilsson
Lennart Nilsson is associate professor at Lärarhögskolan (the Institute of Education) at the University of Gothenburg. His research concerns vocational training and learning in the workplace. He was responsible for the development of the "work place pedagogics" used in the Uddevalla plant. He is an advisor to the Swedish Confederation of Staff Unions on training issues.

Lennart Nilsson
Barry Nyhan is a senior researcher at the European Centre for Work and Society, Brussels, working on the relationships between technological, organisational and competence development. His work has mainly been within the EU Eurotecnet program. He is special research interests are in the field of experiential learning in the workplace from an individual and business perspective. He will soon be moving to work with research issues in the EU Task Force Human Resource Resources, Training and Youth..

Olivier du Roy
Olivier du Roy is a director and senior consultant in the consultancy company AEGIST (Association européenne de gestion et d'intervention socio-technique). They have developed an approach to technology shift and transformation strategies in industrial and public sector organisations based on sociotechnical theory. He was actively involved as a consultant in the Aluminium Dunkerque project. He has a licentiate in philosophy and human science.

Karlheinz Sonntag
Karlheinz Sonntag is professor in Work Science at the University of Heidelberg. He was previously professor at the Institut für Arbeitswissenschaft at the University of Kassel, GhK. He has been involved in several national and EU projects on organisational development and qualification, more recently in the German car industry.

Marie-Claire Villeval
Marie-Claire Villeval is a labour economist and a research fellow in the Economics of Technological Change at the University of Lumière Lyon. Previously she was a member of the research group on education and employment attached to the French National Centre for Scientific Research at the University of Nancy II. She has a Ph.D. in Socio-economics from the University of Paris X Nanterre.

Acknowledgements

This project has been a joint venture between the European Centre for Work and Society, ECWS, Bruxelles and the Institute for Management of Innovation and Technology, IMIT, Stockholm.

This project was initiated by the ECWS, Brussels, the prime instigator being Jack Horgan, director of the ECWS, Brussels. In the course of the project, we have received valuable comments from Gabriel Frangière, Sylvie Osterrieth and Thomas Stahl, colleagues at the ECWS.

The issues focused in the project are central to the Swedish Work Environment Fund's programme on Learning Organisations in which IMIT has an important research role. Valuable comments have been received from Carl Asklöf, Eva Maria Danvind, Roger Mörtvik and Gunnel Skårstedt in the steering committee of the programme.

The first major step in the project was a work shop in Cambridge in June, 1992 when the broad issues in the project were discussed and a number of cases studies were presented. Very valuable input was provided on that occasion by consultants, researchers, managers and programme administrators who did not participate in later stages of the project, namely Antonio Martin Artiles, Arthur Coldrick, Albert Colin, Mike Cooley, Clive Hewitt, Lilia Infelise, Renata Jungeblut, Roger Kings, Chris Lakin, Dieter Lellmann, Clive Smithers and Jos Tilkin.

Further colleagues besides the authors in this book have participated in later work shops and have produced early drafts to further case studies which are not included in this book. They have contributed considerably to the development of the ideas in the project and to the form and analysis of the cases. The colleagues are Millós Argyropoulos, Graham Attwell, Pat Brand, Bruno Clematide, Martin Good, Maria Kandelorou, Nick MacDonald, Michael Pearn, Jaime Rojas, Liam Shanahan, Massimo Tomassini and Philippe Zarifian.

Gaëtane Schellekens and François Bastin of the ECWS and Anita Söderberg-Carlsson from IMIT have provided an expert administration service and helped with the production of various drafts of the report in the course of the project.

We would like to express our warm thanks to all our colleagues mentioned above for their support, inspiration and direct contribution to the book. This thanks goes especially also to our fellow authors, who have not been listed here but who are presented more personally in a specific appendix to the book. Among our fellow authors there are two people who have had an especially supportive role to us as editors and to whom we wish to express especial gratitude, namely Karamjit Gill who has provided constant support and inspiration in guiding this work to practical completion and Christer Marking who has been a close speaking partner in discussions regarding the structure and analysis of the case studies.

Peter Docherty	Barry Nyhan	September, 1994
IMIT, Stockholm	ECWS, Brussels	

Chapter One

Understanding Industry in Transition

Peter Docherty and Barry Nyhan

Introduction: Development in Industry and Commerce

The international literature on industrial and trade developments points to increasing internationalisation and competition in global markets, a steady increase in the formation of corporate alliances and company networks and increased functional and hierarchical integration within organisations. Competition is getting tougher. The pace of technological innovation is increasing. Both customers and business partners are becoming more demanding.

The past fifty years have seen a continuous stream of social, organisational and technological developments in society which have impacted on each other and on individuals in the work place, thereby continually changing the demands and opportunities regarding the worker's acquisition of skill and knowledge. In the nineties the focus on learning and competence issues is emerging as one of the most important and explicit features of organisations requiring top management attention in business strategy development. Organisational survival and competitiveness are dependent on the total commitment of all their members, in particular on their ability to anticipate change, adapt to new circumstances and come up with new solutions and ideas regarding products and production processes. Many authors maintain that learning at all levels in the organisation is not just advantageous for realising its goals. It is imperative for an organisation's long term competitiveness and success.

Where does Europe stand in this context? The state of play in the electronics sectors gives a good indication of the challenges facing European industries. Within this key "new" industrial sector, which is producing the "enabling technologies" which are pervading all economic and social activities, European electronics companies are finding it difficult to remain competitive against the background of fierce world competition.[1] In the semi-conductor industry, for example, work production totalled ECU 55 Billion in 1989 and is expected to rise to ECU 110 Billion by the end of 1994, European companies are producing just 10% of the world output and utilising just 17% of the world output in the manufacture of consumer electronic goods. The story emerging from another global but "older" sector, the automobile sector, is also forcing European companies to sit up and to pay attention. The MIT world-wide study of the car industry concluded that productivity and quality levels of the European companies were significantly lower than those of Japanese companies.[2]

Cooley argues in a FAST report that since European manufacturing is characterised by a highly skilled and flexible working force, its future strength would depend on the development of anthropocentric or human-centred systems which build upon the skill, ingenuity and expertise of working people. It emphasises the need to develop infrastructures, educational forms and means of production which accord with the cultural, geographical, economic and environmental realities of the European community, and build upon the cultural richness and variety in Europe. The role of responsive education and lifelong learning is seen as central to his vision of the future. He also maintains that "developing the skill and competence necessary in the 21st century will require nothing short of a cultural and industrial renaissance".[3]

Another distinctive feature of European thinking of relevance to company development is the discussion of the content of the concepts of efficiency and effectiveness. Table 1 presents the major components of these concepts in the form of a two by two table. The rows in the figure represent the classical business economics concepts of efficiency and effectiveness (or internal and external efficiency) regarding the rational utilisation of resources within the organisation and the degree to which the organisation succeeds in creating value for its customers. The columns on the other hand represent the concepts of static and dynamic efficiency / effectiveness as presented by the Norwegian economist Viktor Norman. His concepts relate the organisation's performance to its assumptions regarding its environment, for example, management may regard the environment as stable or static, or as characterised by change and turbulence. Within the automobile industry the former assumption is referred to as "Fordism" and the latter as "Toyotism". A conscious focus on the dynamic nature of the environment means that flexibility and learning are regarded as essential features of efficiency and effectiveness.

Performance concepts	Contextual Assumptions	
	Static	*Dynamic*
Efficiency (Internal performance)	**Rationalisation** **Productivity**	**Development - Competence**
Effectiveness (External performance)	**Creation of value for customers** **Quality** **Profitability**	**Ability to adjust, develop, innovate**

Table 1. *Performance dimensions*

The necessary focus on learning and the breadth and depth of competence required in individual companies to attain and maintain the levels of static and dynamic effectiveness deemed essential for survival can only be achieved if top management has a clear insight into, and an understanding of, the crucial importance of these factors. This is a prerequisite for top management's wholehearted commitment to and acceptance of responsibility for treating competence as an explicit issue in their strategic planning. Without their insight and commitment, there is little chance that issues of competence will receive the priority and the resource allocation they demand.

A further reason for giving specific attention to the issues of learning and competence development is the fact that the time required to reverse current trends is considerably longer than that for dealing with economic and technological problems. Economic turnaround may be achieved within three or four years. A technological one may take somewhat longer, however, the development of key competencies, especially at a sectorial level, may take decades.[4]

The evolving situation presents Western Europe with different challenges and opportunities. Brödner points out that the limited growth rate in many of our economies changes the character of competition.[5] From supplying expanding market shares, where the suppliers are able to set the conditions to a large extent, competition increasingly depends upon displacing competitors, whereby customers gain power for buying products adapted to their needs. Under these new market conditions of competition by displacement, the price and quality of unified products are no longer the only assets needed to succeed in the marketplace. The abilities to adapt the products to customer requirements with increasing variety and also guarantee short delivery times are becoming rather more important competitive factors.

Optimists maintain that the European industrial core may potentially be better off, in particular those parts with a long experience of "flexible specialisation", with an appropriate production system and a skilled work force at their disposal.[6] While the stagnation in world markets and, hence, competition by displacement prevail, Europe's comparatively favourable position will tend to improve even further.

Organisational innovations are facilitated by technical developments. For example the advent of high performance electronic data processing has considerably widened the range of options for product strategies. Its most important impact is that a new type of high volume production of customised quality competitive goods, or in short "diversified quality production", with the potential economies of scope, has been made possible. The strategy of "flexible specialisation" enables radically improved profitability and competitiveness as traditional mass production gives way to production in smaller batches.

Howard underlines that the starting point in learning processes is to understand how the new emphasis on organisational innovation is a direct response to the profound changes in the competitive environment.[7] The modern organisation is a platform for social and technological innovation. In this context Drucker points out that social innovation is equally important and often more important than scientific and technological innovation.[8] This latter thesis has been confirmed by Hörte and Lindberg in an analysis of innovations in 100 Swedish companies. The improvements in productivity and effectiveness associated with the implementation of social / organisational innovations far exceeded those associated with technological innovations in their follow-up study 2-3 years after the introduction of the innovation.[9] Thus the new emphasis on organisational innovation is a direct response to profound changes in the competitive environment. One of management's main tasks is thus to encourage systematic organisational innovation. At the same time every organisation is always in competition for its most essential resource - its qualified, knowledgeable people. Organisations must earn loyalty by proving to their knowledgeable employees that they offer them exceptional opportunities for putting their knowledge to work.[10]

Competence Development: a Management Issue

Does top management personally involve itself in the issues of competence development and learning? Traditionally it has sufficed to delegate these issues to competent professional specialists who have top management's confidence. This may well be compared to the way in which computer specialists have been given the brief to take care of the company's information technology issues. Competence issues have been dealt with by a professional staff as a business within the business. We maintain that the developments outlined above are of such dignity and import that they demand top management's involvement. They must form an integral part of strategic planning so that business, technological, and personnel/competence issues are dealt with together.

Howard notes that the old competitive environment was characterised by stability - durable products, unchanging customer needs, clearly defined national and regional markets.[11] In such a world the key competitive advantage was where a company chose to compete. In today's business environment shaped by fragmented markets, accelerated product life cycles and global competition, the competitive advantage is less where a company competes than how it competes. The essence of strategy is not the structure, nor

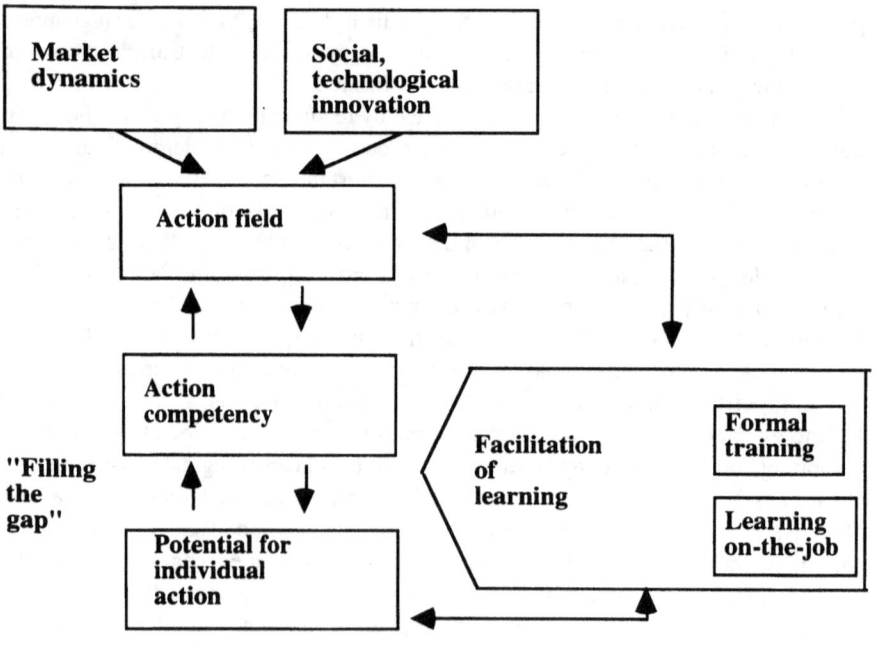

Figure 1. *Competence development issue*

is it a company's products and markets, but the dynamics of its behaviour. He concludes that there must be a shift in how managers perceive their roles. They must become less of "planners", "controllers" and "decision makers" and more of "designers" - creating and designing the organisational context which will stimulate their workers' commitment, learning and creativity.

Figure 1 shows how we view the competence development issue facing management. The action field is made up of the action demands and tasks facing the organisation and its members. This encompasses both demands from different actors in the market and the scope for action or degrees of freedom delimited by existing structures, legal, rule and norm systems. A content of the action field is continually influenced by market demands and changes in social and technological structures. The market demands may emanate from customers, suppliers, competitors and different control agencies.

In order to deal with an action field which is constantly changing, today's worker needs an understanding of the field as an integrated system. This entails a capacity to interpret events, to adapt, and to make judgements, which for example are based on a combined consideration of technological, business and quality assurance factors. The "action competency" required to deal with an action field has a complex nature which integrates different skills associated with understanding, learning and doing. Different professionals working with competence issues have evolved different terminologies, which highlight different features or dimensions of action competency. We will touch on some of these later. The essential point is that the continual changes and the demands and possibilities within the action field demand a responsiveness on the part of the individual in terms of development and adaptation of his or her action competency.

Each individual in the organisation possesses a potential to act and needs to be actively involved in the process of acquiring a competency to act. The organisation (management) must provide conditions that facilitate individual, group and organisational learning to "fill the gap" between the individuals' potential to act and their action competency. These conditions may include both the formal training system within the organisation and the facilities for on-the-job learning which are embedded in such features of the individuals' work situation as job design, work organisation, planning, management and follow-up systems, and incentive and reward systems. On-the job-learning needs to be given special attention in this context as it answers for the main part of an individual's learning at work.[12]

It is essential that the learning facilitation system encompasses subsystems for the continual monitoring of changes in the action field and in changes in individual potentials. Otherwise there are severe risks that, for example, the training systems will fail to provide people with the action competencies which are in line with those demanded by the company's action field. At worst the training systems may be caught up in their own closed world of formal and "technical content" oriented programs which are not focused on the competencies needed at work.

Recent developments in work organisation towards for example the devolution of responsibility and authority to production groups and the integration of planning and control tasks in these groups reflect endeavours to bring the learning situation closer to the action field in a planned and systematic fashion. This may also take the form of new relationships, divisions of responsibility and joint action between the formal training subsystem and the line organisation in which on-the-job learning takes place. Formal and informal learning activities may then be integrated in a single learning arena which aims to maximise the dynamic efficiency and effectiveness of the organisation.

When the chief executive of ASEA Brown Bovery (ABB), the Swiss-Swedish engineering corporation, Percy Barnevik, participated in the conference "Work Life in Transition" arranged by the Swedish Work Environment Fund together with ILO in Stockholm in 1991, he declared that ABB in order to meet the competition in the future market place had to redesign their organisation to get people committed to and in charge of the production process. Management control structures at plant level had to be changed fundamentally. The key point is that market variation due to changing customer demands must be absorbed into the production process rather than in the planning department. That change demands both broader and more specialised knowledge from production workers and a more vertically and horizontally integrated organisation.

Barnevik also presented results showing that customers are much more sensitive to how they are treated by the firm they are doing business with, than is usually believed. A negative attitude or approach from the selling firm is by far the most common reason for dropping a business contact. Of course, the attitude employees have to customers is a function of the quality of the involvement of individual employees in the firm. Without real responsibility and corresponding discretion, no one can be expected to have the required involvement.

We are moving from Fordism with mass-production for mass-markets, to neo-craftism with custom-designed, high quality products in an international market place. The overall organisation and the work organisation of production has to be designed in radically different ways. Whereas Fordism perceived people as interchangeable parts in the production process, production within neo-craftism is dependent on the specific skills and abilities of individuals. The competencies that individuals and groups of people develop together in the production process is of fundamental value for that process.

Industrial processes have also strived to minimise the use of scarce and expensive resources. This still holds for neo-craftism. There will always be a conflict between economies of scale and customisation. The new long-term skill patterns that evolve have to be looked for in the interface between production and market. The new short-term skills are demanded when changes take place in the organisational production and in management control systems.

The new work organisations demand both new production skills and new work roles of the production worker. The major changes in work roles concern the power, control, responsibility and accountability dimensions. Efficient and effective production processes demand increased discretion or degrees of freedom on the part of the worker. This also means increased decision powers and responsibility for the worker. Under traditional forms of management control structures, workers were told what to do, how to do it, and were paid for doing it often by straight piece-rate wage systems. Technical and administrative control often left the worker with practically no degrees of freedom. The environmental (market) demands and technical complexity are now such that these tangible formal control mechanisms are self-defeating. New control systems must be evolved.

Competence Development Strategies in European Countries

The aims of the present study

This book presents a study that addresses three questions:

- Which competence development strategies are being used by European industrial companies introducing social and technical innovations?

- Which new competencies are production workers acquiring as these innovations are implemented?

- How does the interplay between management ideas, company structures and processes develop in the course of the implementation of these innovations?

The main focus in the first question is on the management ideas (values and mental models) forming the basis for the action taken in the company. In this context we will define three levels of change in management's ideas which reflect changes differing in depth or significance in management's ideas. These are as follows:

changes in behavioural repertoire
Management extends its behavioural repertoire by utilising new methods or processes in the company which do not entail any modification of management's mental models or frames of reference or their values. In learning terms this would be an example of single-loop learning in which management simply improves its way of conducting business with the conscious aim of doing "business as usual" but better.

changes in mental models
In this case key members of the management group and perhaps even the whole management group modify, develop or radically change their mental models regarding essential aspects of their company's functioning in its environment. This may either be the result of innovative thinking within the management group or through the decision to adopt new models which have been seen to be highly effective and relevant in other organisations. This process may involve the active questioning of current practices and frames of references and as such constitute a form of double-loop learning.

changes in values
The development process may be based on changes in the leading or dominant values in management, or perhaps the clear, explicit articulation of a tacit value, which forms a point of departure or basis for a new vision or strategy formulation process. This may be associated with changes of key individuals in the management team. It may even follow the assessment of changes in the demands placed on the organisation by its environment.

An example of value changes which have currently been the subject of discussion in the management literature is management's basic attitude towards the company's personnel. In many companies management formulates its strategies and plans on the understanding that personnel are an important production factor. This point of departure motivates a classical rationalisation approach to personnel in manning and organisation questions and also motivates the Anglo-Saxon competence development strategy of "mobility". The mobility strategy, as documented by Bengtsson in his study of companies in the OECD, is one in which management regards competence development as primarily a responsibility of the individual - not of the company.[13] The company then recruits individuals with the skills required by the company, laying off those who do not have the necessary skills. Another stand at the other end of the spectrum is to regard personnel as partners in the organisation. Drucker foresees a swing from regarding power as the most important variable distributed in the organisation to its displacement by the variable "responsibility".[14] Management and personnel are co-responsible for the organisation in a partnership relation.

The design of the study

The frame of reference and the central questions in this study concern the promotion of dynamic efficiency now and in the long term in European industry. The focus is on current efforts to engage and develop personnel in connection with the introduction of innovative business practices. The aim is to identify patterns in the interplay between different factors over time. It is natural therefore to select a number of case studies presented in reasonable detail. Each case study exemplifies what Emery called "the future we are in", i.e. it represents an innovative development which may well be regarded as representing a more general state of affairs in the not-too-distant future. [15] Individually the case studies provide a source of reflection for policy and decision makers in the relevant sectors. Together they provide a base for the identification of the main features of different competence development strategies and features of the organisations related to them.

This study was conceived and planned in parallel with the EPOQUAL project within the European community EUROTECNET program and the Swedish Work Environment Fund's Program on Learning Organisations. The EUROTECNET program was mainly interested in new competence demands on workers following the introduction of new technology. The Learning Organisation Program is mainly interested in management and structural factors and methods and tools facilitating learning processes. Utilising the national expert groups within the EUROTECNET program, the national co-ordinators were asked to suggest companies introducing social and technical innovations which were anticipated to place new competence demands on production personnel and which may be regarded as representing positive developments likely to be emulated by other companies. In addition contacts were taken with national R & D agencies to elicit suggestions regarding suitable case studies. A series of three seminars was organised in which the case studies were presented and discussed within the general frame of reference presented below.

The number of cases identified in the different countries varied considerably. It was difficult to identify cases in countries where the economy is not strongly biased to the industrial sector and which do not have central R & D agencies with a detailed overview of current national developments. The case study authors had different backgrounds, namely:
- management representatives,
- consultants and/or
- university and other researchers.

In most cases the authors had been involved in the development processes they were describing. The authors used the common framework in describing the developments in their company. Several of the case studies discussed in the seminars are not included in the book because of difficulties in producing complete cases in time, either due to current priorities in the company or to insufficient resources for producing the case study.

This book includes eleven case studies: five upon large and medium scale batch production in the mechanical and manufacturing industries and six upon the light and heavy process industries. The cases are drawn from seven European countries: Belgium, France, Germany, Ireland, Netherlands, Sweden and the United Kingdom.

Values, Structures and Processes - a framework for understanding and planning competence development

The basic model in our study is shown in Figure 2. Production and development processes in the organisation, such as learning, are influenced by people's values and mental models. The latter term is used broadly to include individuals' ideas and conceptions about features of the environment, organisation, individual actors and processes and how they are related to each other. In the first instance it is the collective aspects that are of interest here, i.e. values and models that may be regarded as being shared by in the first instance management, or even the majority of the members in the running of the business, directly or indirectly. Thus ideas regarding people and the relations between people, e.g. behaviour towards people, is a central value area. This is not restricted to seeing people as employees, i.e. personnel policy issues, but also sees people as customers, competitors, and citizens.

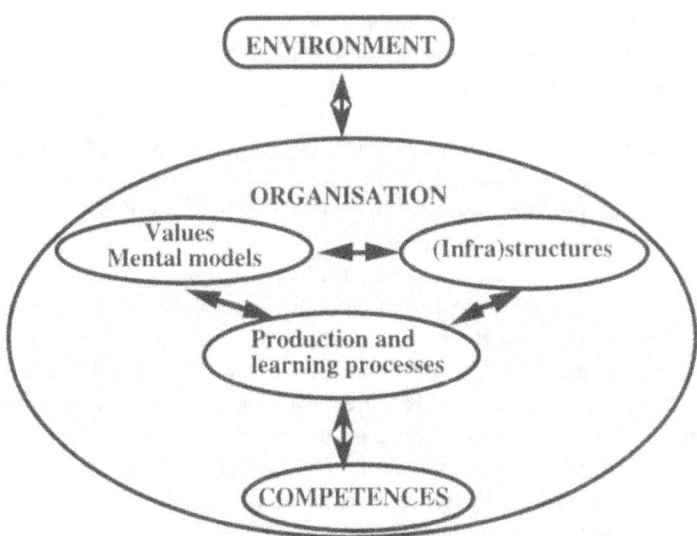

Figure 2. *Frame of reference*

A concept that is related to the sphere of values and mental models is that of company culture. Culture is in itself a difficult concept, not least because many authors use the concept giving it different definitions. Some times the concept is used very loosely as a convenient labelling of the rest variance in an analysis, i.e. that which cannot be explained by relationships to concrete phenomena in the analysis situation is simply explained diffusely by referring to culture. In addition there may well be a number of different cultures that may be regarded as important in a specific context, for example organisational, professional or national cultures. The fields of values, cognitive models and culture have in common that they are by nature of an intangible character and are mainly available through subjective data or secondary indicators.

The topic of culture has been the subject of much serious research within organisational theory and is naturally of importance, both within the context of the European union as well as in a broader scale within the context of the global economy.[16] The aspect of culture is not explicitly focused in the case studies presented here, but is addressed more fully in the concluding chapter in the book by Karamjit Gill.

The second main component in our frame of reference is the structures in the organisations. These are the tangible expressions of values and mental models, even in cases where the forming of the structures has not been consciously related to these values and mental models. Naturally the mental models are more likely to be formally articulated and shared in a senior management group prior to decisions on structures than are their values. Research in such areas as, for example, the development and implementation of information systems, an important type of infrastructure in an organisation, has shown that designers tend to base their designs not on their own values or the perceived values of system users, but on their impressions and interpretations of the values of senior management.[17]

The structures include the formal division of power, responsibility and accountability in the organisation as reflected both in the overall organisation and in the work organisation. It includes the formal goals, strategies, plans, policies and guidelines in the company. Infrastructure includes the main systems utilised in the processes in the organisation. These cover the processing of all resources, materials, information, capital and personnel. Materials systems concern the production operators. The other systems concern the different management planning and control systems, including both computer-based and non-computer-based information systems.

Some new management systems may be introduced as simple, if even radical, improvements of the structures embodying or expressing values and/or frames of reference of models already well-established in the organisation. They may thus simply reflect a generation shift in technology, and a response to action taken by competitors or other efficiency and effectiveness measures. The structural change need not denote or follow any cognitive value change. This may be the case in the adoption of such currently popular systems as Total Quality Management (TQM) or of Time-Based Management (TBM). The system may be adopted without any deeper analysis of, or reflection on, the values and ideas embodied in the system and their eventual compatibility or non-compatibility with those currently prevailing in the organisation. The immediate need to solve a serious crisis may, for example, hinder such reflective action.

On the other hand the structural changes may be the result of a revaluation of values and mental models. Top management may, for example, decide that instead of principally adopting a market positioning view in its strategic thinking, as in Porter's model, it should use a resource-based model such as Quinn's or Prahalad's[18].

The third area in the model is the processes of both production and development. The process or flow view of organisations forms the basis of one of the latest rationalisation methods, business process re-engineering (BPR)[19]. A process is defined in this context as a series of activities that takes one or more kinds of input and creates an output that is of value to the customer. In most organisations it is possible to identify between 10-20 processes in most organisations, These processes both generate competencies and are enhanced by the competence of the work force.

Competence, the fourth area in the model, should not be seen and treated as something separate from the organisation as such, or be equated with technical knowledge and/or formal training. It is more than that. Competence is an individual's ability to execute his tasks and to meet the external demands in a practically designed fashion in relation to the current situation.

If an individual is to carry out certain tasks and to meet external demands in a purposeful way in relation to prevailing conditions, the individual must have the knowledge required to execute the tasks. Knowledge acquired through training may be called reproductive, i.e. knowledge transferred from others, while knowledge that is generated from experience is in one sense unique, i.e. it is the individual learner herself that has developed the knowledge (quite independently of whether others already have this knowledge or not).

Knowledge is thus generated both by training and by experiential learning. Training may enable an individual to structure and give meaning to her experiences, whereby the individual develops new, personally unique knowledge. When an individual influences her environment, the impact of that influence must be visible for the individual if she is to be able to develop and learn from it, i.e. she must receive feedback. Feedback upon the results of action taken is an essential component in the learning process.

The Dynamics in the Overall Development Process

In reference again to Figure 2, the coupling from the environment to the organisation indicates in this context that the values, structures and processes within the organisation are influenced by the structure and processes in the environment. In this context we are interested in events and developments in the environment which may have acted as triggers or pressures initiating or maintaining the developments within the companies studied.

The double-headed arrows in Figure 2 indicate that we regard the relations between the various areas as interdependent, e.g. the mental models influence structures and structures affect mental models. The developments in individual companies will be very complex with parallel processes proceeding in different parts of and at different levels in the organisation at the same time. However a certain limited number of factors, events and processes are probably regarded by the members of the organisation as being the salient ones in the overall development process. It is these and the temporal ordering of the main steps that are of main interest here.

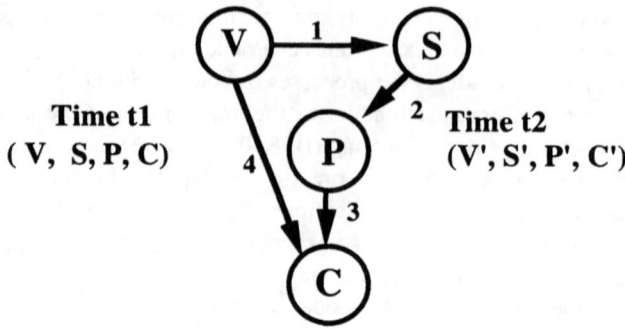

Figure 3. *The dynamics of the overall development process: a schematic figure*

Figure 3 indicates schematically the use of the frame of reference to describe the dynamics of the development processes in the case studies. The initial situation at the point of time t_1 consists of the constellation of values, structures, processes and competencies (V, S, P, C). At the end of the period reported in the case studies, the situation in the companies concerned may be expected to have developed to a situation with a different set of values, V', S', P' and C', depending on what has happened in that company. Naturally changes may not have occurred in all areas. The temporal sequence of the changes in the different areas and the relations between them are indicated by the numbers of the arrows in Figure 3, in which the development process began with the change in values that led to a change in structure to attain a change in work processes, and so on.

With regard to the interpretation of the individual case studies presented in this volume, we consider a development process as having been initiated by a change in values or mental models only if that change has been articulated and communicated at least to the parties and actors involved in the company and has been presented by management as a basis for other action regarding changes in structures and processes. This is one clear way of differentiating between value- or model-based initiated changes and changes in structure and process that have not been preceded by management taking a new or revised position in the value issue. Apart from the issue of initiating processes, later stages in a development process may entail value changes of the clarification and articulation of existing values.

Management's Strategies for Competence Development

Our general frame of reference encompasses structures and processes for competence development. The critical actor who is the focus of attention in our study is management. What strategies, stances, or paradigms characterise management's handling of competence issues? The key component in the frame of reference is management's values and mental models. These are of great import in:

- guiding management's perception and evaluation of the environment, or as we have also referred to it, the action field;
- the choice and design of structures within the organisation;

- the forming of the processes within the organisation.

Management's definition of competence development needs will be strongly related to its perception and evaluation of demands on and opportunities for the company in the market place. These demands and opportunities must also be seen and judged from a competence perspective. It is not sufficient that these judgements are reactive - then there is a strong risk that the company's responses may be too late. It is essential to strive to be proactive and exert as much influence as possible on developments in the market place. Competence is not solely a resource to realise business strategy, but is also a prerequisite for developing new strategies. In order to keep one step ahead management must have the ability to identify and interpret weak signals in the environment and to form visions of desirable futures for the company. This must be a continuously ongoing process.

Management must also have the ability to communicate its insights and visions. It is not unusual that top management groups may have a clear realisation of the importance of a competence strategy without communicating this to lower levels of management in the organisation.[20]

Insight into and commitment to the development of competencies must naturally follow through the whole hierarchical chain from top management to workers on the shop floor. All members of the organisation must feel responsibility not only for their own work tasks but for the business, its development and the development of their own competencies. This condition is the only sound indicator of the integration of business and competence development in an organisation. Integration at this point has become part of the organisational culture.

The individuals in the organisation must not only be committed to their own personal development, they must be also be provided with the opportunities to realise this development. Individuals must, for example, be given the opportunity to understand the prerequisites and conditions for the success of their company and especially regarding the contributions of their department or unit and of their own contributions within their unit. Insights into the changing demands on the company provide one of the main incentives to the self questioning of the appropriateness and adequacy of one's own skills and knowledge at work. This self questioning needs to take place within the context of a supportive dialogue between the individual, his or her peers and immediate superior. Learning opportunities should not be confined to formal training but may even include a mentor system, new tasks, participation in projects, job rotation, etc. It also requires suitable channels through which each individual may make known to his or her superior his or her legitimate aspirations regarding personal development, that newly acquired competencies are rewarded and that opportunities are provided to put these competencies into practice.

These last comments imply that management's values, goals and strategies for competence development must be supported by the infrastructure or support systems in the organisation. Such subsystems concern goal formulation, planning, management control systems and consultation systems between management and unions.

Business development and competence development display a kind of "chicken-egg" relationship to each other; it is difficult to say which comes first. At the same time it is clear that one cannot exist without the other. Both must be related to changing demands on the organisation in its environment. In that sense competence development is environmentally driven. At the same time management must develop insights into the demands and opportunities of the market and act accordingly. In this sense competence development is a management-driven issue. Even the individual employee, and personnel as a whole, must perceive these changes in demands, needs and opportunities and have sufficient degrees of freedom to be able to take the required initiative. In this context competence development is a workplace-driven issue.

Transition to a New Paradigm of the Learning-Oriented Work Organisation?

As has been stated earlier companies are subject to significant pressures for change from the market place. These pressures are being met in a wide variety of social (organisational) innovations and technical innovations. Different researchers have naturally focused the social and technical innovations but there is now fairly general agreement on the high degree of interaction between these innovations and that these innovations entail demands and opportunities for extensive competence development on the part of production workers. These developments entail a "re-professionalisation" or "re-qualification" of production workers. The new technology demands that they acquire more general or theoretical knowledge regarding production processes and the basic scientific knowledge concerning their industrial base, for example metallurgy in the mechanical industry or cellulose technology in the paper industry. The organisational innovations bring with them the opportunities and demands to acquire new social skills, and even in some cases, business skills. Survey studies, such as that of Bessant, would indicate that these changes are well on the way - if not already in place.[21]

However, other authors, such as Senker, present less flattering results which would seem to indicate that there are still many organisations which have not realised the potential of the available organisational and technological innovations.[22] In this study we present a number of in-depth case studies with the object of illustrating the processes of management adaptation that may result in a new paradigm for a learning-oriented work organisation.

The Structure of the Book

In Chapter 2 Docherty and Marking present some of the current trends in social or organisational innovations, technological development and learning approaches, and the demands and opportunities these provide for the development of worker competencies. A brief overview of some of the different classifications of individual competencies is also presented together with the schema utilised in this study.

In Chapter 3 Docherty and Nyhan present an analysis of the eleven case studies with respect to our three main questions. The competence strategies emerging may be regarded as reflecting distinct phases in the progression to a new paradigm of a learning-oriented work organisation. The progression indicates the steady expansion in a number of features of the organisation which are regarded as relevant to, and are integrated in the competence strategy. There is also a shift in management's perspective and values regarding its work force and in the responsibility and authority the latter may shoulder. This is also coupled to the tasks they are allotted and the knowledge and skills these require. On the other hand the patterns in the processes by which these strategies emerge and are implemented are less clear in the number of cases studied and would appear to be very subject to local conditions, individual histories and the particular actors involved.

Chapters 4-15 present the case studies. Each case study rounds off with an analysis using the common frame of reference.

Olivier du Roy describes the setting up of a new aluminium plant in Dunkirk by the Pechiney group over a three year period. The plant was a "state of the art" plant both regarding its technology and work organisation. It included self-supporting teams of workers with planning and maintenance tasks and clear competence ladders for the personal development of individual workers. The manning of the plant entailed recruiting and reskilling unemployed local labour one year before the start of the plant. Each worker received several months of training before entering the plant. The competence development system in the plant provides individual skill-progress plans for each worker.

Sean Mistéil and Michael Lawlor describe the turn-around in the semi-state peat production company, Bord na Móna, in Ireland conducted over a five year period by a new management team within the framework of a radical negotiated partnership with trade union representatives. The changes involved significant investment in development, innovation and quality. Much of the success to date stems from the focus put on the job itself as a learning environment, respecting natural groupings and their location when forming new teams and tapping the unused potential of boglands to reshape the company's future.

Wim Heine describes the development of performance through entrepreneurship at Sara Lee in the Netherlands. The company is the European-based subsidiary of an American consumer products company. The case describes the reorientation of the training and development department to support the performance of business units in the best possible way. Their "performance improvement program" focused on development of non-technical competencies. These new competencies, such as initiative, cooperation, goal setting, and communication are difficult to learn individually. Therefore the program aimed at the development of "organisational" competencies collectively. The model required the improvement of business results especially the perceived quality of three distinct business processes: policy deployment, client orientation and project management. An important aim was to teach middle and lower management to act as entrepreneurs who can scan the environment for opportunities and make the best use of them.

Peter Docherty describes the formation and implementation of a capability-based strategy in the French plastics company Manducher, a major supplier to the French car industry. Following the formation of a new vision focusing on worker competencies, the company introduced a new team-oriented work organisation, new forms of plastic and paint technology, and new incentive and reward systems together with a comprehensive learning program covering basic skills and planned progressive on-the-job learning and evaluation in five key skill areas.

Thomas Engström, Dan Jönsson, Lennart Nilsson, Kajsa Ellegård and Lars Medbo describe and analyse developments of Volvo Auto Uddevalla factory from the conception of the idea until it was running as the corporation's most productive unit in Sweden. The formation of the vision of a work organisation offering individual workers more meaningful and qualified work was followed by an extended search and learning process to develop methods and solutions that would enable this vision to be realised. This included the development of unique production and work structure in principles.

Karlheinz Sonntag and Mikael Freiboth describe the introduction of semi-autonomous working groups at Audi-Volkswagen. The organisational change also involved the integration of production and maintenance tasks in one group and the integration of metal workers and electricians in the same groups. The competence development efforts concerned cognitive, communication and co-operation skills and technical knowledge. New methods were developed for cognitive training for the improvement and performance of controlling tasks and fault diagnoses and for decentralised work-based training for flexible manufacturing cells.

Michael Kelleher describes the impact of a total quality management (TQM) strategy on worker roles and competence at a Cadbury factory producing chocolates. He focuses on new occupational competence emerging from the demands of technological change, work organisation and improvements in product quality. The developments are characterised by a progression from a low skills, low trust, low training culture to one where continual learning, co-operation and commitment are central features of its manufacturing culture. It provides valuable insight into how firms might innovate in the broader national context of poor training and adversarial industrial relations.

Ludger Deitmer and Uwe Köstner describe the introduction of the production island principle at Felten and Guilleaume in Nordenham, Germany. The company embarked on a long-term change process to attain greater efficiency through a complete organisational renewal. The production island concepts were introduced throughout production and administration and required extensive services of an in-house team of change agents. A new company strategy involved the step-by-step removal of the distinction between manual and mental work and active participation in organisational personnel development through life-long learning with the help of the island concept.

Marie-Claire Villeval presents the development of "collective intelligence" at Autoplastique, which is the pseudonym for a progressive SME manufacturing plastic components. The company introduced a new organisation including such components as a new JIT-system, production teams as profit centres and new management systems. The worker core competencies focus on anticipation, reactivity, communication and co-operation and the ability to build cognitive strategies. The new organisation focuses co-operative learning through project teams, problem solving meetings, one-to-one learning at the worker place, tutoring, and so forth. The case study focuses on a number of paradoxes or trade-offs, for example the balance between the "right to error" and the goal of "zero defects", which require subtle balancing if conditions for the learning organisation are to be maintained.

Christer Marking describes the informal learning processes which took place on the shop floor when flexible manufacturing was introduced into Byggtransportekonomi, a medium-sized company, as a means of tackling difficult production issues without being coupled to a formal competence development strategy.

Franz Ghyssaert describes the evolution of management thinking on production systems at the Belgium subsidiary of the American company Clark International, manufacturing heavy transmission units. He describes the step-by-step development in the work organisation and worker competencies resulting from the changes in technology introduced into the company. These reflected a gradual increase in the autonomy and influence of the workers on technological development.

The final chapter in the book Karamjit Gill presents an overview of some of the central ideas which have formed the basis for the European FAST program which has been a key source of inspiration to many of the company initiatives reported on the European scene. The program has focused on the prerequisites, capacities and needs of the individual worker as a basic point of departure in the design of manufacturing technology. Different authors have labelled this approach anthropocentric, human-centred, socio-technical and contrastive. [23] In our final chapter, Gill also takes up several important factors in a societal and European context which have not fallen within the scope of this study, namely the importance of the cultural factor in a European context and the relevance of the issues illustrated in this study in large companies when dealing with the development of small and medium sized enterprises.

Notes

[1] Commission of the European Communities (1991). <u>Information and Communication Technologies in Europe</u>, Luxembourg: Office for Official Publications of the European Communities.

[2] Womack, J.P., Jones, D.I. and Roos, D. (1990) <u>The Machine that Changed the World</u>. New York: Maxwell Macmillan International.

[3] Cooley, M. (1989) <u>European Competitiveness in the 21st Century</u>, Brussels: FAST, EEC. Cooley maintains that the harnessing of the inherent cultural diversity of Europe could create a permanent way of creativity and innovation which, culturally as well as economically, will yield a global competitive edge for European industry - somewhat comparable to the "Japanese miracle".

[4] Saias, M. (1992) <u>The Learning Organisation.</u> Key note speech to the European Foundation Conference on Learning Organisations in Brussels, November 1992.

[5] Brödner, P. (1990). Technocratic and Anthropocentric Approaches Towards Skill-based Manufacturing. in Warner, M., Wobbe, W. and Brödner, P. (editors) <u>New Technology and Manufacturing Management.</u> Chichester: J. Wiley & Sons.

[6] Piore, M. & Sabel, C. (1984), <u>Beyond the Industrial Divide: Possibilities for Prosperity</u>. New York: Basic Books.

[7] Howard, E. (1993) <u>The Learning Imperative</u>. Cambridge, MA: Harvard Business School Press.

[8] Drucker, P. F. (1992). <u>The Post Capitalist Society</u>. Oxford: Butterworth-Heineman

[9] Hörte, S.Å. & Lindberg, P. (1994) The Impact of Human and Organisational Development and Technological Development on Productivity and Performance, <u>International Journal of Human Factors in Manufacturing.</u> No.1(1994).

[10] Drucker, P.F., op. cit.

[11] Howard, E. op. cit.

[12] Current studies indicate that the formal training structures answer for somewhat less than 20 % of the individual learning which takes place at work. See for example Masick, V.J. and Watkins, K.B. (1990) <u>Informal and Incidental Learning in the Workplace.</u> London: Routledge.

[13] Bengtsson, J. (1985) <u>Human Resource Strategies in the O.E.C.D.</u> Presentation to the Swedish Work Environment Fund Workshop on "New Technology, management and Working Life" at Djurönäset, August, 1985.

[14] Drucker, P.F., op. cit.

[15] In his report <u>The Future we're in</u> (Sydney: Quantas, 1972). Emery argues that today's highly innovative companies can in many cases be regarded as advanced examples of regular good practice 5-10 years from now.

[16] Alvesson, M. (1993) <u>Cultural Perspectives on Organisations.</u> Cambridge: Cambridge University Press.

[17] Magnusson, Å. (1974) <u>Participation and a Company's Information and Decision-Making Systems</u>. Stockholm: EFI at the Stockholm School of Economics, Working Paper No. 6022; Hedberg, B.; Björn-Andersson, N.

[18] Porter, M. (1980) <u>Competitive Strategy. Competitive Strategy</u>. New York: Free Press;

Quinn, B.J. (1991) <u>Intelligent Enterprise</u>. New York: Free Press;

Prahalad, C.K. & Hamel, G. (1990) "The Core Competence of the Organisation", <u>Harvard Business Review</u>, Vol. 68, No. 3,;

Stalk, G. , Evens, P. & Schulman, L.E. (1992) "Competing on Capabilities, the New Roles of Corporate Strategy". <u>Harvard Business Review</u>, Vol. 70, No. 2, pp. 57-69.

[19] Hammer, M. & Champy, J.(1993) <u>Reengineering the Corporation. London</u>: Nicholas Brealey.

[20] Dilschmann, A., Docherty, P. & Stjernberg, T. (1994) <u>Competence Strategies in the Civil Service.</u> Stockholm: National Agency for Government Employers.

[21] Bessant, J. (1993) "Towards Factory 2000: Designing Organisations for Computer-Integrated Technology". In Clark, J. (ed.) <u>Human Resource Management and Technical Change.</u> London: Sage.

[22] Senker, P.(1992) "Automation and Work in Britain". In Adler, P. (ed.) <u>The Future of Work and Technology.</u> New York: Oxford University Press.

[23] Cooley, M. (1989) op.cit. (anthropocentric and human-centred)

Emery, F. E. & Trist, E. L. (1969) "The causal texture of organisational environments". In Emery, F.E.(Ed.) <u>Systems Thinking.</u> Harmondsworth, Middlesex: Penguin

Pasmore, W. A.(1990)<u>Designing Effective Organisations: The Sociotechnical Perspective.</u> New York: John Wiley & Sons. (sociotechnical)

Volpert, W. (1988) <u>What working and learning conditions are conducive to human development</u>? Swedish-German workshop on the Humanisation of Working Life. Stockholm December, 1988.(contrastive)

Chapter Two

Understanding Changing Competence Demands

Peter Docherty and Christer Marking

Introduction: What affects competence?

Our basic notion about the determinants of competence in a business organisation is illustrated in Figure 1. The main determinants of the competencies needed are considered to be the business idea, the available technology, the work organisation and the people employed. Clearly, core skills and competencies vary with the business idea. Work organisation and technology are chosen to create the means to fulfil the overall business idea. Very often these choices are dependent on dominating contemporary "models" of best practice. People are recruited according to the needs of the other determinants - it is very seldom that individuals, even if they are unique, innovate organisations. Still there is no one-to-one relation between the different components in the model. There is considerable freedom of choice when determining the work organisation, even if the technology is considered as given.

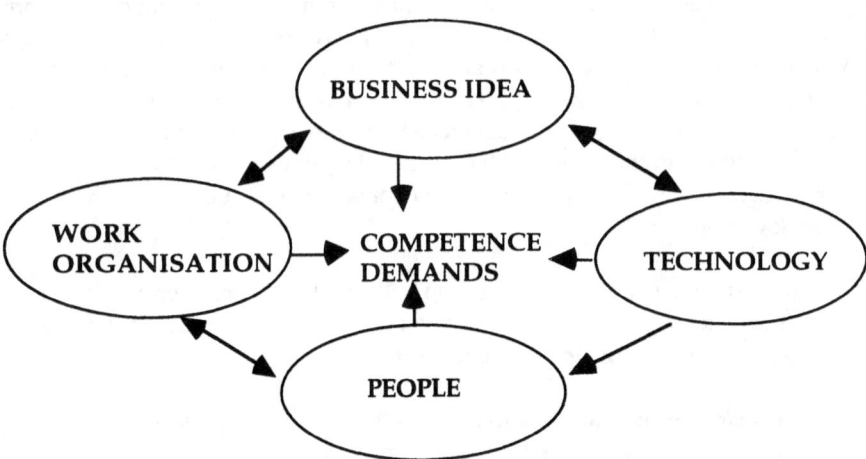

Figure 1. *Factors affecting competence demands*

The concept of choice in the design of a work organisation could be seen in relation to the idea that there is "one best way" to do things and that this could be revealed by scientific methods. This position regarding the design of production systems was first formulated by Taylor nearly a hundred years ago and has survived to this day. Ideas based on Taylor's view about how to organise production have been very influential. Although not generally the "espoused theory" of all managers, they all too often show themselves to be placing the "theory in practice".[1]

In a tradition, such as the Tayloristic tradition, problem solving very often takes the form of the unreflected application of "contemporary theory". Solutions to new problems are sought for in the light of the well-established theory. Reassessing traditional problems within theory could lead to new solutions. In practice, however, these seldom result in more than marginal adjustments to current practice. Yet within the tradition there are substantial variations from company to company, not least in the type of equipment used. What is new in one company is ordinary practice in other companies.[2] Radically different responses to traditional problems demand major changes in theory. New patterns of responses to production problems therefore hint at major changes in theory.

One of the critical pivoting points in organisational design, where traditional theory has given clear cut recommendations, is the trade off between management control and worker discretion. Traditional theory gives no leeway for interpretation: management control should reduce worker discretion otherwise workers could gain bargaining power by acquiring control over production processes. Efforts in this direction have been dubbed Taylorism and Fordism. This is not only the case in the manufacturing industry but even other industries. The control systems are built into technical and administrative control routines. Already in 1950 Drucker complained about the use of man as "a badly designed single-purpose machine-tool".[3] Noble maintains that the "management control" principle was one of the guiding forces in the original development of computer-supported technology in manufacturing.[4] This is also the basis of what Bainbridge calls "the irony of automation": Automated technology has been (and even in many cases still is) explicitly designed to reduce the discretion of the production worker in the production process, at the same time as the worker is responsible for handling contingencies when the automated equipment breaks down.[5] Volpert gives behavioural scientists their fair share of the blame for these developments:

> "mainstream general psychology and traditional ergonomics provide the theoretical superstructure for "the irony of automation" through their use of the von Neuman computer as the principle metaphor of man."[6]

Other researchers have noted management's focus on the competence dimension instead of the control dimension in an effort to minimise the costs of personnel as a production factor. Thus Senker notes the tendency of most British users of computer-supported manufacturing equipment to devote a great deal of attention to making their systems "idiot proof", rather than rely on the availability of a competent work force or the need to invest in training such a workforce in the company.[7]

Reports from all over the world indicate that traditional control systems do not work well when the variability in the surrounding environment of the firm is growing. When demands from the clients or customers are put directly to firms and swift response to these is demanded, traditional forms of organisational control are dysfunctional in most cases.

When new patterns of problem solving are applied, when the organisation is transformed to a more integrated form, the balance between management control and worker discretion must also alter. An integrated form of work organisation signifies an organisation where vertical and horizontal partitioning of work in the traditional form no longer exists. To handle short lead times in production as well as in product development, a new distribution of responsibility and power to define and solve problems is applied. This may be taken as a major challenge to traditional management control theory. This also reflects current Japanese practice. Koicke reports how the scope of discretion of Japanese production workers has been systematically extended from the simple execution of production tasks to successively include maintenance decisions, planning decisions, quality control decisions, problem solving in production and participation in product development activities.[8]

Cole's work in Japan confirms Koicke's findings to a large extent. Non-routine problems, even in industries thought to be dependent on routine technology, are far more common than is generally recognised and stem from changes in product and labour mix as well as production methods. Thus the Japanese have chosen to tackle such problems by immediate on-the-spot resolution by the workers involved, finding this a far more efficient approach than that embodied in referring them to separate specialists. To the extent that professional engineers are needed to help resolve more complex problems, these engineers are located close to the shop floor and are expected to be responsive to the problem solving needs for production workers.[9] The capacity to solve both production problems and social problems in the enterprise is critical. Unless the growth in the relevant competencies is supported by management the new organisation will not be viable.

What is competence?

Management has a basic responsibility for the development of an organisation's competence. They should develop their organisations into learning organisations. Most authors writing on these topics evolve their own definitions of these concepts depending on the specific features of these complex issues they aim to focus upon. One key dimension is the unit of analysis chosen: does the competence discussion refer to the organisation as a whole or to its individual members? Already thirty years ago an American sociologist, Selznick, defined an organisation's distinctive competence as:

> "the competence the company has that results in customers approaching the company and not its competitors"[10].

Strategy theoreticians regard an organisation's core competence that is difficult to define and difficult to imitate as being of decisive importance for its success. Representatives for the "capability-based strategy" school maintain that a company's strategy should not be based on products or markets but on competencies that are difficult for competitors to emulate. Prahalad, one of the founders of this strategy school, expresses the aims of the competence orientation in the idea that an organisation should identify and organise itself around what it does best. He points out:

> "core competencies are the collective learning in the organisation, especially regarding the ability to co-ordinate different production skills and integrate different technologies. It is not sufficient to be a learning organisation, a company must have the ability to learn more effectively than its competitors"[11].

The only way to be more effective in its learning than its competitors is for a company to have more knowledge of underlying processes, assumptions and points of departure and goals. The only way of gaining that knowledge is by analysing basic components of the organisational core. Efficient learning is based on correct learning, which means developing what one does best in order to maintain a long-term competitiveness. Prahalad points out also that competence never wears out but increases in value with use.

The manufacturing strategy school reasons in a similar fashion around the determination of strategic goals and how these goals may be realised through the procurement, dimensioning and improvement of different types of "resource" within the company. These activities which are in agreement with the strategy and which lead to utilisation and development of company resources are regarded as "value-creating activities". A basic requirement for the adequate execution of these activities at different levels in the company is the availability of requisite competence.

Competence is time and context specific. One cannot assume than an organisation which is effective and competent at one point in time will remain so if it lacks the ability to learn. Learning with a future orientation is a key aspect in this context. Senge in fact defines a learning organisation as:

> "one that is continually expanding its capacity to create its own future.... to create the results (its members) truly desire, where new and expansive patterns of thinking are nurtured, where collective aspiration is set free, and where people are continually learning how they learn together"[12].

This learning aims to increase the company's ability to analyse, and successfully master the different types of new or changing demands in the market place.

The concept "Core Competence" at the organisational level has a completely different structure from the concept of core competence applied to individuals. Different authors provide different definitions of what the central components are in the concept of organisational core competence. What is very interesting is that the authors indicate that structural properties of the organisation are important elements in core competence. The components named in the most common definitions are:

- the individual competencies of the members of the organisation;
- the values characterising the organisation for example regarding the company's employees, customers and the environment, how work should be carried out, etc.;
- the organisation's structure and infrastructure (work organisation, management systems, planning and control systems, reward systems and production systems);
- key activities.

Dorothy Leonard-Barton points out that identifying a company's core competence profile gives the opportunity of dealing with the other side of the coin, which she names "core rigidities". An all-too-exclusive focus on core competencies can unconsciously create an environment which only attracts a small spectrum of the knowledge and skills which precisely match and harmonise with the organisational core competence as they are defined at the moment. This can inhibit a sound "double-loop learning" which entails a healthy questioning of existing structures and practices. This is particularly risky in dynamic and rapidly changing situations where the concepts of success can quickly become obsolete. She points out that it is important to be aware of these core rigidities if they are to be dealt with.[13]

As with many other things, the analysis of core competencies is a strategic exercise that must be constantly repeated. Considering individual competence, researchers and consultants have formulated different definitions and concepts. Our definition of competence is illustrated in Figure 2. Competence should not be seen and treated as something separate from the organisation as such, or be equated with technical knowledge and/or formal training. It is more than that. Competence is an individual's ability to execute his tasks and meet external demands in a practical and designed fashion in relation to the current situation. This definition expresses a focus on the individual as an interpreting, acting and problem-solving being. Competence will be expressed in action in a given situation, with a certain meaning in the given context in a given environment. Knowledge is not synonymous with competence but is one of its components. An aspect of competence which is not explicitly included in the figure is "will" or "motivation" which we also regard as being of key importance in the concept.

Given the importance being attached to learning and competence in different contexts, it is no wonder that there is an emerging plethora of definitions of individual concepts and an overlapping in the meanings attached to different concepts. This has special relevance in the

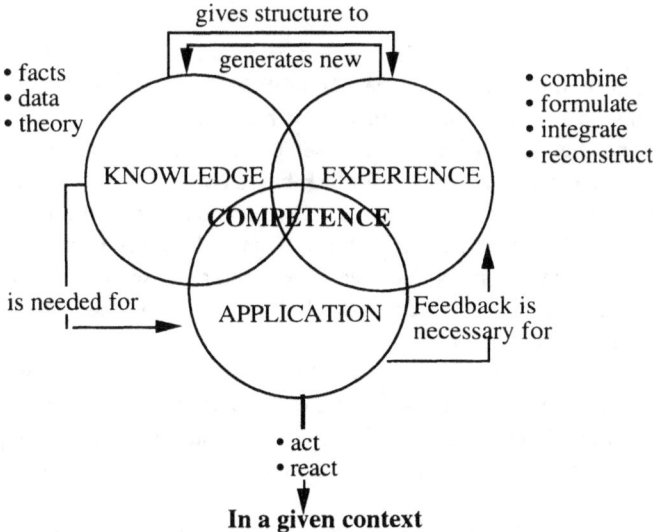

Figure 2. *Competence and the learning process*
(Source: Docherty & Dilschmann (1992) [14])

European community which is striving towards common concerted action in this area and where the national debates are conducted with a terminology which naturally reflects different cultural nuances. Real communication in the European arena is only guaranteed if people have a capacity to relate the terms used to the meaning they have in their "sitz im leben", in their specific cultural context. In addition the situation is somewhat complicated as the meaning of words is always changing. As T.S. Elliot put it "words slip and slide and lose their meaning, they don't stand still".

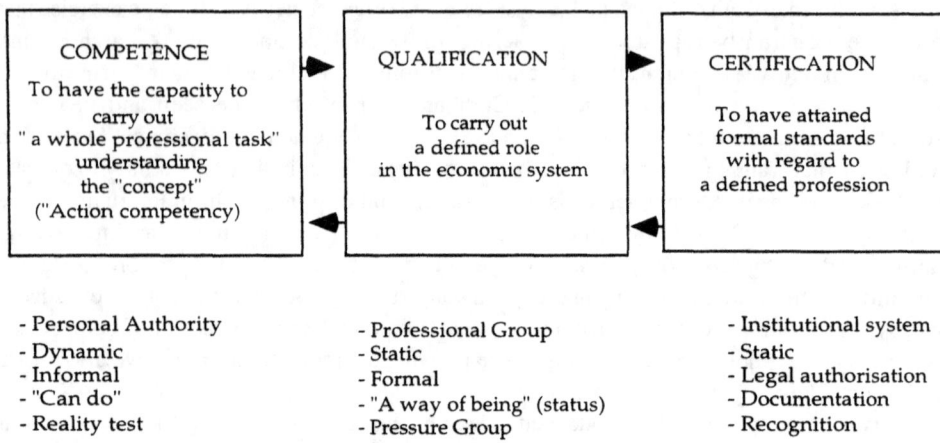

Figure 3. *Relationships between concepts of competence, qualification and certification*
(Source: Nyhan (1993))

In this context we would like to indicate how we see the relationships between three concepts, namely "competence", "qualification", and "certification". Figure 3 indicates relationship between these concepts as has been defined by Nyhan.[15] Competence is an individual-based concept, i.e. competence is defined in terms of an actor's capacity for action. Qualification is a work or task-based concept. It is defined in relation to actions or activities which are to be carried out. Certification is an institution-based concept. It relates the capability of meeting certain formal standards agreed upon by specific institutions. The German debate and much German research has focused on the concept of "qualification"; which is concerned with work tasks. In France there has been more focus on competencies and the individual actor or worker. In the United Kingdom the word "skill" is used at least as much as the word "competence" and refers to separate work-based abilities. In the United Kingdom the word "qualification" tends to be restricted to the notion of certification. In this study the focus is on the action field of the enterprise which provides the acid test of a person's competence, in whatever sense one interprets the term, either formally or informally.

With the individual as the unit of analysis, the discussion of core competencies has centred on a number of skills which contribute to a person being "a self-managing person". They refer to a set of complimentary competencies which enable a person to carry out a "whole action". They relate to "the capacity to act in responsible manners" with regard to complex tasks. They include such components as self motivation, self learning and self control. It is clear that these can only come to expression in a work organisation context in which people are requested to behave in an autonomous or independent manner.

Views of competencies

As noted earlier most authors writing on competence evolve their own definitions and typologies depending on the specific features they aim to focus on. We comment on three such typologies before presenting the one that will be used in this study, which naturally overlaps with those presented.

The basis of the Norwegian researcher Nordhaug's typology is the concept of human resource idiosyncrasy or specificity which refers to how narrow a group of tasks a competence is relevant. A competence with low specificity can be exercised in many different situations. Referring to Table 1, Nordhaug calls his most general group of competencies "meta-competencies". These include such competencies as those related to managing people and symbols as well as analytical problems, communication skills, co-operative competence and "carrier competencies", i.e. skills in acquiring other skills. Meta-competencies represent a sort of genuinely basic or underlying infrastructure of knowledge and skills that are broadly applicable and form a crucial foundation for work performance in general. The fact that they crosscut different tasks and constitute a potential for the mastering of emerging and future tasks makes them especially critical for organisational performance and change. Traditionally, the formal educational system has been viewed as the main transmitter of firm non-specific competencies. However, this applies to a much lower degree to meta-competencies. Many of them are likely to depend, at least to an equal degree, on other sources, such as heredity, primary and secondary socialisation processes, work experience and various leisure activities.

		FIRM SPECIFICITY		
		LOW		HIGH
		INDUSTRY SPECIFICITY		
		LOW		HIGH
TASK SPECIFICITY	LOW	I Meta- Competences	II Industry Competences	III Intraorganizational Competences
	HIGH	IV Standard Technical Competences	V Technical Trade Competences	VI Unique Competences

Table 1. *A competence typology*
(Source: Nordhaug (1993) [16])

Industrial competencies are characterised by low task specificity, low firm specificity and high industry specificity. The ability to analyse the specific competitive conditions of the industry a firm operates within is an example of an industry specific competence. Industrial competencies are carried chiefly by personnel in higher level managerial jobs, but it is favourable for employees at all levels in the organisation to possess basic knowledge on the industry, the firm's competitors and their strategies.

Type III, intraorganisational, competencies exhibit low task specificity and high firm specificity. The importance of these skills has mainly been in management and leadership literature and in politically oriented organisation theory where the focus has been on skills in internal networking, knowledge of and capacity to manage firm specific symbols, and knowledge of the culture in different parts of the organisation. These competencies are acquired and developed mostly by every day learning in the work place through interaction with and observation of individual colleagues and groups of colleagues.

Standard technical competencies, the fourth type, exhibit high task specificity, low firm specificity and low industry specificity. The important generators of standard technical competencies are the ordinary educational system, vocational education and training for adults. It is also frequently supplied by technology vendors.

Technical trade competencies are task specific, industry specific and firm non-specific. Consequently they are portable across firms within the industry.

Unique competencies are highly firm specific and task specific: they apply to the one task or a very few tasks within one firm and include knowledge and skills related to operation of unique technology and routines such as the operation and maintenance of customised technology.

In chapter one we broached the importance of the concepts of static and dynamic efficiency. The tendency for western countries to focus on static efficiency is reflected in a training context in the prescriptive professional human resource management and human resource literature, which recommends a focus on training to generate standard technical competencies - and, to the degree that they are needed, unique competencies. Thus the recommended focus is directed at the creation of a static fit between the employees and current work tasks. It is not aimed at developing individual and organisational flexibility through the generation of meta-competencies and intraorganisational competencies which are regarded as the most important in managing organisational transformation processes as those induced by changes in the external environment and those which are crucial to employees' overall capacity to cope with change.

In the context of our own study we are also particularly interested in the portability of the skills acquired by workers. The Swedish researcher Forsberg presents a somewhat different grouping of competencies in four dimensions:

- *professional technical*: includes theories, methods, skills related to the technical execution of the job;
- *functional* competencies related to problem-solving, rather than routine, abilities to learn, cooperate and organise;
- *strategic* competencies regarding understanding, and overview of the environment, the business idea, goals and the organisation. It also includes the ability to perceive whole systems;
- *personal* competencies regarding ethics, values and responsibility; this includes the ability to make decisions regarding right or wrong.

The distinctive contribution in Forsberg's typology is the explicit definition of "personal competencies". This deals specifically and explicitly with ethical issues and is an area which is now finding its way into university curricula and management development programs following the business and political developments related to "incompetencies" in this field in the 1980s.[17]

Figure 4 shows the four categories of competencies we have used in our analysis. The typologies presented by Nordhaug and Forsberg aim to cover competencies required in the labour market, i.e. they are aimed at all levels in organisations and all sectors in the economy. Our categories are somewhat more restricted to the personnel in focus in this study, namely production workers in the mechanical, manufacturing and process industries. The categories we use are:

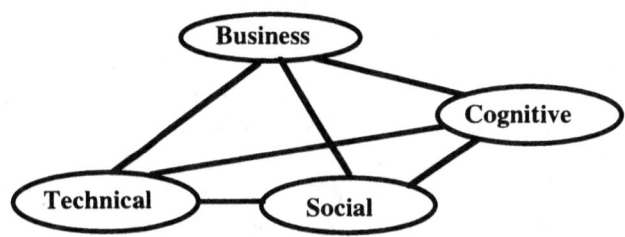

Figure 4. *Skills grouping in this study*

Technical competencies
This refers to knowledge and skills needed to utilise in an efficient way the tools, machines and systems used in the production process. In this context we have been especially interested in whether the training and support organisation in terms of manuals, multimedia, self-learning materials, tutors and supervisors, are designed and organised to facilitate rule-based or knowledge-based behaviour.

Cognitive competencies
These refer to analytical, planning, problem solving abilities which enable the workers to shoulder responsibility for the planning and control of production and for handling contingencies that may arise.

Social competencies
These refer to the interaction skills of the workers in production groups with each other and with people outside their groups. These include communication, co-operation and conflict resolution.

Business Competencies
These are specific skills used in exercising responsibility for the business performance of the production group. In this context we focus on two specific aspects of business performance: responsibility for the economic result of the group and responsibility for direct relations with customers. Thus responsibility for quality control in which the workers ensure that certain predetermined technical performance criteria are met before

finished items are sent to another department or to storage is regarded as a technical skill whereas quality control in contact with customers to ensure that products delivered to them meet their needs is regarded as a business skill. Similarly scheduling the orders to maintain a steady production is regarded as a cognitive skill, whereas planning the production to minimise capital bound in work in progress, a key economic performance criterion, is regarded as a business skill.

We began this chapter by pointing out that the competence demands emerging in industry will be a reflection of the demands arising from business ideas, work organisation, technology and personal needs. The main theme emerging now from the business debate is the partial eclipse of the scientific management paradigm by a post-scientific management paradigm which emphasises the creation of customer value. If scientific management has Anglo-Saxon roots, then the new paradigm may be said to have emerged from Japan, where Toyota has played a prominent role. That company's intensive and highly focused attention on eliminating products, services and activities that do not clearly and tangibly contribute to customer value has resulted in a logical series of developments in that company from the efficient changing of tools and dies in production to kanban, Just-in-time, Time-based Management, lean production, Kaizen, Total Quality Management, benchmarking, Business Process Re-engineering.[18] The key concepts emerging with this paradigm are customer value, time and quality. These form key values and elements in the mental models management is striving to imprint in its personnel. They form a basis for the application of all competencies but have even led to the demand in some companies for the specific business competencies we have mentioned above.

In the following sections of this chapter we will examine some of the latest research results regarding the impact of work organisation and technology on emerging competence demands. Finally worker abilities to cope with these demands will be addressed by a learning perspective.

The Implications of the Work Organisational Perspective

Today's new work organisations demand both new production skills and new work roles of the production worker. The major changes in work roles concern the power, control, responsibility and accountability dimensions. Efficient and effective production processes demand increased discretion or degrees of freedom on the part of the worker. This also means increased decision powers and responsibility for the worker. Under traditional forms of management control structures workers were told what to do, how to do it, and were paid for doing it, often by straight piece-rate wage systems. Technical and administrative control often left the worker with practically no degrees of freedom. The environmental (market) demands and technical complexity are now such that these tangible formal control mechanisms are self-defeating. New control systems must be evolved. With reference to our frame of reference presented in the previous chapter we can say that the physical controls of the production workers behavioural repertoire are now being replaced by "cognitive control systems" which regard production workers' mental models and values. [19] These approaches can entail organising production groups/cells more or less as profit centres or "mini companies" with the members of the work group as small company entrepreneurs taking a personal pride in the performance of their own group, exhibiting a loyalty and dedication in effort mostly associated with the self-employed.

Much of the training provided in the production groups which have been given a high degree of responsibility for their own performance is directed to providing knowledge and models which will enable this knowledge-based behaviour when faced with new, unique, deviating, contingency situations. These models may concern planning, problem solving, budgeting, quality control, capital rationalisation, and so forth. The value-oriented influence is exerted by increasing the production worker's understanding of the goals of the organisation, the conditions under which it operates and how it functions internally, especially with regard to where the production group and the production worker fit in the overall picture. This entails mapping out the goals for the production group in relation to the company goals and how the efforts and actions of the individual members of the group can contribute to and control the realisation of the group's goals.[20]

Important prerequisites for the establishment of a company-oriented knowledge-based behaviour on the part of the workers entails modifications in the company's infrastructures in terms of management planning and control systems. This will entail, for example, the development of local planning systems at the disposal of the production groups. It should also entail a modification in the incentive and reward systems so that members of the production groups see clear relations between their efforts related to factors under their control and the rewards they receive from management, not least in economic terms, for example via profit sharing, shareholding and other performance-related schemes.

German research, for example by Kern and Schumann, has shown that firms need particularly well-qualified workers who are both manually and theoretically competent, both able to diagnose and act effectively; workers who process to an equal degree, metal cutting and electrical and electronic knowledge of basics. They maintain a new kind of skilled production worker is emerging in Germany. They are anxious to dispel the misunderstanding that there is a shift from a practical worker to a theoretical worker. The new worker is not "either/or" but "both/and". Schumann maintains that according to their findings:

> "empirical knowledge has retained its major importance alongside increased
> theoretical experience. But the firm requires, as in previous times, the practical
> person who first acquired his necessary assurance in action through his daily
> dealing with machines, with sequences of production process and with the
> materials to be processed. The "trouble-shooter" who can sniff out problems
> before they happen and anticipate hiatuses in a sequence of production before they
> result in disruption is still needed, as well as the manual "Jack-of-all-trades"
> and "bright boy" who can jump in if production breaks down and who can produce
> a satisfactory improvisation. Using a combination of theoretical know-how,
> experience and manual dexterity, he must be in a position to compensate for
> weaknesses in the technical systems by practical action"[21].

The new production worker can, however, still be far less content than the traditional craftsmen with his once-learned knowledge and ability. The intellectual ability to learn permanently and go on learning, that is, being able to cope with the high grade dynamics of the production process, is the important specific new demand being made of him. Schumann maintains therefore that we are seeing a tendency towards a "re-professionalisation" of production work. Referring to the irony of automation he agrees that the skilled worker will still remain irreplaceable as a source of correction for the still imperfect technology, that is, to offset the remaining deficiencies in theory and control. The worker here helps to plug the gaps which are no longer of mechanised but of automated production technology, but with totally different tasks.

Similar tendencies have been reported from developments on the Swedish scene. In summarising the results emerging from the Swedish Work Environment Fund's development program on new technology, management and working life, which was carried out in the 1980's and in which forty companies and public agencies participated, Docherty notes the following shifts in the principles being applied in work organisation which constitute positive preconditions for competence growth on the part of production workers:

- a tendency to replace the principle of "redundancy of parts" by that of "redundancy of functions" in job design.
- a tendency to decentralise management planning and control systems, especially regarding goal setting, planning, problem solving and the provision of feedback to production workers.
- a tendency to move away from uniform, across-the-board organisational solutions, in preference for polyform or multiprinciple organisations in which different work groups in the same work place were organised according to different principles, for example mixing foremen-led groups with autonomous working groups.
- a tendency to replace "single-loop learning" conditions where workers had no opportunity to question or comment on current practices, to "double-loop learning" conditions in which workers were encouraged to come with constructive comments and ideas on the improvement of current practices and structures.
- from a "steady state orientation" in which jobs and working groups are designed on the assumption that the production conditions are stable and the level of uncertainty and turbulence are low, to a "disrupted-state" orientation in which jobs and the organisation are designed on the assumption that the work place must handle a considerable degree of turbulence and uncertainty.[22]

Naturally, a number of complimentary shifts have emerged in the competencies required of production workers in the companies participating in this program. These include:

- the shift from "niche specialisation" (one man, one task) towards broad integration in which individual workers carry out a number of tasks within a group;
- a shift from "rule-based" performance towards "knowledge-based performance";
- the shift from a "puzzle-solving" orientation, in which the worker identifies "the one solution" which is relevant in the situation, towards a "problem-solving" orientation in which the worker is free to select or design one of many possible solutions to a situation;
- a shift from individualised knowledge where knowledge is related to the individual worker, towards collective knowledge in which knowledge is related to production groups.

Similar results were also obtained by Hirschhorn and Mokray in an analysis primarily of American studies. [23] Tables 2 and 3 show their results regarding the changing nature of problems to be solved by workers and technology's impact on the nature of skills required. The changes are all in the direction of increased complexity and "fuzziness". The skills required were all more abstract cognitive or knowledge-based skills.

From	To
A few parameters	Many parameters
Correcting variances	Preventing variance
Sustaining levels of output	Sustaining quality
Puzzles: a single piece	Patterns: the flow, the linkages
Within a single operation	Across several operations

Table 2. *The changing nature of problems to be solved by workers*
(Source: Hirschhorn & Mokray in Adler (1992, p 23))

From	To
Doing	Controlling
Responding	Planning
Tacit knowledge	Explicit knowledge: knowing what you know
Enacting one's knowledge	Remembering one's knowledge
Awareness	Awareness of one's awareness

Table 3. *Technology's impact on the nature of skills required*
(Source: Hirschhorn & Mokray in Adler (1992, p 24))

They identified five "layers" of cognitive functions ranging from lower - to successively higher - order skills. The layer closest to the work itself is "doing", the actual performance of the task. The next skill level above this is "controlling" and the third level is "learning", which entails reflection on the results obtained during the control process. The fourth level of skill is "design", introducing chain following learning. The fifth and final level is "evaluating", understanding how to evaluate alternative designs. These levels in themselves may well be compared with the different phases involved in experiential learning as proposed by Kolb.[24]

Present pattern	Factory of the future
Single skills	Multiple skills
Demarcation	Blurring of boundaries
Rigid working practices	Flexible working practices
Operation mainly by direct intervention	Mainly supervision of advanced operations
High division of labour	Moves towards team work
Low local autonomy	High local autonomy and devolution of responsibility
Training given low priority	Training and organisational development given high priority

Table 4. *Patterns of work in present and future factories.*
(Source: Bessant and Senker (1987, p. 162))

Table 4 shows the results of Bessant and Senker's study on work patterns which also point clearly to rising skill demands requiring more flexibility, more formal education, more frequent training. The workers also need to be provided with the opportunities to maintain good learning habits.

The Implications of the Technology Perspective

The Technology-Organisation Interaction

The idea that a specific technology always leads to the same effects, and that a technology's impact on its users and their organisations is deterministic, was regarded by the majority of people as true in the 60s and 70s, in much the same way as the majority regard this idea as obviously false today. [25] Technology and work organisation are two factors which management may use as control systems to determine the individual degrees of freedom or scope for action at work.

Brytting & Löwstedt studied the impact of one particular computer-based application in similar situations in different European countries.[26] They studied the impacts of computer-supported automatic analysis systems in hospital laboratories on the work organisation and professional roles of the laboratory assistants. Professional roles were categorised in terms of administrative, caring and scientific/technical roles. The weight associated with these different aspects of the profession of the laboratory system differed between the participating countries which were Belgium, Germany, Hungary, Italy, Sweden and the United Kingdom. In each country the introduction of the new technology led to a reinforcement of the dominant dimension in the profession in each country.

Tidd names technologies that can be deployed in a wide variety of patterns, such as numerically controlled machine tools, flexible manufacturing systems (FMS) and robotics as "configurational" technologies.[27] Tidd argues that it can be misleading to look for the "impact " or "implications" of configurational technologies on skills and work organisation, because the experience of users and suppliers of robot technology in the United Kingdom and Japan indicates that the existing work organisations and skills are taken into account in the design of the systems. Swedish experiences have not always been as fortunate as those of the British. In Sweden there has been a tendency for designers to utilise the latest technology when designing new plants instead of using an "appropriate technology" adjusted to the competencies available in the work force.[28] Often the changes demanded are radical, and demand a "quantum leap" which the management is not aware of when it is designing its personnel development strategy. As a consequence, it is often inadequate.

It is often conscious or unconscious decisions on the part of the management and the designer which determine to a large extent how technology will influence the users. Examples of important factors in this context are as follows:

Technology as a bearer of values
The important factor of this context is management's view of its personnel, their commitment to their work and their company, and their competence. If management has little trust in its personnel, their competence and commitment, regarding personnel instead as the main source of the so called "human error factor", that disconcerting risk factor in production that is so difficult to control, then it is natural that technology will be utilised to minimise the workers' discretion and influence on production. On the other hand if technology is regarded as a means of supporting and facilitating the competence and discretion of the user, systems which achieve these ends can be designed. These values form the point of departure for the R and D projects on anthropocentric production systems within the ESPRIT and FAST programme in the European community[29].

Technology is a mirror of the available or utilised knowledge
Docherty has established that the systems designers were often completely unconscious of many of the shortcomings of computer-based systems in failing to meet their users' needs and capacities at work. They were often highly dismayed and upset when they were informed of the problems which their systems had lead to in the users' working conditions. Analyses of the formal educational courses for systems designers in, for example Sweden, show that only a few universities offered optional courses in such areas as organisation theory, psychology and economics - the designers had little or no relevant knowledge to apply in their work[30].

The Impact of Technology on Skills

Some people have seen technology as a way of solving the insufficient supply of qualified personnel: automation would guarantee industrial and commercial growth. Others have seen it as a possibility to emancipate and develop people by being a means for learning. Experts have mainly indicated three possible lines of development: downgrading, upgrading and the polarisation of skills and competence within the work force. If technology was mainly regarded as a means for reducing personnel inputs as a production factor and increasing management's control over the production processes, it is natural, for example, that the introduction of different decision algorithms in production systems should aim at deskilling. Evidence of deskilling among local and government civil servants as a result of the introduction of the computer based system has also been reported on the European scene. On the other hand automation could alternatively be used to relieve qualified employees from much routine work, giving them more time for qualified tasks. The third line of development is a combination of the other two: in practice it results in a growing gap between high and low skilled workers, a polarisation. Some personnel categories, for example academics, can look forward to a more stimulating job supported by advanced computer-based systems, whereas other groups' work mainly acquires an instrumental value, i.e. is seen by the workers primarily as necessary for their personal economy, i.e. the money it generates. Reviews of the available literature have shown evidence of all three trends.

Attewell maintains there are several indications that the deskilling approach to numerical control has become less common over time, and that the practice of encouraging operators to set up, proof out and edit is spreading. Earlier experiences in the 60s and 70s of utilising unskilled labour to man numerical control machines proved to be inefficient and ineffective. Later generations of these machines are now designed to be programmable at the machine. Attewell makes the point that automated machines and modern integrated work processes are not necessarily more error prone than earlier technologies in the sense that errors occur more often than in less automated or less integrated machine systems. However highly integrated systems tend to be more error sensitive in the sense that chain reactions may occur through parts of an interdependent system giving rise to more complex and difficult problems.

New Demands from the Technology

A number of researchers have pointed out that the new technology does not lead to deskilling but to reskilling, i.e. that the new technology demands quite new skills that operators did not previously possess.[31] The complexity of the new technology and the stresses and strains to which it is subjected, result in the technology being non- predictable; it functions in a stochastic rather than in a deterministic fashion.[32] This gives rise to new uncertainties regarding the types of problem that may arise and when they may occur. This in its turn means that operators must be given greater discretion for action, greater autonomy and a broader competence for handling contingencies.[33]

The new technology also results in the work becoming more abstract.[34] Previously an operator received information as the basis for his actions from his concrete working situation in the form of sounds, and visual and kinetic signals. Now this information may be provided by various instruments in the form of abstract symbols and numbers. These symbols and numbers may be further processed in a computer-based model and "hands on" control of the machines is now replaced by key-punching at a keyboard or control panel.

Supervisors and operators must now display high levels of cognitive skills: to draw conclusions from large amounts of data, for example in statistical production, to integrate information from different sources, to visualise and create for themselves mental models of the processes in a work situation, to understand the complex systems which the work situation is a part of, to verbalise and convey descriptions, analyses and interpretations of the work situation to others. In addition the new technology in many contexts, has led to increased demands on attention, concentration, endurance and speed in decision making and actions, i.e. what Masusch calls "Intensity Skills".[35] The technology can introduce new forms of work discipline and pacing. In summary, concrete motor and physical skills are being replaced by conceptual, cognitive skills, based on an abstract understanding of the work.[36] Operators are being required to manipulate mental models, create for example block or flow diagrams or models over the process they are working with. There are marked similarities with what Zuboff calls "data-based reasoning", to be able to extract relevant information from large amounts of data in order to be able to interpret what is happening in processes.[37]

Docherty & Dilschmann noted three distinct stages in the individual's learning when new information technology systems are implemented. In the first stage, attention and learning are concentrated to mastering the equipment itself and the basic routines in the system. These issues absorb the user's full attention. The length of this phase depends naturally on the user's previous relevant sensory-based skill level. Following the first stage, this attention will then become focused on the actual application, its different functions and relations between them. First in the third stage the user will begin to utilise the application as a tool in order to be able to do his job in a better fashion. Phases one and two can be quite extensive, e.g. over one year.[38] Naturally this depends on such factors as previous experience of information technology and the organisation and resources allotted to training and support systems.

The design of the interface between the system and the user determines to a large extent the cognitive demands made of the user. Hacker points out that the interface should place as low demands on the user - novice or expert - as possible.[39] The interface should be simplified and made transparent to allow the user to be able to develop a personal working style. The dialogue with the system should only require a minor part of the user's consciousness and mental capacity. The efficiency in the dialogue is dependent on the complexity of the task defined in terms of its scope and its demands for reflection and memory.

Swedish experiments with knowledge-based systems have shown that the design of the interface is critical for the user's motivation and ability to learn the system.[40] Interfaces which are designed to promote efficiency in administrative aspects of the work may be a direct hindrance to utilisation of the system as a problem-solving tool in interpersonal production tasks, e.g. in service tasks.

Implications of a Learning and Competence Perspective

Stern reviews a considerable number of studies which show the absence of correlation between school taught knowledge and problem solving in the context of actual production.[41] Research on "situated learning" suggests that learning through the work process itself may, in general, be the best way to acquire work related knowledge and skill. The following conditions facilitate a person's learning at work.

A "Context for Action"
The work must offer a certain degree of variation or change; either a planned variation, for example rotation between different tasks, or the participation in development projects, or via unplanned variation, for example the delegation of problem solving responsibility for dealing with certain types of contingencies at work.

Goals for and Models of the Production Process

Goals and models constitute the prerequisites for planned action at work. An important assumption here is that work is a goal-directed activity, i. e. it presumes rational behaviour in which a person acts first and thinks afterwards. People in an organisation may, however, have different ideas as to what the goal(s) is (are). Goals provide meaning to feedback. They make it possible for a person to evaluate results of his actions and give guidance as to what action needs to be taken thereafter.

Sandström and Howard noted that people working with complex tasks make few errors if the systems used present information corresponding to the mental models the users have of their work. Bråten found that people who had no clear model of their work or their production process, had much greater difficulty in controlling their work and solving problems because they had little chance of identifying with any certainty important signals in their environment concerning their work.[42]

An early criticism of data-based systems was that the models the systems included were often not available to the users. An advantage with the later technical developments, for example in knowledge-based systems, is that they can make models accessible, for example in graphic form, and that they include explanatory functions. The latter describe in ordinary language how the models are constructed, how the data entered into the system would be used, and how the difference results, for example proposed decisions, have been arrived at. All these functions facilitate learning.

Degrees of Freedom a Scope for Action

Learning requires that an individual can choose a plan of action, having analysed the current situation and his goals and needs. In single-loop learning this is just a question of trimming the execution of a standard routine. If double-loop learning is to occur however, the individual must have a certain autonomy, sufficient degrees of freedom to formulate and test new solutions, in order to develop a personal working style.

An important characteristic of many systems is that they have been designed in order to minimise the discretion of the operator: what could be automated, has been automated. Zuboff uses the term "informating" to characterise the opposite strategy in which control systems are made more flexible and safe by presenting the operator with detailed information which they may use for planning production and maintenance, and for solving problems when contingencies arise. This entails a work organisation which gives the operator greater responsibility and discretion to try out new ways of acting. This is a basic prerequisite for learning.

Feedback

If a person is to learn in a situation where he acts to realise a goal or execute a task, he needs to know relatively soon if his actions to date have contributed to the accomplishment of the goal or the task. Without rapid feedback the individual will loose motivation in his work.

The majority of the feedback from computer-based systems on work processes and their results is only made available to management. In order to facilitate learning other groups of personnel should also receive feedback on their goals and factors in the work process which they can control. This can suitably take place in local planning systems at the disposal of the operators. Such systems have formed an important part of the development work within ABB and are being developed within such companies as Swedish Rail.[43]

Reflection

Having planned, acted and received feedback, the next logical step in the learning process is to reflect on the experiences gained; to compare the plans, the actions and results, and to think through the possible reasons for possible deviations. The reasons may be related to one's own actions, own interpretations of the situation and/or the environment, actions or interpretations of other actors, and so forth. Many work situations give neither priority nor opportunity for such reflection.

A Social Context

The process of reflection can often be supported if it takes place in a group in which workers share their experiences and discuss interpretations. This group process has the advantage of leading to a collective knowledge where the workers build up a common model of important factors in their work situation and how these are related to each other. This in its turn facilitates better communication between the workers (reduces the grounds for misunderstanding) and a more consistent way of acting within the group. This in its turn, provides a basis for more reliable expectations regarding how different members will react in a given situation and thus heightens feelings of security in the group.

In considering learning, it is important to distinguish between what is learnt and how the learning process takes place. Our point of departure is that people relate to their environment in a learning way. They always learn and adapt to their environment. Learning is however not always positive. Many people live in situations where they learn not to get involved, where they in fact cannot learn, and feel they are incapable of more qualified tasks.[44] Thus it is important to differentiate between learning to adapt and learning for development and change.

How can one classify different aspects of the learning situation in the work place? We wish to discriminate between different types of learning in terms of the factors that delimit what could be learnt. Table 5 shows four such learning situations. In reproductive learning, both the task and the method to fulfil the task, as well as the result of the activity, are determined in advance. The learner should learn certain ways of handling the task to achieve a given prescribed result. In rule-based productive learning a goal and method are given but not the result. Problems are solved by the application of specific methods that one can be trained to master. In goal-directed productive learning you have to find or develop your own methods to achieve a result that meets the demands formulated in the goal. In creative learning basically nothing is given. You determine the goals as well as the means and assess the results.

Learning in industrial settings, in the work organisation, can easily be related to the cases in Table 5. In fact most jobs in traditional work organisations at the shop floor level only offer opportunities for reproductive learning. In the most extreme forms of new, transformed work organisations, tasks, methods and results are sometimes open even at the shop floor level. In extreme cases, learning is an entirely open process as depicted as creative learning in Table 5. This concerns how people orientate themselves in partially unknown environments. Swift adaptation in new environments heightens the chances of survival.

Aspect of the learning situation	Levels of learning			
	Reproductive learning	Productive learning		Creative learning
		Rule-based	Goal-based	
Task/Goal	Given	Given	Given	Open
Method	Given	Given	Open	Open
Result	Given	Open	Open	Open

Table 5. *Four types of learning as a function of the discretion of action there is in the learning situation*
(Source: Ellström in Marking (ed.) (1992) [45])

How do people handle their environment and in what way does it need different skills in the four cases in Table 5? The Danish researcher Rasmussen has described different levels and types of skill-based behaviour.[46] The first and deepest skill level, requiring no conscious reflection, he calls "sensory-based behaviour" in which the individual, on noting a relevant sensory input, automatically executes the appropriate response. This is typical of physical skill performed in the production process; for example by a turner using a lathe.

The second level is what he calls "rule-based behaviour" in which sensory signals may more or less consciously be regarded as relevant cues which initiate a search for the relevant standard response in the individual's repertoire. These standard or "by management pre-defined legitimate" responses reflect the traditional form of management control.

The third level is "knowledge-based behaviour" when the individual registers a signal which is deemed to require response which is either totally new or of such non-standard or infrequent character that it requires special, conscious handling. In this case the response to the signal is specifically tailored to match the unique situation it constitutes. The solution is formulated on the basis of the individual's knowledge in the area (mental models) and his knowledge of the company (production group) goals.

If he/she can, the worker will design a plan of action to handle the situation. Having executed the plan of action, the consequences it gives rise to are observed. When the worker feels he/she has gained control of the situation, the successful actions are incorporated in his/her repertoire of sensory or rule-based behaviours.

If the worker does not manage to sort out the situation that has arisen, he/she is faced with a problem solving situation. This requires reflection in relation to his/her evaluation of the overall task or goal that demands action. It is simply a matter of trying to solve the problem with what he/she knows or the knowledge available to him/her from other sources. Gradually, or more usually, suddenly he/she sees things clearly. He/she gets an idea of what he/she might do to handle the situation. This could be an active response, such as "press the stop button", entailing a direct regression to sensory-based behaviour. More typically for knowledge-based behaviour the reflection leads to a consciously formulated intention to take action which is incorporated in a plan of action and so forth. Action is assessed and judged to be functional or not and the process repeats itself.

Referring to Table 5, some new features emerge. In the rule-based learning mode you activate all the levels in the Rasmussen model when learning to handle the task. The intention is that you, as a trainee, shall ultimately attain skills so that you perform at the sensory-based level. On the other hand, in the creative learning mode, you will always activate knowledge-based performance. There are enormous differences in demands on the individual and the learning loads between these situations. It clearly indicates that the variability in the environment of the organisation is one crucial factor and the organisational design to respond to that variation is a crucial point for learning in the work place.

Ciborra and Schneider give the examples of workers using manufacturing resources planning systems at an aircraft instruments plant. The workers must make skill judgements, based on projections about the repercussions of their actions rather than simply according to fixed rules. They maintain:

> "to accomplish this, the workers need at least three distinct cognitive skills:
> - a formal abstract knowledge of the system itself - its logic and rules;
> - a highly concrete knowledge of the work organisation - how different department's function, what their formal procedures and informal practices are; and
> - the capacity to make their organisational models explicit and available for reflection, so they can better relate them to the formal model of the work organisation embodied in the software."[47]

Ciborra and Schneider differentiate between two levels of learning which they call:

1. *"Incremental learning"*; whereby organisational knowledge is increased by the re-performing or refining existing routines within a stable context that attaches the same set of meanings both to old and new routines.
2. *"Second-order learning"*; whereby the context of meaning is changed. Old routines loose their original significance and acquire completely new meaning, and routines previously ignored, suppressed, or unimagined are put into place and executed.

Second-order learning implies regarding disturbances and fluctuations as opportunities for new emerging designs, and not as objects for control or elimination. They regard second-order learning as being related to the organisation's "formative context", "mental and behavioural commitments to technology, personnel and methods in the organisation, not easily or quickly altered".[48] They maintain that learning -by-doing, for example, on the part of production workers, only leads to revising routines within given contexts. On the other hand second-order learning implies the revising of contexts. Thus they recommend a number of actions to facilitate second-order organisational learning and successful business renewal which include: sanctioning local experimentation, developing an institutional infrastructure based on loosely coupled networks, to enhance co-ordination and the flexible sharing of information and innovation.

[1] The American social psychologist Chris Argyris defines the terms "espoused theories", i.e. the theories or ideas that a person openly states are the bases for their actions, and "theories in practice", i.e. the ideas and theories emerging from an analysis of what that person does in practice. See Argyris, C. & Schön, D. (1978) Organisational Learning: A Theory of Action in Perspective. Reading, MA: Addison-Wesley.

[2] Bright, J.C. (1958) Automation and Management. Boston: Division of Research, Graduate School of Business Administration, Harvard University

[3] Drucker, P. (1950) The New Society. New York: Harper & Row.

[4] Noble, D. (1978) The Design of America, Cambridge, MA: MIT Press.

[5] Bainbridge, L.(1983) "Ironies of Automation". In Johansson, G. & Rijnsdorf, J.E.(Eds.) Analysis, Design and Evaluation of Man-Machine Systems. Oxford: Pergamon.

[6] Volpert, W. (1986) "Contrastive analysis of the relationship between man and computer as a basis for system design". In Docherty, P. et al. (Eds.) System Design for Human Development and Productivity: Participation and Beyond. Amsterdam : North-Holland.

[7] Senker, P. (1992) "Automation and Work in Britain". In Alder, P.(ed.) The Future of Work and Technology. New York: Oxford University Press.

[8] Choice, K.(1984) Human Resource Development on the Shop Floor in Contemporary Japan. Stockholm: Arbetslivscentrum

[9] Cole, R. (1992) "Issues in Skill Formation in Japanese Approaches to Automation". In Adler, P. (Ed.) The Future of Work and Technology. New York: Oxford University Press

[10] Selznick, P. (1949) TVA and the Grassroots. Berkeley: University of California Press and Selznick, P. (1957) Leadership in Administration. Evanston, Ill.: Row and Peterson.

[11] Hamel, G. and Prahalad, C.K. (1993) "Strategy as Stretch and Leverage", Harvard Business Review, Vol. 71, No. 2, p. 75-84

[12] Senge, P.M. (1990), The Fifth Discipline: The Art and Practice of the Learning Organisation. New York: Doubleday

[13] Leonard-Barton, D. (1992) "Core Capabilities and Core Rigidities: A Paradox in Managing New Product Development", Strategic Management Journal, Vol. 13, pp. 111-125

[14] Docherty, P. & Dilschmann, A. (1992) Lärande med förhinder: När teknik stöd blir teknikstyrning. Stockholm Arbetsmiljöfonden MDArapport 1992:12.

[15] Nyhan, B.(1993) Emerging Patterns of Qualification and Learning. Presentation at the European Centre for Work and Society Workshopin Dublin in December, 1993.

[16] Nordhaug, O. (1993) Human Capital in Organisations: Competence, Training, and Learning. Oslo: Scandinavian University Press.

[17] Forsberg, B. (1992) Lärande arbeten i teorin: en analys av förutsättningar för meningsfulla lärprocesser i arbetet med utgångspunkt i fyra olika forskningstraditioner. Stockholm: Arbetsmiljöfonden, Programmet för lärande organisationer

[18] Lillrank, P.(1994) T-50 på ABB-ett svenskt svar på den japanska utvecklingen. Stockholm: European Institue for Japanese Economic Studies och Arbetsmiljöfondens program för Lärande organisationer.

[19] Barker, J.R.(1993) "Tightening the Iron Cage: Concertive Control in Self-Managing Teams". Administrative Science Quarterly, Vol. 38, No. 3, pp. 408-437; Weick, K.E. and Roberts, K.H. (1993) Collective Mind in Organizations: Heedful Interrelating on Flight Decks. Administrative Science Quarterly, Vol. 38, No. 3, pp. 357-381. The news is not the development of "cognitive control systems " per se. These have been reported long ago, e.g. in geographically dispersed organisations (cf. Kaufman, H. (1960) The Forest Ranger: A Study in Administrative Behavior. Baltimore: Johns Hopkins University and Resources for the Future Inc.) It is rather the renewed interest in and conscious, widespread adoption of the strategy that is new.

[20] Considerable research has shown that production workers' own cognitive models of how the company functions often differ considerably from the models of senior (and even middle) management. It would be naive to assume that simply informing workers of management's models would be sufficient to guarantee that the workers would simply disgard their own models and adopt management's. Establishing a joint model requires an intense dialogue.

[21] Schumann, M. (1990) "Changing Concepts of Work and Qualifications" in Warner, M. , Wobbe, W. and Brödner, P. (eds) New Technology and Manufacturing Management. Chichester: John Wiley & Sons.

[22] Docherty, P. (1990) IT and Organizational Change in Sweden. Paper to the MIT Activity Meeting 22/23 November 1990, Public Management Service (PUMA), OECD, Paris.

[23] Hirschhorn, L. and Mokray, J. (1992) "Automation and Competency Requirements in Manufacturing: A Case Study" in Adler (ed.) Technology and the Future of Work. New York: Oxford University Press.

[24] Kolb, D.A. (1964) Experiential Learning: Experience as a Source of Learning and Development. Englewood Cliffs, NJ: Prentice-Hall

[25] Löwstedt, J. (ed.) (1989) Organisation och teknikförändring. Lund:Studentlitteratur.

[26] Brytting, T. & Löwstedt, J. (1986) Organisationsfrihet-visst finns det! Stockholm: EFI

[27] Tidd (1991) Flexible Manufacturing Technologies and International Competitiveness. London: Frances Pinter.

[28] See for example Roland Steen (1982) Progress Review of the Development Program on New Technology, Management and Working Life. Stockholm:Swedish Work Enviroment Fund.; Hörte, Sven-Åke (1987) The Development Project at the D III Factory in Gothenburg. Gothenburg: Institute for Management of Innovation and Technology.

[29] See for example Rosenbrock, H. (1990) Machines with a purpose. Oxford: Oxford University Press and Rosenbrock, H. (1989) Designing Human-Centred Technology Berlin: Springer-Verlag.

[30] Docherty, P. et al (1974) Hur man lyckas med systemutveckling: En analys av fem praktikfall.Stockholm: EFI.

[31] Björkman, T. and Lundqvist, K. (1986). Yrkeskunnande och datorisering. Stockholm: Statskontoret

[32] Hirshhorn, L. (1984). Beyond Mechanization: Work and Technology in a Postindustrial Age. Cambridge, MA: M.I.T. Press.

[33] Davis, L.E. & Taylor, J.C. (1976) "Technology, Organization and Job Structure" in Handbook of Word, Organization and Society. Skokei, IL: Rand-McNally.
[34] Weick, K. (1990) "Technology as Equivogue: Sense making in New Technologies" in Goodman, P.S., Sproull, L.S. and Assoc. (ed) San Fransisco: Jossey-Bass
[35] Masuschs, M. (1974) Unddannelersektorens politiska ekonomi-lära arbetet och lönearbetet i kapitalismen. Köpenhamn: Rhodos
[36] Gerwin, D. & Kolodny, H. (1992). Management of Advanced Manufacturing Technology: Strategy, Organization and Innovation. Chichester: John Wiley & Sons
[37] Zuboff, S. (1989) In the Age of the Smart Machine in the Future of Work and Power. Oxford: Heinemann.
[38] Docherty, P. & Dilschmann, A. (1992) Lärande med förhinder: När tekniksstöd blir teknikstyrning. Stockholm: Arbetsmiljöfonden MDA Rapport 1992:12.
[39] Hacker, W. (1987) "Computerization Versus Computer-Aided Mental Work" in Frese., M. H., Ulich, E. and Dzida, W. (eds): Human Computer Interaction in the Work Place. Amsterdam: North-Holland
[40] Beckman, J. & Steineck, J. (1991) DUS-projektet vid Centralstudiemedelsnämnden. Stockholm: Statskontoret; Docherty, P. & Dilschmann, A. (1992), op. cit.
[41] Stern, D. (1992) "Institutions and Incentives for Developing Work-Related Knowledge and Skill" in Adler, P. (ed) Technology and the Future of Work. New York: Oxford University Press.
[42] Bråten, S. (1983) Dialogens villkor i datasamfundet. Oslo: Universitetsförlaget.
[43] Mårtensson, L. (1987) Developments at ASEA Distribution. Stockholm: Arbetsmiljölaboratoriet, Royal Institute of Technology Stockholm. Forss, P. and Ehn, P. (1992) Local planning systems in Production at Swedish Rail. Stockholm: IMIT
[44] See, for example, the literature regarding Learned helplessness including, for example Lennerlöf, L. (1986) Kompetens eller hjälplöshet: Om lärande i arbete: En forskningsöversikt. Stocholm: Arbetsmiljöinstitutet.
[45] Ellström, P.E. (1992) "Kompetens och arbetsorganisation" in Marking, C. (ed.) Kompetens i arbete. Stockholm: Publika.
[46] Rasmussen, J. (1986) Information Processing and Human-Machine Interaction. Amsterdam: North-Holland.
[47] Ciborra, C. U. and Schneider, L.S. (1992) "Transforming the Routines and Contexts of Management, Work, and Technology" in Adler, P. (ed) Technology and the Future of Work. New York: Oxford University Press.
[48] Ciborra and Schneider (op. cit.) maintain that their concept "formative context" is different from the concepts of mental models and organisational culture, though their distinction is not clear to this author.

Chapter Three

Meeting the New Challenges

Peter Docherty and Barry Nyhan

Introduction: Competence Strategies

What competence development strategies are being implemented by the European industrial companies who are introducing social and technical innovations? How are they adapting their strategies to the rapid changes occurring in their environments? We are especially interested in the ideas of management (values and mental models) which are forming the basis for the action taken in companies. In this context we have defined three levels of change in management's ideas which reflect their different depths or significance, namely changes in behavioural repertoires, changes in mental models and changes in values. These have been presented and defined in Chapter One. Figure 1 shows the strategies corresponding to these respective levels of change in management with regard to selected companies. These companies are presented as case studies of such developments or strategies in the later chapters of this book.

Problem-solving Strategies are based on management's insights that the company is faced with clear, specific and pressing problems which may be solved by measures which, in varying degrees, require competence development efforts. It may well involve utilising tools, methods and models which have shown themselves to be successful in other companies facing similar situations. The adoption of a problem-solving strategy requires specific measures in order to meet current problems and needs. There is no question of management regarding the situation as needing a radical re-evaluation of current strategies and policies or its basic ideas about how it should do business. This may be a reflection of the fact that management is not prepared to re-evaluate its ways of conducting its business or simply that it does not regard such a re-evaluation as relevant. This may also reflect a deep caution regarding change.

Model-based strategies are another type of strategy, reflecting deep changes, in which management adopts a frame of reference or cognitive models which have been developed in other companies and which have been shown to be very successful. Examples of the types of models and strategies that have aroused wide interest in management circles are service management, time-based management, total quality management and Kaizen. Management's decision to adopt the frame of reference, thereby changing its previous models for the development and running of the company, is based on a conscious evaluation process which may vary greatly in the number of people involved and the resources used. The adoption of a model-based strategy for competence development usually involves more than limited specific measures and is more characteristic of a transformation.

The vision-based strategy entails a deeper or more fundamental change in management, concerning value issues. The strategy is based on a clear management vision regarding the role of the company in the market place and the roles and responsibilities of personnel in the company in the future. The vision is essentially based on values. It is not unusual that there are few, if any, relevant or easily accessible experiences from other organisations that may function as bench marks for the making of decisions in this context. On the contrary the formulation of a vision-based strategy may be the point of departure for an extensive learning process which requires considerable risk taking on the part of management. It is not a question of easily retreating when difficulties are encountered. Rather a vision-based strategy implies a basic change in perspective and culture in contrast to the adoption of existing models and perspectives. It is a question of seeking new ways and models rather than implementing existing ones.

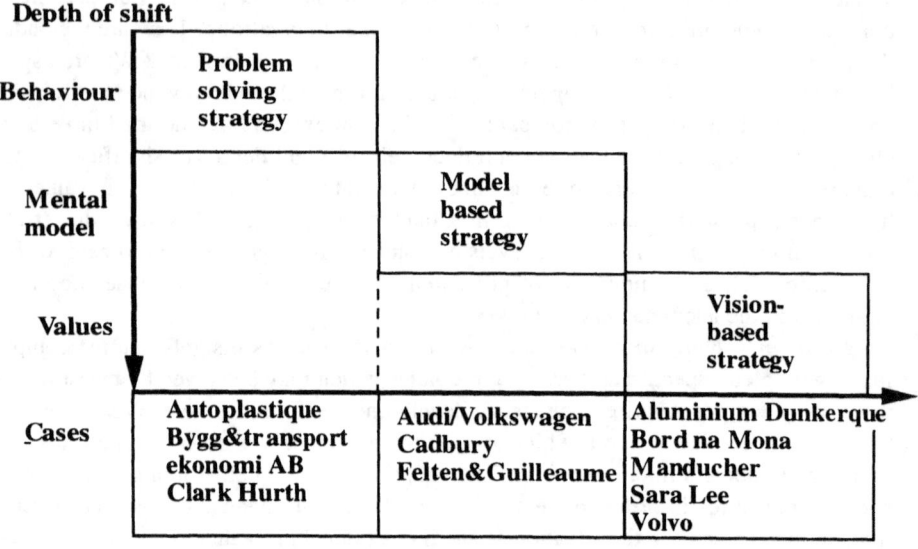

Figure 1. *Competence development strategies*

Problem-solving strategies

Of the 11 case studies presented here, three are examples of problem-solving strategies. These are the French plastics company Autoplastique, and the Swedish and Belgium manufacturing companies Bygg & Transportekonomi AB and Clark Hurth. In these cases the competence development strategies have been clearly limited for different reasons. In Autoplastique, management regarded the situation with which they were faced as simply requiring a decision on a shift to a new technology generation. They were not prepared to re-evaluate their own current position regarding models and values. In the Swedish case management's actions reflected a more short-term ad hoc handling of the issues arising. Top management support for competence development issues was weak and there was a certain dynamic conservatism in middle management towards a more radical or innovative development of the roles and skills of production workers. In the Belgian case, management's approach to change and competence development was characterised by extreme caution.

The changes involved in a problem-solving strategy may be regarded as being minimum adjustments to be made when circumstances demand. In only one case, that of Autoplastique, did the competence development strategy involve the provision of basic preparatory training for the workers to ensure their ability to participate in the main changes. There was only one case of any systematic learning at work, as distinct from formal training. There were no systematic pilot activities, nor were any adjustments made to the incentive and reward systems in the company. Similarly, systematic co-operation and an overhaul of joint agreements between union and management did not occur in these cases.

Model-based strategies

Model-based strategies for competence development were introduced in three companies: a British confectionery company, Cadbury's, and two German manufacturing companies, the car-manufacturing corporation Audi/Volkswagen and the engineering company, Felten & Guilleaume. Considering the models being adopted, Cadbury's was introducing total quality management (TQM) and was coupling its competence development activities to the British system for "National Vocational Qualifications", NVQ, a system for the general certification of worker skills aimed amongst other things at heightening the portability of skills between companies. The German companies were introducing different variations upon the production island system involving teams with integrated production skills on the shop floor.

In each case the competence development strategy was based on detailed models and concepts which form the basis for radical, large-scale changes in the companies which were associated with considerable risks. In each case they constituted radical changes in existing plants. The change processes were characterised by a pragmatic co-operation between the social partners, the local unions and management, related to mutual gains. The cases benefited from considerable external support. This took partly the form of researchers and consultants who provided frames of reference and methods to implement the changes. In the German cases the companies also received financial support from regional and national R&D programs such as the Arbeit und Technik program.

A number of features of the competence development programs which were found in isolated cases in this group were:

- the development of a competence-related incentive and reward system;
- the development of a competence portability system (the NVQ system);
- the development of a system to support learning within the organisation;
- the joint evaluation of the developments by management and the local unions.

In none of these cases were there any reports of a more general basic preparatory training program for the workers to provide a competence platform for their eventual participation in the proposed developments. This was probably unnecessary in the German cases as the German manufacturing industry is in many respects a European benchmark regarding the vocational training of skilled engineering workers.

Vision-based strategies

The most radical, all embracing and fundamental of the competence development strategies we have observed in the case studies is the vision-based strategy of which five examples are presented in this volume. They include the development of a new aluminium processing plant in Aluminium Dunkerque, a radical re-organisation of the production in the Irish state-owned company, Bord na Móna, the introduction of a new entrepreneurial management system in the Dutch subsidiary of Sara Lee, the introduction of a capability-based strategy in the French plastics car component company, Manducher and the development of the Uddevalla plant in the Volvo company.

Management, and often clearly identifiable members of top management, have taken a value-based initiative which entails a marked shift in management's conceptions of the roles and value of its work force. This vision usually encompasses the work force as a whole, i.e. is non-elitist, and entails competence development opportunities being made available for all employees. The ideas in the vision can lack practical examples or directly available experiences although they may often be well-grounded in a theoretical framework, for example social-technical system theory. Thus, in the Volvo case, the improvement of the status of production workers and the enrichment of the content of assembly work were two essentials in management's vision. This was to be realised by evolving radical alternatives to the assembly line. Taking the craft worker as a point of reference, a new car plant was designed in which individual workers would be responsible for assembling major systems in a car, or even the entire car, thereby extending the work cycle for the car worker from several minutes, through the "limiting barrier" of twenty-thirty minutes, to several hours. The capability-based vision in Volvo extended the "vision of the possible" far beyond that which had been reported at any other car factory.

Aluminium Dunkerque, Manducher and Volvo have in common that the competence development processes started with a vision regarding the critical role to be played by line production workers in the achievement of business goals. The competence and innovativeness of the workforce were seen as key resources.

Another feature of the vision-based competence development strategy is that they were the result of a very close and deep co-operation between management and the unions from a very early stage in management's thinking about the new changes. This co-operation was often regarded as being "unusual" within the general context of the industrial relations prevailing in the country concerned. The social partners concerned succeeded in these cases in establishing "virtuous circles" in their interaction. Management's initiative was, to say the least, compatible with the values and goals of the union. This is not to say, however, that some of the change processes were not the subject of intense and extensive negotiations with the unions as in Bord na Móna or that the development processes could be simply characterised as "joint ventures". In Manducher, for example, management made it quite clear that they had the initiative to take action and the experiences gained formed the bases for joint evaluation and negotiation, often resulting in new joint agreements covering successive developments.

This strategy requires an intensive and continuous support from top management. Thus, the owners of Manducher specifically recruited the consultant responsible for their strategic analysis to be the designer and champion for their new capability-based strategy. After this strategy had been launched, the company has been taken over by a German corporation and is now part of a multinational European consortium. However, the director of social affairs and the capability-based strategy he designed have received the full backing of the new owners and the strategy is now valid for the consortium as a whole.

Management must give high and continued priority to concretising the vision in specific measures which can be perceived by broad groups of personnel as relevant, important, challenging and achievable. The vision is conveyed to the personnel via local (regional) programmes as in the case of Aluminium Dunkerque or through a partnership programme as in the cases of Sara Lee and Bord na Móna. In the latter cases personnel were regarded as partners in the business and the competence development programme entailed providing them with specific business skills. Important features of the information process between management and personnel is establishing clarity and understanding regarding basic features of the competence development programme and the new strategy, for example regarding the necessity of an extended learning process, the risks involved and the demands made and management's commitment to "not going back", i.e. not to abandon the strategy.

A frequent feature of the vision-based strategies is a provision of a basic preparatory educational program which will enable those personnel who have gaps in their basic education to complement their knowledge and skills so that they can participate in the general competence development programme. These programmes even include the basic "3 Rs": reading, writing and arithmetic. They may also include the basic technical skills relevant to the industry in question.

The vision-based competence development strategy is not however, simply a matter of designing a sufficient number of relevant, high quality courses for different groups of personnel. Important aspects of creating the learning organisation include:

- the systematic design of learning projects in the organisation;
- a design of systematic follow up and evaluation processes to monitor the development of individual workers;
- the design of incentive and reward system so that the individual worker knows precisely the benefits he or she will reap by shouldering responsibility for his or her own development and the development of the business.

Steps towards a new paradigm

We feel that these broad strategies may be regarded as stages in a progression towards a new competence-based work organisation paradigm. The separate strategies refer to basic elements which will characterise the new paradigm, i.e. new behaviours, cognitions and values. However, the transitions between the separate strategies may be expected to be somewhat fuzzy as successive new features emerge or are adopted in individual companies. The progression in the strategies is characterised by a steady growth in the breadth and depth of the strategy, steadily encompassing more features and more stakeholders within the company:

- from behaviour to cognitive models and values;
- from management as a sole stakeholder to include different categories of personnel and their unions;
- from a special cluster of job skills, to basic skills and finally even to business skills;
- from solely formal training programs to also include systematic on-the-job training on the shop floor;
- from existing organisations to new work organisations with decentralised decision making;
- from existing management control systems to new systems including new incentive and reward systems.

The driving goals in the vision-based examples in this study have in all cases been business effectiveness and business goals regarding customer value, product quality, reduced lead times and higher productivity. A key shift has been the shift in the role of workers from being a simple production factor or human resource to being a partner, capable of exercising discretion, responsibility, business acumen and self development. The aim of the companies is then to develop competencies needed for business - a capability-based strategy. Competence development has not been motivated as an independent goal per se. The establishment of a learning organisation has not been seen as a goal in itself, e.g. "to have a good personnel policy", but has been regarded essentially as a means to attain business goals.

Competencies in demand

Which are the new competencies the production workers are acquiring when technical and social innovations are implemented in European industry? Table 1 shows the results of the 11 cases presented here. In our frame of reference we refer to four distinct clusters of competence; social competence, including conflict resolution, cognitive skills such as planning and problem solving, technical skills related to the technology in the industry in question and business skills regarding various forms of economic planning and evaluation and more social competence directed to the personal interaction with customers. In addition to these specific competence clusters the table also presents a number of other features of the competence development in the cases.

The trend towards team organisation is an international phenomenon. All the cases reported that the technical and social innovations in their companies led to workers acquiring more social competence, e.g. communication and conflict resolution, and cognitive competence, e.g. planning and problem solving. The competence development was limited in some of the problem-based strategy companies "to those whom it may concern, or "on a need to know basis". Thus in AB Bygg & Transportekonomi the competence development efforts concerned those workers assigned to a FMS-cell and not to the other workers on other stations in the production flow.

Competence issue	Competence strategy		
	Problem-based	Model-based	Vision-based
Social/team competency	All	All	All
Cognitive competency	All	All	Several
Technical competency	Several	Several	Strongly emphasised
Business competency	None	None	Several cases
Holistic Perspective	Limited	Examples	Several
Multiskilling	----------	All	All
Competence ladder	----------	Clear examples	Clear examples
Competence portability	----------	UK-case	Some cases

Table 1. *Competence characteristics of different competence strategies*

New technical competencies were required in most cases, irrespective of the competence development strategy, but it is interesting to note that they were especially emphasised in the vision-based cases. However the vision-based strategy cases show clearer differences from the other strategies in the other aspects of the competence picture:

- They include the only cases in which employees are required to develop *business skills*. This is congruent with the "partnership" values underpinning this strategy. These included both economic skills and customer-handling skills;
- The include the majority of cases characterised by an *holistic perspective* regarding the employees' work situation, i.e. the workers are given the opportunity of handling all the important features of the work and the problems arising in it;
- There were a number of clear examples in this category of the *competence adders*, i.e. management offered the workers clear opportunities for their future development in the form of the successive development of their competence by acquiring new levels of competence in current skills or by acquiring new skills. These career paths are clearly available to all, though often on a voluntary basis (at least initially);
- There were several cases where *portability* was regarded as an important aspect of competence acquisition, i.e. the company provided certification so that the skills acquired could be verified and utilised if and when the individual left the company and wished to take up a position in another company.

The idea of holistic competence has attained special significance lately due to the increasing complexity of work situations. The worker must be able to relate the specific task he/she is dealing with at any moment to the overall task being carried out by other members in the team and the organisation. It requires a kind of helicopter perspective and a feeling of contact with different parts of the system. Such attributes were previously seen as only applying to management. It is necessary for the worker to be able carry out "complete jobs" or "long cycle" work in a relatively autonomous manner. This was particularly emphasised in the studies of Aluminium Dunkerque, Audi/Volkswagen, Felten & Guilleaume and Volvo, and from an unique perspective in Autoplastique.

In Aluminium Dunkerque, worker development was conceived in terms of moving successively along different levels of complexity within a "field of related jobs", instead of learning compartmentalised jobs related to discrete functions. One begins by carrying out normal operations regarding different stages of the work process from start to finish, while gradually extending the depth of one's theoretical and practical knowledge, so learning to handle variance and attain mastery.

The notion of "handlungskompetenz" (action-competency) which is a key attribute of workers in Audi/VW and Felten & Guilleaume, refers to the ability to conceptualise, plan and execute all aspects of a complex job in an independent manner.

In Volvo the emphasis was placed on being able to assemble complete subsystems or even several subsystems in a car. This gave work cycle times of several hours.

Multiskilling was reported in all the cases pursuing model-based and vision-based strategies. The character of the multiskilling confirms that reported by Schuman, i.e. the workers were required to master both theoretical knowledge and practical skills. The social, cognitive and, naturally, business competencies were related to handling the increased complexity in the workplace and were thereby directly related to improving the efficiency and effectiveness of the business, e.g. through reducing lead times, heightening product quality, facilitating maintenance and problem solving, quickening responsiveness to customer requests.

The main coupling between the emerging competencies and strategies lay in the devolution of management tasks and authority to the workers as management's trust in and understanding of the workers increased. Thus, already in model-based strategies the workers began to acquire cognitive skills and what we in Chapter Two called secondary and tertiary tasks / skills, i.e. both a responsibility for problem solving in production and for participation in the development of the products and the production processes.

First in the vision-based strategy, when the individual is not simply regarded as a "human resource", were the employees given responsibility for business decisions. However, this did not involve any specific training in the field of ethics, either defined in terms of general moral norms in business or as company-specific values determining the character of the company culture. In some countries, such as the United States, there has been a gradual shift since the fifties in the composition of top management in the manufacturing sector from consisting mainly of engineers to economists. This contributed to the increased focus on short-term economic indicators as key performance criteria, at the expense of longer term technical development criteria. (This shift has been given as an explanation of the decline of the American car industry in the face of Japanese competition in the seventies.) Indeed the focus on financial performance on paper exerted a compelling fascination for management, especially in the eighties. This strongly contributed to the severe economic decline the financial sector and business in the late eighties and early nineties. This in turn has led to a strong interest in ethical issues, in a broad sense, in management and management development. Our cases in this book are probably too early in their origins (most originate from the late eighties) for this issue to have surfaced properly on the agenda regarding worker development. Several current examples of such training are available, e.g. in the Swedish Work Environment Fund's programme for Learning Organisations.

Figures 2-4 show different examples of the competence profiles emerging with the different social and technical innovations being implemented. Bord na Móna and Sara Lee, both adopting vision-based strategies, introduced social/organisational innovations in work organisation and management systems that placed special emphasis on social and business

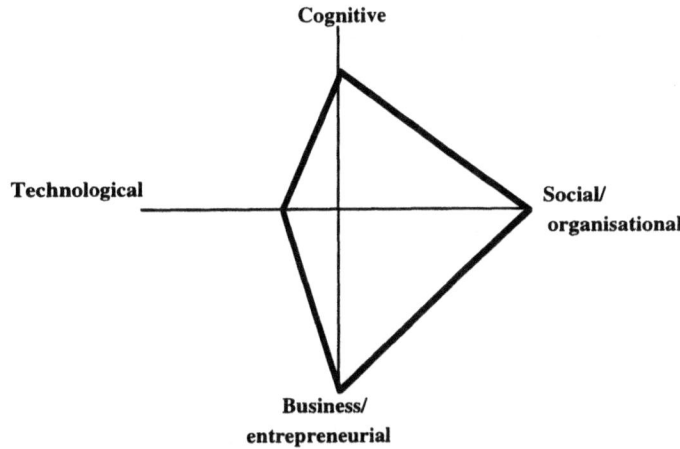

Figure 2. *Competence profile at Bord na Móna and Sara Lee*

competencies and somewhat less on technical skills, although in Bord na Móna the teams had full responsibility for the running and maintenance of the production machinery. The business skills in Bord na Móna focused on the financial management --"understanding basic finance was seen as central to the success of the team". Broad business management skills, such as cost management, forecasting, planning and in particular risk taking, were also seen as essential. In Sara Lee, the emphasis was on employees developing an entrepreneurial spirit, taking initiative and responsibility.

The concept of "key qualifications" was central to the notion of worker competence in the two German companies, Audi/VW and Felten & Guilleaume, which were both pursuing model-based strategies. In this context the key qualifications concern cognitive, social and technical skills. In these companies, the cognitive skills include observing/ listening to and interpreting the running of the production machinery, reading and interpreting drawings and numeric data. This also requires knowledge of the structuring of the programmes in the computer-supported machines. The communication and co-operation skills include mutual information exchange and joint problem solving. The technical skills in the teams included electrical and electronics, hydraulics and pneumatics. These were interpreted in relation to "handlungskompetenz" which means bringing all these qualifications together in an integrated way to carry out a whole job.

Aluminium Dunkerque, BT, Cadbury, Clark-Hurth, Manducher and Volvo also have competence profiles that highlight cognitive, social and technical competencies, similar to the German "key qualifications". Manducher also included social business skills to handle customer contacts.

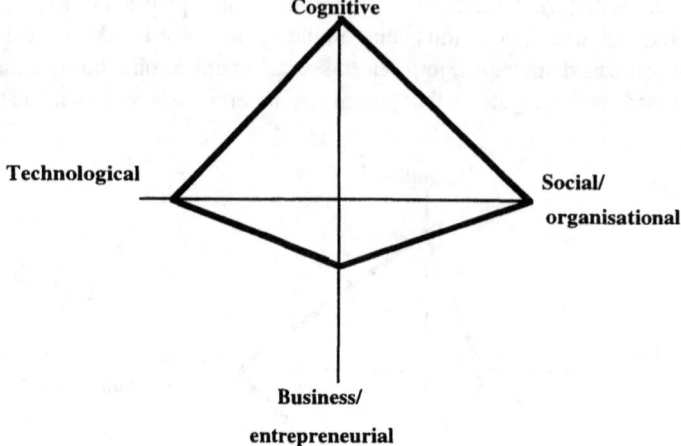

Figure 3. *Competence profile at Audi/VW and Felten & Guilleaume*

In Autoplastique, a company pursuing a problem-based strategy, workers developed core competencies for "Collective Intelligence". This required skills of a cognitive character and social and communication competencies to share knowledge and know-how. Among the cognitive competencies mentioned were the ability to anticipate and react, problem formulation and solution and decision making.

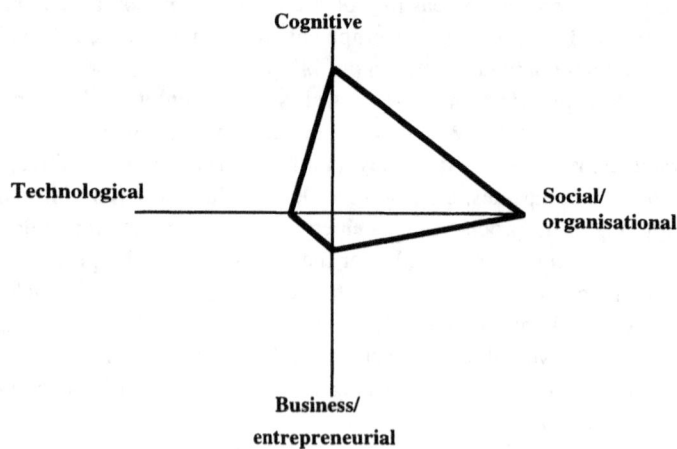

Figure 4. *Competence profile of Autoplastique*

The Development of New Competencies

How did the companies go about facilitating the acquisition of the new competence required by their social and technical innovations? A few observations may be made here.

Seven of the cases made special efforts to ensure that everyone had a good opportunity to participate in the "learning drive", either by arranging a initial training programme to trim up individuals' basic competence, or by arranging pilot projects to test and make people familiar with the basic ideas to be implemented in the restructuring of the companies in the coming solutions. The programme at Aluminium Dunkerque comprised 1100 classroom hours in scientific, social and technical skills. At Manducher this programme lasted 125 days, divided into three main blocks, a basic refresher (35 days), basic company and job knowledge (50 days) and a specific job course (40 days). The Bord na Móna programme was focused on cost-management skills. Regarding the pilot projects, work organisation experiments were carried out in Bord na Móna, Felten & Guilleaume and Volvo. Sara Lee conducted a number of "developmental projects" including a training course for first line management.

When the serious changes began, to what extent was formal training complemented or replaced by "informal" learning at the workplace? The latter term, especially in union circles, is often interpreted as meaning "no training -- sink or swim as best you can". In this context we are interested in the extent to which learning in the workplace has been supported in a planned, systematic fashion with its own infrastructure and resources. Here we find there is quite a spread in the options adopted by the different companies:

- Personnel at Autoplastique and BT were given no formal training and had to scavenge for themselves, creating their own degrees of freedom and finding their own resources. Learning took place exclusively within the team;
- Following the initial formal training at Bord na Móna, the teams were "thrown in at the deep end" and had to fend largely on their own;
- Training needs at Clark Hurth were identified by trainers by means of formal contacts with work groups and informal contacts with individual operators and tutors. Technical work groups were set up under the supervision of the trainer to resolve special problems;
- Felten & Guilleaume used learning circles with line managers as coaches/tutors. The circles identified the learning needs and agreed on training programmes;
- Cadbury used formal training and self-instruction package modules, with the assistance of external consultants and training bodies to assist in the development of cross-trade technical skills at craft level;
- Audi/Volkswagen used "learning-oriented flexible manufacturing cells" and cognitive learning strategies such as "heuristic rules" and "Leittextmethode" (guided discovery learning texts) to facilitate learning;
- Manducher used experienced workers or supervisors as teachers /tutors and used "distributed formal training" by placing training rooms on the shop floor where classes could be held continually by different groups of workers leaving their work stations for an hour or more;
- Volvo used "cascading" where newly trained workers, having gained practical experience, trained new recruits until the factory was manned. A special "work

place pedagogics" was developed so that workers could learn to assemble major subsystems of a car by perceiving them as cognitive wholes;
- Aluminium Dunkerque followed a "planned on-the-job-learning" programme (according to eight stages in a job) with continuous learning based on reviews of performance in "real work situations". Learning in teams was co-ordinated by middle management with staff and consultant help;
- Aluminium Dunkerque, Cadbury and Manducher used joint assessment of the progress of the developments by unions and management as a meta-learning exercise.

The Competence-Based Strategy Development Processes

The nature of the development sequences

The third question posed in this study was how does the interplay between management ideas, company structures and processes develop in the course of the implementation of the social and technological innovations that require or lead to new competencies and competence levels? The sequence in the stages in the development processes in individual companies naturally took different forms. In the cases presented here there was considerable variation in the course and structure of the development processes and the emerging patterns are preliminary. That is, the study of the limited number of cases here did not indicate any clear and marked patterns in the order in which changes in the different areas were implemented within the different strategy categories or between the strategy categories. This result may be dependent on the small number of cases involved. We present however a number of observations from these companies.

The companies pursuing vision-based competence strategies were prime movers, charting courses in unknown waters. In several cases they formulated new values explicitly at the outset of the development process. In others the values were latent and became clearer and explicit in the course of the process. In three companies, Aluminium Dunkerque, Manducher and Volvo (Fig. 5), the process started from a clear vision of the critical role to be played by line production workers in the achievement of business goals. The competence and innovativeness of the workforce were regarded as key resources. The further development of structures and processes followed from this.

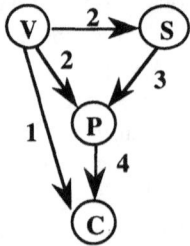

Figure 5. *The vision-based strategy process at Aluminium Dunkerque, Manducher and Volvo*

The developments at Aluminium Dunkerque started with the premise that unemployed people in an economically depressed area can be retrained to play an essential role in a process plant. Manducher changed its work organisation to increase the discretion and responsibility of the workers - a change that was in agreement with their wishes as established in a survey at the outset of the change process. Volvo started with a vision of a factory in which workers' creative craftsmanship skills (planning, controlling, "sense of ownership of the product") were mobilised to make a maximum contribution in a technologically advanced production situation.

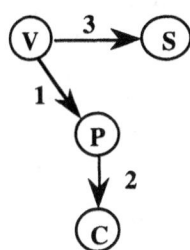

Figure 6. *The vision-based strategy process at Sara Lee*

In the case of Sara Lee (Fig. 6), the initial focus was on the competencies of the business units which would enable the company to innovate, to try new ways of doing things thus ensuring continuous improvement. This was regarded as a *value clarification* process in which the fundamental value of regarding the personnel as business partners capable of shouldering responsibility for the development of the business was to be brought more clearly in focus. A company-wide training programme was implemented which had the business units at the centre, but which was conducted in a total organisational context, looking upwards within the organisation and outwards at its external environment. It linked individuals roles in the business units to clear performance goals and criteria.

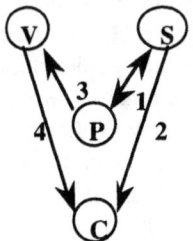

Figure 7. *The vision-based strategy process at Bord na Móna.*

Bord na Móna (Fig.7) arrived at a similar value position as Sara Lee, but not on the basis of a proactive value clarification process. A chronic company crisis forced top management to take radical steps. The new and painful measures were implemented through intensive and extensive negotiations with the trade unions on a step-by-step experimental basis, partly to maintain the relations between the social partners and partly to allow the evaluation of the radical changes being adopted. The company introduced autonomous business units and found that they were very successful, The system was ratified and the new implicit value system was explicitly clarified and accepted by both management and unions - workers were partners in the organisation and as a result business skills became essential worker competencies in the new organisation.

The companies with model-based competence strategies were basically secondary movers. They adopted models or solutions from others' experience. The changes which took place in the two German companies can be seen in the context of Germany's national research and development programmes concerned with working life - previously the Humanizerungprogram and now the Arbeit und Technik program. These programmes have fostered a close co-operation between academics and practitioners and have lead to the introduction of models, methods and tools from the academic sphere to industry. Some examples include such concepts as autonomous groups, "production island" manufacturing principles and networks. The changes in these cases also involved the use of new instruments for work-based learning with competence development seen as a central strategy.

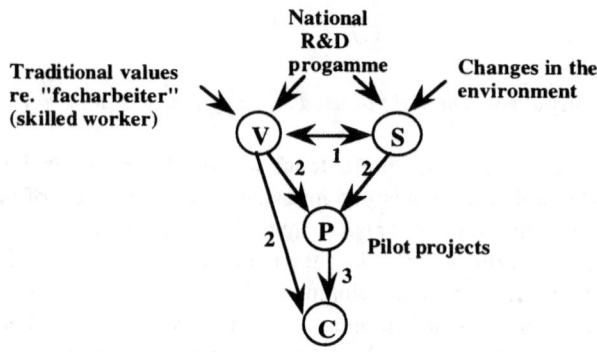

Figure 8. *The model-based strategy process in the two German companies*

In Audi/Volkswagen, the introduction of semi-autonomous multiskilled teams with machinists and electricians was supported by researchers, providing analysis and development methods and instruments, while the developments were strongly influenced by traditional German values regarding the central role of "facharbeiter"(skilled worker) in manufacturing companies (Fig. 8). In Felten & Guilleaume there was similar support from action researchers in the introduction of production islands. Both projects were supported by the German national and regional R&D programmes.

In the case of Cadbury the management's main transformation strategy (Fig.9) was based on the adoption of a Total Quality Management approach involving the adoption of a quality stance or perspective, including the value adjustments and the focus on new skills as distinct, for example, from the more simple introduction of a set of highly standardised routines as in the ISO 9000 framework. The Cadbury process also took place at the same time as the British authorities were pushing for the evaluation and certification of individual competencies within the National Vocational Qualifications (NVQ) framework, which was also adopted in this case.

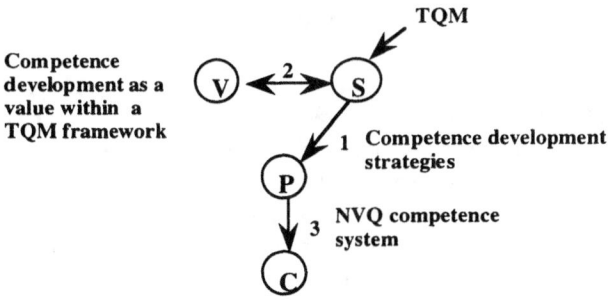

Figure 9. *The model-based strategy process in Cadbury*

The three cases presented here display a problem-solving strategy (Fig. 10) which entails a limited competence focus. Although radical changes were introduced in their work processes and some personnel groups acquired new competencies, the impact made on management structures and values was limited. Bygg & Transportekonomi introduced an FMS group into the production line, but it retained the character of an experimental group. The competencies acquired by this group were difficult to pass on and develop in other groups in the company.

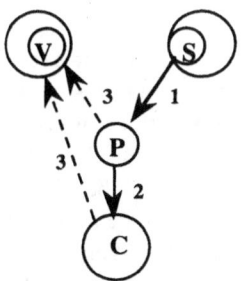

Figure 10. *The problem-solving strategy process*

In the case of Autoplastique, even though the adoption of new management tools gave rise to dynamic learning patterns, management seemed incapable of changing its image as being a centralised, and rather autocratic controlling body. They saw the changes as having to do with the implementation of new techniques without any corresponding significant changes in values.

The Clark Hurth case illustrates an extended change and learning process. The change depicts a rather tortuous piece-meal change process in which management gradually allowed more autonomy to be given to the workers as more advanced technology was introduced. This had significant repercussions for their competence development. The overriding caution of management did not allow radical changes to take place.

Distinctive features of competence-based strategy development

The different strategy categories identified in the above cases are regarded as phases in a transition towards a competence-based strategy. Such a strategy will be characterised by a number of features, some of which have been noted earlier in this chapter. The features emerging in this study are presented in further detail here.

Before discussing these features, it is important to note the time scale involved in establishing these new strategies. The cases described cover periods of four to ten years. This is because the establishment of a new strategy often involves changes in values, mental models and culture, i.e. changes in deeply rooted properties of individuals and organisations. An awareness of the longevity of the process of developing and implementing competence-based strategies is a facilitating factor. Realistic expectations about the feasible rate of progress in the process stimulate patience and endurance to see the process through inspite of eventual hold-ups or set-backs. Short-term opportunism and rapid changes of course and priorities are unlikely to facilitate the establishment of the strategy.

Dynamic visionary leadership and support by senior management

This feature underlines the key role played by top management in providing the value-based legitimacy for the risk taking, the extended trial-and even error and the cost in money, time and personal effort that the development of a new strategy takes. An example not included in this study is the corporate-wide transformation process initiated six years ago by the Swiss-Swedish engineering firm Asea Brown Boveri.[1] In their T-50 programme they launched a campaign to halve lead times in all their companies. The means used to do this had been advocated within the company repeatedly within the past fifteen to twenty years. Why did the T-50 programme succeed to the extent that no previous transformation effort in that company had done? The main reason given by all parties is the clear, explicit and continuous emphasis given to the programme by the corporate managing director, Percy Barnevik.[2]

In this study, all five companies were classified as driven by competence-based values and as "prime movers" who had inspired senior managers to be committed to creating degrees of freedom and control to be exercised by their employees. By the same token, the senior management of those companies that remained at the problem-centred solution level, seemed reluctant or afraid to initiate a policy based upon removing traditional management control systems.

The key figure or driver in such a strategic process is the chief executive. The personnel director can only initiate real change on the condition that he/she has the full backing of the chief executive and senior management colleagues. The significance of the role played by the chairman and directors in initiating such changes is clearly illustrated in the case of Aluminium Dunkerque, where the plant was specifically designed from the start to give prominent roles to front line production workers.

Manducher illustrates how close co-operation and trust between the chief executive and the director of social affairs facilitated an efficient change process. The senior management of Sara Lee reinforced the new orientation of their company by ensuring an environment in which middle management (business unit managers) felt fully involved in the company decision-making process. Thus they appeared to have avoided some of the problems that middle management in Aluminium Dunkerque and Felten & Guilleaume had with their new roles vis-a-vis the line workers.

In the case of Sara Lee, the corporate strategy focused on the concept of entrepreneurial management, encouraging managers to feel and act like the owners of the business unit they were responsible for. A visionary image was utilised to communicate the new management philosophy and inspire the employees to adopt new ways of working. Similarly the new production process at Volvo was driven by a new vision of the car worker as someone who can build a complete car on his/her own, being articulated by the company chairman. At the same time one can conclude that it was the failure of many managers to share this vision that contributed significantly to the closure of the Uddevalla factory.

Autoplastique illustrates a solution which many managers may be tempted to adopt - introducing new production and learning techniques within a traditional framework - putting new wine in old bottles. The result in that company was an uneasy co-existence of prescriptive management practices alongside open learning ones, not an ideal framework for sustainable development.

Faith in the commitment and competence of the workers and their unions

The top management values which characterise an extended and strong commitment to a competence-based strategy concern the dual aspects of business performance on the one hand and conceptualisation of personnel on the other. The new features in this context are the appreciation of the potential skills, commitment, initiative, creativity and responsibility of personnel and the willingness to regard personnel as partners in the organisation and not simply as a resource to be utilised (and even developed). Thus the management of Bord na Móna regarded "the creative tension between the old control and the new autonomy of the teams" as a central feature of the new organisation. The chief executive decided on this inspired, yet pragmatic decision in order to ensure the survival of the company. It meant "a total culture change for the company which involved setting up businesses within the group, carving out their own identity and direction and transferring leadership to the teams". Team-based activities as such were not new to the company - "what was new was the focus and the centrality of the teamwork". Even though management's risk taking resulted in a "fragile consensus" with the impact of the new values still reverberating within the company, the strong feeling of the workers after six years was that "there is no going back". The stability of the "fragile consensus" which management and unions referred to in Bord na Móna can be contrasted with the uneasy "trade-off" type of agreement in Autoplastique and the volatility of the consensus achieved in Volvo which was felt to have contributed to the decision to close the factory.

Felten & Guilleaume made a dramatic change from developing the workplace in its factories solely on the basis of a technology-centred investment policy to the introduction of a more sociotechnical approach centred on the concept of "production islands" - a concept of which they had no personal experience, but which had been shown to be very fruitful in similar contexts to their own. Basing the new solution on this concept meant a radical shift from reliance on technology to reliance on the workforce.

The problem-based strategy cases reveal the obstacles to such commitment. This may be fear of losing control as in the case of BT and as has been described in so many of the sociotechnical projects in the 50s, 60s and 70s. These projects often resulted in experiments in individual business units or departments of a company - experiments that often attracted considerable attention among managers and academics at home and abroad, but which were rarely emulated by others in their own company.[3] On the contrary, they were often isolated from the rest of the organisation. In Clark Hurth the hindrance was extreme caution or uncertainty about trying new ideas.

Management's positive mental model of the individual employee, when well-established, seemed to lead to a positive mental model of the personnel collective, i.e. of the unions and the relations between management and the unions. These were often characterised by mutual respect and understanding, not least understanding of the different frames of reference and values forming the basis for each party's position on different issues. This was often characterised by hard and extended negotiations at the company level, in some cases before, in other cases after management's initiatives or decisions, partly dependent on the national industrial relations patterns. Even the tougher cases, such as Bord na Móna, Cadbury and Manducher, the social partners could not be described as following adversarial industrial relations strategies.

Existence of an overall framework or model for the strategy process

As we have already noted these strategy development and implementation processes took several years from the start-up phase to the achievement of a significant objective. We encountered no examples of rapid "re-engineering". The processes had the character of evolution rather than revolution. In this long-term context a soundly based framework or model is of great use to keep the project on track. This may be provided, for example, by broad conceptual organisational change models developed within the company as in the case of Bord na Móna, Manducher and Sara Lee, or between the company and external consultancies or action researchers as in the Volvo case.

Similarly the two German cases, Felten & Guilleaume and Audi/Volkswagen, both co-operated with researchers on new qualification models to respond to the introduction of new technology and forms of work organisation. Aluminium Dunkerque relied on sociotechnical thinking and drew on the theoretical ideas on "l'organisation qualifiante" (the learning organisation) developed by such researchers as Zarifian.[4] The Cadbury company adopted a TQM. framework within which the overall competence development programme took place.

Common ownership of the development process

Management and unions at Bord na Móna regarded the development of an "informal understanding and mutual respect" between management and employees as a key element in the success of the whole process: everyone became involved in a significant way. The extensive meetings between the two parties evolved a shared vision given the title "Teams - Partnership for Progress". The deep level of trust and understanding that had grown in the company meant that this phrase symbolised common ground and was not a mere slogan.

One aspect of this is that management's vision must become a *shared vision*. This is a goal that requires considerable activities. Sara Lee focused initially on developing this shared vision on a company-wide basis and within each business unit. The arranging of company-wide communication meetings was an critical element in this process. The shared vision then provided a basis for the setting of performance standards for individuals who then perceived themselves as "partners in the business".

Another means that may contribute to the common ownership of and commitment to the development process is to proceed in an incremental stepwise fashion so that:

- the individual employees can develop the skills required to participate meaningfully in the process;
- the employees see that they will be given the opportunity to learn and adjust to the new conditions;
- the employees and their unions will have the opportunity of evaluating the effects of the changes and testing, and hopefully deepening, their trust in management.

One such stepwise approach is the use of *experimentation and pilot projects*. For example, Bord na Móna, Felten & Guilleaume, Manducher and Volvo tested their basic ideas in a single department or with a group of employees. The design of subsequent stages then proceeded on the basis of the joint evaluations of the outcomes of these experiments. Sara Lee also utilised this joint evaluation procedure, though with representatives of management, supervisors and the workers.

Another means used to foster common understanding and trust was *cross-functional teams*. These teams could be composed to represent both different functions and different levels in a company. In Cadbury's, for example, these teams were called "Quality Action Teams" and were made up of people from different occupational grades, who met regularly to ensure that all of the interested parties were au fait with current production and maintenance problems.

Clark Hurth set up "ad hoc" project groups along the same lines, but they were composed of training and production personnel. These had the aim of devising relevant work-based competence development systems. In the case of Aluminium Dunkerque, planning and development responsibilities, such as personnel development, were handled by management on a cross-departmental basis, while the line management functions in the different departments were handled by less senior staff. This is the reverse of the traditional arrangement in companies.

A further feature of union management relations in this context has been the local development of a *pragmatic co-operation* which was not inhibited or restricted by central agreements. Thus in Bord na Móna, the workers could determine their own pay levels within bounds of a "gain-sharing" principle. Similarly, Cadbury realised that higher levels of competence gave higher quality and greater flexibility in production, hence it altered the incentive and reward systems by the introducing new pay structures to reward learning through the acquisition of new skills. Possibly French companies attach special attention to incentive and reward systems when reviewing learning and competence issues. Manducher, for example, offered all its workers the opportunity to participate in a competence development programme where five basic skills in production were defined on different levels and the pay system was coupled to this. An innovative aspect of the system was that workers were remunerated for their competence, i.e. what they could do -- not what they did, and management was rewarded for its ability to utilise the workers' competencies.

Other factors impinging on the development processes

We have already had occasion to mention the roles played by consultants and researchers in many of the projects. Especially in France and Germany, central and regional programmes have made not only knowledge and competence available to individual companies, but have also, through specific programmes, brought together other companies dealing with similar issues with whom contacts may be made and given financial support for the actual development process. Even the companies we contacted in the United Kingdom referred to the professional assistance provided by the National Council for Vocational Qualifications. This provides instruments and methods for the assessment and certification of job skills. However the British political strategy seems to differ from the French and German in that it is result-oriented and not process-oriented. It addresses what skills people have, not what are relevant skills are in any given context nor how they should be acquired.

Several of the projects have been carried out in a more general social context. The two French cases, for example, took pains to come to grips with the development of less privileged workers. The Aluminium Dunkerque case illustrates how unemployed people in an area of industrial decline can be retrained and successfully integrated in a modern work environment, demanding advanced social and technical skills. Manducher made similar investments with similar success with immigrant workers who had little formal education. The Bord na Móna case demonstrated how workers from a rural background who had become accustomed to Tayloristic work practices including adversarial industrial relations, were able to actively co-operate with the company management in implementing radical changes. The management and workers in Cadbury successfully negotiated a transition from a negative industrial relations culture to one built on pragmatic co-operation.

While Felten & Guilleaume shows how existing older workers can be retrained so as to adapt to new technology and modern practices, the more common and more traditional solution that would at first sight appear less demanding and less costly for a company, namely simply displacing older "untrainable" workers by younger ones, emerges in the problem-based companies, such as Autoplastique and Clark Hurth.

Although the management in many of these cases was experiencing business pressures to change, Bord na Móna was the only one experiencing a distinct survival crisis in which the board had appointed a new managing director with the simple brief of achieving an immediate turnaround.

Most of the cases were "brown-field" sites. Manducher included both "green-" and "brown-field" sites, whereas Aluminium Dunkerque and Volvo Uddevalla were both "green-field" sites, i.e. new factories.

Some Reflections on the Competence Development Strategy

In this section we discuss the cases from the viewpoint of a number of structural issues that have emerged in the course of the competence development strategy development and implementation.

The character of the control strategy

As we pointed out in Chapter 1, the traditional control practices in companies have revolved around technical and administrative routines. Control has also been a central task for first line supervision. The increasing complexity of the production process and the need for a high level of responsiveness to the many unexpected and prioritised changes in customer needs requires the devolution of management discretion to worker level in the name of efficiency and effectiveness. This reality has shown itself to hold in many of these cases -- the workers have received much wider mandates to make decisions and to conduct "business", e.g. to discuss scheduling, delivery times, quality levels, directly with customers. This has been accomplished by heightening the workers' awareness and understanding of the business goals of the company and their competence in business issues. The close co-operation between unions and management has also led to common formulations of goals and policy principles. This can be termed "cognitive" or "conceptual control": the workers' actions are guided by goals, policies, and models that they have learnt from or together with management. In many cases the work team functions as a small independent company. The management information systems provide the teams with feedback on their performance that allows self-evaluation and corrective action as necessary. These conditions prevail to a large extent in the five value-based strategy companies and to a certain extent in the model-based companies.

The character of the evaluation and reward system

The incentive, evaluation and reward systems are really an important component in the company's management control system. Only a few of the cases made specific adjustments to these systems in order to promote worker interest in his/her own personal development, i.e. to reward competence development explicitly. These adjustments were mainly in the form of competence adjustments to the hourly rates, e.g. in the Manducher case. It is less clear from the cases what form bonus systems took, what proportion of the monthly salary the bonus formed, if they were calculated for each team or each business unit.

The development of the remuneration systems is yet another example of the gradual but steady elimination of the differences between blue- and white-collar workers. In some sectors in some countries these groups are already integrated within the same trade unions, e.g. in the United Kingdom. In other countries, such as Sweden, there is a clear, historically based dichotomy between blue- and white-collar worker unions. Some of the major blue-collar worker unions in Sweden have severe misgivings regarding management's application of the "white-collar" control and reward systems to blue-collar workers. They are disturbed by the risk that these control and reward systems will foster attitudes that are dysfunctional or damaging for worker solidarity which plays so important a role for the worker collective. However we can provide no systematic evidence as to whether these misgivings are justified.

The character of worker influence

Participatory models for organisational and technological development and the devolution of responsibility and authority to the shop floor have, as one important goal, the engagement of the interest and the commitment of the individual worker in his/her job, so that his/her initiative and creativity will in turn benefit the company. These approaches are very effective in achieving these aims, though they are regarded as having some less positive effects at the same time if there is a tendency for management to adopt an "either/or" approach to worker influence, instead of a "both/and" approach. The two types of worker influence in this context are: direct, individual influence (as exemplified above) and representative, collective influence as exercised by the workers through their unions. A factual basis for unions' fears of the utilisation of direct influence as an alternative to, or a means for undermining union influence has been documented in many different national contexts. This study, however, does not include any clear examples of this kind, but rather several clear examples of the achievement of "both an enhanced union role and an enhanced individual role". These examples include Aluminium Dunkerque, Bord na Móna, Cadbury, Manducher and Volvo.

In some industrial relations climates there is an historically based antipathy on the part of the social partners to the general idea that unions should interest themselves or be allowed to interest themselves in the affairs of the owners and their management. Such antipathy is not a marked feature of the cases presented here, though there are a number of cases in which management has not given the unions any prominent role, but focused more on direct participation. Sara Lee is a case in point.

However the issue that has been raised in these cases is the reverse one: how far can the social partners, who represent such basically different interests, co-operate without there being a real danger that they will lose sight of their distinctive interests? The co-operation described in a number of the cases presented here has reflected such mutual trust and understanding and resulted in agreements that, even in their national context, give rise to bewilderment and even consternation, e.g. Bord na Móna. (There are even cases where management has introduced changes without consulting unions, which are so radical that few unions would have wanted them and few managers would accept, e.g. Sara Lee.)

The case studies shed no light on where a line should be drawn in these contexts as the limit for "safe" co-operation. Rather they indicate that it is probably possible to achieve more than one imagined through co-operation as long as the social partners are clearly aware of their distinctive interests and goals they are representing and that they have the full backing of their members and superiors respectively.

The character of the learning process

One feature of the current interest in learning in organisations is the issue of the subject who/which learns. When we talk of learning in the organisation, do we refer mainly to the individual employees who are learning, to the groups learning collectively or to the organisation itself that is learning? All three forms are important for the competitive power of the individual company.

The main focus of this study has been the production workers in the companies, i.e. the learning of individual employees. However, some American researchers who have been engaged in comparative studies of American, European and Japanese companies, note a tendency for European companies to focus their attention on individual learning generally and on vocational training in particular, at the expense of organisational learning. This is reflected in the fact that on-the-job learning and organisational learning are scarcely mentioned in the current European research programmes. Similarly the Volvo Uddevalla factory has featured in an extended debate on individual versus organisational learning in the Sloan Management Review in 1994. Here it was established that the Volvo factory provided excellent opportunities for individual learning but that its organisational learning was inferior to that of such factories as the Toyota/GM Nummi factory in California.

Several of the other case studies indicate that the company infrastructures in terms of management planning and control systems have been developed in a manner that would facilitate organisational learning, for example, by providing relevant performance feedback to different groups. However a closer review of this issue would require a new study.

Notes

1 Lillrank, P.(1994) T-50- Ett svenskt svar på Lean Production. Stockholm: The European Institute of Japanese Studies at the Stockholm School of Economics.
2 'European Manager of the Year" in International Management (1994).
3 Miller , E.J.(1975) Sociotechnical Systems in Weaving 1953-70: A follow-up study. Human Relations, Vol. 28, No. 4, p. 349-86; Philips, Å. & Stjernberg, T.(1983) Attutveckla arbetsorganisation: Långsiktiga effekter av 70-talets försöksverksamheter Stockholm: Economic Research Institute at the Stockholm School of Economics.
4. Zarifian,P. (1993) L'organisation qualifiante dans l'industrie agroalimentaire: L'exemple
du groupe BSN. Noisy-le-Grand: Université Paris Val-de-Marne;
Zarifian, P.(1992) "L'organisation qualifiante: de quoi parle-t-on?" Le Monde, 09/09/1992

Chapter Four

A New Plant Designed as a Learning Organisation: Aluminium Dunkerque

Olivier du Roy

Introduction

The industrial group Pechiney which launched this project is the world leader in the sale of aluminium reduction (electrolysis) technology and the third largest producer of primary aluminium in the world.

Aluminium Pechiney decided in 1988 to build an aluminium smelter in France in a joint venture with Electricité de France, the French state-owned electricity company. The site chosen was in the Dunkirk region near the Gravelines nuclear power plant. The plan was that the smelter would produce 215,000 metric tons per year and employ 550 people. Pechiney was, for the first time, installing a 300,000 potline technology in an industrial situation. The old Noguères plant, in South West France, was to be closed down and some of the employees re-deployed on the same site for new industrial activities (aluminium cans) and others taken on by the Dunkirk plant.

Pechiney's Chairman, Jean Gandois, wanted this plant to demonstrate a new industrial policy:

> "It is time that efficient management of human resources be considered a key factor in ensuring company competitiveness ... there is no ideal organisation ... the best organisation is one which actualises and develops people and utilises techniques efficiently, thus providing client satisfaction under the most favourable conditions. The new plant in Dunkerque ... is an important venture in this respect" (an interview in Le Monde on 16 November 1990).

The company wanted to be innovative with regard to three areas, listed below. The case study deals with the last two areas:

- respect for the environment;
- work organisation;
- social and economic integration in the Dunkirk region.

Group Pechiney

The Pechiney Group employed 27,000 people in France and 36,600 abroad (totalling 63,600 people) at the end of 1992. The Aluminium Metal division employed approximately 7,500 people. The Aluminium Pechiney company has six aluminium reduction plants and one research centre in France employing a total of 3600 people. Aluminium Dunkerque is part of the Aluminium Metal division employing 550 people.

Why Did Pechiney Implement a New Policy ?

There are three reasons behind Pechiney's desire to make Dunkirk the symbol of radical change, establishing a policy aimed at both industrial performance and employee satisfaction, the one strengthening the other.

1. *Staff training and qualifications alone do not suffice to transform work organisations*
The Pechiney group, and in particular the Aluminium Pechiney company, had for the past ten years implemented a dynamic training policy in its plants, and as a result of its very close collaboration with the Education Nationale (State Education Authority), enabled its trainees to obtain nationally recognised diplomas. To implement this policy the training was innovative in that complete "descriptions" for each particular job were created and skills were assessed in the working situation.

It was noted however that increasing the level of qualifications alone would not enable progress to be made in industrial performance, or allow the complete initialisation of the skills acquired, unless the acquisition of qualifications was linked to considerable changes in work organisation. Hence the qualification issue was placed within the framework of a complete redesign of the work organisation at Dunkirk.

2. *Existing plants did not reach their productivity expectations because they tended to almost rely entirely on technical innovations*
Pechiney builds and supplies the technical know-how for nearly all the new aluminium smelters in the world and has developed almost one per year in the recent past. It was noted however that technological progress was not equalled by the quality of working conditions, levels of employee qualifications and responsibilities, and harmonious organisational methods. Technical changes only were accomplished: pot size and regulation, improvements to emission treatment and waste recycling methods etc.

In Dunkirk's case on the other hand, productivity gains are estimated 30% higher than a classical smelter of the same size, with half of the gains due to technological developments and the remainder due to organisational ones.

3. *Pechiney wanted to show that heavy industry in Europe could be competitive*
Pechiney's other recent smelters had been built in countries where the price of energy was low, Australia, Canada, or in countries where labour costs were low and/or energy superabundant: Bahrain, India, South Africa.

Thanks to a unique partnership between Pechiney and Electricité de France (the reduction in energy costs, representing 30% of the aluminium cost price) and to new work organisation, Jean Gandois set out to demonstrate that it was still possible for heavy industry to exist in Europe and be competitive.

The project was initiated thanks to the political impetus of the main decision makers at Pechiney. It was the brainchild of Pechiney's Chairman, Jean Gandois and his Assistant Manager, Martine Aubry - who became Ministre du Travail et de l'Emploi (Labour and Employment Minister) in France in 1992-1993. The project was implemented by a project team, who were supported by consultants.

The Impact of the Work Organisation on the Jobs of Operators

A Plant Designed to Enable People to Realise their Potential

At the launch of the project at the end of 1988, Pechiney outlined the following objectives:

- to start with highly-skilled staff;
- to create an organisation which favours the development of skills such as self-management, teamwork;
- to ensure high quality working conditions for everybody in all sectors of the plant;
- to design an integrated plant in contrast to the old factories which were often composed of three or four distinctive units on the same site;
- to provide career prospects for all.

In order to apply these objectives three project groups set to work.

Architects

Architects designed the traffic flow for workers and machines, to meet the challenge of creating a whole plant which, whilst having its three production departments built over an area of 17 hectares, would be a friendly and a pleasant place in which to work.

Ergonomic Specialists

Ergonomic Specialists undertook a "reference study" at the St. Jean de Maurienne (in Haute Savoie, France) and Vlissingen Smelters (in the Netherlands). Their mission was to reduce the five "black spots" located in each department. Over and above this, they assist the project engineers with negotiations on the schedules for equipment installations, and with the design of the computer systems.

Training Specialists

Training Specialists, together with Education Nationale, the Regional authorities and the trade unions, created a programme to bring the manpower available in the Dunkirk region up to the required educational standard. This manpower in the main comprised unemployed workers from the local steel and shipbuilding industries. A training programme totalling 1,100 hours was carried out by GRETA, AFPA (the French National Training Agencies) and the consulting bodies before hiring. 350 candidates were registered for this programme of which 273 were hired, 85% of the candidates achieved the CAP level (*Certificat d'Aptitude Professionnelle*, Certificate of Professional Competence).

When work started on the building at the end of 1989, the following three foundations of the "human" aspects of the project were already in place:

- the design of the different working area;
- the ergonomic layout of the work stations and machines;
- the operators' initial training.

Work Organisation - the Key Area of Innovation

The assistance of AEGIST (*Association européenne de gestion et d'intervention sociotechnique*) was requested in the conception and implementation of the innovative work organisation. AEGIST firstly helped the project team, and subsequently the management team, in the creation of a model organisation which met the defined objectives and broke completely with all previous organisational concepts in place at the older Aluminium Pechiney plants.

AEGIST operates within the framework of the Tavistock Institute's socio-technical model, as it developed in France in the early seventies. It supervises investments in technological change from a socio-technical viewpoint, and it facilitates the evolution of "learning organisations" (Organisation qualifiante: see writings of Phillipe Zarifian). Its approach is similar to those of several other French consultancy groups such as CISTE (Grenoble), IECI (Strasbourg), and CEMIS (Lyon).

Seven Themes Characterising the New Organisation

The characteristics of the organisation project, as it was set up by the project team are as follows:

Self-managing teams of operators

This company is made up of teams of operators, doing shift work, with a great deal of autonomy, without foremen as in the old plants. Every team is in charge of part of the process (electrolysis, anode oven, metal casting in foundry, etc.). There are about 25 teams of this kind in the plant and each is made up of eight to twelve individuals. They have their own objectives and result indicators. They share out the work among themselves by referring to standard job-outline documents. There are no shift foremen: the teams are self-organising and versatile: each operator in turn carries out all technical operations. What is at stake is mastery of the "complete field of jobs".

"A complete field of jobs"   (des métiers complets)

All the "jobs" in the plant are described, following the same scheme in relation to eight major stages which cover all the dimensions of a complete mastery of the work (see Figure 1). In each category there is an identification of know-how (following several complexity levels) which allow for:

- the implementation of appropriate training;
- an assessment according to an objective or a "reference".

What are the eight major stages ?

1. <u>To be able to gather information and to situate oneself</u>
   to be able to look up information, use data bases, technical documents, and operation modes, and to be able to situate one's function and post in terms of the whole process of the plant.

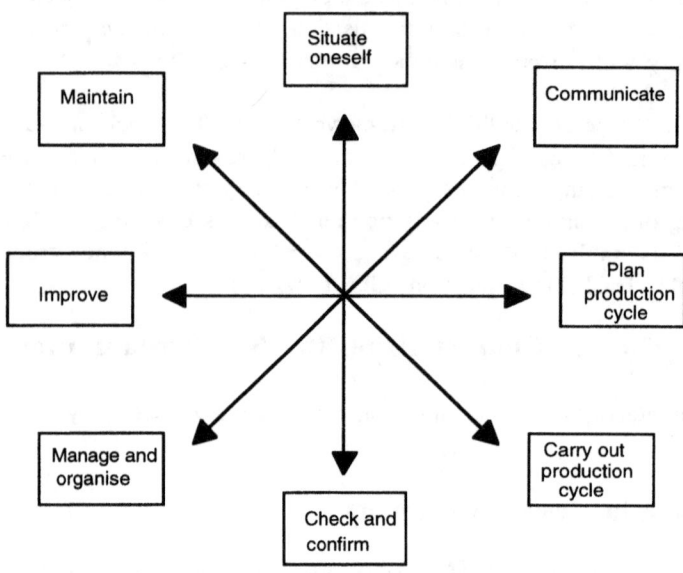

Figure 1. *Eight steps in undertaking a job*

2. <u>To communicate</u>
   To be able to write out an intervention or a shift work report; to be able to explain to superiors or the maintenance team the circumstances of a breakdown; to be able to work in a team, etc.
3. <u>To plan the production cycle</u>
   To be able to plan one's own work or the team's work, to prepare the tools or the supplies, to plan and register the equipment in need of repair, etc.
4. <u>To carry out the production cycle</u>
   To be able to carry out the technical actions needed for the running and regulation of the plant, in usual or unusual situations.
5. <u>To check and confirm</u>
   To be able to evaluate, to sample, to read results, to do Statistical Process Control, to check the product quality, to check the running of the plant.

6. <u>To manage and organise</u>
   To be able to manage technical management indicators, to read results, to define corrective action plans, to organise one's own work and the team's work.
7. <u>To improve the process</u>
   To be able to take part in "problem-solving" groups, to define improvements of the product or in the production process, to justify them to the hierarchy or technical services, and to implement the improvements.
8. <u>To carry out maintenance</u>
   To undertake maintenance of equipment; to define problems so as to enable the maintenance service to carry out more advanced technical operations.

The organisation of work for each team gives every operator the possibility to acquire all the skills related to the complete field of jobs. The traditional "job" hierarchy no longer exists. Each operator can carry out all of the tasks but with different levels of professionalism (see Figure 2). At level one (E1) they are able to do all the tasks in a normal operating situation; at level two (E2) they can also handle important operating malfunctions; At level 3 (E3) they are able to master the complete job sufficiently and to be able to pass on their know-how to others.

Figure 2 shows the contrast between old and new forms of worker development. Traditionally workers in an electrolysis workshop progressed from a non-qualified post to a post demanding better qualifications. Basic operators sometimes waited a long time before reaching posts where more sophisticated technical tools were used.

In the new work organisation all operators have a complete task from the start to run the plant fully and carry out all operations in turn: those requiring higher qualifications but also the manual ones. The workers progression is no longer linear, but within the same function, based on the mastery of new competencies new aspects of the job, for instance the ability to cope with difficult situations (breakdown of the process, major incidents, etc.).

All skills within a team relate to level IV of the "Education Nationale Française", (i.e., the Baccalaureate level, the end of secondary school) and can be ratified in the form of a diploma of the "Education Nationale". The necessary steps to obtain the diploma have been taken by 140 operators to date.

Alternating roles to serve the team

The job of shift foreman no longer exists, only the Shift Manager who oversees the whole plant. This means that outside of normal day-time working hours there is only one member of staff to supervise the plant. However, each operator takes his turn in a specific role to enhance the efficient operation of his team: co-ordination, quality and recycling, and safety. This role is not hierarchical but serves the team with a view to ensuring good collective performance. This authority comes from the team and is in the hands of any one member for two months only.

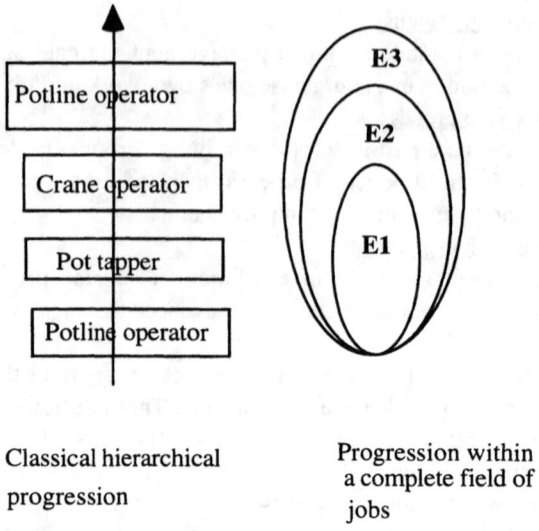

Figure 2. *Linear versus holistic competence development*

A rigorous system of career progression

By means of the DIPC (Individual Skills Progression Dossier), each operator can control his own career progression. The way is marked out by complete job descriptions and by co-evaluation protocols. These consist of working situations or problems in which rigorous handling can be observed through the co-evaluation procedure. The "craft's guarantor" (the Technical Advisor), and the operator can see together which skills have really been acquired and also agree on the supplementary training necessary.

Such a progression system, based on competencies rather than on functions, requires a great deal of rigour. That is the reason why tests are carried out in real professional situations and not in a traditional school based environment.

Three different tests exist:

- Observation situations (e.g. setting up the workshop);
- Following up activities (Those last several weeks; e.g. the development of a quality pattern using SPC controlling cards);
- Problem solving situations- in which the operator must be methodical and rigorous in dealing with the problem.

Shared maintenance

Some maintenance areas are included in the production operators' complete jobs. Other maintenance tasks are undertaken by a specialised Maintenance Department. However, the innovation in this field is the "shared" maintenance, because it is carried out by production operators who are seconded to the Maintenance Department for periods of two months per year.
There are three different levels in maintenance tasks:

- M^1 = maintenance tasks which are *integrated* into the production jobs skills (20%)
- M^2 = *shared* maintenance (60%) tasks which can be carried out either by the Maintenance Department teams, or by the production operators regularly seconded to Maintenance for two month periods (second job apprenticeship)
  - programmed tasks;
  - breakdowns and diagnostics;
- M^3 = *specialised* maintenance (20%) requiring highly specific technical ability or heavy equipment.

A common culture and a sharing of know-how is generated. One can hope eventually for a real breakdown of the traditional barriers between production and maintenance and a new type of co-operation.

Department management teams

Overall Department management is ensured by a team led by the Head of Department. In this team there are four "Supervisors" - who could be former traditional foremen or young engineers. Each Supervisor is responsible for two or three fields of management:

1. quality and process;
2. production, safety and training;
3. human resources and administration;
4. equipment installations and recycling.

Each of these also acts as a Pilot for two or three teams of operators. The pilot guides the team performance by means of fixed objectives and progress plans. Alongside the Supervisors, are the Technical Advisors whose mission is to advise and train the operators. These are qualified experts who assist the management teams or the operator teams. They do not act in a hierarchical fashion, but rather as assistants, trainers and resource individuals.

Overall plant management team

The total plant is managed by a team of Directors, assisted by a Plant Committee. Organisation topics are followed closely. One of the Deputy Directors is responsible for work organisation and conducts audits of the system regularly. One Plant Committee meeting per month focuses on a particular organisational issue. Many inter-departmental committees exist with the members coming from each plant -departmental managers and operators. Each of these committees deal with one critical issue: safety, quality, recycling, communication, training.

The management philosophy is based on the following three principles:

- each departmental manager should work at *his own level of responsibility only*, without being distracted by short term operating problems;
- a sense of *responsibility by means of self-management* with objectives and result indicators is promoted at every level, including, and in particular, at operator level;
- the *possibility of the continuous evolution of the work organisation* is allowed for as employees gradually master their jobs within a structure which promotes complete jobs as well as the possibility of mastering a second job.

The application of the basic principles of self-management and responsibility is made possible through the existence of a friendly and accessible management information system using MACINTOSH computers.

The Training and Skills Development Plan

Training before start-up

Two actions were undertaken:

upgrading of the future operators from the Dunkirk region, to bring them up to the standard required by the project: comprising 900 hours of maths, sciences, written and oral expression, technical subjects.

training in methodologies: problem solving in groups, introduction to computers, safety, economics, etc. (approx. 200 hours).

Training during start-up

Two actions were also undertaken here:

• *technical training in aluminium industry related jobs* three months shared between classroom and practical on site training; the training material had been prepared over many months by the Technical Advisors, in co-operation with an educational methods team. The task was to create a real programme of training by objectives, favouring self-learning and team-training techniques, in order to prepare the operators for the self-management skills which would characterise their future work;
• participation by each team of operators in *training sessions on the "operation of self-managing teams"*, by means of production process simulations. These sessions were created animated by AEGIST consultants.

Learning based on dealing with "real life situations"

Towards the end of the plant's first year of operation, consultants began training actions in real working situations on site. These actions consisted of simulations of certain working situations such as "shift changeover" between operator teams. This training also helped all the different participants in the organisation (Operators, Supervisors, Shift Managers, Technical Advisors) to be aware of their respective roles and to decide on rules for efficient operation.

Additional training to facilitate the introduction of the new work organisation

Integrated Process Regulation Training For Potline Operators

At the beginning of 1992, it became clear that the potline operators needed a more thorough command of process regulation. It was tempting to create an intermediate level of operators, called "Process Assistants" in other smelters. But the wish to make all the skills of the complete job accessible to everybody, and not reserve certain more qualified tasks for a few, led to the creation of an accelerated training programme involving groups of ten to twelve operators who had to become competent in the following areas: identification of the condition of the pots; diagnosis of anomalies, planning and realisation of the necessary actions for their correction.

Training principles on which this particular programme was based, supervised by a Training Consultant from Québec, Jean Lemay, are as follows:

"Training should:
- exploit to a maximum, the real work situation;
- subscribe to a logical approach, working from reality towards the abstract; in other words, always begin with observation and pot readings and then work back to rediscover the technical theories and principles (which corresponds to the mental activity that an operator must master);
- favour an attitude towards the problems to be solved, the activities to be carried out and the objectives to be reached which places the operator in a thought process where he acts "for, on behalf of, and to serve, his team");
- include a large part of self-learning and self-evaluation to facilitate the development of the operator's autonomy and his sense of responsibility, key factors necessary for the working activities he will carry out on site ..."

Continuous training, resource centres, self-learning and co-evaluation

During the first eighteen months of plant operation, regardless, of the different start-up problems encountered, the operators gradually discovered and mastered their jobs, often entirely new to them. They learned these new jobs with the help of technical advisors, but also by using the self-learning and resource centres which were available to them.

The training system was based on the idea that the operator must act as the leader of his own learning. So he must be completely aware of what the organisation expects from him by using the "job description reference" which identifies all the required competencies.

As soon as they feel ready, operators can ask to be co-evaluated. This consists of assessing the different skills of the job, by means of three kinds of reference situations: observation (real time), activities (long term) and solving real problems encountered in their working situations.

The term "co-evaluation" is used because the operator assesses himself at the same time as he is assessed by a technical advisor, both using the same guide and the same evaluation protocol.

Management training

In 1993 an important management training programme was implemented. This was prepared during the second half of 1992 by a "think-tank" group which looked at middle management a category of staff which has proved difficult to position in the new type of organisation.

Summary and Analysis of Company According to the Common Framework

Right from the beginning the directors of this company decided to pursue an organisational design policy which was based on "high levels of competence and responsibility" for process operators. Investment in Human Resource Development was the outstanding value which gave direction to this green field site plant (see Figure 3, 1^1 and 1Δ below). This was implemented following socio-technical design principles. Management also put frameworks in place to begin to build a Learning Organisation.

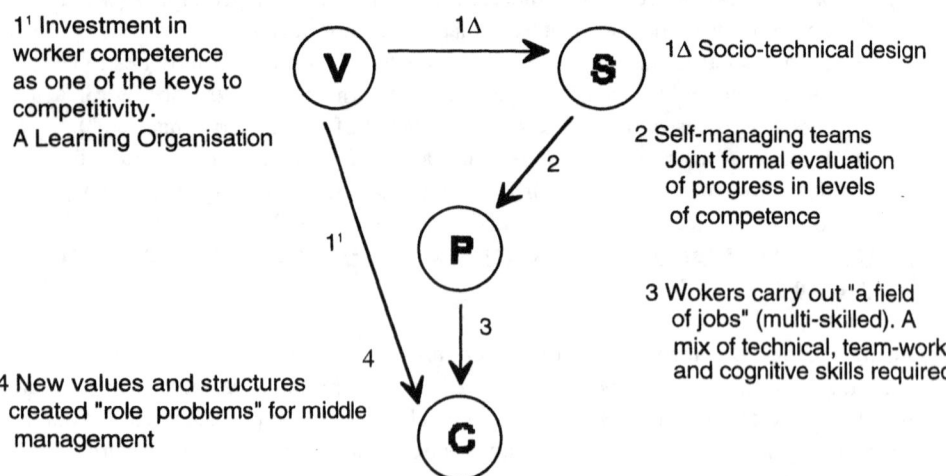

Figure 3. *A green field site plant based on a competence based strategy*

The socio-technical design system envisaged 35 self-managing teams with a matrix type middle management structure (Figure 3, 2). A prerequisite for this was a massive general preparatory training programme to bring the future employees (75% of whom had been unemployed) up to a basic level so that they could start in the company. "Planned on the job learning" at the "start-up" phase was accompanied later on by continuous self-assessment based learning programmes which gave the workers career progression possibilities (Figure 3 n°2).

Operators learnt to handle a "field of jobs" initially at a basic level, with the opportunity and support to gain deeper competence levels, giving them complete mastery over the jobs including the ability to teach others (Figure 3, 3).

At the time of writing, the plant has been in full operation for about two years. It is therefore difficult to draw definitive and overall conclusions. Some departments are further advanced in organisation compared to others. This may be due to the fact that they encountered fewer technical problems during the start-up period. One thing is certain: the teams developed the ability to work together in an autonomous and self-managing manner soon as they assimilated the basics of the different technical jobs. Indicators are at the present time being implemented to measure their progress towards complete team self-management.

As regards the progression of skills acquisition, 50% of the operators were ratified at Level One by June 1993 and 75% at the end of that year. In other words, they have reached the standard aimed for (mastery of the complete job and the equivalent of level IV, Education Nationale).

Chapter Five

From Workers to Business Partners: Response to a Crisis in Bord na Móna

Seán Mistéil and Michael Lawlor

Introduction

Bord na Móna (the Irish Peat Development Board) is the major producer of peat and peat-related products in Ireland. "Móna" comes from the Irish word "móin", meaning peat or turf. Peat is a natural product of plant origin, comprised of decayed roots, stems, leaves and flowers, forming in layers for centuries. The vegetation of peat bogs absorbs and retains water and as the peat layers increase, contact with the mineral nutritional soil is sealed off.

Over 2,000 people are employed full-time with average numbers employed rising to over 2,500 at peak production. The Company is divided into four distinct businesses. These include a peat energy division, which, as the core element of the company's operations, supplies peat for the generation of electricity; a solid fuels division, which sells primarily to the Irish market; and a horticultural and an environmental products division, which operate in a world-wide market.

The company has operated with a workforce which is almost totally unionised, operating traditionally in rural communities, particularly in the midlands and to a lesser extent in the west of Ireland. Its employment-creating role within these communities since its establishment in 1946 has been significant. A number of villages and small rural communities were created and thrived for over a generation due to the company's level of operation. The company's contribution to national economic development has, therefore, been substantial.

Since the mid 1980s, Bord na Móna has been transformed organisationally while maintaining its rural base and its identity with peat processing as a core business. It has undertaken major changes in structure, work design and operations. In adopting these changes, it has become a group of distinct businesses with a common commitment to being customer-focused, market-led, and profitable in a commercial environment.

Company Organisation - The Old and the New

Up until this recent transformation, the company was a traditional bureaucratic, centralised semi-state organisation operating in over a third of the counties of Ireland, and with a small base in the UK. The main focus of its work was - as it had been for 40 years - the production of different types of peat for sale to peat-burning power stations, for peat briquette (solid fuel) factories, and for horticultural produce.

Government policy in response to the energy crises of the 1970s included a major focus on peat as a native fuel. This led to major investment in a new expansion programme and in private enterprise bog development. A new briquette factory was built and site development on a further (fifth) factory followed. Thus company borrowing increased at a time when volatility in energy prices was a fading concern.

Further difficulties which followed adverse weather conditions in successive seasons of production led to a severe shortage of peat supplies, and a failure to meet customer needs. At the same time, world energy prices continued to fall, depressing competitiveness in both solid fuels and peat energy and reducing overall profitability. Urgent action became necessary to save the company.

This case history will address some of the key elements of what has been comprehensive organisational change in Bord na Móna since the mid 1980s. The impetus for change and the manner in which agreement was reached about the nature of many aspects of the proposed change are explained. The role of management and unions in agreeing and introducing new work forms and the contribution of various initiatives - especially in the development and training area - to shaping the change achieved to date, will be emphasised.

The Turning Point

Organisational change in Bord na Móna stemmed from three factors: a very poor financial performance, a rapidly changing competitive environment, and the arrival of a new managing director who was determined to turn around the fortunes of the company.

The abnormally poor production seasons of 1985 and 1986 for milled peat (39% and 78% of target, respectively) were new low points in the history of Bord na Móna. Briquette production was cut back and sales were rationed. Reserves of stock were depleted to such an extent that deliveries to power stations in the first half of 1987 were halted for a period. Improved harvesting conditions that summer were followed by an extremely mild winter with consequent reductions in briquette sales.

A crisis occurred in the wake of this disastrous period. The threat of possible major redundancies and rising company debt provoked the Board of the company into a radical examination of the need for change in the way Bord na Móna operated. The assumption of an executive role by the company chairman, followed by the appointment in mid 1987 of a new Managing Director, heralded a major redirection of the Company to being market led and customer driven.

On his appointment, the new Managing Director proceeded to initiate a major examination of options to address what were agreed as threats to the future viability of the company. Production methods used by Finnish peat producers, for example, were closely studied. Company development plans were also critically reviewed.

In 1988 - faced with accumulated losses over the previous four years and a sharply rising deficit - the Board acted decisively by agreeing to:

- adopt a series of targets aimed at improving productivity;
- negotiate with the trade unions about new structures;

- adopt a redundancy and early retirement package, and
- close a number of non-viable operations.

The Board also indicated that if the Company were to continue unchanged, it would not survive another five years. While staying in its core peat-related businesses, new products and markets would have to be found and developed, and all operations would have to be upgraded.

To advance these decisions, a task force approach was adopted, actively involving line management and specialists in the process. All aspects of the company's operations were scrutinised and evaluated. Reports were prepared based on the restructuring or divisioning of the company, changing production methods, and assessing marketing, finance, and technical services.

After considering these reports, the Managing Director in the autumn of 1988 proposed a number of initiatives designed to radically increase competitiveness and to reduce fixed overhead costs. These proposals included the creation of independent enterprise units and the contracting out of peat production, bringing about major increases in productivity and profitability.

Contract-style working would be supported by a decentralised organisation structure - more sensitive to market needs. A new framework of relationships would be sought with employees and their representatives, customers, banks and government.

From the outset, agreement on new forms of harvesting and producing peat was identified as pivotal: without change in this one critical area, any other proposed changes - even if unanimously agreed upon - would be relatively insignificant.

Communicating the Need for Change

The Managing Director launched his proposals with a direct communication to all employees, outlining the impact of - and need for - proposed changes. These proposals centred on operations such as production and transport as well as maintenance being carried out by enterprise units.

The key change outlined by the Managing Director involved former employees who had availed themselves of a voluntary redundancy package, setting up these new units. Members of units would be required to invest in those units as would the Company, both sharing risk and opportunity. A programme of work would then be agreed on a contractual basis with payment based on output and quality.

The Managing Director and other senior management also addressed the need for change in a series of meetings with groups drawn mainly from those midland communities in which the company operates.

In particular, school groups in these communities were addressed concerning the changing job opportunities now emerging. Apprenticeship with Bord na Móna had long been an almost guaranteed route to a career for many early school-leavers in these communities. The Company now sought to encourage longer participation in full-time education as apprenticeship opportunities were anticipated to fall rapidly, to be replaced by more selective graduate recruitment.

Within the company itself, the Managing Director, since his appointment, regularly meets employees at each location to hear their views on the ongoing changes and on business performance. Senior management also regularly meet the Group of Unions on these issues.

Agreement on Change

The Group of Unions

The Group of Unions in Bord na Móna represents all unions with membership in the company. Five main unions represent the workforce, from general workers to administrative, professional and technical grades. Faced with the challenges of revolutionary organisational change described in the communication by the Managing Director, the Group of Unions recognised the need for action - particularly through addressing the severe financial pressure facing the Company. They realised the threat to the viability of company operations. In response, the Group of Unions proposed a system of direct labour enterprise in which basic pay and conditions would be guaranteed, and they sought the introduction of a direct labour system on a trial basis.

The Group received important support from an industrial officer of the Irish Congress of Trade Unions (ICTU) in developing this alternative to the company management's proposals. ICTU's major contribution to the debate on new forms of work was reflected in a discussion document issued in 1993[1].

Partnership for Progress

Following the announcement of the company's proposals for major changes, a period of intense discussion followed during which major differences emerged concerning these proposals and the direction which the company should follow.

When negotiations eventually started, the approach adopted by senior management and the Group of Unions helped to ensure that at the highest level the interests and concerns of employees regarding job security and losses would be addressed. It also provided for a consensual approach to major organisational change particularly in terms of its impact on traditional work practices.

Sustained and difficult negotiations took place over a period, which included intensive consultation with the affected employees. This culminated in April 1989 with a framework - known as the _Partnership for Progress_ -between Bord na Móna Management and the Group of Unions. This framework provided for the introduction of "new work forms" in the 1989 production season on a pilot or experimental basis. Initially, there were two types of unit or team proposed, _Employee Enterprise Units_, and, _Autonomous Work Groups_.

Employee Enterprise Units were a modification of the original proposals by management to encourage employees to sever formal links with the company, set up their own companies as independent peat producers, and enter into contractual agreement with their former employer. The main change from the original proposal was to allow for secondment of employees to this type of unit.

Autonomous Work Groups bore close resemblance to the proposal of the Unions to introduce a direct labour system of production in an effort to reduce fixed costs while protecting wage levels.

In order to monitor the effects of the new work forms, a joint evaluation process was agreed, initially for a period of one year. In 1990 it was agreed to continue the experiment initiated in 1989 and to move to team based production across the organisation on a phased basis. This agreed process shaped the emergence of a third model - autonomous enterprise groups - introduced in 1991.

The Enterprise Concept

What has been introduced in Bord na Móna takes as its model or paradigm the *Open Socio-Technical System* which has been applied in many other industrial contexts world-wide. The social needs of employees working on a task and the technical nature of the task in question were reflected in the "enterprise" concept put forward initially and in the compromise proposals that emerged from negotiation.

In all autonomous teams, a balance of both social and technical aspects of the work is required. In Bord na Móna's case, three main aims which relate to socio-technical systems were sought in the agreed experiment:

1   that the work be, or remain, personally meaningful through a combination of skill and task variety in particular;
2   that each team be responsible for its own results - through a degree of autonomous working; and
3   that teams have satisfactory knowledge of their achievement of targets through speedy feedback of results.

Given the traditional work practice in Bord na Móna of large bog production groups, the use of teams as the basic unit of work design fitted both employee and company needs.

What has been attempted in Bord na Móna, however, amounts to applying a socio-technical process in an agricultural setting. Natural team and area affiliations have been acknowledged and largely respected. Large work groups have been succeeded by small core teams with a reduced number of seasonal workers being employed. Seasonal workers are normally engaged in the production period between April and September.

Areas of bog which are assigned to teams follow traditional geographical identity to such an extent that teams are typically identified by area or place name. This area "identity" and the smaller numbers responsible for areas of bog also bring with them greater physical isolation than heretofore.

The new work systems did benefit, of course, from the greater availability of new and better machinery. New responsibilities, however, included greater formal responsibility for environmental care (through, for example, silt control) as well as for health and safety.

Traditional work practices and large work groups shaped the old company culture. Introducing risk and reward, self-management and greater devolved responsibility meant changing roles, rules and relationships. It meant, in effect, a reshaping of identity with work itself and with the Company. Significant for those employees entering autonomous groups was the fact that virtually all started their working lives with Bord na Móna and knew no other working environment. Mobility to them - unlike that of urban workers throughout North Western Europe - meant little more than the distance to and from the workplace. That workplace was a dark expanse of land stretching many kilometres in all directions. They knew no other workplace for up to ten years before moving to another similar environment.

The main aim of bringing enterprise into peat production was to reduce the cost of production and to vary the operational cost base by linking payment of wages to results or production achieved. That aim was, and remains a fundamental element of the movement to autonomous enterprise working.

Technically, the Company needed to rationalise and manage its cost structure. Socially, it was necessary to ensure that team based skills and the necessary level of commitment and motivation were present to meet production targets within the standards set.

Quantitative (e.g. tonnage) and qualitative (e.g. moisture content) measures would be standard factors in determining payment.

For employees, the enterprise approach involved both risk and reward, measurable autonomy and control over an assigned area of operations. In socio-technical terms, a definite level of interdependence or "technically required co-operation" existed. Given the common interest in achieving success, autonomous working meant an opportunity for "*gainsharing*" - where the Company and those in autonomous units shared the benefits of reduced costs and increased productivity.

Socio-technical work systems require a re-balancing of autonomy and control. In Bord na Móna, this meant the supervisory role giving way to a support/facilitative function with the new teams being, effectively, self-regulatory. This transformation in the role of foremen and supervisors is dealt with later in this paper.

For teams, other critical forms of support from outside would include management support and administrative, informational and technical services, especially at the local level.

How the Autonomous Work Models Operate

Since 1989 three models of autonomous working have been in place in the production of peat. All three types of production team share many common features.

The concept of autonomous working is centred on a core group of between three and six people, drawn from the workforce, based on their group cohesiveness, mix of individual skill and experience. This core group - to be known as *team leaders* - took responsibility for all operations within their own area of bog ranging from production to drainage, silt control, and plant and equipment maintenance. Each member of the group had team-leadership responsibilities, so that the group was referred to as "team-leaders". The local Bord na Móna works carried responsibility for support services such as fuel supplies, spare parts, training and administration, and offered back-up maintenance. They also dealt with wages, and with tax and other relevant deductions. These services were costed and provided for in the budget of each team.

The team leaders were selected by local management in consultation with the Group of Unions. Typically, a core team would be composed of four or five team leaders - one a former supervisor, another a craftsperson, and two or three semi-skilled employees. Thus provision was being made for a balance of experience and skills to sustain the new autonomous operation. Use of the term "team leaders" derived from the centrality of the work group in the socio-technical system on which the teams were originally modelled.

Each team had decision-making responsibilities for its employment needs. These included the recall and layoff of those employed on a seasonal basis, working hours, the allocation of work and the degree of operational flexibility required within that team.

Type one: Autonomous Working Groups

These teams are perceived as the relatively low risk-takers. They elect to keep greater job and pay security and receive a reasonably high guaranteed minimum wage. Real "take-home pay" for all members of the team, including seasonal employees, is calculated by adding a productivity bonus to the guaranteed wage. Originally, this type of work group closely resembled the direct labour based team envisaged by the Group of Unions in their proposals, with the emphasis they put on protecting wage levels.

A budget, covering all operational costs - from wages to machinery - is agreed between each team and works management. Differences associated with each bog area - such as production history, peat density and the size of each area - are reflected in each agreed budget. There is no profit element built into the price of produced peat agreed with Bord na Móna. In a good weather year, the set price for an autonomous work group would produce the cheapest peat for Bord na Móna while in a bad year, the price could be the dearest.

All accounting is done by the local Works on behalf of each Group. This includes processing of payments for materials and fuels used by each Group.

Type two: Employee Enterprise Units

This was the original and most radical model of enterprise unit in place, carrying the greatest risks for those involved. The structure was as follows: the Team Leaders were seconded to a separate limited liability company in which Bord na Móna took a percentage stake. Each new company then leased an area of bog from Bord na Móna and negotiated a price per ton of peat produced. Terms of contract covering overhead costs were then agreed and the purchase of peat which met agreed specifications was guaranteed.

A salary was built into the price and profit was linked to 100% of production target with break-even set at 80% of target. The harvested peat was paid by the unit on a weekly basis, thus creating significant cash flow during the production period. Bord na Móna, similarly, charged for services provided to the units, on agreed terms. Bonus payment in respect of the price of peat sold by Bord na Móna was agreed at a later date. Weekly pay is determined by output - the daily tonnage - as in the case of the autonomous work groups.

Type three: Autonomous Enterprise Units

The enterprise concept was extended in 1990. The extension related directly to the introduction of a third work scheme - the Autonomous Enterprise Unit. An additional 26 Groups of this type - including one reconstituted Autonomous Working Group - went into operation along with the other eight original teams. More recently, two of the original enterprise units have been reconstituted as autonomous enterprise units.

Typically, an autonomous enterprise unit or team would be composed of up to five team leaders, supported by fifteen to twenty seasonal employees, including a few permanent employees with craft or other skills. A production area of about 1200 or 1300 acres would be allocated to the team with a production target of, say, 120,000 tonnes of milled peat. Responsibilities for such issues as bog drainage, machine maintenance, safety management, and providing protective covering for harvested peat, would be specified for each team. They were guaranteed a rather low minimum wage. Anything on top of that depended on productivity, based on a "gainsharing" principle. They had the possibility to earn much more money than the workers in the lower risk "type one" group above.

This is now the dominant model of autonomous working in peat production in Bord na Móna. The risk and reward involved lie somewhat in-between *employee enterprise* and *autonomous work groups* and reflect the most effective features of the other two schemes and the experience gained within those other schemes.

Significantly, *all* participants in autonomous enterprise units remain employees of the company.

The Link Role of Works Management

Before the introduction of new work forms, the numbers of bog-production foremen and supervisors (both bog and factory) in Bord na Móna were approximately 300 or 8-9% of the workforce. A bog-foreman had responsibility for 40 or more employees under traditional production systems, with a large intake of seasonal employees at peak production. Supervisors reported to foremen under the traditional production system. The numbers involved in supervision have almost halved since 1989 with many ex-supervisors being absorbed into the new teams and many others taking redundancy.

The elimination of the direct supervisory role which followed the introduction of autonomous groups or teams has been addressed in a number of ways. Foremen now have a liaison role with teams, providing guidance on team management issues, checking progress towards agreed targets and standards, and acting as an information and two-way communication channel with local management.

The "Partnership for Progress" agreement involved a restatement of the key responsibilities of local works management following the introduction of the enterprise concept. New administrative systems were devised, for example, relating to payment of wages, performance against team budget and team production records. Works management still remained accountable for property leased to teams and for security of stock.

The need for a coaching and advisory role in working with new teams was identified, particularly in relation to the effective use of team resources and the efficient application of equipment and machinery. This role has been expanded to include many of the development and training initiatives which have been introduced for teams. These and other responsibilities were effectively devolved to the former bog foremen. This newly created role for them - new in that it covers a range of relationships between teams and the main organisation - is characteristic of a flattening and widening structure which has removed layers of control.

Some "controls" still remain. For example, product quality checks- on moisture content of harvested peat- are a responsibility which must be exercised on behalf of the company. Monitoring of safety standards is another area where some degree of control or influence is involved.

Many foremen now liaise with up to three or more teams. Contact with teams is now more a "once a day" contact as opposed to the traditional permanent and highly visible presence of the bog foreman or supervisor.

The new role, therefore, can be summarised as a complex one. There is *facilitation* - active support for teams through formal training and informal coaching and communication, as well as *checking and controlling* - the formal monitoring of operational agreements and standards and legal responsibilities, on behalf of the Company.

The new role is an evolving one, shaped by the experience gained by all parties since new work forms were introduced. The apparent contradictions inherent in the complexity of the role are currently being addressed, particularly from a development and training perspective.

Development and Training

In forming autonomous teams in 1989, it was agreed that the experiment would be concentrated in a small number of locations. *"Natural"* teams, drawing on the homogeneity of small groups and averaging between three and six employees, were formed. These teams were characterised by a balanced blend of experience and skill, either supervisory, craft or technical. There is little doubt that this approach was critical to the smooth introduction and development of autonomous working. Effectively, it shifted the emphasis from the creation of these teams (since the nucleus of most teams already existed) to their potential to prosper which was a common concern of all involved. From a development and training viewpoint, it directly reduced the range of major interventions required initially.

One of the main training interventions in the first year - see Figure 1 - was in the area of finance - explaining the financial model on which the budget for each team was agreed. Training on the interpretation of financial data, and the management of seasonal employees was also included.

Finance	Budgets; interpreting data; the financial model and how it works; clarifying points of information; social welfare implications of autonomous working and temporary lay-offs
Team Development	Formation; working in teams; problem solving and decision-making; team roles- core team, non-core members (permanent and seasonal)
Autonomous Working	What it means- benefits and risks; the relationship with the local works; support services; communication- inside and outside teams; the foreman/supervisor outside the team

Figure 1. *Initial formal training interventions*

In addition to retaining natural teams and blending disciplines, experience and skills, a supportive framework to monitor progress and achievement was put in place. A key factor was a common focus on developing the understanding of socio-technical approaches to work and other options to existing work forms by management and union representatives. This included joint visits to other companies of interest and also to appropriate conferences and seminars.

All training - other than on finance and setting up new business - was provided by internal specialists. The financial training - being perhaps the single most sensitive topic in establishing the credibility of autonomous working - was led by an external consultant who contributed significantly to the design of the financial model and budget plan used initially.

New teams were also provided with training on how teams develop, and on team meetings, communications, and quality. Legal responsibilities in areas such as safety were also covered as were discipline and grievance-handling procedures. Guidance on adapting to and coping with the change from traditional to autonomous working arrangements was also provided.

In the second year of operation, additional training took place on the financial management of team operations as well as refresher training on many of the other topics covered in the first year. Problem-solving and decision-making in teams, as well as safety and health were also addressed.

As teams mature (into their third and fourth years of operation), the emphasis is changing to developing team and individual skills. This has led to a stronger focus on updating technical skills of individual team members and improving group cohesion in areas such as conflict handling.

An external research study group were commissioned in late 1990 to review the progress of the experiment[2]. When the researchers raised the issue of training requirements, team leaders highlighted perceived learning needs in such areas as planning and decision-making. The importance of existing cohesiveness in these teams was emphasised in areas such as leadership and decision-making. Initially, those team leaders drawn from a supervisory background, tended to emerge as nominated representatives in contacts with local management. Overall, team leaders showed low recognition of the need for expanding their personal or team skills.

There has been growing emphasis since 1991 from team leaders on improving the basic skills and knowledge - both interpersonal and technical - of individual members. This is reflected in the participation of team leaders in sessions as diverse as: handling new machinery, safety and health, employment law and social welfare. The involvement of former bog-foremen and line managers in the provision of training has increased in that same period. The development and training and functional roles are now increasingly perceived by works management as being complementary.

New teams in the start-up phase each year are now benefiting from the company's evaluation of the effectiveness of training provided to more established teams, and programmes continue to be revised on that basis. In addition, the role of seasonal workers is being re-addressed and new emphasis is being put on the potential of teams to innovate and achieve continuous improvement in their work programmes.

The new foreman role - referred to earlier - was addressed at some length as part of an extensive programme for managers, foremen and supervisors, which started in late 1991. Focused initially on the background to socio-technical systems in the workplace, this programme involved a number of task teams working on improvements to practical issues affecting or involving autonomous working.

The next phase of development and training will include a major emphasis on team skills and an extension of the focus on the new roles for foremen and managers. The initiatives on team skills will seek to integrate the progress made with team-based work systems and with innovation and quality in recent years. Other initiatives will help to deepen the external market-awareness of team leaders in particular and also their commitment to the company itself.

The development training intervention carried out to date with teams are summarised in Figure 2.

Finance	Budgetary performance review; agreed revision of budgetary framework; further interpretation of financial data
Team development	Team "growth"; interdependence; developing new skills; managing differences; improving team performance

Figure 2. *Developmental initiatives with autonomous teams*

Innovation and Quality

Alongside the initiative on enterprise, a major programme on innovation and diversification was launched. Both *incremental* innovation, focused on existing operations, and *radical* innovation - emphasising the potential to diversify into potentially profitable activities through ideas generated by employees themselves - were encouraged. A strategy and a structure were developed to support these processes and a manager appointed as full-time coordinator dealing with innovation.

Multi-disciplinary teams were put in place throughout the organisation to facilitate the flow, development, evaluation and implementation of ideas. These teams are composed mainly of general operatives and craft workers and they operate as part-time teams in addition to their formal roles. They meet regularly to progress ideas put forward by employees at each location.

There have been considerable advances in quality improvement in the company since divisionalisation. National quality awards, (Q-Mark), have been made to horticultural products and solid fuels factories and works. The international standards ISO 9000 have been achieved by Horticultural Products Division. Solid Fuels and Environmental Products Divisions are now being attested for ISO standard.

New Business Development

In the five years up to 1993, a number of small business ventures had spawned through the innovation process in Bord na Móna. These businesses and projects included bog wood sculpture, a bog railway tourism venture, engineering services, and an international consultancy on peat production. Several other ideas have reached feasibility study stage. The number and the quality of suggestions and ideas put forward by employees rose sharply over that period. Significant savings have been achieved even with only local implementation of ideas for improvement.

A major programme of development and training has preceded and accompanied the advances achieved on both innovation and quality, ranging from awareness-building and basic information sessions to skills-based programmes. Groups of managers and employees throughout the company have participated in business start-up programmes. These participants include people who are developing business ideas as well as managers in a coaching or support role.

A significant related initiative was the setting up in 1992 of a New Business Development Fund into which employees voluntarily contribute what will in a short period amount to seed capital for starting new business ventures. Within one year of its launch, over 60% of employees were contributors.

Outcomes To Date

The significance of the changes proposed in 1987 is shown at a glance in Figure 3 below which compares Company performance data. The pace of change indicated by these figures may be perceived as slowing somewhat over this period. However, while average numbers employed, for example, are falling more slowly, profitability has been achieved for a third successive year as turnover dropped slightly. Overheads continued to fall and overall debt fell for the first time in years.

Year	Average Employment	Staff Costs (IR£00)	Operating Costs/ Turnover (%)	Profit/ Turnover (%)	Production Target Achieved (%)	Productivity per Person (Milled Peat)/Tonne
1987/88	4,795	74.9	88	(4)	101	1,800
1988/89	3,835	59.1	96	(76)	66	1,300
1989/90	3,152	54.6	83	2	135	3,600
1990/91	2,673	52.3	80	-	119	3,550
1991/92	2,387	48.5	79	2	103	2,850
1992/93	2,297	46.1	71	(7)	70	1,954

Main Source: Bord na Móna Annual Reports[3]

Figure 3. *Company performance 1987 -1991: some comparisons*

The Contribution of New Work Forms

In the 1993 production season, a very high percentage of the Company's peat harvest has been supplied by autonomous work groups which have been in operation for over three-to-four years. Throughout the Company, other payment-by-results systems are in place. These developments, along with reduced numbers in the production and maintenance areas, have led to significant productivity gains over this period.

The growth of teams and the numbers involved is significant. From nine teams comprising 114 (including seasonal) workers, the numbers have grown to 52 teams and an overall total of over 700 full time and seasonal workers on autonomous work in harvesting peat (see Figure 4).

	1989	1990	1991	1992	1993
No. of Teams	9	34	41	47	52
No. of participants	114	448	572	653	720+

Figure 4. *Autonomous teams on peat production*

Critically, the Company has succeeded in transforming itself and at the same time maintained good industrial relations against a background of major job losses among full-time and seasonal employees and the closing of many traditional operational works.

The direct impact of autonomous working can be singled out as the greatest contributor to change in company performance and prospects in the past five years. Autonomous work teams now account for all horticultural peat production. In 1993, over 85% of milled peat production was provided by autonomous teams, as compared with 14% when these teams started in 1989.

The growing influence of "teamwork" has continued in parallel with the increase in teams on the bog. The concept of payment-by-results, which shapes autonomous working, has been introduced in several areas of activity, notably in factory and workshop environments. Payment-by-results systems have been successfully introduced in such areas as fabrication units, machine shops and transport, while shift factory production teams in briquette factories are working on a group bonus system.

An estimated 1300 permanent and seasonal employees now work in either autonomous teams on the bog or in payment-by-results or bonus based work systems. Average employment figures are now under 2,300. Increases in productivity in that period have been significant as production costs have fallen and uneconomic operations have been closed. On the other hand, economic investment in organisational change has been costly, ranging from the cost of redundancy to the purchase of new machinery and technology. Working profits have been achieved, however, and maintained.

Independent research was initiated on the new work systems in 1991 to evaluate their impact and a joint monitoring group reported the same year on the progress made by new teams. A major review of new forms of work design within the company, chaired by an external independent labour relations official, started in the autumn of 1993.

Given that weather conditions remain a critical factor in the performance of autonomous teams, the challenges of adjustment and change continue. In addressing possible changes in the operating system of autonomous working, the company, the team leaders, and their union representatives, will be very much influenced by the continued fluctuation in team earnings, which are the main incentive in autonomous working. In addition, the maintenance of adequate company stocks of produced peat will be critical to the company's viability.

As an illustration of this weather influence, the summer of 1993 was a difficult challenge. With only 70% of target achieved in 1992, an even worse performance appeared likely entering the last week of August 1993. At that stage only 45% had been reached. Within four weeks, however, following a very dry spell of weather, production ended with 85% of target achieved.

Developing New Job Competencies

The impact of the complex structural and role changes on behaviour is apparent in practically all spheres of company activity. The job skills sought and now being developed within autonomous work teams are also demanded elsewhere. Areas as diverse as sales and marketing and management information systems are very much driven by work group or team development issues.

Team activity where rewards are output or performance-based, requires both *enterprise* in terms of improvement and innovation, and *interdependence* of resources. This demands a degree of adaptability from team members which many would not have been required to show in the past. Increasingly, teams are becoming multi-skilled and multi-functional in capability.

While many of these developments reflect the design elements of the job restructuring, they can only now - as it were, *after the event* - be catered for in development and training interventions.

The emphasis placed on natural teams as the building block for autonomous teams seems to have worked as a safety net for both the company and for those "braving the new world". This allowed the newly-formed teams to concentrate on issues such as interpreting financial reports, and understanding basic employment law, rather than dwelling on the role of, or the interaction between, individual team members.

Organisational change was signalled with the arrival of the new Managing Director in 1987. Autonomous work teams formed a pivotal *part* of that change. For team members, therefore, factors external to their immediate working environment - such as the need for greater cost competitiveness - were reshaping their jobs.

Most of the training provided "pre-change" was descriptive, instructive and motivational - such as the relationship between teams and the Company, new work liaison arrangements, and especially, budgetary and financial procedures. *The* major adjustment for most team leaders was the new relationship signalled by the "creation" of the new teams. Development and training interventions "post-change" seem to have the effect of formally acknowledging or affirming a culture change process.

Relationships, roles and rules are now different, and are still evolving. Different competencies - in areas such as innovation and problem solving - are emerging alongside the much anticipated entrepreneurial role of autonomous teams.

The Future

What has been achieved in terms of change is still a fragile consensus - it could falter easily. As yet, what has been embedded is a structural change. The production process is now carried through by much smaller numbers in much smaller units of operation. Key attitude changes (such as the perception of the role of managers and foremen/supervisors in particular) have yet to be clarified. This is reflected in the tendency or inclination on the part of some to assert a control rather than a facilitative role when faced with conflict or disagreement over details of what is now a contractual relationship with teams.

The change to autonomous working became a necessity; the most tangible benefits were financial ones; against that was the loss of employment if change was not accepted. For team members, this was a major issue. Given the vagaries of the Irish weather, they have already faced lean financial years. By common consent, this taste of "adversity" was to be the "acid test" for many teams and for autonomous work systems.

Team based activity is not new to the company; many factory-based and maintenance operations were already shaped on shift teams or crews, before the advent of this crisis. What is new is the extent, focus and centrality of teamwork and, especially the productivity potential of team-based production.

As they enter the sixth season of the new teams, the future remains uncertain for many players. What seems certain is that while relationships and results may vary in terms of success, there really is "no going back" to the traditional work methods which shaped the organisation for four decades. That fact appears non-negotiable.

Analysis According to the Common Framework

Nearly all the major actions and decisions taken by Bord na Móna, as well as the set of company values that are reflected in those actions, can be related to the crisis which the company faced (see Figure 5, 0). There is no evidence that the radical restructuring of the company, nor the changes in work operations and relationships that form the core of the case study would have been attempted without a major and enduring crisis. Equally, we can only speculate now as to whether the former senior management of the company, had they continued in post, would have faced the crisis with the same conviction as did their successors.

Indeed, the key actors - both management and union leaders - in the agreed framework ("Partnership for Progress") approached the question of change as one of "crisis". Ultimately, all that was agreed was a framework within which new work forms were introduced on an experimental basis (see Figure 5, 1). Joint monitoring of the experiment was also agreed at that time after which a wider implementation of the Autonomous Enterprise Units took place.

Decisions on divisionalisation and decentralisation can be viewed as one of emerging consensus, given the "task force" framework adopted by the new senior management team in late 1987.

The Dynamics of the Change Process

The values of the old organisation - such as job creation in remote and underdeveloped rural areas and power generation from native fuels - had stood intact and unchanged for forty years.

The response to the crisis of the mid 1980s ended that long period of stability. The new processes led to a restatement of company values. The emphasis on maintaining employment had to be dropped in the interest of survival, cost management and profitability. The company closed a number of small "non-viable" operations in communities identified with (and even "created" by) the company, breaking, in some cases, a link that spanned the life of the company. Most of this change was expressed in terms of redundancies.

Adaptability and team working were now to be supported by the concept of "gainsharing" i.e. the benefits would accrue to members of teams accordingly as the levels of productivity and increased efficiency were reflected in costs savings and profits.

Some traditional company values found continued expression. Employee identification with their community or area of work was acknowledged in the formation of teams. Most teams are identified by area of operation and composed of members with affinity for their area.

The manner in which change has been introduced owes a great deal to the relationship between the key actors on both the management and union sides. The agreed framework conceals the fact that a detailed negotiated agreement on permanent change was never concluded. What emerged was a deep understanding and a mutual respect which is formally expressed in the framework but, critically, upheld informally by both sides in the employee relations climate they have fostered in recent years. The apparent smoothness of the change process is the result of considerable and complex work by principal players on both sides, involving prolonged periods of persuasion and sensitive discussions.

The learning environment that has emerged is, in many respects, a very informal one. For instance, most training associated with the change has had a very practical bias, and where possible, has been away from the classroom. Risk-taking is a central feature of the "new" Bord na Móna with a creative tension between the old controls and the new autonomy expressing itself in the relationship between manager, foreman or supervisor, and the core members of the production teams. This tension is also a feature of the core team - seasonal worker relationship.

Competencies

The skills to manage a bog operation are, in many respects, agricultural practice and mining skills. The company had "grown" a workforce of loyal, dedicated people with respect for peat as the source of their livelihoods. The knowledge and experience they acquired was continually refined through changing technology in all aspects of the process of peat production.

The depth of experience and practical knowledge of members of teams was a critical advantage in shaping the early success of new work forms. The experiment is essentially built around these competency factors. The change in work structures demanded new types of business and team-work competencies on the part of the workers which they developed through an informal and formal training programme (see Figure 5, 2).

The concept of the "natural team" was important, alongside experience and knowledge. This refers to a group of employees who were drawn together into an autonomous environment having shared common experiences working together in the same or similar bog operations. This may be seen as minimising the risk of failure for "new" teams. However, it also reflects careful consideration of team composition and the ability of individuals who were previously in larger groups (of say, eighteen to twenty) to work well together when reshaped as a small core team of three, four or five.

The new operating structures signalled through divisionalisation, reduced numbers and performance-based pay, heralded the addition of new competencies to complement or sharpen the existing base. Cost management, forecasting and planning, and, critically, risk taking were now added to the "must knows" of each unit of operation.

New Processes and Structures leading to New Values

On the management side, information flow had to be improved in both content and timeliness, and complementary changes in style were necessary, such as from being a boss to being a coach. Immediate or speedy feedback on team performance against set targets is now essential. This has led to major change in some instances. For teams, this early reflection of how well they were performing was also an expression of their capability - as compared with other teams - and a test of the resolve of management to deliver critical information as promised and required.

The introduction of an agreed financial model relating to operating budgets for teams was much highlighted in the early phases of setting up autonomous work teams. Many employees saw the outlined model as providing the stamp of autonomy. Leadership and organisation now lay within teams.

Summary of the Change Process

The process of change can be summarised as follows. The new Managing Director proposed new working processes to respond to a severe company crisis. Following negotiations with employee representatives, new work structures based on autonomous work groups were introduced, initially on a trial basis, but afterwards becoming more widespread (see Figure 5, 0 and 1).

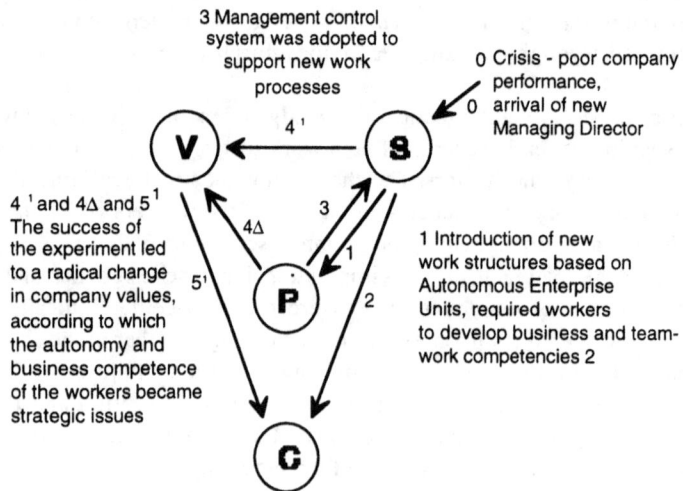

Figure 5. *A crisis resulting in the adoption of radical new values*

In order to perform effectively in the new teams, workers required business and team-work competencies (see Figure 5, 2). Facilitative rather than controlling management systems were put in place (see Figure 5, 3).

The overall success of the experiment led to a radical change in the company's values, according to which the autonomy of teams, and the business competencies of the individuals within those teams, became issues of strategic importance (see Figure 5, 4[1] and 4[Δ] and 5). The realignment of work process and management structures with the new values continues to have an enormous impact on the company.

Notes

[1] New Forms of Work Organisation - Options for Unions, Irish Congress of Trade Unions, 1993.
[2] Faughnan, P. (1991). The Dynamics of Work Group Operation in Bord na Móna, Social Science Research Centre, University College Dublin.
[3] Bord na Móna Annual Reports, 1987-1993 inclusive.

Chapter Six

MANDUCHER: A CAPABILITY-BASED STRATEGY IN THE PLASTICS INDUSTRY

Peter Docherty
Institute for Management of Innovation and Technology, Stockholm

Introduction

Manducher is a medium-sized French company that has been developing and pursuing a capability-based strategy for the last six years in an integrated approach which embraces the strategic, administrative and operational levels in the company. As part of this strategy, the company appointed a new director of social affairs. This appointment was accompanied by the formulation of a visionary strategy which held the development of competence at the centre. It was concerned with improving the worker's understanding of the business, and aimed at improving economic performance. The new values, embodied in this strategy, were consolidated by new management recruits at plant facilities and an extension of the social director's brief. Developments led to a revision of both the production and the management structures, involving the introduction of new technology, a multiskilled team organisation supported by new supervisory roles and learning structures which integrated both formal training and on the job learning on the shop floor. The new management system included a new incentive and reward system whereby workers were paid according to their capacity and managers by their ability to utilise worker capacity. The transfer of knowledge from older workers was also deemed to be important.

Manducher: A Manufacturer of Plastic Components in the Car Industry

Manducher primarily produces components for the French car industry.[1] Its main products are bumpers, dashboards and dashboard components, door panels and elements, inner roofs, and hub caps. In addition the company also produces some disposable items such as plastic sacks, coverings and wrapping film. The company is a major supplier to all French car manufacturers. Production is carried out 24 hours a day, and six days a week. The capitalisation in the plants is intense, amounting to 10-13% of the turnover. The company produces roughly 25% new products each year. Car manufacturers contact 3-4 suppliers for each function and 1-2 suppliers for the pre-development phase before selecting the supplier of new components. The company has increased its R & D staff from 20 to 120 in the last 6 years. The purchasing policies of car manufacturers are extremely complex and challenging. Their prices drop by 3-5% per year. Manducher introduces a new production line into one of its plants roughly every six months.

The company has a turnover of roughly 400 million FF (1993/4). Its cost structure is:

Materials:	45 %
Capital costs:	7 %
Depreciation:	7 %
Distribution:	16 %
Personnel costs:	25 %

The company has 6 plants in different parts of France. Three of these have between 100 - 150 employees and three have between 400 - 450 workers. A number of these plants have been obtained by buy-outs or take-overs, and two were built in the period 1988-1991. The plants differ considerably from each other in the local labour market, in their work practices and at the technological level. However, the development of a new and common company culture has been one of management's main aims since the mid 1980s.

The company was established in 1901 under the name ETS Grasset. It was taken over by E. Manducher in 1921. Since then the company has been run as a typical family enterprise in which management exercised a benevolent and firm control. In 1991 Manducher was in its turn bought up by the German company Klöckner-Werke which, until 1993, produced steel, and now only produces machines and plastics. Manducher exercises considerable autonomy, although major policy and economic decisions must be cleared with Klöckner.

Manducher has recently become a part of a European group, Eurotec, which comprises roughly 20 plants in Europe. The group is the most important European supplier of plastic products to the European car industry. The aim of the group is to generate considerable synergy in product development and company efficiency while each member of the group retains primary responsibility for the delivery of components to its national car industry. Other members of the group are Peguform (Germany), Inerga (Spain) and Plastimat (Czeckien). The former two participate 100 % participants in the group, and the latter, 51%.

Manducher's headquarters are based in Oyonnax, a small city in the Jura region which has been the centre of craftsmanship for products which since the 12th century were made of horn and bone, but today are made of plastic. There are over 400 plastics companies in Oyonnax, together with the only plastics engineering polytechnic in France. Although this gives the company close proximity to the latest know-how in plastics technology, the demand for ordinary labour exceeds supply. Thus the company recruited extensively from Italy and North Africa in the post war period. Over 90 % of the workers in its Oyonnax plant are immigrant workers who have a poor education and in many cases speak poor French.

The total number of employees in the company at the end of 1994 is roughly 1700. The average age of the workforce is 35 yrs. 35% of the labour force is female and 40% are unskilled. Roughly 25 % of the workers at Manducher are unionised either in the socialist CFDT or the communist CGT. Management has very good relations with the unions.

Although the unions may be regarded as militant, management feels that they have kept them fully informed as to the current status of the company and feels that unions have more legitimacy than they did a few years ago. Unions and personnel receive extensive company and financial information at regular intervals. The financial state of affairs is published monthly. An example of the trust existing between the parties was of how management kept labour fully informed of the developments which eventually led to Klöcker's take-over and the commitment of employees who had been prepared to invest their money in Manducher in order to avoid the take-over.

The company is committed to having a very strong internal communication policy which backs up a belief in "doing it together" firstly and then "speaking about it together" to confirm common understanding. Management's openness regarding information on current and past issues is somewhat in contrast to its more restricted practice regarding information about its future plans for its plants. Such information is provided only for the short-term and consultation on the company's different plants is conducted on a highly controlled basis. This policy has worked very smoothly with the major changes the company has implemented in the last five years between 1988 to 1993, during which time they were introduced under the guidance of a joint steering committee. All the steps taken have been recorded and published, and all the information generated during this process has been shared.

Creating a Capability-based Strategy

In 1987 management felt that "things could be better" and contacted a research team at the University of Grenoble to conduct an in depth study of the company's organisation and working conditions. Management was considerably dismayed by the results of the study which showed that, amongst others things, the workers felt that they had very little discretion in an extensively hierarchical organisation. In addition the market place was putting the following new demands on the company:

- quality must be improved;
- material logistics had to be reformed, for example in line with the developments in "just-in-time" techniques;
- prices must be reduced, for example by at least 2 % a year; and
- there is a need to carry out heavy investments in technology.

Until then the company had mainly used plastic injection technology. Now there was a need to use even extrusion and compression technologies and utilise the latest developments in paint technology. The transformation from being a user of injection plastics to being a functional supplier in the plastics field necessitated the development of new core competencies. There was a need for a concerted effort to form and implement a new vision with a new infrastructure.

The professor who led the study was persuaded to join the company as its director of social affairs with responsibility for designing a strategy for dealing with the organisational and human resource issues he listed in his study. Since his initial appointment in 1988 he has become Managing Director of Manducher. In addition he has appointed members of his former staff at the University of Grenoble as personnel managers in the different French plants. Following the formation of the Eurotec group in 1991 he has become Director of

Social Affairs for the group as a whole, and in this role he is formulating human resource policies for the major plastic component suppliers to the French, German and Spanish car industries.

The director is formulating a vision based on the corner stones of economic effectiveness and human-centred values regarding the nature of work organisation and working conditions. Three basic components in his strategy are:

- the radical lifting of the level of competence of production employees through extensive integrated programs of formal training and on the job learning;
- the introduction of a new work organisation based on multi-skilled teams;
- new management and reward systems.

His programs are simultaneously being implemented in the brown-field sites, such as the production facility in Oyonnax, and in the green-field sites, such as the production facility in Burnhaupt. (Two new plants were built during the period 1988-1991.) Another feature of the company's strategy is to work in close co-operation with public professional agencies by undertaking joint ventures to ascertain, analyse and prioritise problem areas and to evolve strategies and programs for their solution. For example the design and setting up of a new plant in Burnhaupt was conducted together with ANACT (the National Agency for the Amelioration of Working Conditions). The Burnhaupt project focused on:

- the introduction of new automated technology;
- the improvement of the work organisation and environment, with a focus on increased decision discretion and job enrichment for production workers.

The project was conducted with a high degree of worker participation and resulted in a reduction in the number of levels of middle management, and the creation of multi-functional teams which included such tasks as quality control, maintenance and problem solving. Nowadays in large plants there at the most 3 to 4 levels of management and in the small production units (comprising 200 persons) it is usual to have three levels, i.e. plant manager, production manager and team members.

In 1989-1990 two research teams, one made up of sociologists, the other of cognitive psychologists, conducted studies of worker competencies. A steering committee was formed for this project which consisted of four representatives for management, four for the unions and four for the National Centre for Scientific Research. Contract research studies in the last three years have cost approximately three million French francs, divided approximately fifty-fifty between the company and the French state. Similarly the French state has contributed to roughly 40% of the costs of developing a training package for developing unskilled workers. To confirm the rise in standards the company has benchmarked its activities by examining its competitors in different parts of the world. At least ten visits, with the unions, have been undertaken to confirm their standing.

The vision entails increasing the learning capacity of the organisation so that it will be able to adapt to and take advantage of the changing conditions in its environment. This requires a high degree of autonomy for the individual production facilities. Senior management formulates values, models and strategies which are to be applied by local management with discretion. Local interpretation is essential to both learning and effectiveness. Standard across-the-board solutions are not the order of the day. Plant managers are expected to co-operate with their personnel managers in the interpretation and implementation of the vision. The objective of the change programme was to increase the learning capacity. This was a significant lever for change upon top managers. Some managers left the system and this provided a clear message to everyone. Now all the plants have been reorganised.

Competence: A Necessity for Business, Technology and Organisation

In the years between 1988-1991 there were a number of important parallel development processes linked to the creation of a new work organisation, the introduction of new technology and the creation of a basic competence platform which would enable the learning developments required of and offered by the new work organisation.

The New Work Organisation

These developments involved the introduction of new technology for extrusion and compression plastics technology. Major changes were made at the "brown-field" sites, such as that at Oyonnax, and new factories were designed in co-operation with experts from ANACT, for example the factory in Burnhapt. In Oyonnax the machines were grouped in cells to enable a certain degree of job rotation between work stations. This re-grouping also facilitated communication between the members of the new teams. Within the teams, members had to perform a range of tasks. This offered a possibility for individuals to continuously learn whilst working. This would eventually lead to the worker being multi-skilled. It also offered the opportunity for employees to be involved in problem solving and decision-making. In order to meet customer demands for higher quality, and precision in delivery times, management delegated more responsibility to the teams for quality control and delivery control. The size of a team is normally between 8-15 persons.

These changes were regarded as both challenging and demanding as the work force was poorly educated and low skilled. Employees basically performed standard operating procedures commonly associated with machine minding, manually feeding plastics into the machine and picking and placing finished products in different containers. The development of employees was based on two main parallel activities, namely, the development of formal educational programs, described later, and discussion circles.

Discussion circles were introduced in 1989 at the same time as the new layout of the factory was introduced. The idea for groups was based upon the principles of quality circles and aimed at developing the individual worker's ability to articulate his or her ideas about problems and possibilities for development in the work place and improving the communications between workers, and between the workers and management. The discussion circles provided an opportunity for learning. They allowed the workers to describe a problem and reflect together about why it had occurred and how it could possibly be solved.

In 1989, 15 older employees went into part-time retirement instead of fully retiring. They were retained on a part-time basis as trainers or tutors for the groups. Their backgrounds were diverse, and they included departmental managers, quality managers, foremen and skilled workers. A tutor was appointed to each group to provide information and knowledge about production processes and the underlying technology in response to the workers queries about specific problems. The object of talking through problems towards a solution was to provide workers with valuable insights and a common understanding of the production processes and facilitate their learning. This in turn enabled them to identify the first signs of problems and to take appropriate remedial action. A natural development in the groups was for the workers to adopt a more proactive position in the sense. They were active in making suggestions for improving work processes, and for technological developments and quality improvements. The development function in the factory was also adapted to provide the workers with an active opportunity to participate in and even initiate such developments. For example, the teams were provided with development budgets.

Each team had a team leader whose role was different from that of the traditional foremen. A sub-theme in the development activities was the evolution of the role of the foreman. A major training program for foremen was carried out between 1988-1992. Each foreman received two months training during this period. Some foremen are no longer coupled to specific teams but are organised as separate groups in the factory. Each foreman has a personal contract which defines his/her new role of being responsible for co-ordination, learning and new product implementation on the shop floor. Their role is regarded as being in "permanent evolution".

Creating a Basic Platform for Learning

At the same time as the market place was placing a pressure for new levels of competence within Manducher, the company was tackling the problem of a relatively unskilled workforce and a poorly educated available labour force available. Thus an important element in the company's competence development strategy was to develop a basic formal education program for new employees. This consisted of three main blocks:

1. A basic refresher course which is an obligatory prerequisite for the other two blocks. The block as a whole lasted 35 days, 25 days of which formed a sub-block dealing with the subjects of mathematics, statistics, logic and French. This was followed by a 10 day "project mobilisation" which prepared the participants for next set of blocks.
2. A basic company and job knowledge block. A fifty-day course aimed at teaching technical knowledge about plastics and plastics production (injection moulding, spray painting), and general knowledge about the company (its products and production processes), production control and statistics, group work, production flow mechanics, quality control and electricity.
3. A job specific block which is a forty day course providing the necessary skills and knowledge for work in specific work stations. This covered such topics as parts and components, the technical environment, group work, quality control and first level maintenance.

Special courses have also been developed in the technical areas of:

- polyesters;

- painting;
- plastic injection technology;
- plastic compression technology.

These courses are roughly 20 hours long, divided into lessons of 1-2 hours, which are spread over several weeks. A wide variety of educational materials have been developed to facilitate the teaching of these courses. For example, brochures have been designed using cartoon figures to explain how a machine works and its position in the overall production process. Educational posters and handbooks have been produced, as well as video films. These explain the production processes in different parts of the factories. Special training rooms have also been set up on the factory floor. This basic educational program for the development of advanced skilled workers was financed with the aid of state grants (2.2 million French francs). In 1992 Manducher sold the training package, called "Moulding people", to the plastics sector training organisation for 4 million French francs.

Training itself has been identified as a profit-making concern. Training tools for understanding plastics technology, operating production machinery (in the plastics industry), and the development and implementation of training processes themselves have been developed and sold. The company also currently employs two social science research graduates with a brief to monitor what is happening in the world of work both within and outside. In-company training will continue to be packaged for sale within identified markets and thus contribute to the recovery of training costs.

In the "green-field" sites the first group of workers completed the full education program before getting practical experience of work in the factory. A follow-up of the group showed that many of them felt that the contrast between work in the factory and their preparation in the classroom was so great that they had difficulties in coping with the work situation. They felt they had been left too much to cope on their own in the factory. The basic classroom training has been alternated with experience on the production line for the later groups. They have not experienced the frustrations of the former group and have been able to form more realistic expectations about the nature and content of the jobs they will be assigned to.

The development of these training packages and the organisational mechanisms for on-the-job learning are characteristic of Manducher's general policy of making competence development an internal company concern. The ability to facilitate learning is itself a company core competence. The company aims to develop its know-how in defining, designing, implementing and evaluating training projects.

Motivation and Reward Systems for Competence Development

The company's general policy is to encourage employees to improve their competencies. But as the managing director points out "there is no point in offering a drink to someone who is not thirsty". A basic issue is thus to stimulate or motivate workers to be interested in competence development. One basic approach adopted by the company is to reward individual workers for their competencies. More specifically, it pays workers for their established knowledge and skills, rather than for the ability the company has to utilise that knowledge and those skills. The onus on the employee is to develop and maintain relevant skills and the onus on the employer is to provide facilitating circumstances for the development of these required skills and to provide opportunities for their application.

Hence, the management introduced a new pay scheme based on an assessment of an individual worker's skills.

The initial mapping of competencies was carried out in collaboration with experts from ANACT. Further tests and evaluations were carried out within the company in a joint project between management and unions. Each employee was given the opportunity to make a personal decision about whether to participate in this exercise. The aim of individual assessments was to establish possible "white spots" in the individual's knowledge and skills. The individuals were assessed in relation to the field and levels of knowledge and skill required by their particular department in the factory. If the team leader had an opinion which differed (either positively or negatively) from that of the assessment consultant he was required to register this in writing on a special form in the assessment file.

The voluntary nature of the exercise was partly due to management's wish to stimulate motivation and partly because the unions' objected to attitude testing. The assessment also covered the individuals' learning capacity and their possibilities for developing in their present or alternative profession or part of the factory.

The Key Competence Structure

The individual workers' wage classification was based on the concept of the so called "espace du qualification".[2] The concept of the "qualification space" is based on a graphical representation utilising five axis radiating from a common origin (see Figure 1). Each axis symbolises a key competence in the production worker:

1. product skills: the degree to which a worker masters all the operations within a particular technology for making a product;
2. quality: the degree to which the operator can independently conduct quality control on different products using different technologies;
3. process skills: the degree to which the operator masters the parameters of the production process and can act on it;
4. planning skills: the degree to which the operator can master production process planning;
5. communication and social skills: the degree to which an operator possesses community and social skills required for working in a group.

For each skill area or dimension management has defined four levels of competence. At the lowest level, the operator will have mastered the basic skills in the particular area. At the highest competence, the operator has sufficient mastery of the area such that he or she can teach others. A number of points are assigned for each scale point on a dimensions and the individual's wage is determined by the sum of points. A worker who reaches level 3 on all five scales would have a sum total of 145 points. A worker who reaches level 4 on all five scales would have a value of 155 points. Of the 1950 employees in the company at the moment roughly 1200 have reached the 145 point level and roughly 600 have expressed their desire to achieve the 155 point status. In management's view all personnel should be able to achieve the 155 point status within a period of 7-15 months, irrespective of their standing at the outset. A premium of 15% of the basic wage is paid to individuals who have achieved the 155 point status.

When 60% of the workers in a group have reached level 4 on four of the five competence dimensions they are allowed to make direct contact with other (corresponding) groups both within and outside the company in order to get their work done, e.g. customers or suppliers. They do not require clearance from a supervisor before making such contacts.

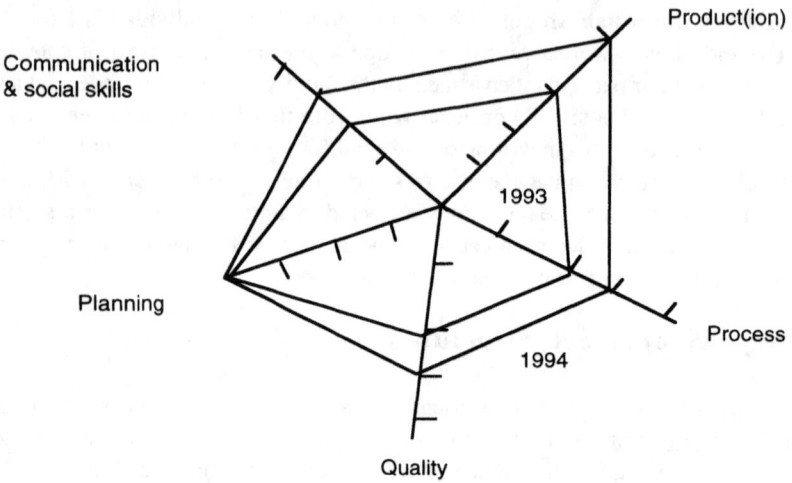

Figure 1. *Key components and their assessment*

The training which is required to move from one competence level to the next on the different competence dimensions is integrated into the production process. A number of training rooms have been located on the shop floor, in the factory, which can be booked by different tutors to hold tutorial or training sessions for different groups of workers at times agreed on with the individual participants. In autumn 1993 there were roughly 50 "démultiplicateurs" working as tutors or teachers. A démultiplicateur may be a team leader, a highly qualified worker or a part-time retired expert who has retired early. To carry out their tutorial role they are released from other duties in production for an agreed time to supervise the training of specific training groups in specific topics. The membership of a specific training group will be distributed amongst different production teams. The tutor will book a time for each meeting in consultation with his group's participants and their teams.

One example in the Oyonnax production facility is of the three training rooms which serve 10 job families. The teams are made up of 8-15 people, including the team leader. The employees work in three 8-hour shifts from Monday to Friday and two 12-hour shifts over the weekend.

The resources required to carry out all this training are largely acquired through rationalisations of other activities and the external marketing of training products. For example, prior to the quality training and delegation of responsibility to the groups Manducher had 150 quality controllers. Now they have 30 quality facilitators supporting the teams. Similarly where previously 35 people were engaged in planning and logistics as separate functions, there are now two people.

Revisions of an individual's competence compensation is based on the assessments of the individual's capacity made by three people. These are the individual, his team leader and his tutor or démultiplicateur. Their assessments are then passed on to the personnel department.

Personnel development meetings are arranged between employees, their immediate superiors and the head of personnel. In the course of these talks the functioning, the evaluation, the aspirations, ambitions and training needs of the employee are jointly discussed. The discussion results in a report which is signed by all participants.

An interesting feature of the Manducher approach is that while workers are rewarded for developing their competencies, management is rewarded for utilising these competencies. Thus a manager's remuneration is related in part to the way in which he has succeeded in using the competence of his employees. The problem facing the company in 1994 is how to improve management performance in these matters.

A Human-Centred Strategy and the Test of Turbulence

The early 90s has seen a marked recession within the car industry. In Germany the market has declined by 20-25 %. In France the decline has been 16 %. For Manducher's part it has meant a drop of 5% in 1993. Though 1993 is seen as a very bad year, the company expects to recover and make profits again in 1994. The company's efforts to improve efficiency and to meet the sharply falling demands from the market are clearly reflected in the downsizing of the company which has occurred during the 90's. The company's employment figures are:

1991:	2,381 employed
1993:	1,950 employed
1994:	1,700 employed

Thus in 1993, 350 workers were laid off. However, this was done within the general framework of the human centred personnel policy at Manducher. Attempts were made to retain as much competence in the organisation as possible. Alternatives were offered to those being laid off:

1. 30 people were offered a year's sabbatical leave without wages. If they used this year for undertaking social service or service in a third world country they were offered a stipendium of 40,000 French francs (which may be compared with the average worker's taxable yearly income of 78,000 French francs).
2. 170 people, between 50-70%, became part time workers.
3. 25 people between the ages of 55 and 56 years 2 months were offered part-time work as teachers and tutors in the organisation.
4. 50 people who had reached the age of 56 years 2 months were offered early retirement.
5. 160 people were given the normal severance benefits.

Klöckner's top management agreed to these measures which cost the company 32 million French francs. A follow-up study in which 150 of those workers who were laid off in 1993 were interviewed showed that 55% of them had already acquired new jobs. The company interprets this as an indication that people who have been developed as competent team members in Manducher are in demand upon leaving the company.

Manducher's management feels confident that the present vision of a broad based effort to improve key competencies in the work force is sound business. For example while the corporate average for labour costs at different production facilities is 25 %, the levels for the innovation leaders in Oyonnax and Burnhapt are 18 % and 19 % respectively. Similarly between 70% and 80 % of the calculated benefits expected in a five year period for these plants have already been realised after two years.

Conclusions

The robustness of Manducher's visionary strategy, centred on competence development, is related to a number of interdependent and, in this case, mutually supporting factors:

- The vision is value-based on a positive management conception of the will and abilities of the workforce to develop themselves and the business.
- This is coupled with management's readiness to give the workforce and their unions an adequate position" in the running of the business, involving at the individual level, the shouldering of responsibility for quality control and customer contact. At the representative level the unions participated in joint evaluations of management initiatives which led to new joint agreements.
- The values forming the cornerstones for the vision were clearly formulated by a new member of the top management team who was formally responsible for the organisational transformation of the company.
- The transformation process was facilitated by a co-operative, as distinct from adversarial, relation between management and the unions. The process was designed to be accessible and achievable by the entire workforce. The individual's participation in the process was on a voluntary basis. At the same time, a basic education program was carried out to ensure that the workforce had the necessary prerequisite knowledge and skills to participate in the developments in a meaningful fashion.
- The transformation was clearly based on an holistic approach:

    - clear vision and policy statements;
    - clear champions in every plant;
    - clear organisational changes with the introduction of multi-skill teams;
    - clear technological changes with new production process technologies;
    - clear changes in the management systems with new supervisory roles and new incentive and wage systems.

- Five basic key competencies were identified, operationalised and calibrated. They were also "valued" by being directly coupled to a competence component in the workers' remuneration system. Competence development was also mutually assessed by the employee concerned, the team leader and the tutor.

Figure 2 shows some of the basic steps in the development process which have taken place in Manducher over the last five years. The appointment of a new director for social affairs led to the clear articulation of human-centred values in the organisation and the clear formulation of a competence or capability-based perspective on business development. Two kernels of this business vision were:

1. The in-depth realignment and development of the basic structures in the organisation. This included the adoption of new forms of plastics technology, and the realignment of the work organisation around multi-skilled teams. A management system was developed in which supervisory roles, together with the new tutorial and teaching roles, created an organisational infrastructure to support competence development on the part of the individual worker. This was also supported by the introduction of a new reward system which included clear competence components.
2. Formal educational programs were launched to raise the basic competencies of the workers to enable them to function and develop in the new system.

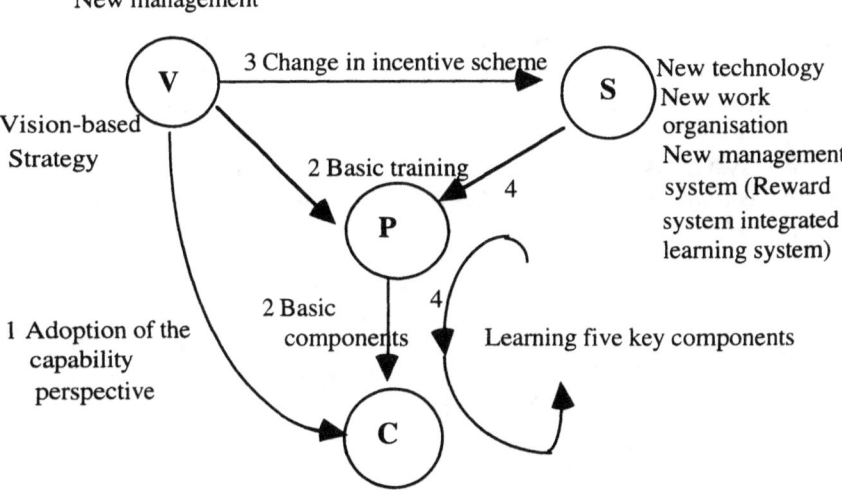

Figure 2. *A new value-and vision-based strategy leading to an in-depth structural re-alignment in the company*

Upon acquiring the basic competencies, the identification of the main key competencies in production formed the point of departure for systematic learning and competence development for an increasing proportion of the workforce. Although the strategy was implemented on the basis of voluntary participation, between a third and a half of the workers have already become fully committed to it. The level of commitment shown by them probably reflects the fact that management and unions together undertook the "internal marketing" of the plan.

Furthermore these initiatives have been accompanied by the signing of some 19 collective agreements on non-wage issues by management and unions in the last four years. Amongst others. These include agreements upon:

- work classification;
- further vocational training;
- flexible working time;
- equality of opportunity between men and women;
- opportunities for handicapped workers;
- provisions for work council meetings and;
- union recognition rights.

In March 1994 the company and the unions entered into a new series of negotiations on "the evolution of the system".

Notes

1. The Manducher case was recommended by Dany Wijgaerts of the European Centre for Work and Society in Maastricht. The Maastricht centre had conducted a study of ten learning-oriented companies. The report from this study has been published in Flemish.

2. The new system is succinctly described in French in a recent publication from the company: *Evolution Professionelle: Les Nouvelles Classifications.* Eurotec/Manducher, Oyonnax, 1994

Chapter Seven

Improving Performance through Entrepreneurship at Sara Lee/Douwe Egberts

Wim Heine

Introduction

The rapid changes confronting Sara Lee/Douwe Egberts in recent years compelled the Training & Development department (T&D) to find a new direction. It transformed itself from being a traditional department with a focus on individuals, to one which assisted business units to become more effective.

A model approach was developed to carry out this task which is known as the "Performance Improvement Programme". This programme in fact consists of smaller programmes and supporting activities, which focus on the practical involvement of employees, at all levels, in formulating and realising the primary goals of the organisation.

In the approach described here typical characteristics of Sara Lee/DE are examined, as well as the role of Training & Development and the different parts of the programme. It is a snapshot of a development process of which the final results are as yet not visible.

Sara Lee/Douwe Egberts

- Sara Lee/Douwe Egberts, known as Sara Lee/DE, is part of the Sara Lee Corporation with its headquarters in Chicago. The Sara Lee Corporation (SLC) has an annual turnover of 14 billion dollars. It has 112 000 employees, and ranks among the top companies in America (1991). SLC is an international organisation which produces and sells consumer goods. The four product categories are: Personal Products (pantyhose, leather goods, sportswear and underwear); Packaged Meat and Bakery (deep frozen cakes, pastries and packaged meats); Coffee and Grocery (coffee, tea, tobacco, rice, nuts and snacks) and Household and Personal Care (washing powders, toothpaste, baby care, skin care, shoe and car care, air fresheners and many other similar products).
- Sara Lee/DE is situated in Utrecht (The Netherlands) and is responsible for the purchasing, manufacturing, packaging, distribution, marketing and selling of consumer products in the categories of Coffee and Groceries and Household and Personal Care.
  The most important markets for these product-categories are in Western and Eastern Europe and to a lesser extent Africa, North America and the Pacific Rim. Eastern Europe, Central America and the Pacific Rim are considered to be the most important areas for potential

growth. Sara Lee/DE has an annual turnover of c. 4 billion dollars and has c. 25,000 employees (1991).

Features

The specific features of the organisation are its abundant growth (c. 300% during the last 5 years), the drive for new markets, the development and improvement of brand products, and powerful financial management.

Sara Lee/DE is a very decentralised company consisting of many small and medium sized business units (100 to 400 employees). These business units are sometimes merged into subsidiary companies, depending on the market and products. These different subsidiaries, formed by the business units, have a relatively large amount of operational autonomy. However, the areas where cooperation takes place is on the increase.

Recent developments

Largely due to its rapid growth and changes in markets and market positions, the company is faced with a number of challenges which have drawn management's attention to the quality of the internal organisation [1].

A number of the most important challenges for development of the organisation, are listed below.

- the increase of international competition in our traditional markets requires that the company should produce (even) more efficiently and cheaply (globalisation);
- rapid changes in consumer preference and shifting trends in new and existing markets, require constant attention and measures to increase the effectiveness of the business units (individualisation);
- the increasing complexity of systems and structures, resulting from the growth of the company and the segmentation of products and markets, has led to a trend where decision-making is transferred to lower levels of the organisation;
- the availability of technology creates opportunities for the improvement of job related information and the strengthening of linkages between functions.

The above challenges are not equally important in every business unit and need not apply at the same time. Market developments, the position of different brands and local management's reaction to these developments, play an important role.

New Competencies

A direct consequence of the above challenges and the (intended) reaction of management is a shift in demands made on employees. This is evident in management's increasing interest in issues regarding entrepreneurial management such as leadership, team building, responsibility for results, performance management and a new focus on business processes resulted in actions like Total Quality Management, ISO 9000, client orientation, core competency, etc.

In our view, the nature of this interest and the resulting activities, herald clear changes in the job demands made on non-executive employees, and lower and middle management, in particular. Before going into this in more detail, the job structure of an average Sara Lee/DE business unit is illustrated below. In a production unit this structure usually has four levels:

- senior management: responsible for the end results of the business units. Minimum educational level: university or equivalent;
- middle management: responsible for the results of a department within a business unit. Minimum educational level; university or equivalent;
- lower management: responsible for some of the production process within a department. Minimum education level: technical college or equivalent;
- workers: responsible for carrying out specific tasks within the production process; Minimum education level: secondary education.

From our observations, changes in job demands were just as important for the more technical aspects of a job as for the non-technical aspects, such as team work, communication and other related qualities.

What was noticeable was that business units which were heavily under pressure from external developments paid relatively more attention to developing the non-technical aspects. The most important reason for this was, in our opinion, a lack of trust in the more traditional means of improving productivity in organisations, such as restructuring, cost-cutting or other methods of using raw materials and capital more efficiently. In short, there was a search for more effective means of reaching the desired results.

This should result in a unit whereby the flow of activities is closely tuned to the fast changing desires of customers, while at the same time keeping costs at the same level, or preferably lower, than those of competitors.

This new orientation by Senior Management in particular to the productivity of their business units led to a need for strengthening competencies such as:

- speed of response;
- initiative;
- cooperation;
- involvement;
- fulfilment of obligations;
- communication (especially listening);
- responsibility taking;
- self development.

An increasing number of managers believe that an improvement in these areas will, in time, lead to a substantial improvement of company results. Furthermore, they recognise that the period required to make the desired changes seems to be in conflict with the short-term attention to financial results. However, they expect that Human Resource Development may provide a solution to this problem, in which short-term targets are realised and long-term organisational potential is developed.

Training and Development

Within Sara Lee/DE, Human Resource Development is the responsibility of local management, which is supported by local personnel departments. At a central level there is a small staff department for 'Training and Development', which consists of the corporate staff. Until recently, this department's task was to develop and offer training programmes for individual employees attached to various business units.

The most important reason for this was a change in the expectations of Management. Until then, the product portfolio was based, in particular, on conclusions of managers that their subordinates were not capable of fully realising their job demands. In nearly all the cases this conclusion was reached retrospectively. It became increasingly obvious that managers preferred an approach in which future competencies for realising business objectives were clearly stated in advance. Consequently, the development of the necessary competencies was considered a prerequisite for forecasting business results. These changes compelled the Training & Development department to take a more active approach, rather than the reactive support they had hitherto been giving. This created new and unprecedented demands for the department, and led to the reorganisation of personnel within the department. A new head and a number of new staff members were appointed (all of whom had experience with operational personnel) and the staff was reduced from 6 to 4 members. The first task of the new department was to redefine its role and objectives and to present its new work method and work plan.

Starting Points

The role which the department enacted has two aspects:

1. To support business units in realising training policy;
2. To design, present and execute common development activities for the entire company.

The most important starting point for the department is that:

> "The development of the competencies of employees should be directed towards the realisation of improved company results."

This implies that the individual employee or a group of employees is still the object of a certain development activity. However, the success of an activity of this type should be primarily measured in terms of the (improved) results of the unit in which the employees work.

In this context the term "company" refers to that part of the organisation in which the development activity is taking place. This may be the entire company, as in the case of a general management training, or a department, as in the case of a team training.

Company Performance

The company's performance is dependent to a large degree on the possibilities offered by the environment (opportunities and threats), and how the company responds to it (strengths and weaknesses). The activities of Training & Development in recent years has been geared to supporting business units both in analysing opportunities and threats, and using the existing means effectively at all levels within the organisation.

In developing and carrying out its activities, T&D differentiates between two groups of employees, namely:

1. employees who traditionally contribute the most to creating added value within the organisation (i.e. workers and supervisory employees); and
2. employees who bring about the conditions which make it possible for workers and supervisory employees to perform (middle and senior management).

Our attention is increasingly focusing on employees in the first category. They must, after all, deliver the results that can enable the company to improve its performance.

Such a performance is only possible, however, if management creates the necessary conditions. In other words, only an integrated approach with attention equally divided between both categories will be successful. Therefore, in Sara Lee's approach, relatively the same amount of time is devoted to workers and supervisory employees (approx. 50%). This, incidentally is not only because of their role in creating added value, but also because they were relatively behind in efforts aimed at enhancing personal skills.

Organisation

An effective organisation is more than the sum of the individual competencies of employees. The most important challenge for Training & Development was to create such an added value by connecting the improvement of individual competencies of employees to those of the organisation as a whole. In our opinion this was, to a large extent, the result of open co-operation between employees within an organisation working towards a common vision [2]. This means that the development of individual competencies must be dealt with collectively.

To coordinate these activities we make use of a model based on the classical determinants of an organisation, namely, Strategy, Structure and Culture. To these determinants we have added the determinants for the quality of individual employees, mainly based on the work of Boyatzis, Schroder and Katz [3a], and the characteristics of successful operating units, based on Wissema, Bartlett & Goshal, and Kotter & Heskett [3b].

The relationship of determination within different organisational levels are presented in the following model (Figure 1): The competency model was used as a basis for deciding upon a dual approach of development. It was based on the (present) limited knowledge of developing and carrying out training and organisation-development programmes. The approach also included information obtained from recent publications on the transfer of training experience at the work place [4].

Company	Business unit	Employee
Strategy	Vision	Direction
Culture	Leadership	Cooperation
Structure	Core Competence	Technical competence

Figure 1. *An organisational and individual development model*

Dual Approach

This dual approach focuses upon two fields of interest:

1. The *functional development* of employees, where the emphasis is upon improving the technical skills of individual employees.

In light of the extensive experience of local management in this field, Training & Development is hardly required, except in the area of "Core Competencies"[5] which determine the competitiveness of the organisation to a large extent. Specific communal programmes for this area are being developed.

2. The organisational development of business units, where the emphasis is upon the collective advancement of knowledge and skills with regards to:

    (a) the setting and realisation of a 'vision' for the business unit and directly related individual 'objectives' of department and/or employees.
    (b) the 'Leadership' of the unit manager and his team and the cooperation in and between various departments of the organisation.

An adequate strategy was required for both fields of interest. Here the discussion is limited to organisational development.

Transfer

The creation of a vision and the development of effective relationships within an organisation are disciplines which, according to Senge [2], are inherently collective in nature. "Only groups can engage in these activities. The principles must be understood by groups. And the essences are states of being experienced collectively". Other authors have expressed similar views [6]. This knowledge added to the experience we had already gained with various open training programmes, persuaded us to carry out training activities only with the various groups within the organisation. We therefore chose subjects directly related to the day-to-day work of participants. The programmes were organised, as far as possible, on these premises.

Initial Development Projects

Prior to 1989 the involvement of the Training and Development department in various company sectors was negligible or non-existent. Consequently, there was little expertise in this area. Therefore, a number of development projects were initiated to assess the extent of the problem (need for training) and to take stock of possible solutions. Four development projects were defined:

- Total Quality Management;
- lower management;
- absence through illness;
- Management by Objectives.

Various project groups were formed, consisting of participants from a variety of departments within the Central Staff (Company Medical Services, Quality Support, Occupational Psychology, Organisation Design, and others).

It became evident that "Total Quality Management" and "Lower Management" were the most important and relevant projects. These projects were exceptional in that they made it possible to have an integrated approach to various organisational problems. The other projects were equally important, but were more focused upon specific problems.

Total Quality Management Project

In recent years a lot of time and energy has been devoted to Total Quality Management in various staff-departments. The reason for this activity was the need to determine what "Quality" might imply for certain departments at Sara Lee/DE in the near future. There was also a need to coordinate activities in this field, which were taking place in various sectors of the company. The results of this effort are:

1. greater insight into the meaning of "Quality Management" and underlying theories;
2. an overview of the activities in this field in various business units;
3. an inventory of instruments which might be used in further development of company sectors; and
4. better coordination between departments which were involved in Certification (ISO) of subsidiaries and whose objective was the improvement of cooperation and goal setting in those sectors.

This last point, in particular, contributed to the presentation of a joint project proposal from Training & Development and Quality Support [7] for a production unit. In this project, lasting 30 months, the first part is largely devoted to effective behaviour (such as goal setting and team work). The emphasis of the last part is upon strengthening the technical skills necessary to obtain an ISO certificate. We think that this approach helps us to disavow the belief that the ISO certificate may be obtained by merely constructing a technical plan and subsequently enforcing it. Although this approach has its advantages and may lead to qualitatively better products in the long run, it does not contribute to an efficient and solid organisation, or rather, it may do so only partially. In light of the excellent quality of the products at present, it seemed more logical to focus upon behavioural aspects.

An application for a project subsidy from the EEC (European Social Fund) was made at the end of 1992. A substantial part of the total cost, about Dfl. 1,000 000 was received from Brussels to cover the start-up of this project.

Lower Management Project

One programme from the "old style" period of Training and Development was a successful training programme for recently appointed Floor Managers and Supervisors (Supervisory level). The programme had a modular design plan and paid a lot of attention to the work environment of participants. However, we were not completely satisfied with the transfer of the theory into practice. The participants reverted to their former behaviour patterns too rapidly and no improvement was apparent in the results of the department. In our view, the reason for this was the negligible acceptance of the significance of the skills learned in the training. Too often this led to a reversion to former behaviour patterns.

A new programme was sought which would both enhance the leadership qualities of the younger supervisor and increase the acceptance of those enhanced qualities in the work environment. It was our belief that the latter could only be achieved via a collective approach, in which the entire unit was involved. After searching intensively in the Dutch training market we were forced to conclude that a programme of this sort was not available. However, due to a lucky coincidence, we found a sizeable government project in England which was experimenting with a programme which seemed to fulfil our needs. It was based on the latest training and management techniques, such as "Action Learning", "Team building", "Participative Leadership" and "Quality Control".

Having made this discovery, contact was made with a training institute, which was prepared to become a licence holder for the Dutch language area and to translate the mass of training material. As a result of these preparations we were able to launch a pilot project in one of the subsidiaries of Sara Lee/DE in the Netherlands. The execution and supervision of the 16 month programme was in the hands of a duo, consisting of a consultant from the licence holder and a training advisor from Training & Development.

The success of the programme surpassed our wildest expectations. After a hesitant start participants and staff members, with whom they worked directly, became so enthusiastic that they devoted a substantial part of their free time to preparing and developing the programme. An evaluation in mid 1991 showed that the high costs of the programme (c. 100 thousand guilders) would be earned back within a year. Certainly not a bad result for a training programme.

This success did not go unnoticed and soon other unit managers wanted to implement the programme in their organisation. However, the question was raised as to which criteria had to be fulfilled within an organisation as prerequisites for the successful implementation of the programme. The English institute which had developed the programme could provide no answer because they had as much experience with the programme as we did.

The decision was made to commission an external training bureau to develop a so-called "preparatory programme" and implement it. This programme was intended to clarify the operational objectives which the unit management and the unit in question had set itself. This information served as input for the English programme, which was called "First Line Management" (FLM). Following a seemingly successful implementation of the preparatory programme and the introduction of FLM in one business unit, it became apparent that major problems were arising in other units. These problems were all related to the ability of the bosses of the participants to adapt to the new style of leadership. It became evident that the preparatory programme was inappropriately linked to FLM and that its content and depth did not meet our expectations.

We asked ourselves how this misjudgement had come about. This evaluation led to the decision to investigate the pilot organisation. It soon became clear that this business unit, in contrast to the second unit, was more advanced at the cooperation level. Furthermore, this unit had already stated its objectives and had gained support for these objectives within the unit. The link with the FLM programme was remarkably strong. In short, the success of the first programme was largely based upon qualities which were already present amongst managers and employees in this organisation. Our conclusion was that we should direct our attention towards creating favourable preconditions which would guarantee the success of the implemented FLM programme (this will be discussed further in the description of our operational model).

Evaluation of Development Projects

Experience gained with two FLM programmes, an extremely successful Project A (First Unit), and a less successful, Project B (Second Unit) is presented here. In comparing these projects and evaluating their effect upon workers, the following characteristics become apparent:

Project A

First FLM programme, implemented under perfect conditions (in retrospect):

- Participants in the FLM programme, hence referred to as FLMs, were stimulated to delegate more tasks to their staff, due to the intensity of the programme.
- FLMs made more use of the knowledge and experience of their staff; experiments with regards to improvement were set up jointly from the start. For example, all staff members whose work would be influenced by a new automation project, were involved in its progress from the beginning to the end.
- There was more attention for training and education in various teams. FLMs personally worked as trainer/instructor, and time and space were provided for extensive training for the new computer system. FLMs set themselves the goal of re-initiating training amongst staff members who were considered to be 'no longer trainable'. As a result they were able to stimulate staff members in the 50-plus age group to take a course in reading and writing.
- There was more consultation and a greater exchange of information: FLMs became convinced of the importance of good (steering) information.
- FLMs made improvements whereby:
  - a night shift, during which less pleasant work had to be done, could be dropped;
    The employees were given more interesting work in return;
  - there were fewer communication problems with other departments;
  - the new computer system was installed without a hitch; and
  - the traditional, unhealthy rivalry between different teams decreased considerably.

- Owing to the personal development which the FLMs had undergone, they were more open to suggestions from staff members.
- The role and significance of the FLMs within the organisation is increasing.

Project B

Second programme where a number of criteria were not met:

- Half a year had passed and the delegation of responsibility was still limited. True delegation was rare in this sector of the company. FLMs were therefore unable to find role models.
- At the level of FLMs themselves contact was improving. However, at lower levels this improvement was negligible.
- FLMs were developing an interest in the development of their staff. However, the translation into activity was still limited.
- The reaction of FLMs to their colleagues and staff was becoming more positive and business-like; instead of solving conflicts, problems were being recognised earlier and solved in interactive consultation. Their attitude towards staff members had undergone general improvement, but at a slower rate than we had been led to expect by the first programme.

In both projects it is evident that the behaviour of the FLMs was initially a reflection of that of their managers. However, they gradually began to show a greater ability to adapt and develop than their bosses. The most important conclusion that may be drawn from the comparison of the two projects is that, although the process should be a top-down one, once the programme has reached a work floor level the involvement of middle management should be stimulated. Only an integrated approach, where linkages back to earlier phases are constantly made, can lead to a process of development in which the participation of all members of the organisation is ensured. We believe this sort of approach is a precondition for maximum results.

With such an approach, account should be taken of the task allocation of middle and lower management. In other words, there has to be enough job security for middle management if the need for their work decreases as a result of the growing influence of the FLMs.

New Model for Organisational Development

An operational model was developed, which served as a guideline for further development (see Figure 2). It was based on the knowledge gained by various project groups and the experience gained in the development and implementation of various pilot projects. This model is referred to as the "Performance Improvement Programme", which implies that this approach is directed towards the improving the results of the organisation. The model is based on the view that the quality of the internal organisation is largely dependent upon the quality of three distinct processes.

1. policy deployment (PD);
2. client orientation (CO);
3. project management (PM).

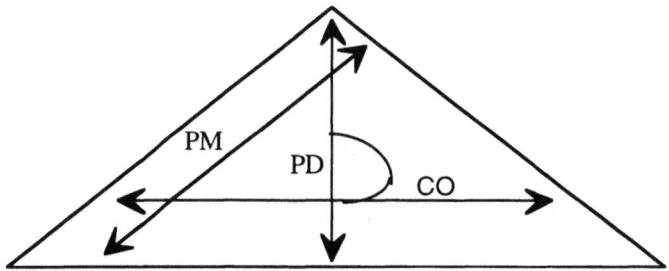

Figure 2. *Organisational development model*

Policy Deployment [8] may be described as the development of a vision, with regard to the future position and significance of the company sector in question; the translation of this vision into concrete, quantifiable and acceptable objectives for all staff members, from senior management to the shop floor. In addition, it entails the provision of feedback to the top level about the experience and results gained at various levels. At best, this process will constantly repeat itself. However, before this point is reached a great effort will have to be made to improve the cooperation and communication between different groups in the organisation.

Client orientation implies that the norms applied to determine the quality of products and services are those of the consumer. For the sales department this criterion is a matter of course. However, this is not the case for other departments working in support of sales, for example, in the timely production of goods; or, in the case of a training department, the opportune and effective training of various employees, who are all links in the chain which ensures the added value of the organisation. In other words, the core of Client Orientation consists of the management of functional relationships between departments (interfaces) and the training of employees which takes into account the expectations of the internal and external clients.

Client orientation also implies the cooperation of employees, working at different levels and/or in different disciplines. This involves solving operational problems, which may be outside the domain of a specific department. The most remarkable feature of this cooperation is that:

1. the "leader" does not necessarily have a formal authority over group members;
2. for most part the cooperation between the members is on an informal level.

The structure of such a group varies from a formal project team with its own budget and authority to a loose network with an entrepreneurial "idea holder" and some interested supporters. An example of the latter would be a research officer who wants to realise a certain idea. But to do so he needs the cooperation of marketing, production and senior management. In short, he needs everyone's support without their formal authority. There is a growing need in my company for improving skills in this field.

Interrelationship of Development Programmes

The development model and the various programmes it is composed of were not all developed at the same time and were not co-ordinated according to a set plan. The programmes, which make up the already mentioned company processes, were either developed separately or purchased on the basis of the specific requirements of the management of the company sectors. It was not until later that we began to perceive the inter-relationship of the different processes, which became apparent following extensive consultation with local management. The consultation with employees working at different levels in a variety of related organisations, offered the unique opportunity to compare problems and to seek joint solutions to these problems. At present (1994) we are trying to optimise the model, as three of the pilot programmes are being completed.

1. Employment policy	1. Course determination
	2. Coaching for commitment
	3. Performance development
2. Client orientation	1. Client and result orientation
	2. First line management
3. Project management	1. Project management

Figure 3. *The performance improvement programme*

Although the programmes should preferably be applied in the order given in Fig. 3, in practice it does not always work like this. The reasons for this is that the management may have already undertaken activities without any reference to the development programme. We try to adapt the programme to these activities as far as possible when applying the programme. This sometimes means a somewhat different start or even a different order. A similar, flexible filling-in of the model has, it would appear to us, only a limited effect on the result, provided that the starting points of activities already underway are comparable to those in the model.

The different instruments of the model are discussed briefly in the following sections.

Policy Development Programme

The *course determination* programme serves to formulate a shared objective (mission) and organisational philosophy for the business unit, based on the "Sara Lee/DE Golden Rules" and the norms and values determined by local management.

This serves as a point of departure for an analysis of strengths and weaknesses and the formulation of between six and eight quantifiable operational objectives. These objectives should be achieved by a business unit over two to three years, together with a set of six to eight basic values. The teams in this programme have taken a keen interest not only in the result, but also in the process. A crucial phase in the programme comes at the end of the "course determination". This part is known as the "communication-meeting". The unit manager gives an account of the (provisional) results of the course determination at this meeting, in which all executive employees and specialists within the unit take part. At the same time the manager explains the next part in the model, in which a large part of those present at the meeting will be involved.

The programme, "Coaching for Commitment", is run in conjunction with the course. The coaching programme also consists of short modules, presented at 2 to 3 week intervals, which are attended by members of the management team and other employees. The content of this programme is made up of two parts:

1. the first part focuses upon the translation of general organisational objectives into departmental objectives. This part includes an abridged analysis of the strengths and weaknesses of the department in question. To this end, much attention is given to the so-called SMART principle [9];
2. the second part entails the application of coaching techniques, such as the giving of positive feedback, the stimulation of initiatives, the delegation of responsibility and the development of shared plans of action.

After the first part of the programme has been completed there is another communication meeting. In this meeting, participants present, to each other and their managers, the (provisional) goals they have set. After discussion, the goals are then fixed, although not yet properly adapted. The possibility to adapt is just as relevant to the results of the "course determination" presented earlier. All lower ranking participants, who did not work on the (provisional) course determination, have the opportunity to suggest areas for improvement. The management teams decides if it agrees with such a proposal. Until now our experience has been that employees and management teams deal with these proposals very constructively.

The *performance development* programme for middle and lower-middle management builds on the Coaching programme, and aims to develop a framework of performance standards for employees. The learning objectives are to:

1. define *what* performance standards a department should achieve for each of its objectives;
2. formulate *how* the job should be done by creating a set of behavioural standards (job demands) which are directly linked to the basic values of the unit;
3. deepen the coaching techniques of the previous programme.

The effectiveness of the development programme may also depend upon the nature of the employee's work. For example, it is difficult for secretaries to formulate individual goals based on departmental objectives, because they are generally too detached from the primary organisational process. However, it is possible to formulate job demands based on the three aspects mentioned previously, namely conceptual, human and technical competencies. For secretaries this may imply: the improved ability to work with a word processor (technical competence) or an improved interaction with the boss (human competence) or the formulation of priorities (conceptual competence). To visualise the relationship between competencies and business results, we use the scheme outlined in the Figure 4 below, which is primarily based on Patricia McLagan and Debra Suhadolnik [10].

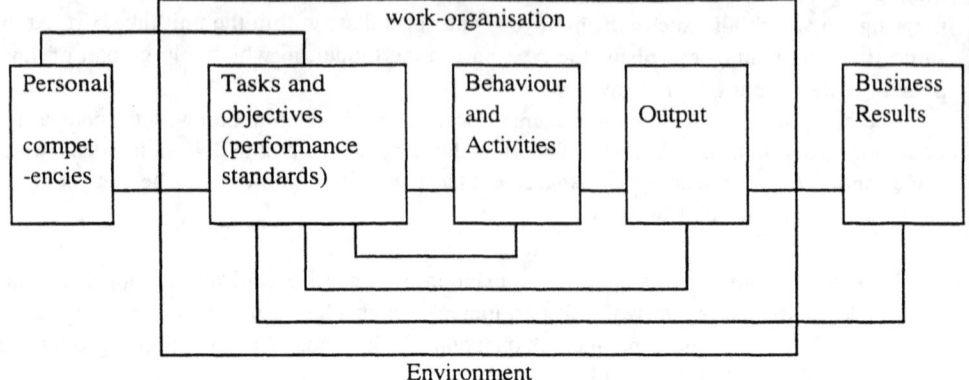

Figure 4. *Link between competencies and the achievement of business results*

Client Orientation

At present two client orientation programmes have been developed:

1. Client and Result Orientation;
2. First Line Management.

The first programme was developed in collaboration with an external bureau for organisational advice, to improve the organisational efficiency of one of the subsidiaries. The greatest problem confronting this subsidiary was the lack of communication between various company sectors.

The second programme was purchased from an English publisher (at present the rights are in hands of Henley Distance Learning Ltd). Essentially, the First Line Management programme is not purely a Client Orientation programme. It is a hybrid, containing elements of Policy Deployment (it includes standards and objectives) and Client Orientation, in that it explicitly analyses the interaction between various departments and its significance to internal clients. The fact that the programme integrates these two areas may be seen as a strength, however, in practice it has proved difficult to develop a comparable situation at higher levels of the organisation.

As well as the difference mentioned above, there is also a distinction with regard to the target group. The Client and Result Orientation programme is intended for staff departments and service organisations. The First Line Management programme is intended for the production organisation. The first programme focuses upon internal client-supplier relationships and their improvement; while the second focuses on the knowledge, skills and behaviour required to lead a department.

Client Orientation Programme Content

In principle, the *Client and Result Orientation Programme*, which is above all aimed at improving internal client orientation, requires that all employees in the organisation answer four questions. The answers should be given within the normal structure of the organisation, i.e. the members of each operational team must provide a joint answer.

Each question is accompanied by an explanation and brief instructions. In addition, a team may consult one of the professional supervisors, in order to solve a specific problem. The questions posed to the teams are listed below.

1. Who are our clients?
2. What can we improve?
3. How can we make these improvements?
4. How can we make the results visible?

Depending on the nature and magnitude of the proposed improvement, implementation is initiated. This may imply that the proposed goal is immediately realised (simple improvements); an investigation is started (complex improvements); or a procedure is started in order to shift decision-making to a higher level of the organisation (extensive improvements).

Our present experience has shown that, upon completing the programme, a quarterly report is presented in which progress and renewal of improvements are monitored and adjusted by means of a system of operational indicators. The programme lasts approximately for six months.

The *First Line Management Programme* forms the core of the development model proposed by Training & Development. The participants are first-level leaders who often have many years of work experience within their own field but have not participated in any form of training outside this field. The programme is based on self-study and the direct implementation of the new skills in the work place. In each of the five modules, the participants and their direct superior formulate departmental and individual objectives. The aim of this programme is to transform leaders at the lowest level into client oriented managers, who are constantly involved in improving quality. The programme lasts c. 16 months and consists of 35 two hour meetings. At the end of the programme the participants should have the ability to:

- apply the principles of TQM in the day to day functioning of the organisation (the goal being to increase efficiency and profit);
- analyse and improve internal and external relationships between the supplier and the client;
- assess and improve the delivery and quality of goods produced in their work area;
- analyse and improve the processes in their work area;
- provide the necessary social preconditions to allow for effective teamwork towards a shared objective and approach;
- engage in self-evaluation, in order to initiate a programme of self-development which will contribute to better leadership;
- perceive the necessity for change and to take the necessary steps to realise change;

- make, implement and supervise new plans, in close consultation with the team which he/she is leading.

Project Management

In the field of project management two programmes are used:

1. Working in Projects;
2. From Ideas towards Results.

The first programme is more-or-less a standard approach for the organisation and implements rather well-designed project. In such a project a number of specialists, mostly from different departments, work closely together to realise a complex task. The delivery of this programme is in the hands of outside consultants. The second programme is quite different in nature. Its aim is to give specialists in marketing, engineering or R&D a tool kit which they can use to improve the change to realise a promising idea. The tools are specially designed to gain support from other managers/specialists, who are not under one's control. This programme was implemented in April 1994. An outside consultant, who designed the programme, and an internal advisor from Training & Development, will run the programme the first time round.

Delivering the Programme

Although the content of the programmes is an important factor determining the success of the *Performance Improvement Programme*, the leadership of the unit manager and the involvement of all other employees is of major significance.

It is for this reason that the first step of the implementation is formed by an assessment of change qualities of management and the cooperation within the team that they are leading. Should either of these factors be of insufficient quality, they will have to be attended to. In the case of the unit manager this may take two forms, which may supplement one another:

1. participation in an external 'Personal Development' and/or 'Change Management' training;
2. intensive personal support, provided by a training advisor from Training & Development, during the entire Performance Improvement Programme (from one-and-half to two years).

At present there has only been one instance where the results of our standard approach seemed insufficient. We therefore decided to link and integrate the 'Course Determination' programme with an external team building programme. Based on the information available to us This move produced more than satisfactory results.

A special feature of the programme is that upon completion of the Policy Deployment, and certainly after client orientation, a steering mechanism develops which is largely based upon operational indicators (Activity Based Management). These indicators are drawn directly from the substantiated departmental objectives. These indicators are particularly useful for middle and lower management, because better feedback can be obtained about organisational processes, in contrast to the financial indicators which are often used. It is evident that this information has a marked effect upon the motivation of the employees. This is largely due to the fact that they have a personal influence upon the results which the indicators are based upon [11].

Lessons Learnt

Human Resource Management

The development model, as described above, did not merely come about according to some preconceived plan. It came about through a learning process, which resulted from a growing realisation amongst management that the success of business units depended upon the improvement of internal communication and the motivation of the employees. It was also due to the increasing insight into Human Resource Management and possible ways of meeting this challenge.

Although there had been rapid changes in the size and structure of the company, it became clear that it was possible to develop new initiatives and provide support for existing ones. In retrospect, it is evident that these initiatives followed a certain pattern and were related in some way. This is not wholly coincidental, but rather a fortunate combination of an extensive debate in Human Resource Management and a high level of practical knowledge in the Training & Development Department of involving large numbers of employees in developing and implementing strategies. This, coupled with the increasing experience in the implementation of programmes amongst operational management, has created a climate in which the model can be extended and improved.

The ultimate objective is to develop a variety of instruments which may be used to enhance the competence of various company sectors, whereby the company may react more effectively to the challenges of the environment.

The Role of Training and Development

The role of the training advisors who are employed in Training & Development is not limited to the (joint) development of various programmes or supporting unit managers. Their task is primarily to guide the entire process from start to finish. An advisor should develop a position of trust with the management of the unit; he/she should become an 'oracle' and expert. This may be realised in a number of ways:

1. Develop good relationship with the unit manager to support his/her leadership in the development process [12].
2. Act as co-trainer in all programme phases; the emphasis being upon:
   - thinking in terms of possibilities and chances;
   - not pointing fingers at others, but personally initiating improvements;
   - seeing the future as the primary object for improvement (instead of harping upon the mistakes of the past);
3. Giving feedback on development process to the unit manager and management team.
4. Organise related activities, if these are useful and necessary for the process.

With regard to co-trainership, there are other issues to be considered besides the supervision of the development process. It has become evident that it is not feasible to yield the whole responsibility for activities which have a significant influence upon the culture of the organisation, to external advisors. It is the joint task of the central staff department, to guard against unintentional changes in culture taking place, which may be contrary to the views of the top management of the organisation. They should apprehend these kinds of developments, and should see that appropriate steps are taken.

Conditions for Success

The development model described here, requires certain organisational preconditions for its implementation. The most important ones are listed below:

1. there must be a definite need for change; without this pressure nobody will feel motivated to devote time to a process of change;
2. there must be a will to change; without tension between the vision of management and the reality perceived by them, every effort to change will be doomed to fail;
3. there must be sufficient ability amongst management to initiate, perpetuate and complete the process;
4. there must be a certain amount of stability in the organisation, i.e. there should be no major changes projected in structure or manpower; should changes be planned, they should be realised first before initiating the process;
E5 the make-up of the management team should be stable, i.e. it should not undergo any considerable change during the course of the process.

An important pre-condition for an effective implementation of a Performance Improvement Programme is a very competent unit manager. This means that such a manager should have a passion for achievement and the skills to think strategically, to communicate effectively and should be able to involve people in decision making processes.

Although the above preconditions may seem unattainable in these turbulent times, it is evident that, preceded by careful preparation, they hardly ever form a problem.

How Sara Lee/De Fits into the General Framework

Values

The process as described in the case above was initiated some four to five years ago when Sara Lee/DE put a strong emphasis on business values like team spirit, initiative, responsibility, dedication and so on. This culminated in a new corporate strategy called "Entrepreneurial Management".

This renewed focus on values was not preceded by any organisational restructuring programme nor did it lead to changes in the balance of power in the organisation afterwards. It was and is far more regarded as naturally belonging to the existing business unit structure. Such a structure, in which the smaller units operate in regions and markets far away from the centre, needs managers who feel and act like owners of the business they are responsible for.

The new corporate initiative was also aimed to be a counter force to the tight discipline of the existing financial reporting system. A major disadvantage of trying to meet strong financial targets and having detailed information systems is risk avoiding behaviour. In a turbulent and competitive marketplace such behaviour was not considered as desirable in the eyes of top management.

The emphasis on values created by rapid changes in markets in combination with tight controlled management information systems, increased the demand for methods and tools to implement a more value driven style of management. The problem was however where to find such instruments and, if you finally find a successful approach, a new problem emerged concerning the assurance of its effectiveness in your organisation. In other words, what were the conditions for its success?

We were lucky to discover a very useful external programme to find a senior manager who had the guts to give us the opportunity to deliver a very lengthy and costly pilot programme, and fortunate to find out the most important conditions for success.

Process

The success criterion we discovered was that Value Management, a way to discover the driving motives in a unit, was particularly effective in our company when its implementation was linked to Strategic Management. We developed methods and tools which were aimed to create a shared vision and mutual values for a business unit and we were able to couple these towards performance standards of the individual jobholder. This coupling was actually done in a very participative way. Starting at the top of the unit, a process was facilitated for each level in the organisation in order to create its own performance standards within the limits formulated earlier by the higher management echelon. The results were a very consistent set of performance indicators for everyone in the unit.

The statements of higher management were however no dictates. Lower layers in the organisation had a genuine opportunity to bring forward proposals for change. This process of mutual involvement was carefully orchestrated by the project manager in close cooperation with the unit manager. The major vehicle for such an involvement was the "communication meeting". After every phase in the process a meeting was organised in which all the key players in the organisation (management, supervisors and workers-representatives), had been informed about the results of the completed development module. In this meeting everyone had the opportunity to participate in small discussion groups, question the outcomes of that particular module and eventually bring forward alternatives. The final remarks of the combined groups created a real impact on the provisional results. These adjusted and agreed results were the starting point for the next phase. To symbolise the commitment to the results of these meetings, all participants placed their signature on the cover of the written agreement.

Structures

The discussion meetings also had some unexpected results. The participants discovered that regular conferences with all key players created a mutual framework of references about the organisation, which in itself was an excellent building block to strengthen good communication. Units in which the programme had been implemented had continued these discussion meetings. Another advantage of these meetings was the need for a unified way of reporting the progress of various departments. This already led, in two cases, to a new reporting system based on operational indicators (time and quality based). Such indicators give, on a quarterly base, feedback about the extent in which the agreed goals were already realised. This reporting system was added to the existing financial reporting system.

Summary of the Development Programme in Relation to the Change Process

The change process began with a "values classification" exercise at a senior management level, as a result of which the focus was placed on Entrepreneurial Business Units (see Figure 5, 1).

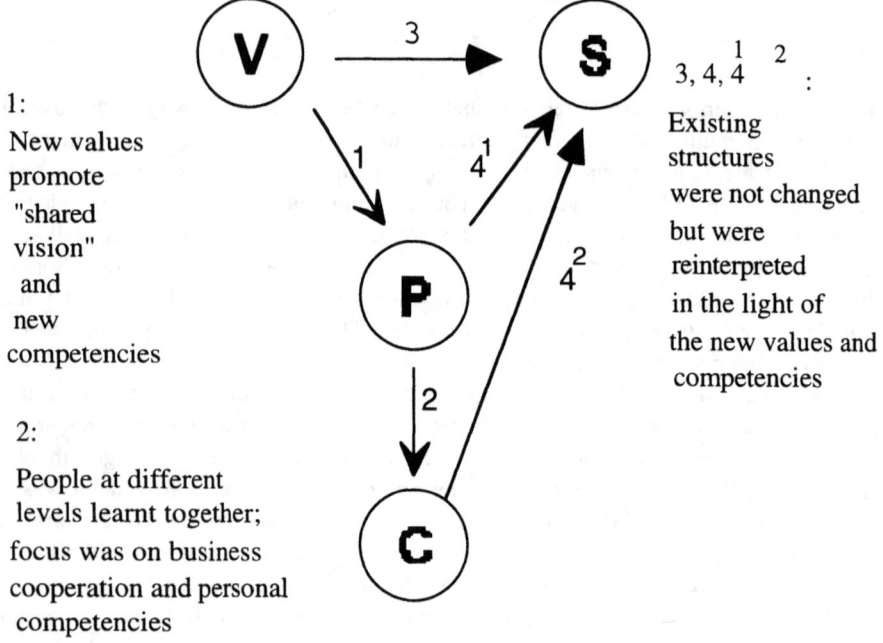

Figure 5. *An entrepreneurial development programme*

A "partnership in business" philosophy was adopted, meaning that each business unit had responsibility for creating its own future. A major organisational development programme was implemented with an initial objective to generate a "shared vision". People at different levels in the business units learnt together. In that way links were established between corporate strategic goals, business unit goals, and individual goals and objectives. Business, individual and cooperation competencies such as initiatives and responsibility were developed (see Figure 5, 2). Even though the existing structures were not changed they had to be formulated in the light of the new values, processes and competencies, which were now driving the company (see Figure 5, 3, 4^1 and 4^2).

Notes

1. See Sara Lee/DE Annual Report 1991-92
2. Not only in our opinion but also in that of a well known writer as Peter M. Senge. See The Fifth Discipline by Peter M. Senge, Doubleday: New York, 1990
3. See (a) clusters in The Competent Manager by Richard E Boyatzis, New York: John Wiley & Sons; the division in competencies in Managerial Competencies by Harold M Schroder, Dubuque: Kendall/Hunt Publishing Company; and (b) the findings of Robert L. Katz quoted in Developing International Managers, published by IMC Research Study, Geneva, Nov. 1992.
4. See article "Why change programs don't produce change" by Michael Beer, Russel A Eistestat and Bert Spectator in Harvard Business Review 1992
5. See article "The Core Competencies of the Corporation" by C. K. Prahalad and Gary Hamel, Harvard Business Review, May/June 1992
6. See article "Training's role in a learning organisation" by Ton Kramlinger in Training, July 1992
7. Internal Staff Department charged with carrying out company processes within the Division Research and Development
8. See the remarks about Quality-programmes made by Jenny Bowles and Joshua Hammond in Beyond Quality, Berkeley Books: New York 1991
9. SMART means: Simple, Measurable, Acceptable, Realistic and Timely; for more information see also article "Wie Sie Ihre Mitarbeiter elektrisieren können" by Adrian F Menz in Gablers Magazin 11.12.91.
10. See Modules for HRD practice by Patricia McLagan and Debra Suhhaddolnik, American Society for Training and Development, 1989.
11. See article "The Performance Measurement Manifesto" by Robert G Eccles in Harvard Business Review, Jan/Feb 1991 and "Creating a Comprehensive System to Measure Performance" by Robert G. Eccles and Phylip J. Pyburn in Management Accounting, October 1992.
12. See articles "Positioning Training" and "Development Departments for Organisational Change" by Graham Stichland in Management Education and Development, Vol. 23, 1992.

Chapter Eight

Developing Unique Production and Work Structuring Principles through a Creative Search and Learning Process:
The Volvo Uddevalla Final Assembly Plant

Kajsa Ellegård, Tomas Engström,
Dan Jonsson, Lennart Nilsson and
Lars Medbo

Introduction

The discussion and analysis of the assembly line, as practised in the automotive industry, tends to be dominated either by researchers from a "human-centred" orientation or by writers who have adopted a point of view inspired by economic models, organisation theory and management literature. In our view, this has led to a bias in defining problems and their considering solutions.

The negative social effects of assembly-line work were noted at an early stage in its development, when the production principles required for the realisation of alternative production concepts had yet to be fully developed and recognised. As a consequence, technology came to be seen as being unsusceptible to influence. It was also considered futile to focus on just the effects of the prevalent production technology rather than discussing the possibilities for technological change. It was assumed that the negative social effects of assembly-line work could, in fact, be remedied through social change, e.g. attitude change and organisational change. In the 1970s and 1980s the reform of assembly work was accompanied by social changes within the framework of the existing technology and/or with obvious technical restrictions, such as existing material feeding techniques.

This case study questions this approach to industrial change, drawing on the experiences gained in the design and running-in of the Volvo Uddevalla final assembly plant, which is now closed. This plant represents a design approach which was mainly concerned with production technology, and the interaction between social factors and production technology.

The study shows that the creative search and learning process which was initiated at the start of the Uddevalla project and continued throughout the entire period of its operation led to irreversible design decisions, implying certain production and work structuring principles. This creative search and learning process continued up until the closing down of the plant, and led to a total change in the technical and administrative preconditions for the assembly line on the basis of unique production principles and non-traditional production techniques.

In this paper we will briefly discuss and report upon the search and learning process itself, and on the production principles implied by the design decisions established during this process and on the application of principles for work structuring. We will conclude by considering some experiences from the Uddevalla plant and prospects for further development and diffusion of the Uddevalla concept.

Volvo Uddevalla

Within the last two decades several innovative final automotive assembly plants have been established in Sweden, for example, the Saab Malmö plant, the Volvo Kalmar plant, the Volvo Tuve facility and, most notably, the Volvo Uddevalla plant. These initiatives have to be seen against the background of product markets, labour markets, industrial relations and other specific socio-economic conditions that characterised the Swedish automotive industry and the Swedish society at that time. Some of these specific conditions are now rapidly changing, while others continue to apply.

With regard to product markets, the Swedish automotive industry is strongly export-oriented. It is similar in some respects to the German automotive industry but it is in marked contrast to both the North American and the Japanese industries which are oriented towards the low-volume production of luxury automobiles. The new facilities in Malmö and Uddevalla, for instance, were built at a time when it was widely recognised that Volvo and Saab could not survive as independent low-volume producers of automobiles by following in the footsteps of North American or indeed Japanese high-volume manufacturers with their huge domestic markets.

Japanese automotive manufacturers have established a number of plants in foreign countries largely due to market restrictions. They have applied their own production principles and created "copies" of Japanese production facilities outside Japan, which have been described as "transplants" (Berggren, Björkman & Hollander, 1991). However, when Swedish plants have been established abroad, alternatives to the assembly line have been used in plants with small production volumes, e.g. in Southeast Asia, and some practical knowledge of using alternative production principles has been gained, albeit on a small scale.

Industrial relations in Sweden have traditionally been more productive and have posed less of an obstacle to the introduction of new production principles than those in most other countries. Industrial relations in the United States, for instance, continue to exhibit the classic conflict between labour and capital. As a consequence, the idea of local problem-solving based on mutual understanding has had little effect there. Swedish trade unions have long ranked among the strongest in the world, but there has also been a tradition, since the 1930s, of cooperation and mutual understanding between employers and trade unions. Mutual understanding is regarded both as a way to bridge immediate conflicts and as being conducive to results that exceed those that would otherwise have been possible.

With regard to labour market conditions, unemployment rates have, until recently, been very low in Sweden, and large wage differentials and individualised wages have been resisted by Swedish trade unions. Hence, unlike as in other countries, it has not been possible for Swedish automotive manufacturers to recruit and retain a high quality work force by offering relatively high wages, or by using seniority based individual wages to reduce employee turnover. This may be a decisive factor behind the Swedish automotive manufacturers' attempts to attract employees by creating more satisfying jobs without compromising productivity.

The initiative to develop and build the Uddevalla plant was thus mainly labour-market driven. At the time, labour was in short supply in Sweden and assembly work with cycle-times of two minutes was not particularly attractive to young people. Management sought ways to make assembly work more attractive by, for example, extending work cycles. Extended work-cycles, in turn, required increased operator competence. Initially such competence development was not seen as a means to attain higher productivity. However, management was not aware of the fact that parallel long-cycle assembly is inherently more efficient than serial, short-cycle assembly due to reduced loss inefficiencies (Wild, 1975; Karlsson, 1979).

To summarise, the main problem as perceived by management was the unattractiveness of short cycle time assembly, not its inherent inefficiency. Competence development was originally seen as being related to the aim of improving the work content. During the course of the design process, however, the role of competence development as a prerequisite for more efficient production principles, based on the parallel extended work cycle assembly, gradually became evident to those involved in the design process.

The Uddevalla plant

The Uddevalla final assembly plant was situated some 90 km north of Gothenburg. It was designed for a one-shift production capacity of 40,000 cars per year, but owing to a decrease in sales the full production-capacity was not utilised. Late in 1992, 708 blue-collar workers and 108 white-collar workers were employed at the plant. The age and sex distribution of blue collar workers is shown in Figure 1.

Age	Male	Female	Total
24 years and younger	64	65	129 (18%)
25 – 45 years	306	187	493 (70%)
46 years and older	66	20	86 (12%)
Total	436 (62%)	272 (38%)	708

Figure 1.*Distribution of age groups of the blue-collar workers at the Uddevalla final assembly plant at the closing down period*

A stated aim of personnel's policy was that the number of employees of different ages and sexes should reflect their representation within the Swedish labour market. In specific terms, the aims were: 60% male workers and 40% female workers; and 25% workers younger than 25 years, 50% workers aged between 25–45 years and 25% workers who were older than 45 years.

In the Uddevalla plant, the flow patterns, materials feeding, and information systems were technically designed to facilitate the learning and the development of knowledge. New aids and tools for materials-handling were developed. This fundamentally new interplay between technology and human beings had positive social effects. Jobs became meaningful, entailing a more extensive work-content which could only be mastered by competent and skilled members of the organisation. Furthermore the new production principles resulted in ergonomic improvements in the assembly area.

These positive social aspects and consequences of the production principles adopted in Uddevalla have been over-emphasised in many presentations and discussions of the Uddevalla plant, especially those directed at a broad audience. What has not been realised is that what makes the Uddevalla plant pioneering is the simultaneous emphasis on social consequences and their technical preconditions. The failure to understand this fact probably contributed to the decision to close down the Uddevalla plant, although the official reason given was the sharp decline in sales experienced by Volvo.

According to Volvo, in November 1992, the Uddevalla plant, as a whole, took on average 32.8 hours to assemble one automobile (Tidningarnas Telegrambyrå, 1992). This figure included the materials handling and feeding work.

The productivity in Uddevalla was not achieved at the expense of product quality. On the contrary, the specific model was manufactured to the highest quality. It should also be noted that individual workers and work groups achieved performance levels exceeding the Volvo figures. For example, work groups, as well as certain individual workers, assembled entire vehicles in 10–14 hours (Nilsson, 1991; Idag, 1993). The traditional Volvo assembly line plants which manufactured similar products did not match this productivity. It is also worth noting that this level of performance was reached in a plant where the running-in took place in parallel with the extensive development and implementation of new and unique production principles.

Owing mainly to the continuous individual and organisational learning process taking place in the plant, which amounted to a continual refinement of the production principles and redesigning of the production techniques, a productivity growth of about 30% per year was achieved between 1989 to 1992. There was no sign of the rate of growth levelling off. Similarly, product quality which was measured by the number and severity of defects detected at the post-assembly inspection improved steadily by about 20% per year.

The decision to close the Uddevalla plant does not affect the validity of the unique production principles which were introduced there. Neither does it detract from the usefulness of the creative search and learning process through which these principles were elaborated.

It would be fallacious to conclude that because the Uddevalla final assembly plant provided, as it was designed to provide, an attractive work environment, it was necessarily less efficient than the plants which used traditional production principles. The Uddevalla plant has provided conclusive empirical evidence that by creating suitable technical and administrative preconditions for assembly work, it is possible to simultaneously gain efficiency, flexibility and improved working conditions.

A Creative Search And Learning Process Leading To Irreversible Design Decisions

The planning and design of the Volvo Uddevalla plant (Fig.2) was original and non-traditional. It involved a flexible search and learning process with three different interacting resource centres. One of these was an experimental workshop in Gothenburg, where practitioners and researchers co-operated. Another one was a training workshop in Uddevalla and the third was the project group responsible for the design of the plant. This group gradually incorporated the new experiences gained.

The Uddevalla project was initiated in 1985, and development work in the experimental workshop was also commenced that year. The basic production principles developed in the experimental workshop were subsequently verified in practice together with personnel from the training workshop. They demanded long cycle time work, involving an extensive work content.

Experience and knowledge from the assembly work was gradually transferred to the project group, who in turn developed and modified their plans and layouts. During certain periods turbulence within the project group was admittedly so great that new experience gained in the experimental and training workshops could not be incorporated into plans and layouts. However, certain decisions in line with the newly developed production principles eventually had to be made.

The training workshop, which pre-dated the Uddevalla plant, started on a small scale in April 1986 and attained full-scale operation in October 1987, remaining in operation until late 1988. Workers received training in building automobiles according to new principles of learning which were based on principles of work-structuring on the shop floor. The experiences they gained were adapted and transferred to the product workshops as they were gradually put into operation (starting in 1988). In this way the difficulty of co-ordinating and training the whole work force at the same time was avoided.

The material workshop in the Uddevalla plant (which prepared and supplied the final assembly kitting fixtures containing components for individual automobiles) was started first, because it had to deliver materials to the training workshop and then to the product workshops. It was in many respects based on conventional storage principles. Here, job redesign and development activities had to be suspended during certain stages of the planning and design work, as well as during the running-in process, in order to guarantee a reliable supply of materials.

At an early stage, (1) an existing building was used for the material workshop and (2) automated guided vehicles (manufactured by a Volvo subsidiary) were used to supply automobile bodies and materials fixtures. These decisions separated the materials-handling work from the assembly work. In this connection, it is worth pointing out that the automated guided vehicles (AGV) were not essential for the implementation of the new production principles. AGV would not have been needed if materials handling and assembly work had been spatially integrated.

With regard to the product workshops on the other hand, there was a prolonged internal discussion, based on the experiences gained in the training workshop, concerning the merits and disadvantages of different production principles.

One of the most important restrictions on the design of the layouts in the product workshops was created by the equipment needed to test the automobiles and to add media

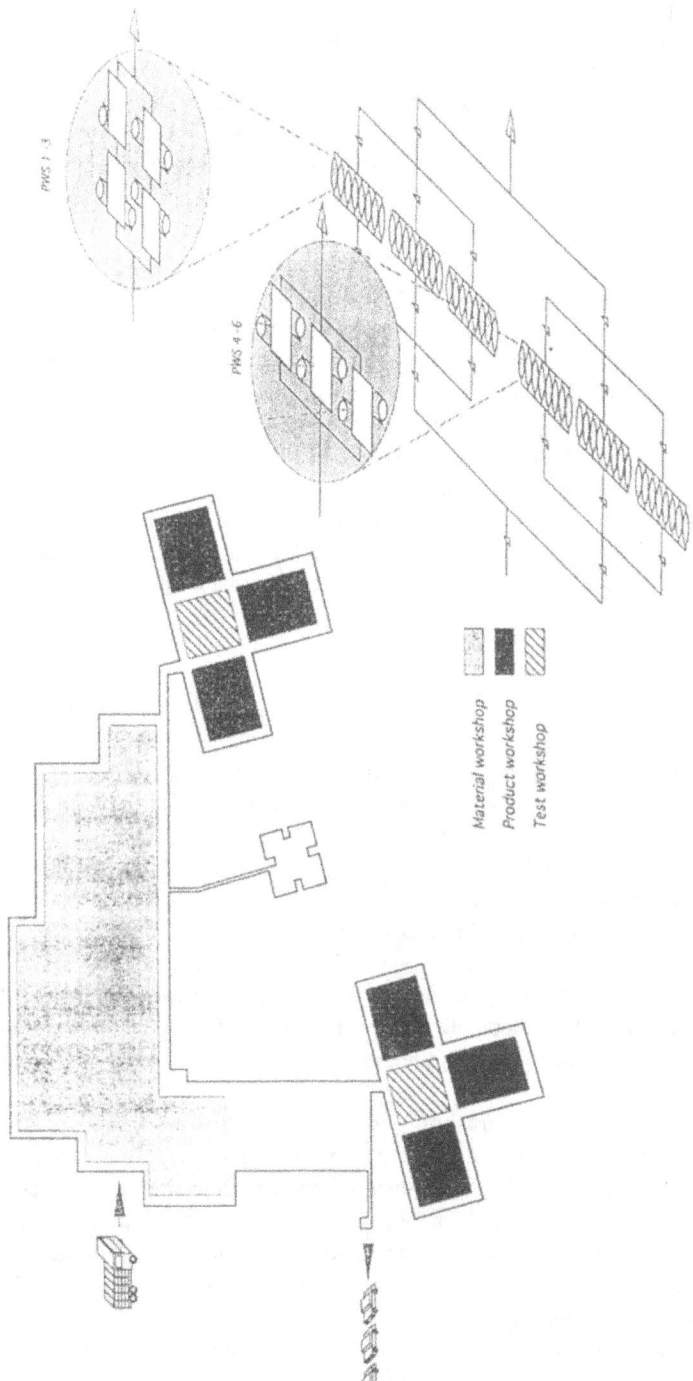

Figure 2. *The Volvo Uddevalla plant with its six parallel product workshops for final assembly (note that the workshops were not entirely identical, since experience from the step-wise running-in process were taken in account). The product workshops are grouped around two test workshops where petrol, water, freon etc. were added and the automobiles were test driven. The material workshop prepared and supplied kitting fixtures to the final assembly*

(petrol, water, etc.), since this required the installation of expensive hardware. This led to the decision to group the six product workshops around two test workshops.

The general shape of the building, as well as the space allocated for the assembly workshops and the interfaces between the assembly work and the AGV, were also defined at an early stage. In particular, the number and positioning of the stands for fetching and leaving materials and automobiles were specified. These stands had to be identical in all the product shops, because the common AGV-system and the same kitting fixtures were used to feed materials to all the product workshops.

The final layout inside the first set of workshops was not decided until the very last moment. The layout was slightly modified for the next set of workshops. In fact, no two workshops were identical, although only two principally different layouts were used.

When the product workshop buildings were almost completed, it was found to be impossible to meet the targeted production volume within the given space by applying traditional production principles. Fortunately, the researchers associated with the experimental workshop were then able to show that it was indeed possible to reach the production target if a non-traditional flow pattern was applied. This also meant that the work-content had to be extended considerably. The decisive factor at this critical stage was therefore the more efficient use of space allowed by the application of the new production principles. The whole of the planning and design of the plant became an irreversible search and learning process.

Summary

In retrospect, the sequence of events in the planning and design of the Uddevalla plant seems clear, and the interaction that took place between the experimental workshop, the training workshop and project management is obvious.

The search and learning process initiated many investigations concerning the layout, but many of the initiatives could not be followed through. The project group proposed a number of innovative product-workshop layouts which were rejected by the company management on the grounds of being either too traditional or requiring too great an investment. When the project group left Gothenburg and all its activities were moved 90 kilometres to Uddevalla, a socially acceptable possibility was opened up to those project members who wished to leave the project because they either could not or did not wish to adopt the new thinking.

As the activities in the training workshop and in the gradually forming product workshops in Uddevalla grew, and as the planning and design progressed, it became increasingly clear that knowledge of and experience gained from traditional production techniques was of little use for designing the new plant. In fact, they were an obstacle to innovative thinking. The assumptions about efficient production embedded in traditional production techniques lead to the conclusion that production according to the production principles used in Uddevalla was inefficient.

However, the work of the project group led to an efficient plant based on completely new principles for industrial work. This is proved partly by the activities themselves and partly by the fact that it became impossible to revert to shorter work-cycles due to layout decisions already taken, investments already made and personal commitments gradually built up. Thus, an irreversible creative search and learning process was set in motion.

Production Principles Implied By The Design Decisions

Some of the production principles applied in the Volvo Uddevalla plant were already known, while others were completely novel. It is a well-known fact that parallel flow leads to more efficient work through the elimination of losses associated with a serial flow. Parallelism means work that is independent of machine controlled flow. In addition, it allows for the organisation of autonomous groups in which the skills of the individual members are complementary and the responsibility for quality and quantity is delegated.

Today, Volvo Trucks is expanding its production capacity using production principles similar to those developed in Uddevalla but without the same well-developed material feeding techniques. One reason for these deviations is that the trucks are simultaneously produced in the same plant in accordance with traditional production principles. Incidentally, this has resulted in more efficient line manufacturing since the most complex and time-consuming product variants, with the largest variation in assembly time, are not assembled on the line.

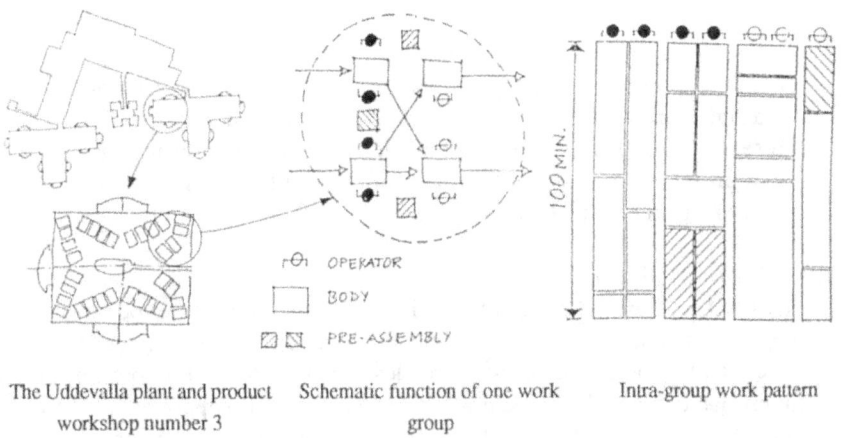

Figure 3. *Schematic description of the final assembly within a work group in Uddevalla where seven operators work on four automobiles. The automobile was assembled in two phases, with a sideways transfer within the group. The labour-intensive subassemblies (doors, engine, dashboard and sunroof) were integrated into the work group in order to increase the internal buffer volumes. The assembly on the automobile body was performed in two phases, with an internal transfer of the body. The four workers in the first phase (A) are marked black, while the three workers in the second phase (B) are white. This phase includes work on the pre-assembly stations for doors (C). The illustration to the right shows the intra-group work pattern and modules of work performed by individuals or in pairs during the 100 minutes throughput time. The worker to the far right is assembling the doors*

The Volvo Uddevalla plant (Fig.3), which had a parallel flow, was based on five newly developed production principles:

1. *Organic Flow Pattern and True Autonomous Group Work*
   The group members carried out assembly work on several automobiles simultaneously, although it was seldom the case that more than two workers were working on the same automobile at any time. Thus it was possible to vary work method and pace, depending on how the work proceeded and what types of product variants were assembled, independently of other work groups work status and variation.

2. *Pre-structured Material Supply to Individual Automobiles*
   The components were brought to the assembly work groups in kitting fixtures. On the kitting fixtures there were a number of plastic boxes containing medium-sized components as well as plastic bags containing small components. The components were grouped in a structured way in the plastic bags. A large number of these small components were needed for a single automobile, and they represented the greatest share of the assembly time. Through grouping and structuring them, a considerable reduction in material-handling time was achieved. Moreover, this way of displaying material will in itself function as a work instruction.

3. *Naturally Grouped Assembly Work*
   Naturally grouped assembly work means that the natural relationships between material display, administrative work description and the method of working are preserved. In the Uddevella plant this led to the development on the shop floor of an expressive professional language and concepts which draw on the designer's work to a greater extent than usual.

4. *A Reformed Product Description System*
   This led to more efficient information handling. Here the product and the work derive from an assembly-oriented material grouping (Engström & Medbo, 1992A) The product and the work were described using a number of pre-defined interrelated "charts". The naturally grouped work was supported and formalised by an information system which is capable of breaking down the product into its smallest components and relating this information to the group-based long cycle time assembly work.

5. *Similar Products to be Similarly Handled and Described*
   Material and production control was based on the principle that products which are similar for assembly purposes are also principally similar when it comes to material handling and product-description, including work-instructions in Uddevalla, so-called "assembly variants". This means there is less need for re-planning and also there is a materials consumption sequence which is more consistent with the planned sequence, leading to reduced buffer volumes, better just-in-time efficiency

and a reduced number of product variants to consider in the final assembly (Engström & Medbo, 1992B).

These production principles exploit the condition specific to automotive manufacturing which is that information about the product is received before the physical materials arrive at the goods reception department. This enables the information and materials to be pre-structured, using the design departments' information as a base, and thus adapted to the method of working in the final assembly. Here, long cycle-time work on a stationary product has the advantage that the product's inner logic becomes apparent in a way that is not possible in traditional production systems.

Summary

The basic assumption behind the planning and design of the Uddevalla plant was that human capabilities and needs and market demands should be the starting-point for the design of technical and administrative preconditions. Hence, it represents a reversal of traditional planning and design.

The nature of the design of the technical and administrative preconditions in the Uddevalla plant was such that the individual and the work groups became, and had to become, increasingly skilled since possessing knowledge makes for an extended technical and administrative autonomy.

Apart from the obvious fact that the parallel flow prevented disturbances and variation from propagating within the production system, the application of these production principles had the following effects, amongst others:

- Reduced space requirements compared to the traditional assembly line, since few products are placed in intermediate buffers between different production phases, and because the need for transport areas is reduced (most automobiles in the product workshops are "assembly active", i.e. subject to assembly work, Engström 1993)
- Reduced need for expensive tools compared to the traditional assembly line for several reasons. (1) The degree of mechanisation is lowered on account of greater work content and more, but less complicated, tools. (2) Fewer tools with a fixture function are required, as the assembly workers in the work group command the whole tolerance chain and are capable of fixing the component, adjusting its position and finally fitting it to the required torque. (3) Expensive production equipment is utilised jointly by several work groups
- The efficient handling of information led to a reduction in the time and resources needed to implement a change of model and to carry out orders. In this respect the Uddevalla plant proved superior to Volvo's other automobile plants.
- There was a gradually reduced need for technical production support (production engineering and supervisory functions) to the work groups.
- Flexible work scheduling, which led to shorter lead times. It became practically feasible to manufacture only those automobiles which already had been sold to the customer.

The fact that the unique production principles used in the Uddevalla plant led to a superior performance confirmed the relevance and validity of the theoretical assumptions which guided the search and learning process.

Principles for Work-Structuring on the Shop Floor

Earlier discussions about learning assembly work have presupposed the atomistic learning of manual skills in individual assembly work. This has led to the conclusion that there exists a definable maximum cycle time of approximately 20 minutes for maintained efficiency for assembling automobiles.

However, later findings, in connection with long cycle-time automotive assembly in Sweden (in the beginning mainly from the experience gained in bus and truck assembly), have indicated the potential for holistic learning, in which manual and intellectual skills are simultaneously developed, and in which human capabilities which normally lie dormant in traditional assembly work are fully utilised. There is also an emphasis on the role of the individual as a member of a work-group.

Product Structure and Work Structure

The experience gained from the Uddevalla plant makes it clear that cycle times of two hours or more are certainly practicable in automotive assembly, from a learning point of view, as well as being economically advantageous. This learning presupposes an assembly-oriented material grouping, implicitly describing the product and work and supporting a holistic product conception. This material grouping is based on a restructuring of the design-oriented administrative product-structure which is almost generally applied throughout the Swedish automotive industry, and not on the bills of materials commonly used. The designer's product-description system is better defined and includes for example a verbal hierarchy which is not present in the "mutilated" bills of materials which are mainly based on part numbers (Engström, Jonsson & Medbo, 1993).

Spatial Orientation and Product Perception

The motor vehicle, like many other mechanical or organic objects displays symmetries which can be used for work structuring (Fig.4). These symmetries facilitate the product and work-descriptions to a considerable degree and create surveyability.

For the Uddevalla worker, the automobile body served as a physical frame of reference, as a "coordinate system", in relation to which each component to be fitted to the body has a specific spatial location defined in terms of three dimensions: "front – back", "up – down" and "left – right". This coordinate system facilitates spatial orientation and makes it possible to establish a congruence between material display, work instructions and practical work. It is noted that in Uddevalla the materials handling work of loading the kitting fixtures posed greater demands on administrative support, since completed products were not present.

The automobile is perceived as an aggregate of components that make up discernible functions, systems or large physical units in the assembled product. When an orientation in

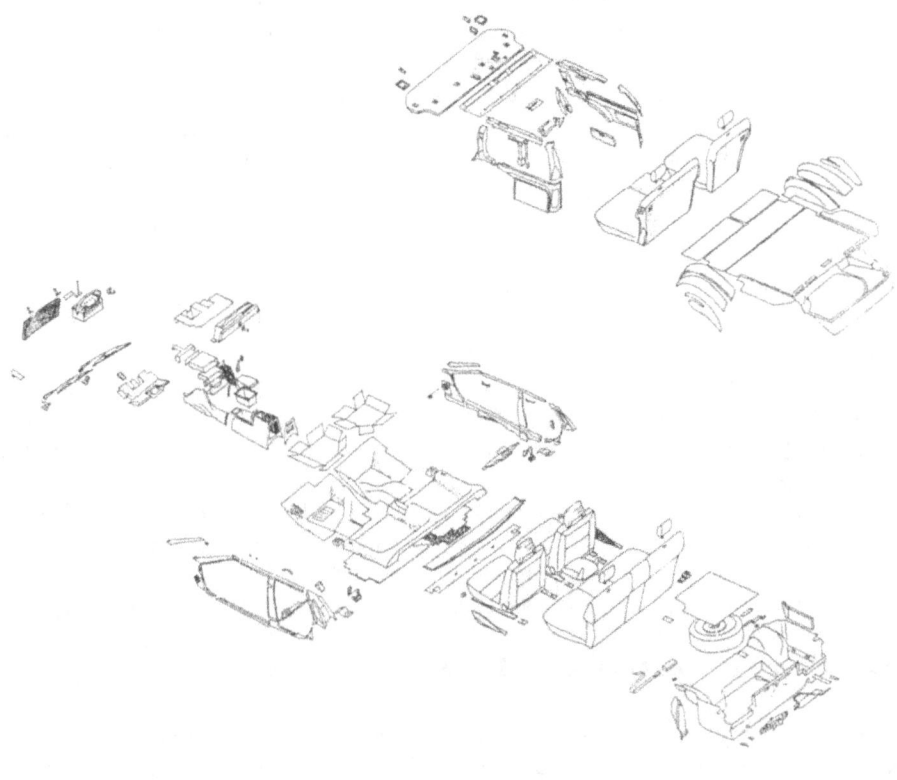

Figure 4. *If one overviews the components needed for about three hour's assembly it becomes obvious that these are related to the symmetries that exist or arise in the product as it is assembled. At the same time the components are related to each other, to causal connections, sequence and variations. The product variants form long chains with varying degrees of clarity during the assembly. The illustration shows the components that differ between four-door (to the left) and five-door automobiles (to the right) in the final assembly of the interior.*

the assembly context has been attained, the description of separate components can be approached.

The components of the automobile form patterns, in which structures and functions can be discerned and related to other structures and functions. Also, if the functions are known, then the components and their relation to each other can be ascertained, so that the functions in the complete product can be maintained.

In practice this was achieved in Uddevalla by a computer-based formalisation of the interrelation between the work-instruction and the materials in the kitting fixtures (the so-called PUMA information system). This information system is based on a single pre-defined point of view, but at the same time it is capable of accommodating many different points of view of the product and assembly work. These points of view were relevant not only to the assembly and materials-handling work but also to other functions, like production engineering, procurement, etc.

Thus, knowledge and experience have been developed which are less susceptible to the influence of "the ravages of forgetfulness" in the mental world of the workers; lasting knowledge is attained in this way. In the product-description systems, the product perception and the structure of the shop floor work will be relatively independent of changes in product variants and new models, because the symmetries in the motor vehicle are always present.

This type of formalisation of the total work in the Uddevalla plant, which was not practised in other Volvo plants, has proved necessary in order to attain increased flexibility and reduce time losses through, for example, the large number of changes made to the automobile over the model year and the ever increasing number of product variants.

Temporal Orientation and Time Perspective

Work structuring obviously involves the time dimension. In the perception of time, the present is related to what comes "before" and "after" it, so that life is not experienced as consisting of a number of "present moments". Reflection, consideration, and forethought assume that the individual is also oriented in the dimension of time.

How humans experience time is connected with the emotional and intellectual content of the activities they perform during a given time period. The experience of time is closely related to the experience of purpose and the significance of these activities. The tasks that the individual performs should contain qualities that contribute to the sense of purpose.

For various reasons people on the shop floor work have a different time perspective. It is known that people's time perspectives can be changed, provided they see purpose of the tasks they perform, and at which they have a fair chance of succeeding (Nilsson, 1981). It is also important that they have the experience of being successful and that this is success is confirmed by others. Their time perspective will then expand and possibilities are created for seeing a purpose in what lies further ahead.

Preparedness, understanding and the realisation of the advantages of forethought are qualities that only humans possess. The work structure must therefore be designed in such a way that it is possible for the individual to attain these qualities and that they are rewarded. The conditions are then created, whereby the assembly worker may acquire an expanded time perspective.

Summary

The use of an assembly-oriented material grouping has the effect that assembly workers and material handlers become the owners of a verbal and visual network connected to the work. It is then possible to handle the predictable and also the unpredictable aspects of the work. Nuances and precision in the world of imagination and reality receive a meaning. For example, support is required from the information system, providing an opportunity for successively formalising one's own experience and relating it to the knowledge of different functions in the plant gained by others.

Learning can thus be speeded up considerably by taking advantage of the human capabilities of holistic perception, pattern recognition and successive activation of mental and motor patterns (cognitive structures as well as work patterns and rhythms). Work elements that constitute meaningful wholes are easier to learn than fragmented, meaningless tasks. It is also important that learning takes place with real objects (Ellegård, Engström & Nilsson, 1991).

For the assembly worker, the reality in the form of products and work becomes subordinated to the visual and verbal networks mentioned above, so that the work becomes an integral part of his professional skill.

The point is that the assembly work itself possesses an inner logic, provided it is described with the predictable product and its symmetries as a basis. The product is in fact defined in detail during the design and pre-production stages. Exploring this predictability provides scope for further development of the principles for materials handling and assembly work.

General Conclusions

Experiences from the Uddevalla Plant and Prospects for Further Development and Diffusion of the Uddevalla Concept

It proved possible, up to a point, to develop new, unique production principles applicable to the final assembly within the Swedish automotive industry. This development was partly due to favourable socio-economic conditions and fortunate circumstances as discussed above.

The Uddevalla plant proved the viability of extended work cycles in automobile assembly. According to wage-related personnel statistics, 64% of the assembly workers learnt to assemble at least half of an automobile at full pace, and 4% were even able to assemble complete automobiles at full pace and proved this by a special test.

At the other end of the scale from the assembly workers who learnt the complete assembly, about 5% had difficulty in learning to assemble 1/4 of a car at full pace. About half of these workers became sufficiently skilled when specially trained in a separate training workshop, whereas the remaining workers moved to other work tasks or quitted the job.

It is noted that the pre-structuring of the materials in the kitting fixtures implied a recommended assembly sequence suitable for various intra-group work-patterns. It was possible to choose different assembly methods, all derived from the same basic assembly sequence. In fact there was a great variety of group sizes and intra-group work patterns. During the closing down period, the work groups in the product workshop consisted of 2–9 assembly workers.

It is also noted that the production principles allowed for this great variation. Neither the equipment nor the tools were standardised, due to the gradual starting up procedure and the continuous refinement of the production principles.

The running-in process involved the gradual starting-up of the product workshops as well as the development and refining of unique materials handling techniques and the information system. Apart from learning to perform the assembly work itself, it became necessary, during the sometimes hectic and tough running-in period, to add verbal and social dimensions to tackle technical and social problems which were present during the whole running-in period

The plant was not fully developed when it was closed down. In fact, assembly work was most of the time restricted by lack of suitable production engineering support. A considerable improvement in assembly performance occurred when most of the production engineering staff left the central administrative office and worked as support functions located in the individual product workshops.

There are however important restrictions to further development and diffusion of the unique production principles used in the Uddevalla plant. Some of these restrictions apply to search and learning processes in the Swedish industry in general, and concern the extension and organisation of such processes. Other restrictions apply specifically to the development and diffusion of the unique production principles used in the Uddevalla plant within the Volvo Corporation as well as the diffusion of these principles to other automotive manufacturers.

In the western world with its general requirement for a quick return on investments, the time-perspectives on changes in industrial activities become necessarily short. Search and learning processes have a time span of a few years at the most.

The learning processes are normally organised as independent projects, in which personnel and external consultants are engaged on a temporary basis. When the project is completed, the project organisation is dissolved. This means, among other things, that the main initiators and driving force ideas often change over to another project at a critical time before the original project has been completed and assessed, and that consultants are trained who later leave the company. The knowledge acquired is often treated as the property of the involved individual or consulting firm.

It can be questioned whether it is possible to change the direction of the Swedish final assembly plants to such an extent that they will become sustainable in the long run, given the fact that, when the Uddevalla plant is closed down, there is no plant to act as a model of a final assembly plant undergoing continuous development.

It is doubtful whether it would have been possible to achieve internal evolution and diffusion of the unique production principles developed in Uddevalla in a traditional production environment given the deep-rooted traditions of fundamentally different production principles. The initiatives that have been taken within Volvo have so far failed in the Volvo Car Corporation (Granath, 1991), whereas the Volvo Truck Corporation on the other hand is successively introducing new production principles and is in fact expanding the production capacity using these principles.

This can be explained by reluctance to change caused by prevailing attitudes, traditions and restrictions, and prevailing technical and administrative preconditions, but also by the fact that today production engineering has turned into a low-status area in the Swedish automotive industry.

When it comes to external development and diffusion of the unique production principles, an extension of the co-operation with other automotive manufacturers is hindered by the misconception that the Uddevalla final assembly plant was a "social experiment" where the expected reduction in personnel turnover due to improved job satisfaction and greater work content would pay for a lower pace of work or increased education costs. The fact is that the Uddevalla plant embodied production principles which are superior in terms of production performance.

The Volvo Uddevalla Process in the common frame of reference

The Volvo Uddevalla process gives a very clear example of the learning character of vision-based developments. The project was characterised by a number of radically new ideas (goals) which in many cases were in stark contrast to established practice and visions-of-the-possible. There were no readily available experiences to emulate. Experimentation with completely new ways of tackling issues and new solutions became almost the order of the day. In addition, specific decisions and events in the course of development - not always under the company's control - created new decision situations and alternatives for action. Thus the process as a whole was definitely not a logical, rational one, in which a plan of action was drawn up and then executed, but rather a continual learning process with successive re-assessments and new decisions (Ellegård, 1989; Granath,1991). The re-assessments aimed to ensure a better realisation of the vision.

The first stage of the Uddevalla project was formally named "the visionary stage". From the outset this was a corporate venture involving both management and the unions. Developing work content and heightening the status of production work were high on the agenda. Elements in the vision concerned quality in production, total efficiency and effectiveness and employee development, to be integrated in the factory as a whole. The plant was to be gradually modified in pace with the increasing competence of the workers. Following this stage the project was handed over to the Volvo Car Company.

Examples of key decisions that formed the solution are:

- he participation of the architects that lead to the direct coupling of the spatial workplace design to the job content and the visions;
- the decision to have a training shop, a unique mechanism for competence development. This also showed those in doubt that it was possible for workers to master workcycles far in excess of 20 minutes;
- the drawn-out negotiations with the governmental concessions board that contributed significantly to the decisions not to go ahead with plans for a chasis and paintshop at the plant; decisions that were later to have dire consequences for the closing of the plant;
- the demonstration of the components of the car in meaningful subsystems achieved by disassembling a car;

- he development of prototypes for the various materials kits for car assembly - especially for small components.

The analysis of the Volvo case.

Considering the general framework of competencies developing in processes within certain structures and value systems, the key features of the Volvo Uddevalla car factory case are the following:

Competencies

The craftsman ideal or vision of the carbuilder is essentially to have an extension of assembly skills in the early stages of the project. In practice this entailed extending the work cycle time of the assembly workers from as short a time as 2 minutes to 11-12 hours (for a worker to assemble an entire car). This was done by grouping the assembly tasks into five broad subsystems. The workers could learn these one at a time. The basic requirement was that each worker master a subsystem. Mastering several subsystems was an issue decided within the work teams. When the assembly skills had been mastered, there followed the opportunities for learning planning, problem solving, communication and coordination skills.

Learning processes

The development of the Uddevalla factory was the latest step in an extended series of projects concerning developments in work and work organisation within the Volvo corporation (it has since been followed by other developments in the car and other divisions). A distinctive feature of the Uddevalla project was the development of a methodology for the analysis and formation of the car into subsystems forming cognitive "wholes" in a learning context, together with the development of a learning method, "craftsmanship workplace pedagogics". The experimental workshop adopted a cascade approach to individual coaching, i.e. A taught B, (A+B) taught (C+D), etc. Finally, upon mastering assembly skills, the workers received training in group processes.

Structures

The development of the Uddevalla car factory was a joint union/management effort. The basic work organisation replaced the assembly line with assembly teams working with an assembly of entire cars within the shopfloor area assigned to each team. The components to be assembled were delivered to the assembly area in special kits which in their turn were made up by special materials' supply teams. Each assembly team was responsible for its own production control and quality. There was an extended initial run-in phase before the company evolved a suitably supportive management structure in the factory.

Values

The efforts to develop the Uddevalla factory depended to a large extent on the social values of the company chairman regarding the workforce and its contribution to the business.

The "carbuilder" vision comprised an extension of what was currently regarded as the limit of the possible, thought to be a cycle time of approximately 20 minutes. This vision was developed together by management and unions. However it seems that many managers and engineers did not share this vision and did not give their full commitment to ensure its realisation.

Other factors

Other factors, not least in the environment, brought about a state of affairs in the company necessitating radical decisions, one of which was to close down the Uddevalla factory. The worldwide crash in the car market, due to the economic recession and a marked overcapacity in production in the industry, left Volvo facing the same problems as its competitors. Production capacity had to be reduced by closing one or more plants. Uddevalla's size, location, and functions outweighed its reputation for being the "best in the corporation" both in terms of productivity and quality. The decision was taken to close the factory. The plant's distinctive ideas regarding the organisation of assembly work were "damned by failure" in the popular media. Whether the innovations pioneered in the "Uddevalla experiment" will be taken up in others parts of Volvo or in other companies remains to be seen.

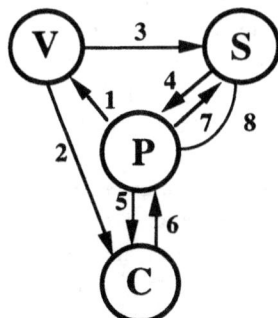

Figure 5. *The process at Volvo Uddevalla*

1. The efficiency and effectiveness of the production process at the traditional Volvo plants were recognised as being in need of radical improvements.
2. The chairman, P. G. Gyllenhammar, became the representative for a joint union/management vision regarding the "craftsman" ideal for workers in the car industry.
3. A new work organisation and materials supply system was developed.
4. New learning and training processes were developed and implemented.
5. Workers acquired the essential assembly skills for one or more subsystems. After some time a number of the workers acquired the skills for assembling the entire car.
6. With their new competencies, the workers had a base for going on to learn other general cognitive and communicative skills.
7. This led to changes in the production and quality control system.
8. Factory management was changed in order to be more supportive of the team organisation.

Notes

Berggren, C., Björkman T. & Hollander E. (1991). *Are They Unbeatable? - Report from a field trip to study transplants, the Japanese-owned auto plants in North America*, Department of Work Science, Royal Institute of Technologies, Stockholm.

Ellegård, K.(1989) *Acrobatics in the Weave of Time: A Documentation of the Development Project for Volvo's Car Factory at Uddevalla*. Gothenburg: Department of Human and Economic Geography, School of Economics and Legal Science,University of Gothenburg Report no.CHOROS 1989:2 *(Ph.D. thesis)*

Ellegård, K., Engström, T. & Nilsson L. (1991). *Principles and Realities in the Reform of Industrial Work– the planning of Volvo's car assembly plant in Uddevalla*, The Swedish Work Environment Fund, Stockholm.

Engström, T. (1993). "Reorganisation of Material Flow for Natural Grouped Assembly Work– some principles and results from action research", in Bennet, D. (Ed.), *International Journal of Technology Management*, Vol. 8, No. 5/6, pp. 384 – 395.

Engström, T., Jonsson, D. & Medbo, L. (1993). "An Assembly-Oriented Product Description System as a Precondition for Efficient Manufacturing with Long Cycle Time Work", in Sumanth, D. J., Edosomwan, J. A., Poupart, R. & Sink, D. S. (Eds.) *Productivity & Quality Management Frontiers– IV*, Industrial Engineering and Management Press, Norcross, Georgia, pp. 453 – 462.

Engström, T. & Medbo, L. (1992A). "Preconditions for Long Cycle Time Assembly and its Management – Some findings", in Karlsson, C. & Rubenowitz, S. (eds.) *International Journal of Operations and Production Management*, Vol. 12, No. 7/8, pp. 134 – 146.

Engström T. & Medbo L. (1992B). "Material Flow Analysis, Sociotechnology and Natural Grouped Assembly Work for Automobiles and Trucks", in Pornschlegel (Ed) *Research and Development in Work and Technology*, Physica Verlag, Heidelberg, pp. 220 – 242.

Idag (1993). "Reine byggde bilen med gasen i botten", *Idag*, 3 Januari, Göteborg *(newspaper)*.

Granath,J.-Å. (1991). *Architecture, Technology and Human Factors- Design in a Socio-Technical Context*. Division of Industrial Architecture and Planning, School of Architecure, Chalmers Tekniska Högskola, Göteborg (Ph.D.-thesis).

Karlsson, U. (1979). *Alternativa produktionssystem till lineproduktion.*, Sociologiska Institutionen, Göteborgs Universitet, Göteborg 1979 (Ph.D.thesis).

Nilsson, L. (1981). *Yrkesutbildning i nutidshistoriskt perspektiv*, Acta Universitatis Gothenburgensis, Göteborg (Ph.D.-thesis).

Tidningarnas Telegrambyrå (1992). "Rekordresultat för nedläggningsbeslut", in*TT:s Nyhetstelegram*, No. 004, 16 December, Stockholm.

Nilsson, L. (1991). "Kraftprovet– Tjejen som växte till helbilsbyggare", in*Volvo Nu*, 10 Maj (newspaper).

Wild, R. (1975) . "On the selection of Mass Production Systems", in *International Journal of Production Research*, Vol. 13, No. 5, pp. 443– 585.

Chapter Nine

Semi-Autonomous Work Groups at Audi-Volkswagen

Karlheinz Sonntag and Michael Freiboth

Introduction

This study is based upon the development of work groups and corresponding training and qualification methods at two companies in the automotive industry. The companies were led to support a major research project because of changes in work structures, new flexible work technologies and the restructuring of the occupational system in the fields of metal forming and electrical construction. The aim of the project was to describe new qualification profiles and emerging qualification patterns of skilled workers in the car industry and to develop training measures to meet the requirements of the new patterns of knowledge, competence in methods, and social competence.

The study reports upon: new task and work-structures of the operative, "Anlagenführer", and the maintenance personnel, "Instandhalter"; emerging qualification-profiles, especially for cognitive requirements, communication requirements, and technical knowledge; new training methods for operatives and maintenance personnel, including cognitive training schemes for improving performance in control tasks and in fault diagnosis, and a flexible manufacturing cell for training purposes which embodies decentralised work-based training.

Factors Influencing the Adoption of a New Human Resource Strategy

The three factors influencing innovative change and the emergence of new qualification profiles of workers at the automotive companies researched were as follows.

1. The increasing distribution of microelectronic devices led to new solutions in the fields of production and control technology, e.g. the use of flexible manufacturing systems, computer-based units and machines. Firstly this affected the skilled workers on the shop floor who had to operate the new units in many different situations such as setting up, putting into operation, monitoring, tending and maintenance. For these activities control technology is an essential component for optimal and flexible operation of the complex and netted production units.

2. Technical developments affect the structure of the interaction processes between man and machine: this leads to the redesign of the work organisation. Rigid hierarchical and the functional division of labour as they still largely exist in traditional production are counter-productive to the use of new technologies. On the one hand companies strive for the adoption of "lean production" consisting of integral and complete work routines. On the other hand they strive to avoid the de-skilling of jobs. Also, progressive production conceptions - especially in the automobile industry - lead to the introduction of team-work which aims at job enlargement and job rotation and forms the basis for further integration of production and maintenance tasks.

3. Technical- oriented organisational changes affect the employment system, and thereby affect the established occupational system. These changes have led to the reform of the structure and content of the occupational system in the fields of metal fabrication and electrical engineering (1987) in the Federal Republic of Germany. These reforms have, in turn, led to the introduction of compulsory regulations for companies regarding vocational education. In this context it is significant to note that these regulations (§§3,4) state that trainees (in German "Auszubildende") should be able to undertake qualified tasks, "that especially include autonomous planning, realisation and controlling". It is the first time that besides instruction in job-specific skills and knowledge, the imparting of "core qualifications" has become compulsory in vocational learning processes, and it is enshrined in law in FRG.

The factors mentioned above describe the 'frame conditions' which inspired the companies to introduce a new strategy of Human Resource Development (HRD). Executive boards and work councils of the companies accepted the new Human Resource Development strategy in order to obtain greater productivity by reducing the division of labour, specifically through overlapping tasks of operating and maintenance work, and by team work. Prerequisites for this process of innovation are skilled workers equipped with the "ability to act", which enables them to cope with complex tasks in a self-confident, reflective and autonomous style.

Our approach towards determining the qualification requirements lies in the practice-oriented analysis of the work-content at the work place. The significance of mental performance for successfully coping with production-related tasks becomes more evident with the introduction of highly complex automated systems. A large number of long term workers now have to live through the technical changes without the necessary qualifications needed for the changing cognitive demands of their profession. There is no way to replace this work-force by a better educated one, and the companies would be ill-advised to neglect the vast expert knowledge that especially older workers have gathered through the years. The obvious conclusion is that the work-force must adapt to the changing mental requirements.

To obtain the optimal work force it is necessary to determine the required qualification level and then develop adequate training measures. This process should be repeated regularly to ensure the adaptation of further technical developments, and to prevent the insufficient and unsatisfactory use of new technologies. In consequence, almost all companies of the automotive sector have understood ongoing training and education of their work-force should be a vital part of their efforts to manufacture economically and cost-effectively in this highly competitive market.

Research Assignment in Two Companies

The vocational training departments of the companies gave the following research assignment to the external scientific research partners:

- to describe qualification profiles for skilled workers (operators and maintenance personnel) in high-volume manufacturing processes which are appropriate to the changes of technical-organisational frame conditions and, deriving from this,
- to work out task-adequate training techniques intended to further knowledge (especially in the field of control technology) as well as competence in methods (problem solving abilities, procedural knowledge) and social competence of the employees (i.e. communication and co-operation abilities). The main emphasis was on (decentralised) work-based training.

The following case study represents parts of the results of a research project supported by the Federal Ministry of Education and Science in Bonn and the Federal Institute of Vocational Education (BIBB) in Berlin. The implementation was carried out by two companies of the automotive industry (Volkswagen AG, Kassel and AUDI AG, Ingolstadt). A detailed final report about the five-year long research activities of the scientific work is available (Sonntag & Heun, 1992). Furthermore initial results of a project sponsored by the German Research Community (DFG) have influenced this article (Sonntag, Bergmann & Timpe, 1991). Both VW and AUDI provided facilities for our research for this case study. VW Kassel (22,000 employees) is a manufacturer of various gear units for cars and AUDI Ingolstadt (20,000 employees) is a car manufacturer with its own technical research and development department. Both companies have progressive production technology and flexible manufacturing systems at their disposal.

The work on such systems represents the future emphasis concerning the employment of skilled workers who will need a general and complex education to fulfil integrated tasks, in particular of the "Industrial Mechanic/Manufacturing Technology" ("Industriemechaniker/ Produktionstechnik"), and who will have to look after operating and maintenance tasks in a team-work context. The case study examined the work structures and qualification profiles of 40 skilled workers (10 Operators and 30 Maintenance Workers, divided into 15 electricians and 15 mechanics) from the flexible manufacturing system ("Flexible Shaft Manufacturing", "body-shop") and the centralised maintenance. Standardised, and partly standardised questionnaires and methods were used for job analyses.

- The "Leitfaden zur qualifizierten Personalplanung bei technisch-organisatorischen Innovationen" (LPI) (Sonntag, Heun & Schaper, 1992) was used to record the tasks and personnel characteristics and the professional knowledge requirements of the job. It was designed as an objective inventory with special regard to control technology. The results give the opportunity to rate and describe the amount and variety of specialised work on devices incorporating control technology for different groups of workers in flexible automated manufacturing systems.

- The Task Analysis Questionnaire (TAI) (Frieling, Facaoaru, Benedix, Pfaus & Sonntag, 1992) was used to record and describes cognitive and motor requirements. It is a standardised and computer-scoreable questionnaire for the description and classification of a wide range of jobs. The inventory integrates a variety of job analysis approaches and psychological theories such as the behaviour description approach, general skills approach, information theoretic approach and others (for further references on these subjects see: Task Analysis Questionnaire Manual). Composite indices that give an overall view of the activities of the workers in their actual working conditions are derived from the evaluation of the information processing and mental work-load aspects of the work-place.

The results can be used to compare different work places and conditions in order to assess the quality of work and the qualification requirements (See the figures below).

The training programs, based on the qualification profiles, were worked out and tested at the vocational training department (Cognitive Training with Heuristic Rules) and at shop floor-level (in Flexible Manufacturing Cells).

Work Structure and Task Allocation

Even in high-volume production, the sophisticated and flexible manufacturing systems have great potential for re-designing work organisation towards integrated task-allocation. This is even more so if the economic success of new technologies is strongly dependent on these systems in maintaining performance and optimal production flow. If the objective is to achieve a change of work-structures in flexible automated manufacturing, then top priority must be given to the maximisation of expert knowledge. This should include the integration of task performance and an opportunity for greater responsibility for the individual worker in a team work environment. Figure 1 sketches the differences between newly designed work structures and traditional structures.

The traditional work structure was marked by a rigid functional division of labour between manufacturing and maintenance, and by a high operator specification level for a single unit or machine within a single production area - e.g. turning or finishing. In contrast to the traditional work structure, the new work-structures are distinguished by task integration, (semi-) autonomous teamwork - 8 to 12 workers with 1 spokesman - and flexible deployment by weekly (or more frequent) job rotation between units and even between manufacturing areas. Only difficult electrical or mechanical faults, e.g. problems of CNC/NCH-controlling, faults of drive electronics, necessitate falling back on the knowledge and competence of precinct or central maintenance. All other faults are handled locally by mechanics, electricians and operators within the teams. The distribution of tasks within a team is shown in Figure 2.

An important opportunity for job enlargement for operators can be seen. Whilst in traditional work-structures operators were occupied mainly with operating and supervising tasks, now within (semi-) autonomous working groups, they have to take over additional maintenance, quality control and optimising tasks (programmes). They have to co-operate effectively with each other in fault diagnosis and rectification, and to support maintenance personnel.

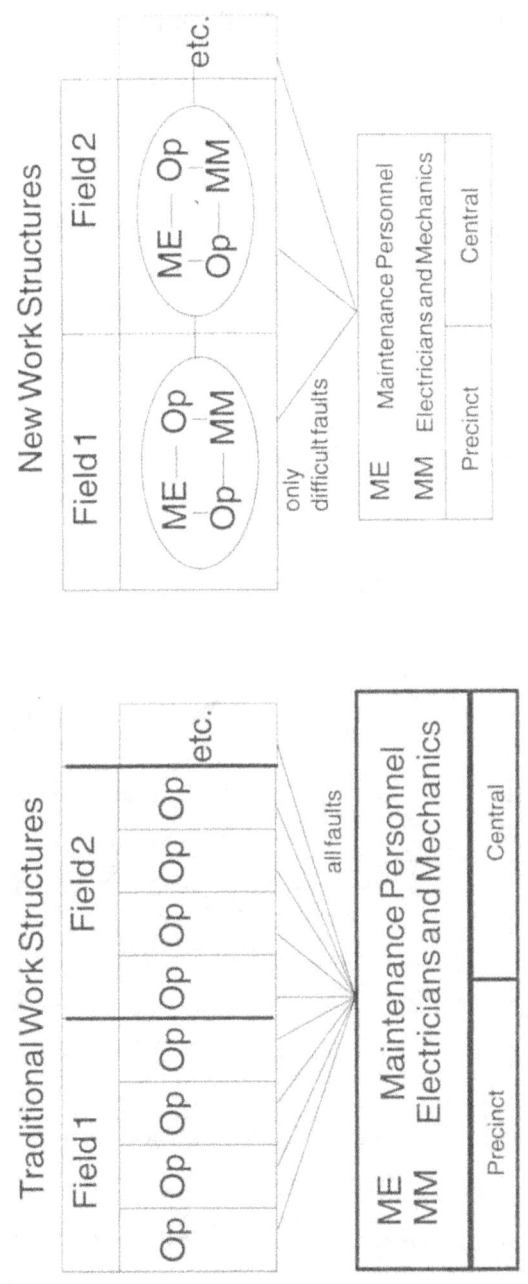

Figure 1. *Comparison between traditional and new work structures*

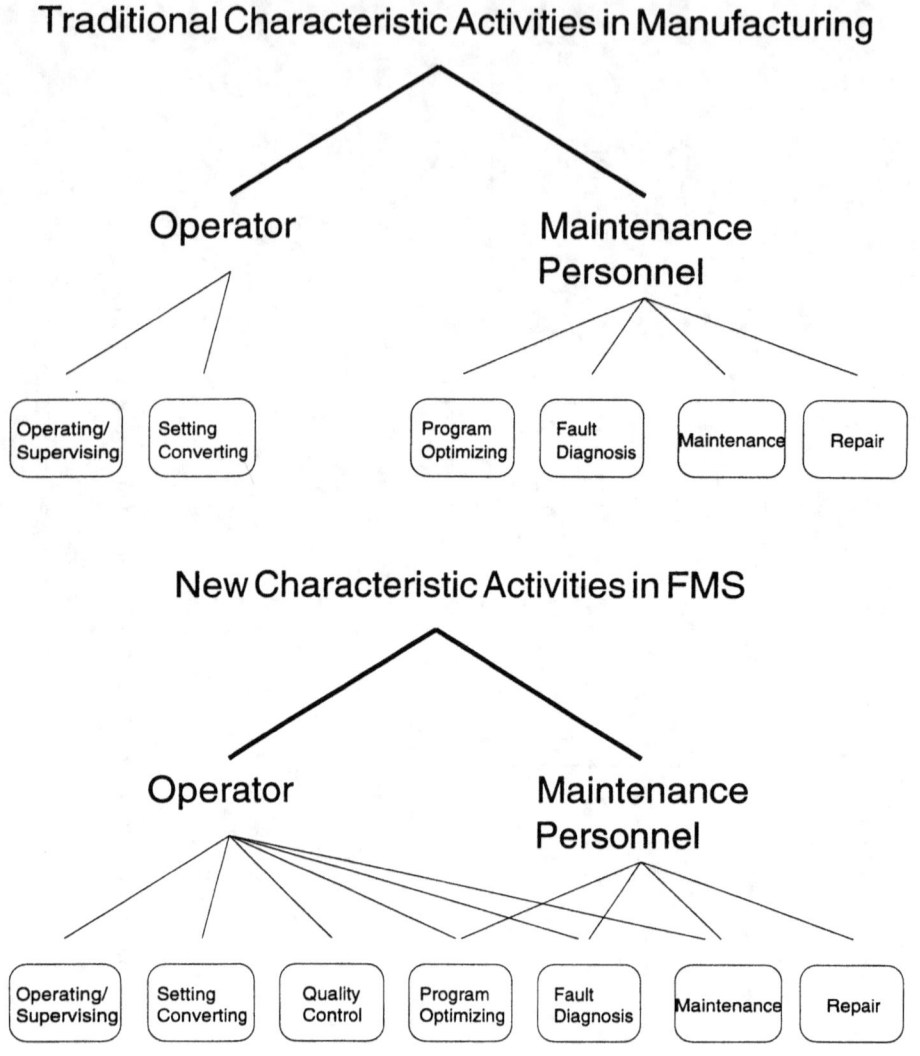

Figure 2. *Distribution of tasks for skilled workers at shop floor level in the car industry*

The main objectives of these working groups are the elimination of faults in the manufacturing process and re-establishing the functionality of the installations. The maintenance personnel in the working groups are, in most cases, also able to take over the operators' tasks.

For the execution of these tasks within teams, qualified skilled workers are essential to the companies. Until recently skilled workers were required to undertake maintenance tasks only, e.g. Energieanlagenelektroniker, Maschinenschlosser, but now the new work structures additionally require operators to gain a skilled worker qualification (Industriemechaniker/ Produktionstechnik). The semi-skilled and unskilled workers common in the high-volume work structures of the past are under-qualified for the new task-spectrum.

Qualification Requirements

Cognitive Skill Requirements

Cognitive requirements were put above the concrete actions of the skilled workers concerning the information intake, e.g. observing, listening, reading of drawings, numbers, programs and texts, and the transfer and output of information, e.g. talking and questioning, making of drawings, calculations, programs and texts. Figure 3 summarises the requirement level of informational tasks concerning fault situations.

An overall higher level of observing and supervising can be found in operators and maintenance personnel. The workers have to identify particular conditions of machines and units from a multitude of various signs and signals. They have to react quickly towards signs that are critical for the optimal production process. They have to carry out adaptations and adjustments or to introduce the right measures during fault situations. Operators are required to undertake low-to-medium range fault diagnosis and repair. These skills are mainly required for the registration of faults, undertaking fault search by comparing nominal and actual values, and the application of simple diagnostics and repair strategies. Those include systematic testing, use of computerised diagnostic systems and recommissioning of the units, to ascertain the level and category of faults, and to identify skilled personnel for undertaking the repairs. The main task for the operator is to support the maintenance personnel on the repair process. Considerable mental performance at fault diagnosis and repair are thus expected of the maintenance personnel.

The main focus is on selecting relevant information and making judgements on the state of the machine and possible reasons of faults. In particular, information has to be picked out from manuals and circuit diagrams and compared with information from other sources - for example signals/displays or verbal information from the operators, and to integrate all information into an overall picture. This picture is then transformed into strategies and actions for diagnosis and repair, independent testing and combining different strategies. Figure 4 shows such information processing strategy during fault management with an example of an electrician (Sonntag & Schaper, 1993).

	Operators	Maintenance Personnel	
Receiving Information	1 low — 5 high	Electricians 1 low — 5 high	Mechanics 1 low — 5 high
Observing/Controlling	5	5	5
Listening	2	2	2
Reading of short notes	2	2	2
Reading of specialist literature (e.g. Manuals)	0	1	1
Reading of technical drawings (e.g. Circuit Diagrams)	1	3	3
Reading of numeric material (e.g. Lists)	0	2	1
Reading of Programs (e.g. PLC-Programs)	0	3	1
Delivering Information			
Talking	3	3	3
Writing of short notes	3	2	2
Writing of specialist literature (e.g. Fault Documentation)	0	3	3
Making of technical drawings (e.g. Circuit Diagrams)	1	3	4
Writing of numerical materials (e.g. Lists)	1	0	0
Writing of programs (e.g. PLC-Programs)	1	3	2

Figure 3. *Level of different requirements on information processing*

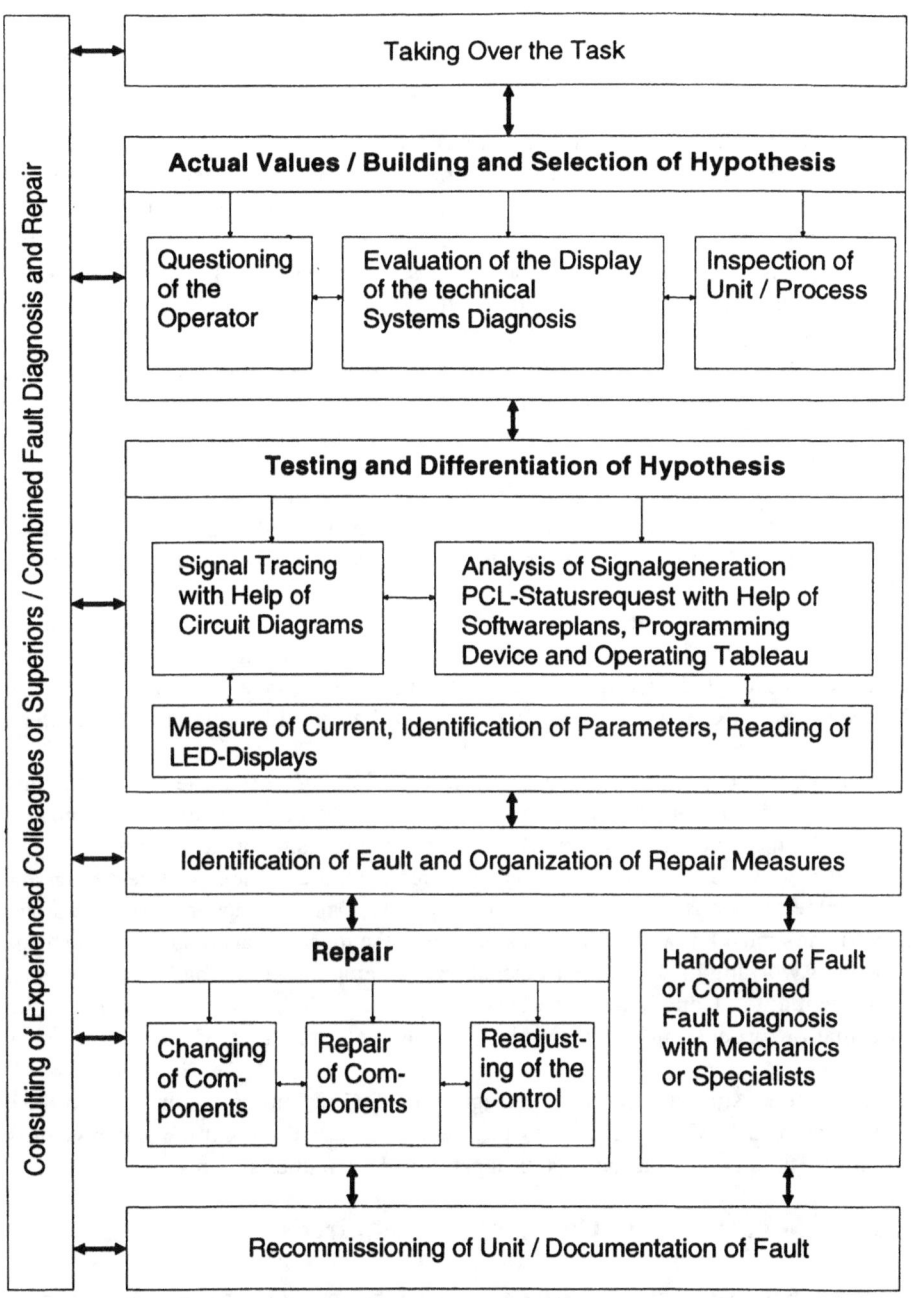

Figure 4. *Process of fault diagnosis and elimination with the example of electrician*

The figure illustrates an information processing procedure for the registration of the normal values, the building and testing of hypotheses on fault finding. It also shows the necessary support of operators and maintenance peers for effective repair actions.

Knowledge

It is presumed that operators should have knowledge of operation and switching units in order to fulfil their tasks in the field of control technology. Knowledge requirements are generally higher in fault situations, and knowledge of the structure and function of the units is necessary. This enables the production personnel to inform particular skilled personnel about repairs or to accomplish small repairs themselves. It is also necessary for the maintenance personnel to have sound knowledge of control technology if they are to fulfil their tasks. They have to understand how to combine various control elements.

Electricians need knowledge of the structure and function of electronic controls, the structure of commands and the feedback loops, as well as the function of the controls in interaction with electrical, mechanical, pneumatic and hydraulic elements of the units.

Usually mechanics have sound knowledge in the fields of pneumatics and hydraulics, and are therefore called upon as specialists for hydraulic and pneumatic machinery. They also have to have knowledge in the fields of electronics and the basic principles of control circuits. Figure 6 shows requirements for control technology in fields of CNC, PCL, and IR.

The operators only need knowledge in CNC-technology as regards operating and program-optimising and adaptation. Programming knowledge in PLC-technology is irrelevant, although they have to understand program structure and programming language. Knowledge of IR-technology is reduced to familiarity with principles of structure and operation.

Maintenance personnel need to operate fault diagnosis systems, based on their knowledge of servicing and maintenance of the machine systems as well as should their elements. An overall high level of knowledge is a prerequisite for electricians.

In the field of PLC-technology it is a requirement that electricians possess programming knowledge to localise faults in the technical process, and to adapt and optimise programs. Electricians must know about the construction of the mechanical components, the handling as well as working modes of the IR including programming knowledge for the optimisation of movements. Concerning CNC-technology, knowledge about program structure, information processing and particularly about the interaction of machine elements is necessary.

Mechanics should have enough insight into PLC-technology to understand the basic principles of a PLC-control as well the electronic activation and the acknowledgement structure of the control elements of pneumatics and hydraulics systems.

Communication and Cooperation Required

An interesting overview based on the example of the operator as a co-operative partner and the quality of cooperative relationships is given in Figure 5.

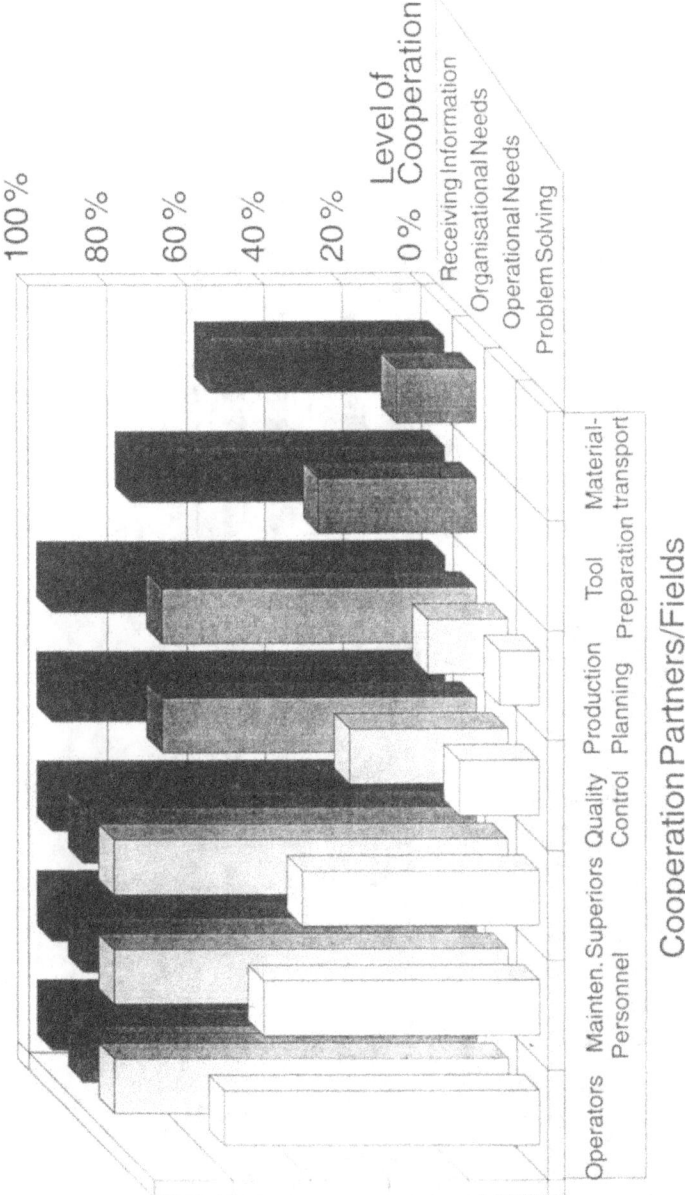

Figure 5. *Communication and cooperation requirements for operators*

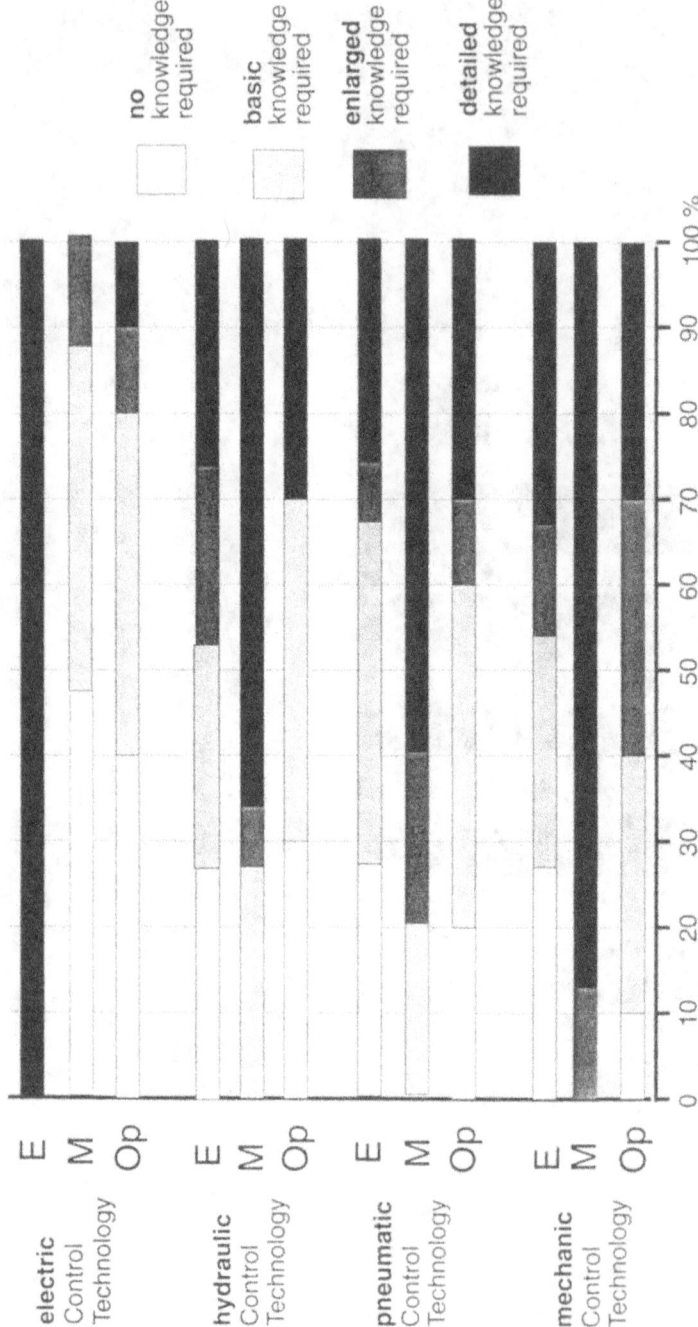

Figure 6. *Demands on different levels of knowledge of control technology I*

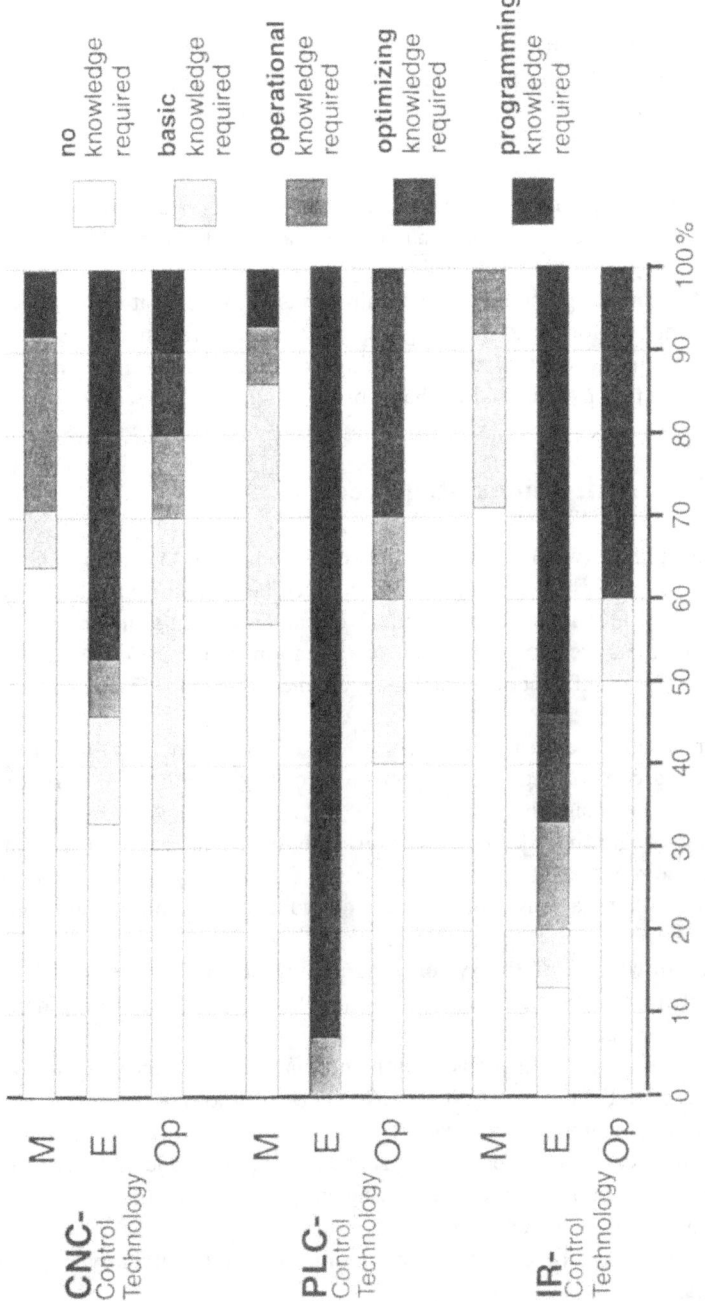

Figure 7. *Demands on different levels of knowledge of control technology II*

The cooperation within the team between the operator and the maintenance personnel is of significance at all quality levels:

- mutual information exchange;
- organisational co-ordination;
- support for repair actions;
- joint problem solving during maintenance.

Co-operation between quality control and production planning is on a smaller scale. Contact with tool preparation personnel and material transport personnel is largely reduced to information exchange and organisational tuning.

In contrast to these high cooperation requirements of the team it is often found that the individual communication behaviour by group members is deficient and hampers effective fault rectification. In this context, deficits in linguistic expression on the one hand, and the filtering of information and holding back of experience on the other, were noted as especially evident.

Vocational Qualifications Required

The reduction of the division of labour between production and maintenance, and the introduction of team work to a changing and enlarged task structure for the operators. The enlargement especially in the work content of fault diagnosis and repair tasks leads compellingly to measures for vocational qualification of (future) production workers. Summarised are the significant qualification requirements (see also Figures 6 and 7):

- requirements regarding thinking and attention performance in the observing/controlling of production processes and in the recording and interpretation of signals;
- demands regarding thinking in fault diagnosis and repair (i.e. planned and systematic procedure);
- requirements regarding willingness and readiness to communicate and cooperate with peers;
- sound knowledge of the system operation; special knowledge of setting and converting the machine systems; CNC-knowledge regarding handling and programming skills;
- sound knowledge of the construction and function of machine systems as well as knowledge in the fields of CNC-, PLC- and IR-technology;
- promotion of planning performance;
- encouragement of target-oriented, systematic and fault-reducing behaviour
- support for autonomous problem solving and task performance;
- fostering team-oriented behaviour;
- effective linking of cognitive functioning and relevant knowledge of control technology;

Training and Qualification Methods

The new training and qualification methods for the skilled worker overcome the inadequacy of simply adapting training programs on their own. Independent and careful handling, planned and systematic action, the ability and readiness for personal development and for team work are held equal to the imparting of skill and knowledge. Only a balanced promotion of knowledge, competence in methods and social competence can satisfy the new and more cognitive-related qualification requirements. In this way the imparting of new subjects of study is strongly dependent on these qualification methods that encourage thinking, imagination and the communication and cooperative skills of the trainees. In the following we introduce two different training methods:

- cognitive training based on heuristic rules;
- production cell for training purposes (decentralised work-based training).

Cognitive Training using Heuristic Rules

Cognitive training procedures enable learners to handle and cope with complex work situations that require high level thinking, planning and decision-making. A possible way to achieve this performance is to familiarise trainees with the use of heuristic rules. Heuristic rules are psychological aids that help to focus thinking and doing, on certain task requirements, by short and clearly phrased advice and rules (Sonntag, 1989). The learner is given instructions to carry out the necessary mental operations, e.g. "Remember the functional principles of wiring before you check!"

In this case study a heuristic training method was developed and designed within the internal company training scheme for trainees in pneumatic control technology (for the development and testing of the training see Sonntag & Schaper, 1988). The case study researchers together with the instructors, analysed fields of activities that determine the performance when building pneumatic switching. The best way to achieve this goal was worked out and written down. A set of heuristic rules were developed and were adapted to the linguistic, intellectual and technical qualifications of the target group.

In contrast to traditional methods we followed different didactic principles to impart the rules. These principles are:

1. Acquiring a platform for working and learning with heuristic rules.
2. Design of a working model that can be used to demonstrate possible problem-solving strategies in the process by both instructors and trainees.
3. Autonomous and repeated training with the aim of gaining experience in the application of rules to solve problems.

We checked the effectiveness of the training with heuristic rules vs. traditional teaching methods using a control group. The results demonstrated that trainees instructed by heuristic rules showed greater and more systematic skills than the control group. Before and during the test they were more purposeful, more systematic at fault reduction and acted more independently in coping with difficulties.

- Get an Imaginary Idea of the Circuit !
- Sketch a Raw Outline of the Circuit !
- Now Sketch the Details !
- Sketch a Step-for-Step Solution !
- Check Your Design with Systematic Tracking of the Signal !

Done ! Systematic Planning Works Out !

If You Encounter Troubles:

- Stay Calm, if it doesn't work out at once:
  Concentrate on the simple parts of the task and make them clear to you !
- Build these simple parts !
- What's missing yet ?
- Sketch a Step-for-Step Solution !
- Use Existing Aids !
- Avoid Random Tries
- Then

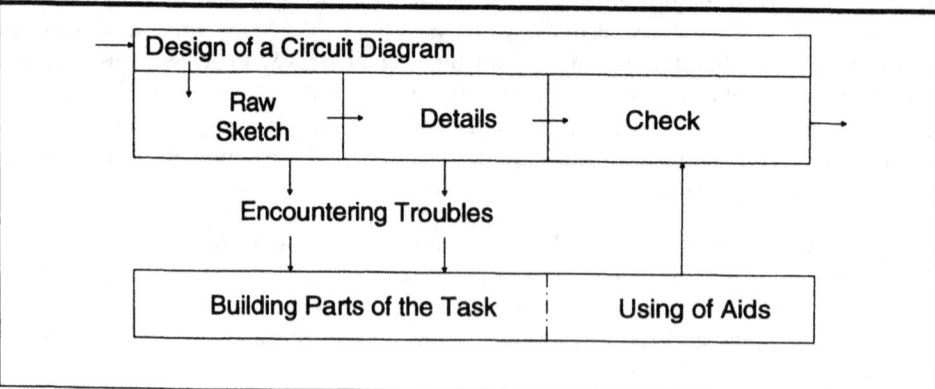

Figure 8 . *Excerpt of heuristic rules for the design of a pneumatic circuit diagram (long and short version)*

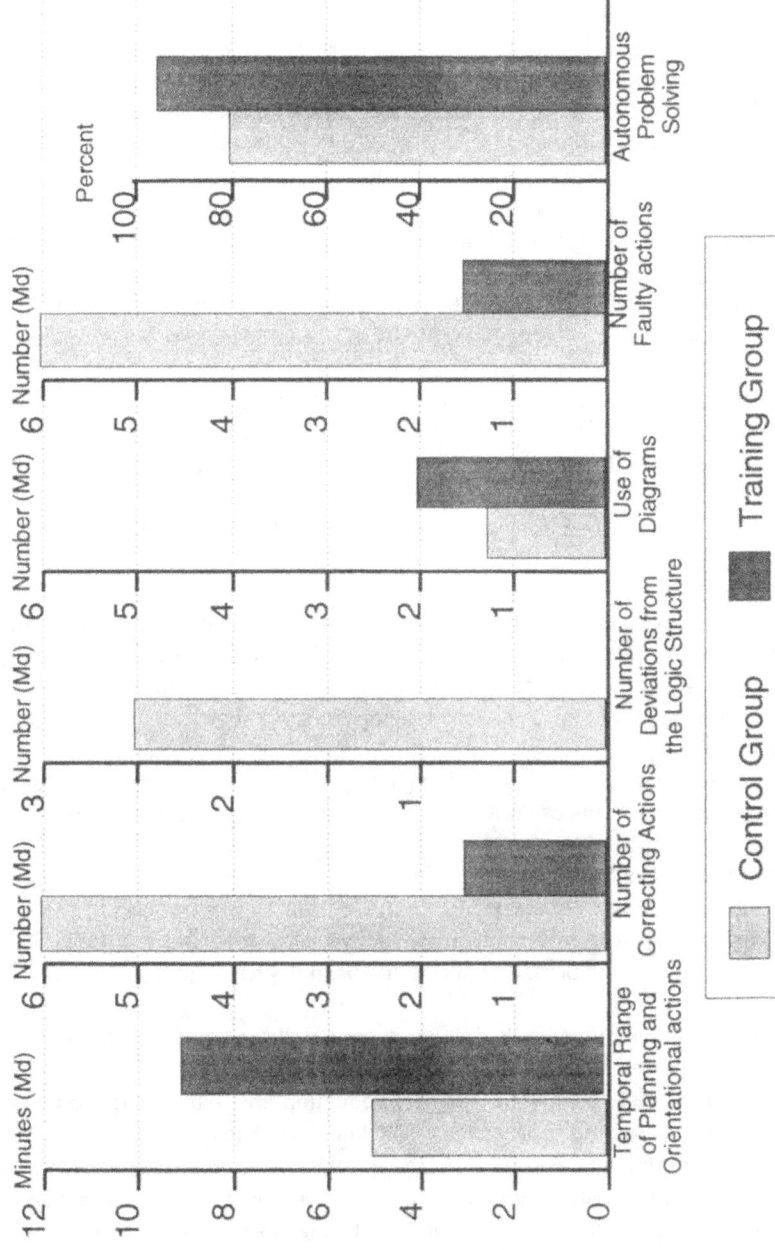

Figure 9. *Test of the effectiveness of training with heuristic rules*

Manufacturing Cell with a Learning Purpose: Decentralised Work-Based Training

New technologies and changing forms of work organisation bring up the question of a suitable location for training within the plant. A more abstract and complex working-world makes "training-on-the-job" on the shop floor level an indispensable prerequisite to acquiring the necessary professional experience and the ability to carry out job-related tasks. This requires the trainees during their work on the shop floor to:

1. practice specialised professional qualifications as reinforcement, e.g. technical knowledge;
2. understand different professional qualifications in considering integrated appliances e.g. to combine knowledge in the fields of pneumatics, hydraulics and electronics from the viewpoint of control technology;
3. be confronted with meta-professional qualification requirements (key qualifications) of every day work, which shape the results of individual action as well as success in cooperation with the team.

Two main constraints have influenced the planning and design of the teaching process: firstly the requirement of proximity to practice which cannot be realised sufficiently in special training workshops; secondly it is hardly possible for economical reasons to mediate maintenance situations immediately at the location of expensive manufacturing units, because that would mean putting them out of order in a real repair situation longer than absolutely necessary. From these "frame conditions" for vocational education arise the demand for training that should be close to shop-floor conditions without hampering the manufacturing process.

The design of the work places for training derives from the developments in technology and work organisation. Trainees must become systematically acquainted with:

- the product being manufactured;
- the manufacturing technology;
- the significance and influencing of product quality;
- maintenance requirements including fault diagnosis techniques.

Volkswagen Kassel developed a flexible production cell for training purposes in order to meet these conditions.

The learning place is integrated with the production area but belongs to the Training Centre with regard to organisational and personal matters. The trainees become acquainted with the specific production area and with the typical installations and units. The shop-floor training prepares them in particular for subsequent employment in the production area.

The handling of problems that arise from interfacing is very important for the mediation of control technology. Ways of combining and the interdependence of different kinds of control technology is expressed most clearly in the training course "Unit-control-technology" through the aforementioned modular flexible manufacturing cell for training purposes.

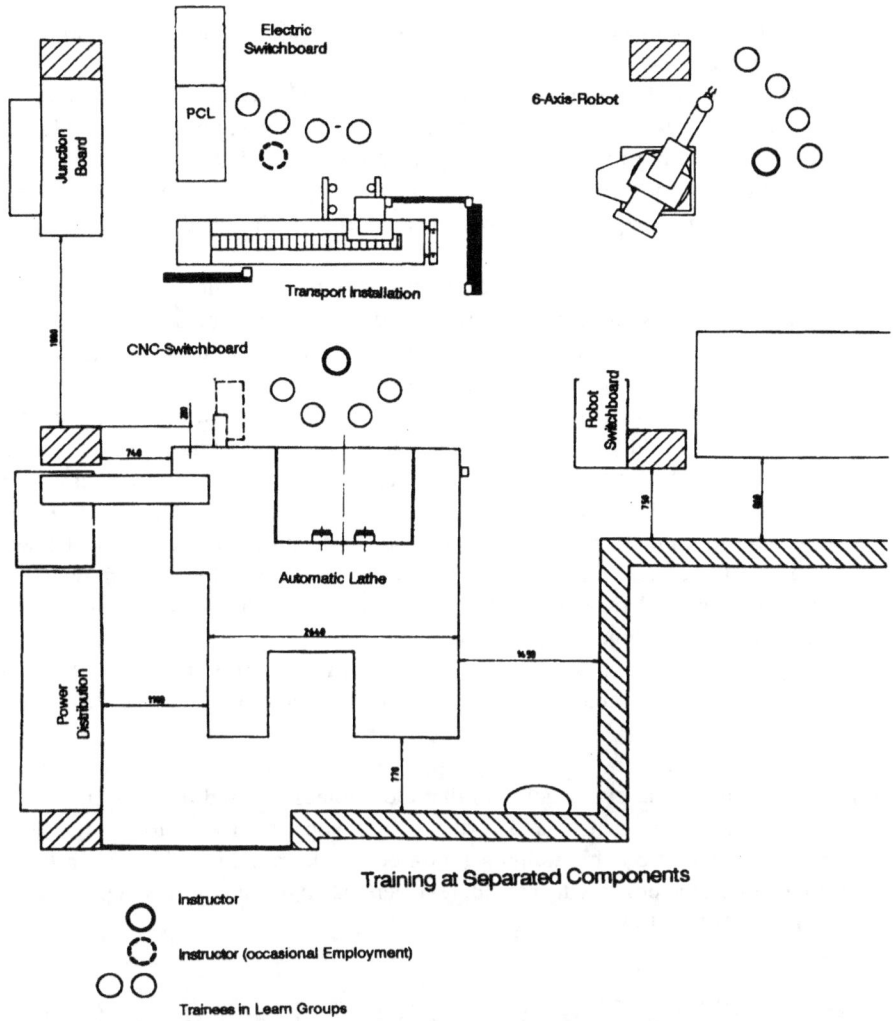

Figure 10. *Modularised flexible manufacturing cell for training purposes*

The system components are:

- a CNC-controlled automatic lathe;
- an Industrial Robot;
- a PCL-controlled transport installation.

The system includes a mechanical device with an electrical and pneumatic power section, and a PCL-controller.

The training is carried through out in a project-oriented way in separate modules of the manufacturing cell. The aim is that small groups will develop and implement a plan for an automatic manufacturing process using production and control technology. Following a general introduction to the functional principles of the flexible manufacturing cell the project-oriented training begins at the separate modules of the installation.

- The first training group (4 trainees) works with the CNC automatic lathe. Based on existing drawings, programs for shafts are developed, executed and optimised.
- The second group learns to operate the robot. The trainees are instructed about the structure, the working principles and functions of the robot.
- The third group works with the transport installation of the unit. The transport process is steered by a PCL controller which at the same time serves as the master computer for the unit. The trainees learn to cope with a transportation task carried out with control technology. The qualification at this module is accomplished through the "Leittextmethode" (LTM). The LTM follows the pedagogical objective of autonomous learning by doing practical work and achieving knowledge and skills by using different information sources independently. The support and guidance of the trainees is pre-structured by the LTM. The instructor's function is mainly that of advisor and moderator. Each learning process is divided into learning and action steps, namely informing, planning, deciding, doing, controlling and estimating.

The main outcome of the evaluation was that the trainees realised that working with the "Leittexte Methode" is positive and furthers their vocational education process. The opportunities provided by this training (autonomous learning, working on a team, to develop their own problem solving procedures) were taken up and this had a positive effect on the motivation of the trainees.

Summary of The Change Process in Relation to the Common Framework

Taking into account the values, deeply embedded in traditional German companies, regarding *skilled workers* ("Facharbeiten") as being central to productivity and quality work (see Figure 11, 1^1 and 1^Δ), the Audi and Volkswagen group initiated an action research project which had the following aims:

- to describe new skills required by modern "skilled workers", and
- to evaluate how these skills could best be learnt.

These new skills were required because of the introduction of microelectronics based flexible technologies and related new forms of less hierarchical work structures. The new regulations on electrician and metalwork occupations in Germany, which laid an emphasis on "key qualifications", influenced the change process as well.

Support was also provided by the German National Institute for Vocational Training (BIBB) (see Figure 11, 0)

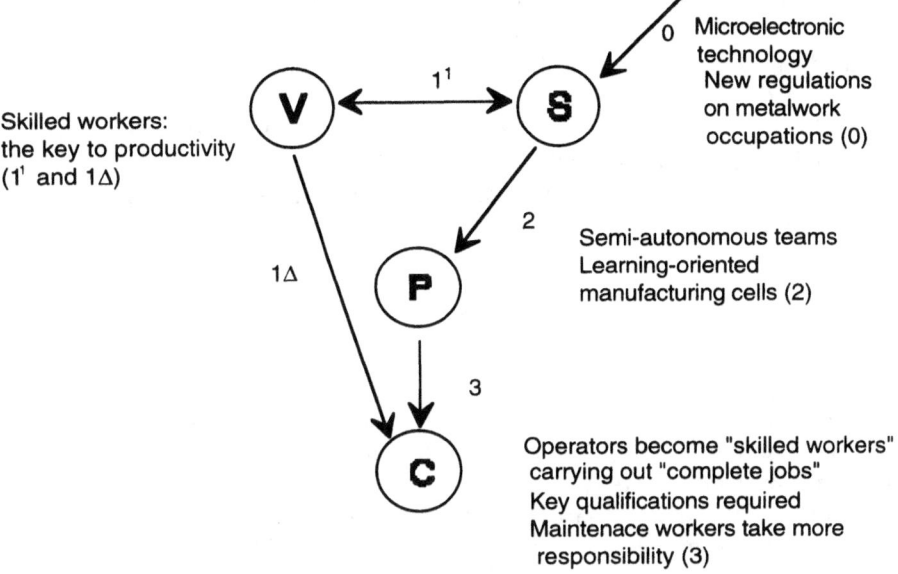

Figure 11. *"Key qualifications" (competencies) required because of new work organisation*

The new work structures entailed a massive reduction in the hierarchical and functional division of labour (see Figure 11, 2). Semi-autonomous teams comprising 8-12 workers with a "spokesman", but not a supervisor, were set up. Work was restructured following the principle of "integrated and complete work routines". There was also job rotation between different manufacturing units and even different departments.

Specially designed "learning oriented manufacturing cells", also termed "decentralised work based training units", were placed in the production area. The learning methods and technique included the use of:

1. heuristic rules in relation to, for example "fault diagnosis" and other problem-solving tasks requiring cognitive skills
2. "Leittextemethode", which means guided "discovery-learning" text-based materials.

The new competencies developed by operators and maintenance workers were as follows:

• Operators took on new roles of becoming skilled workers ("Anlangenfuhrer"), whereas previously only maintenance staff were called skilled workers. This meant that operators had to develop the competence to carry out all aspects of a job ("Handlungskompetenz") including certain maintenance, quality control and programming tasks. The notion of "Handlungskompetenz" means bringing all "one's skills" together in an integrated way to carry out a complete job (see Figure 11, 3).

- Operators and maintenance workers acquired "Key qualifications" (key/core competencies) in the cognitive, social and technical skills domains. Among Cognitive skills are included the ability to observe, read and interpret drawing and numeric data and to identify the structure of PLC programs. Examples of social skills are exchanging information, supporting fellow workers in carrying out maintenance tasks. Technical skills cover the electrical and electronic, hydraulic, pneumatic and mechanical areas.
- Maintenance Workers took on new roles requiring still higher level of cognitive, social and technical skills ("Instandhalter"). Their function is to handle unforeseen or complex maintenance tasks while normal maintenance work is now built into the jobs of operators.

Notes

Frieling, E., Facaoaru, C., Benedix, J., Pfaus, H., Sonntag, Kh. (1992). "Das Tätigkeits Analyse-Inventar (TAI). Aufbau und Nutzungsweisen", in *Zeitschrift für Arbeitswissenschaft*. 46: 51-54.

Sonntag, Kh. (1989)*Trainingsforschung in der Arbeitspsychologie*. Bern: Huber.

Sonntag, Kh. and Heun, D. (1992) "Anforderungsgerechte Qualifizierung unter besonderer Berücksichtigung der Steuerungstechnik", in *Modellversuche zur beruflichen Bildung*, Heft 27. Berlin: Bundesinstitut für Berufsbildung.

Sonntag, Kh. and Schaper, N. (1988) "Kognitives Training zur Bewältigung steuerungstechnischer Aufgabenstellungen", in *Zeitschrift für Arbeits- und Organisationspsychologie*. 32,3: 128-138.

Sonntag, Kh. and Schaper, N. (1993). *Strategies and Training for Maintenance Personnel: Optimizing Fault Diagnosis Activities*. Paper for the Human Interaction Congress 1993. Orlando.

Sonntag, Kh., Heun, D. and Schaper, N. (1992) "Der Leitfaden zur qualitativen Personalplanung bei technisch-organisatorischen Innovationen (LPI)", in *Zeitschrift für Arbeitswissenschaft*. 46: 51-54.

Sonntag, Kh.; Bergmann, B. and Timpe, K.P. (1991) *Analyse und Entwicklung von Fähigkeiten zur Fehlerdiagnose und -korrektur bei komplexen Aufgabenstellungen*. Projektantrag an die DFG. Kassel.

Chapter Ten

The Impact of TQM Strategy on Worker Roles and Competence at Cadbury

Michael Kelleher

Introduction

One of the most important debates in industrial sociology during the mid to late 1980s concerned the possibility of industrialised economies moving away from the production of standardised products with their concomitant narrow job specifications, and low skill requirements, to economies based upon customised products oriented to market demands requiring higher levels of skills and responsibilities from shop floor workers. The emergence of more highly skilled workers, it was argued, could be identified in countries such as West Germany, as it was then known, and several regions of Italy (Piore and Sable 1984, Kern and Schumann 1987). According to Lane's (1988, 1989) comparative analysis of Britain, France and Germany, the institutional systems of training and industrial relations in Germany facilitate the emergence of new types of worker, whereas in Britain, the corresponding institutional systems hinder such an emergence. However, there is a growing body of literature in Britain attesting to the need for new types of skills in manufacturing. In contrast to the belief in a general tendency to de-skill workers in order to gain control over the labour process (Braverman, 1974), recent surveys suggest that employers are increasing the skills of their existing work force and harnessing them to the new microprocessor based technologies (Daniel 1987, Batstone and Gourlay 1986).

There has also been much debate about the extent to which firms have reorganised working practices by introducing greater functional flexibility, broader task ranges and team working. A number of studies have suggested that firms in Britain are beginning to make such changes (IDS 1986, 1988a, 1988b, 1990; 1992)[1].

Despite the timely reminder by Elger (1991) that such work reorganisation may be nothing more than the intensification of labour in disguise, we must now recognise that working practices are undergoing a period of transition in Britain and that a consequence of these changes could be the emergence of the new industrial worker, as predicted by Kern and Schumann, within the British context.

An attempt to analyse the significance of the work reorganisation debate in terms of its implications for skill shortages of skilled craft workers in British manufacturing led to in-depth studies of seven factories with different labour market experiences and different approaches to work reorganisation[2]. The case studies were of firms in six different industries: batch engineering, office machinery, automobile components, materials handling, aluminium cans, and food processing.

In each of these firms, it was found that new types of workers were emerging. In one of the food processing firms new operator-level grades were being developed which required high levels of communication, problem solving and team building skills as well as the technical abilities to carry out normal operator duties. In that firm, and in two of the remaining firms, craft level jobs had been merged and multi-skilled craft workers were being introduced.

In the four other firms, a more radical transformation of working practices was under way. Tasks traditionally undertaken by higher levels of workers were being devolved to lower grades and new personal skills were being made a priority. New grades were being introduced which recognised the higher levels of technical skills involved, plus an additional emphasis on personal skills including communication, judgement, team working and problem solving. Two of these four firms were on green-field sites and as such cannot provide us with an opportunity to examine the dynamic processes of change. Of the two brown-field sites, the automobile components factory has introduced a much more limited range of new skills for its shop floor workers than the final case study which is the one selected for detailed examination here. Before examining the case study in detail, however, it is important to examine its significance in the context of the structure of work and tasks in Britain, and it will be shown that the traditional structure of work consists of strong occupational boundaries reinforced by the socialisation process experienced during initial craft training.

The Traditional Structure of Work in Britain

Work in British manufacturing has traditionally been characterised by vertical and horizontal job boundaries. For instance, four main groups of workers can be identified: engineers, technicians, craft workers and operators. Tasks are allocated to these groups according to a descending level of skill requirements. Thus, engineers' tasks will include the design and draughting of equipment or machines and their related drawings; programming, analysis, software engineering and other computer related work; the design of test equipment and procedures and inspection of equipment and components; the preparation of technical reports and the interpretation of diagrams and drawings and other aspects of internal communication. Craft workers' tasks will include planning jobs by selecting the appropriate equipment; materials, components, operations and their sequence; setting up machines for themselves and others; operating machines and control systems; testing and inspecting finished work (Jones and Scott, 1988: 22-24). Although craft jobs will include these central characteristics, boundaries exist in terms of occupational definitions. Electricians, pipe fitters, turners, millwrights and mechanical fitters are examples of the many occupations to be found at craft level. At the bottom of the skills ladder are the operators, whose knowledge and abilities are relatively limited; the tasks they are engaged on tend to be specific to single products or processes and are more closely supervised. These mainly include the performance of individual operations on a specific piece of equipment, such as the assembly of components or the operation of equipment and the operators require little training.

The importance of understanding the allocation of tasks is that during the process of training craft workers, the key occupational group in manufacturing, the traditional access route to these jobs was through the system of apprenticeships. Young school-leavers would be indentured to a firm, for a period of perhaps four years, in which they would be provided with a combination of theoretical knowledge at a local college and also with practical hands-on experience working with skilled colleagues on the shop floor. During this training the apprentices would be socialised into the norms of solidarity and friendship which surround their occupation (Penn, 1990) and as such the apprenticeship acts as a social as well as a technical system of training. This system of training serves to create an identification with the occupation which tends to be institutionalised in the form of occupationally based trade union representation. The consequence of this form of representation is that not only is management viewed with suspicion but also other groups of workers are treated as a threat to both jobs and skilled status. Any attempts by management to re-allocate tasks have proven difficult to achieve in this climate of distrust and has tended to be negotiated through productivity agreements where change normally accrues financial reward for the workers or penalty for management (Batstone, 1986). Thus the structure of tasks tends to be reinforced by the traditional systems of training and industrial relations which in turn create an identification with occupations making radical innovation in work organisation extremely difficult to implement (see Kelleher (1993) for an overview of this debate). Firms that are able to innovate in terms of work reorganisation provide insights into how change occurs and also act as indicators for potential models of organisational change which have implications for qualifications and learning processes. In this context the Moulded Factory at Cadbury provides a useful example of the type of new occupational qualifications that might emerge and how traditional structures of work and tasks may be overcome.

Cadbury Moulded Factory

Cadbury is a wholly owned subsidiary of Cadbury Schweppes plc. The group produces chocolates, such as Creme Eggs, Flake, Wispa, Fruit & Nut and Roses Chocolates. It also produce sweets, mints, toffees and other similar products as well as soft drinks such as tonic water. Through its links with the Coca Cola Schweppes Beverages division of the corporation also produces and markets other brand leader soft drinks. Through acquisition and merger the group has grown to be possibly the country's leading corporation in the sweets and soft drinks markets. In 1990 group sales were over £3 billion and pre-tax profits amounted to almost £280M. The corporation employs over 35,000 people worldwide. The confectionery stream, of which Cadbury forms a major part, reached sales figures of £1.3 billion and a trading profit of £163M in 1990. Cadbury has three factories in the United Kingdom, two of which are based on one site in Bournville, Birmingham, and the third is situated near Bristol in the South West of England.

Although on the same site, the two factories on the Bournville site are in fact separate business units. Defined by the range of products, the factories have separate management functions and personnel departments. One factory produces varieties of chocolate based sweets for boxes and packets, whereas the second factory produces chocolate bars and other moulded shaped products, hence the name 'Cadbury Moulded Factory'. Despite investing in new technology and signing flexibility agreements with their respective workforces, the extent of work reorganisation appears to have diverged between the two factories. Whilst the former factory has retained traditional divisions of labour with narrow job definitions and skill requirements, the latter factory has undertaken a degree of task integration and a development of new occupational qualifications that makes an examination of its current situation very interesting. At the time of research (mid 1991) the factory employed 1200 employees of which 900 were directly employed on production, 80 of whom were craft workers / technicians and the remainder at operator grades.

During the mid-1980s, at about the time the factories were separated into distinct business units, the market share of the company had been falling. Its own market research had suggested that its name was synonymous with chocolate but its share of the market was only approximately thirty-three per cent (33%). Half of the entire production of its Creme Egg range, one of its biggest selling brands, was exported to Herschey Ltd in the United States, who in turn sold it under franchise in the United States. The concerns of this customer about quality standards, Cadbury's own perceived loss of market share, and increased competition combined to provide an impetus to reform its working practices. The Moulded Factory has several different plants each producing its own brand of chocolate. For example, one plant concentrates on Wispa bars and another plant produces Creme Eggs. The market pressures for reform were felt firstly in the latter plant and the new working practices eventually became the bench mark for changes in other plants. It is the reorganisation of work and the subsequent emergence of new types of skilled worker in the Creme Eggs plant that is the subject of examination here.

These developments can be seen as integrated within the company's overall strategy to improve quality. A 'Manufacturing Excellence Programme' has been initiated that has two key dimensions: Total Quality Management (TQM) and Human Resource Management (HRM). TQM has been designed to reduce the high levels of wastage and improve the overall quality of the production process. Research into TQM suggests that it has originally been driven by the threat of Japanese competition with its high levels of quality and innovation. The essence of TQM is the continuous drive towards greater improvements in quality but its impact on human relations has rarely been examined. The few authors that have examined the phenomenon regard TQM as being directed at managerial grades as well as towards shop floor workers (although we will concentrate on the latter in this paper). However, there appears to be some consensus that TQM affects traditional work relations, in that tasks and responsibilities normally undertaken by higher level grades (management) are devolved to shop floor workers. The process of collating statistical data on the quality of output with the additional obligations to act according to the information acquired becomes, within the philosophy of TQM, the responsibility of shop floor workers. Thus there is a need to make the transition from low-trust to high-trust relations (Collard, 1989; Hill, 1991; Wilkinson, Allen and Snape, 1991).

The change from traditional industrial relations practices to HRM is designed to gain the commitment of employees to company objectives. These attempts to create a new industrial relations environment with an emphasis on commitment, continuous learning, high trust relations and increased employee involvement are consistent with the new HRM paradigm (Storey, 1989; 1992). As yet, there are relatively few case studies of brown-field sites describing the changes from industrial relations to human resource management (Kinnie, 1992) and in contrast to much of the HRM literature which emphasises the erosion of trade union influence and the strategies of direct employee communications by-passing formal industrial relations channels, (Guest, 1987, 1989, 1992), a new culture of co-operation has been developed between management and the work force at the Moulded Factory, which has included the formal trade union representatives.

In order to analyse this case study in more depth we will firstly examine the changes in working practices and the emergence of new shop floor qualifications. The process of how these new qualifications have been introduced will then be analysed.

The Reorganisation of Work

In 1988 the factory introduced new working practices into the plant which produced Creme Eggs. The traditional methods for organising work in the plant were the same as those for all of the other plants in the factory where workers had clearly demarcated job contents. Allocated to different parts of the process, individual workers had narrowly defined job descriptions and responsibilities (see Figure 1).

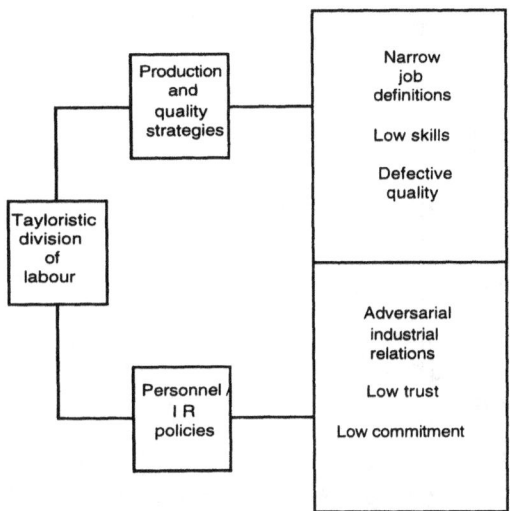

Figure 1. *Model of old organisation*

During the actual production process, individuals had responsibility for specific sections. For example, once the product reached the wrapping stage of the process, operators tended to be dedicated to either a single machine or to parts of a machine. Wrapping machine operators were engaged in a number of discrete tasks including: feeding the wrapping machine, operating the machine, packing cartons, stacking cartons onto pallets. Process operators' tasks were also divided into bringing in the chocolate and monitoring the process, although there was some limited degree of job rotation amongst these workers.

The Tayloristic divisions of labour gives rise to certain conditions which constrain the integration of production and personnel issues. In the old model of organisation each department has distinct functions and the demands of each of these functions culminate in shop floor work which is characterised by narrow job definitions, close supervision and control, and little responsibility for the production process being devolved to operators or craft workers. Management was divided into functional specialisms each of which had its own rationale in terms of reinforcing the divisions of labour on the shop floor. Industrial engineers were concerned with time and motion studies (a Tayloristic device for controlling the pace of work) and production management considered that labour should be directly supervised in their work. Development engineers saw labour as an obstacle to efficiency and preferred to reduce the firm's dependence on workers (see Smith et al (1990), table 10.1, page 348 for a summary of the characteristics of the separate functions and their respective views of management strategies).

After the microprocessor-based new technology was introduced in the mid-1980s, management of the Moulded Factory saw an opportunity to reorganise work away from this Tayloristic division of labour and to create jobs with a broader range of tasks, increased responsibilities and greater skills. The changes in work organisation examined here appear consistent with TQM and HRM's principles of devolved responsibility, continuous improvement and greater commitment from employees (see Figure 2).

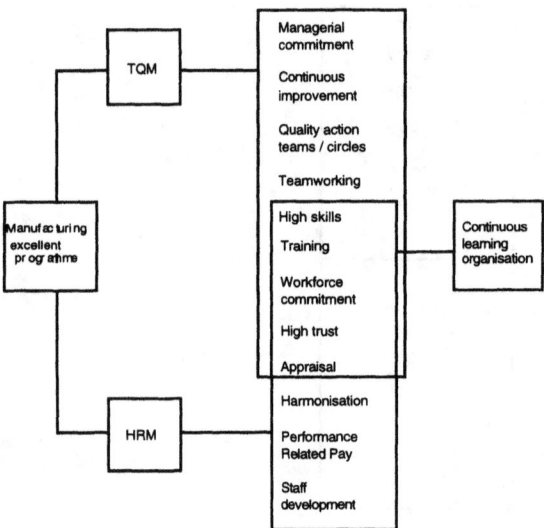

Figure 2. *Model of new organisation*

Figure 2 shows that in the areas of training, industrial relations and work-force commitment, both TQM and HRM synthesise into a strategy for continuous learning. At Cadbury during the mid-to-late 1980s the introduction of new technology, market pressures and the reorganisation of work have acted as agents of change towards a new model with high levels of skills and commitment. Similar pressures are being faced by firms in different sectors of the economy. The new model of *a learning organisation* and its constituent parts may provide a deeper understanding of the processes involved in becoming more competitive. The new occupational profiles that emerge from such a strategy will assist firms adopting this route to remain competitive and perhaps forge ahead[3].

Team working and a four-shift pattern of working were introduced. On each shift there are thirty operators divided into four teams. The teams are delineated by technology: there is one team on the wet end, where the chocolate is processed; at the dry end, there is one team on the wrapping lines and two on the packing lines. Craft workers work with whichever team requires their assistance. The teams have been selected on the basis of skill requirements and also on the basis of personality traits. Where previous organisations of work had involved a "leading hand" deputising for the shift manager, this position no longer exists. There are no team leaders and teams are self-supervisory. The shift manager's responsibilities lie in overtime organisation, costing and discipline.

The new working practices now mean that the wrapping machine operators are not dedicated to any single machine but are flexible across any machine in the plant and have responsibility for quality control using statistical process control (SPC) programmes for monitoring and evaluating the quality of the product. Process operators must now understand computerised control systems and undertake greater responsibility for the production process. This includes ensuring the correct viscosity, temperature, consistency and throughput of the raw materials to the moulds and the final product.

A proportion of the process operators now undertake maintenance of the equipment. Dozens of tasks which were previously the domain of craft workers are now the responsibility of these operators. The following example illustrates the extent to which tasks have been devolved to operator grades.

Sieve lawns are large wire meshes designed to act as strainers and to distribute only the required amount of chocolate to the moulds. Occasionally the sieve lawns need cleaning and this involves several procedures. The operator isolates the machine from the electrical supply and removes various clamps before the sieve lawn can be cleaned. All seals and 'O' rings need to be removed before cleaning and the operator is responsible for their replacement. All clamps and flanges have to be replaced and checked and the operator is responsible for reconnecting the electrical supply, starting up the machine and checking for vibration and leakages. This routine cleaning operation would have needed the presence of an electrician to isolate the machine and check for safe access, and a fitter to remove the seals, flanges, 'O' rings, etc. and check their replacement. The electrician would be needed to reconnect the supply and to ensure the machine started operating again. The operator would have simply stood idle before cleaning the machine and then had to call the craft workers back once the cleaning was complete.

A second example indicates that the devolution of tasks can include fault rectification as well as the more mundane task of cleaning. When moulds jam, for instance, the equipment stops and indicators flash on the control panel. Previously the operator would have simply called for a skilled craft worker to attend the fault: now the operator isolates the supply and frees the mechanism using a ratchet. The rails on which the moulds are placed are re-aligned before putting the machine back into service.

At craft level, a high degree of electrical and mechanical cross-trade flexibility has been introduced. When necessary, workers who had previously been dedicated to mechanical tasks now isolate the supply, disconnect and test motors, and reconnect and restore the supply. Rectification of simple electrical faults are also carried out by these workers. Likewise, mechanical tasks are now carried out by workers who had previously only undertaken electrical work. However, there are limitations to the extent to which the company has introduced a multi-skilling programme. New electrical regulations have rigorously specified the qualifications for undertaking certain more complex electrical tasks. Thus, the old single skilled mechanical workers are restricted to simple electrical work. More skilled electrical tasks remain the domain of time-served electricians[4].

Quality Action Teams

The new working practices have freed the electricians from more mundane tasks and allowed them to undertake tasks previously carried out only by technician level workers. Prior to the reorganisation, Independent Project Groups, consisting mainly of drawing office engineers and technicians, undertook the specification, ordering, installation, commissioning and programming of new equipment before handing over for maintenance, at which time the equipment entered the province of the craft workers. Now, Quality Action Teams, consisting of technicians, craft workers and operators meet regularly and details of the equipment specification and layout are ironed out. Whilst the technicians and engineers still order the machines, the remaining work is carried out by the electricians. This includes the programming of the control software and modifications in the programmes of existing equipment. One limitation to this innovation is that larger projects may need more input from technician grades owing to the small numbers of electricians employed in the factory. Meetings of the Quality Action teams are held whenever specific projects or problems arise - membership of the teams is not defined and team members can sit on a number of different teams, depending on the needs and the issues being dealt with by any team.

New Grades for New Jobs

A key factor in the changing levels of qualification at the factory is the recognition that the new broader range of tasks and skills should be rewarded. At craft level, for instance, a new grading structure has been introduced to acknowledge the new skill requirements (see Figure 3). Grade A is the equivalent of the former single-skilled grade and refers to craft workers who fulfil support roles or who do not progress to the dual skilled role of higher grades.

These workers will include pipe fitters, sheet metal workers, fitters and electricians. Grade A1 is called 'technician'. In order to achieve this grade, workers must be fully committed to cross-trade flexibility and fulfil criteria for both technical and communication skills. These include diagnostic skills, a knowledge and application of confectionery engineering and principles, written and oral skills to complete records and reports for managers and colleagues, a commitment to flexible working practices and initiative to make improvements and undertake training courses. Workers must also have gained at least two years' experience of the company's production processes before being considered for this grade. Grade A2 has also been introduced. These 'Senior Technicians' will be appointed at management discretion from existing A1 technicians.

The role of the Senior Technicians will include judgement, leadership, planning and organisation and problem analysis. Many of these functions are presently carried out by first line management and by more traditional technician grades. To date nobody has been appointed to this grade. The company believes that the creation of such a grade is necessary in order to provide a career incentive for the very best technicians. The factory is planning further work reorganisation programmes to be introduced over the next two years that will call for greater level of skills. Current flexibility agreements cover machines and areas within single plants. The company feels that the Senior Technician skills will be required for future planned developments which might involve flexibility across plants.

Old grades	*New grades*
Single skilled craft e.g. pipe-fitter, electrician	A
Not applicable	A1 Technician *Skilled in more than one trade and proficient in diagnostics, communications and committed to further training*
Not applicable	A2 Technician *Skilled in leadership; judgement; planning; organisation; problem solving*

Figure 3. *Comparison of old and new grades at craft level*

A new grade, located above the previous top grade for operators, has been introduced to the company's grading system that acknowledges the new tasks at operator level. Along with all of the other operator grades in the plant, the new grade needs to develop quality management, problem solving, team working and diagnostic skills. With the exception of the team working expertise which did not exist prior to this reorganisation, these skills tended to be exercised by higher grades including managerial grades within the firm. Thus, an emphasis on changes to core technical skills, which are characterised by the integration of higher level tasks onto tasks of lower graded workers, has been complemented by the need to ensure all shop floor workers develop personal skills, many of which were previously the domain of supervisory grades.

The Change Process

One criticism of the company's previous policies on vocational training has come from its shop stewards who feel that training tended to be limited by the content and availability of courses. These were frequently attended by people who tended to be less involved in the day to day operations of equipment. As a consequence of this policy, shop floor workers failed to obtain the essential training required to ensure an adequate updating of their expertise. Training is now focused on the upgrading of the skills of all of the work force and is more effective.

These innovations in working practices have meant that the company has needed to develop methods to ensure that its shop floor workers achieve the desired standards of technical competency and have access to resources for developing and enhancing their personal skills. During the early phases of the reorganisation the company introduced a training programme to raise the technical competencies of all of its workers. Training at the company is a mixture of both the systematic and informal.

After the introduction of the new technology, the local state organised skills agency was involved in developing the training packages required to upgrade the skills of craft workers and operators. This process lasted approximately twelve months and the agency remains involved in consultation with the factory to develop on-going training initiatives. Each task that has been devolved from craft to operator level was subject to detailed consultation with the craft workers and a modular training programme was devised for each new task which was then followed by the operators at their place of work and during working time. Operators need to fulfil all of the requirements of these modules before being recognised as competent in the tasks involved. Competence is assessed by the person responsible for training the individual, the first line supervisor and the trainee, and is endorsed on a 'unit of competence' as shown in Figure 4.

An internal certification scheme is currently being considered by the company. Operators who successfully complete a course in Statistical Process Control (SPC) are awarded a certificate. Craft workers are also trained using a modular system based on modules of the Engineering Industry Training Board's (EITB)[5]. Once the required number of modules has been completed an internal certificate is awarded. Although distinct mechanical or electrical modules exist, cross-trade training consisted of working through the training programmes of the other trade to the level of competence required by the EITB for that trade.

In contrast to the highly organised approach to training for operators and cross-trade skills at craft level, the manner in which the electricians have developed their new higher level skills has been markedly informal. No formal training in programming skills has been given to the electricians. Although courses were available from manufacturers, these were mostly attended by first line managers. Information and skills tended to be disseminated on a 'need to know basis' when things went wrong. The electricians developed informal self-learning approaches to programming and diagnostics skills. Most frequently, this involved individuals utilising their growing knowledge of the equipment in conjunction with the manufacturer's technical manuals.

Incentives for Continuous Learning

The company has recognised the development amongst these craft workers in terms of their initiative and demand for new skills and access to learning materials, and largely devolves the definitions of learning requirements to the individuals and groups of craft workers. However, amongst operator grades it has taken a more proactive approach to upgrading the skills of its work force. It recognises that the modular approach, as illustrated by Figure 4, are rather mechanical in nature. Once operators fulfil the requirements of each module they were expected to move onto the next one. Once all of the modules have been completed their were no incentives or in-built processes facilitating the continuous upgrading of skills.

Units of Competence	
Description: To accredit the ability to remove, replace and refit sieve lawns used for filtering chocolate before production	
Element	*Performance criteria*
To state accurately	Cracked broken or visibly damaged component parts are reported Isolation procedures strictly adhered to
Toremove the sieve	Excess chocolate is cleaned from sieve Lift collar and sieve upwards and away from plant, pipses and equipment
To refit new sieve	Check handle positions in relationship to clamping device Locking securely to toggle clamps
To start machine	To remove and re-open all isolation procedures Start machine and check for vibration loose parts

Trainer endorsement   Trainee endorsement

Manager endorsement

Figure 4. *Assessment of competence in sieve lawn maintenance*

The weaknesses in this system have been recognised by the company who wish to create an environment of continuous learning where employees have access to and have the desire to continually improve their skill base. To this end, personal computers have been introduced into the work place. Software programmes have been installed in order to facilitate access of workers to educational programmes concentrating on the key changes in skill requirements. A software programme, for instance, outlining the key dimensions of Total Quality Management is available and workers are encouraged to use the computerised learning facilities as often as possible. This development has only recently been introduced and it is difficult to assess its impact on shop floor workers, learning activities. The computers are located on the shop floor or as near as possible to it and the company hopes that operators and craft workers will make use of the facilities as often as possible. To this end it will monitor the use of the computers and develop initiatives to ensure they are used by as many employees as possible.

A further incentive for workers to continually upgrade their skills has been the recent introduction of a skill-based pay system. A number of firms have developed this type of system as a basis for continual improvement. Instead of pay being determined by performance or competency-based criteria, this system rewards the successful completion of periods of training or on-the job learning. A combination of formal training and a period of shop floor practical implementation of new skills will see additional bonuses paid on top of a basic wage (IDS, 1992).

General National Vocational Qualifications

Cadbury believes that the emergence of the General National Vocational Qualification system (GNVQ) parallels their own requirements and the company intends to adopt this new system for its own needs. GNVQ is a new national system for vocational qualifications in Britain which the government believes will provide a framework of vocational qualifications comparable to the existing academic qualifications of GCSE and A levels. The GNVQ system operates at five different levels. For instance, level 3 has been designed to be comparable to the academic A level standard. Within this system, people are expected to obtain twelve GNVQ units consisting of eight mandatory units plus four optional units. An example of one such unit - Maintenance and Control - is given in Figure 5)[6].

In addition to these units a further three units in the core skills have been identified: communication, application of number, and information technology. These three core skills form the basis of GNVQs and are seen as an integral part of the new qualification procedures. Additional core skills have been identified as: working with others, problem solving, and improving one's learning and performance. These latter core skills are in the development stage and have yet to be introduced (NCVQ, 1992a). In order to ensure that workers develop the ability to utilise these core skills in their work, training for these skills must ensure that the skills are integrated into the training for technical skills. Failure to do so will create artificial distinctions in terms of types of qualifications required. If this case study is at all representative of the new qualifications demanded of manufacturing, then it is essential that this point is recognised at an early stage in the design of training programmes.

The extent to which the NVQ system has been adopted in manufacturing industry, and information on how firms are introducing the system is as yet unavailable. However, it is important to recognise the emergence of serious concerns over the ability of the NVQ system to rectify the problem of skill shortages in British industry. Whilst the occupational labour market system prevails, those firms that are reorganising working practices and training internally may successfully tackle their skill shortage problem. The vertical integration of tasks which has been introduced at Cadbury Moulded Factory and the accompanying firm specific skills may not be compatible with a national training system which has been criticised for its low levels of attainment compared to European systems, its rejection of external assessment, and its over reliance on employers to define training needs. This could lead to the introduction of narrow and inflexible qualifications at the expense of the economy's need for people with broader skills (Jarvis and Prais, 1989; Prais, 1991; McCool, 1989, cited in IRS, 1992). Cadbury needs, like other firms considering introducing training towards GNVQs, to take account of these early criticisms of the system in order to tackle the problems at an early stage in their implementation.

At Cadbury, this system is in its infancy, and the company has insufficient experience with which to evaluate its effectiveness. However, it has begun to devolve the responsibility for this learning process to its first line supervisors. This is a part of the process which emphasises that learning and the practical requirements of production become more integrated. Although there has been little resistance to the types of change described here amongst lower management grades, the company has recently introduced courses for first line supervisors on empowerment of shop floor workers and the company hopes that this might overcome any potential difficulties in lower management's attitudes to devolved responsibility.

These developments can be seen as a part of the process towards the emergence of new occupational qualifications. This process is synonymous with the core skills and Attwell suggests that the integration of skill definitions and the process towards their achievement is a part of the 'common core' (Attwell, 1992). However, it is important to recognise that such a model neglects the important role that the work force itself plays in the definition of skills (see for example, Penn, 1984). In order to provide a more detailed examination of the 'core process' we must therefore examine the nature of industrial relations at Cadbury.

The Impact of Employee Relations on Organisational Change

Prior to the separation of the business units the company had undertaken a radical reassessment of its old paternalistic approach to industrial relations in which the trade unions were able to exercise a strong voice in their representation of the work force. In the late 1970s and early 1980s new personnel managers were employed who adopted strong anti-union approaches and whose tactics reasserted the managerial prerogative. Industrial relations in the company at this time could be best described as adversarial which is consistent with Tayloristic work organisation in that any change to the division of labour accrues costs to management and involves lengthy negotiating procedures before gaining agreement. The separation of the two factories into distinct business units has shown that where one factory has successfully managed the changes described, the other factory has retained past working practices despite similar technology and flexibility agreements[7]. This contrast is a direct result of a cultural change introduced soon after the separation. The introduction of TQM and team working marked the beginning of a closer more cooperative style of industrial relations and an increase in the positive participatory role of the trade unions. An example of how the role of trade unions has changed can be seen during the large scale job evaluation exercise undertaken after the new technology was introduced. Although external consultants were used, the unions were involved in designing the structure of the exercise and were present at all of the consultation interviews with their members.

SUMMARY OF RELATIONSHIPS WITHIN UNIT		
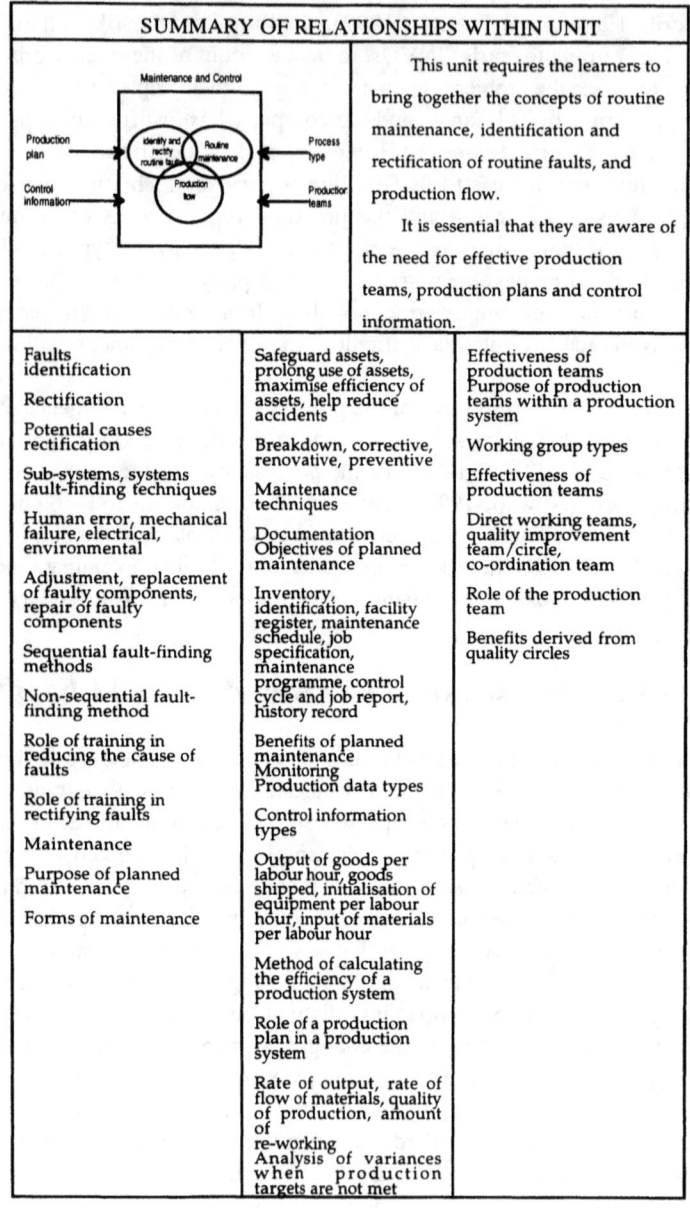		This unit requires the learners to bring together the concepts of routine maintenance, identification and rectification of routine faults, and production flow. It is essential that they are aware of the need for effective production teams, production plans and control information.
Faults identification

Rectification

Potential causes rectification

Sub-systems, systems fault-finding techniques

Human error, mechanical failure, electrical, environmental

Adjustment, replacement of faulty components, repair of faulty components

Sequential fault-finding methods

Non-sequential fault-finding method

Role of training in reducing the cause of faults

Role of training in rectifying faults

Maintenance

Purpose of planned maintenance

Forms of maintenance | Safeguard assets, prolong use of assets, maximise efficiency of assets, help reduce accidents

Breakdown, corrective, renovative, preventive

Maintenance techniques

Documentation Objectives of planned maintenance

Inventory, identification, facility register, maintenance schedule, job specification, maintenance programme, control cycle and job report, history record

Benefits of planned maintenance Monitoring Production data types

Control information types

Output of goods per labour hour, goods shipped, initialisation of equipment per labour hour, input of materials per labour hour

Method of calculating the efficiency of a production system

Role of a production plan in a production system

Rate of output, rate of flow of materials, quality of production, amount of re-working
Analysis of variances when production targets are not met | Effectiveness of production teams Purpose of production teams within a production system

Working group types

Effectiveness of production teams

Direct working teams, quality improvement team/circle, co-ordination team

Role of the production team

Benefits derived from quality circles |

Figure 5. *Example of GNVQ Specification: Knowledge specification GNVQ manufacturing 2M5 maintenance and control*

The two factories operate autonomous collective bargaining arrangements and have different union representatives. In the factory studied, consultation with company Directors occurs regularly and these meetings tend to set the climate for negotiation. The unions feel that they are listened to at these meetings and that their views are often reflected in the eventual detailed proposals from management. Decisions are often taken before the trade unions are consulted, but any proposal from line management is regarded as negotiable. There is a joint union committee that negotiates with management on issues involving shop floor workers. Involvement in a range of collective bargaining issues tends to vary. The unions experience of new technology proposals has led to mixed feelings. They feel that they try to get involved at an early stage but sometimes fail. As regards the work reorganisation examined here, the trade unions were involved at an early stage in the planning of the changes. Although led by management, a joint team guided the introduction of the new working practices.

The unions have frequently been pro-active and the craft unions have developed a five year plan which encompasses work reorganisation, training and pay. This plan is fairly pragmatic in that there are no hard-and-fast timetables or methods set out by which to achieve goals and consists of general objectives, and acknowledges the need to be flexible and adaptable to future circumstances. The unions are extremely positive in their attitudes to training and were keen to be involved at an early stage in the consultation and design stages of the operators' training modules considered earlier. The trade unions have three priorities when confronted with any work reorganisation plans. Firstly, they feel that there is no use in gaining increased pay if jobs are lost. Accordingly security is the primary aim of the trade union negotiators. Secondly, adequate cash inducements are sought. Thirdly, increased job satisfaction is an important goal. Although these are in descending order the trade union stewards argue that they attempt to ensure all three elements are involved before making any agreement.

Employee Communications

The company attempts directly to involve its workers through an extensive employee communication system, primarily designed to promote quality and its "manufacturing excellence programme". Newsletters are distributed regularly and the company's aim is to move away from "identifying with the skill but more towards the product or the company". The trade unions are represented in the Quality Action Teams which allow for direct employee involvement in all matters of production and this provides them with a great deal of information and as a result they are able to take relevant decisions when consequences can be seen for members in other plants or teams. In the event of a trade union representative not being available for the meetings, management provide minutes to the unions before taking further action.

This new environment is characterised by the recognition by both parties of the need to improve competitiveness and use the quality-driven means to achieve this. This climate of pragmatic cooperation is in direct contrast to previous industrial relations within the factory where change would need to be negotiated, and invariably significant financial cost would accrue. The increased productivity resulting from the changes has enabled the company to consider pay incentives, and the new cultural environment means that the work force is more adaptable and even proactive in some elements of it.

Conclusion

It has not been argued here that this case study is representative of manufacturing industries in Britain and in fact it may not be representative of the various sites and plants within the company itself. However, the innovative approach to working practices may act as an illustration of a potential model for future job design. In the national context of Tayloristic divisions of labour and strong occupational identities created by the systems of training and industrial relations in Britain, the type of work reorganisation described in this study challenges both the horizontal and vertical boundaries between jobs and tasks and shows that it may be possible to innovate along the radical lines pursued in this case study.

A perceived quality problem and a recognition that its market share was at variance with its market research has initiated a period of remarkable change at Cadbury Moulded Factory. This change has resulted in the emergence of new occupational qualifications which emphasise higher levels of technical skills combined with new personal skills such as, communications, problem solving and quality control management. The tasks that have been devolved to both skilled and semi-skilled shop floor workers were previously the domain of higher grades and first line management. New grades have been introduced which recognise the new higher levels of skills demanded of the shop floor workers and incentives have been introduced to the pay and grading system to promote the acquisition of skills on a continuous basis.

As a direct result of the changes examined here, Cadbury has firstly stabilised its market share and then showed a continuous improvement in each month of the last two years. In a declining market this is a remarkable achievement and appears to endorse the decision of the company. The strategic decisions of both the factory management and its work force have helped to alter the company's market position and have created a climate of a high degree of trust where change is no longer a major problem.

A new factory culture has arisen to facilitate such radical innovations in which there is an all-embracing philosophy of improving quality whilst gaining the commitment and involvement of the work force. Within this "Manufacturing Excellence Programme", the key dimensions of TQM and HRM have acted as vehicles for the changes described here. TQM demands increased worker responsibility for the collation of quality statistics and the obligation to act according to the information. HRM philosophies include an emphasis on employee involvement and training, and eliciting commitment to the goals of the firm. Locating training at the work place would appear to be the most suitable action to facilitate learning. In this case study, work-place learning has been introduced and although the original modular programme was seen as limiting learning expectations, the factory management has recognised that continuous learning is the key to the acquisition of skills.

Where this case study diverges from other examples of HRM practices is that whilst the Moulded Factory has adopted elements of HRM such as direct employee communication it has also adopted an inclusive approach to the trade unions. As in this factory, firms with strong trade union representation may feel that a strongly anti-union HRM strategy is inappropriate and that pragmatic cooperation may be the best way to facilitate change.

This case study suggests that new occupational qualifications may be emerging in Britain and that firms wishing to innovate in such a radical manner may need to address their approaches to training and employee relations. The introduction of continuous learning process based at the work place and establishment of high trust relationships with employee representatives can create an environment where change is more readily accepted and the acquisition of skills accommodated. Despite the national context characterised by low skills, inadequate training and low trust industrial relations, this case study shows that it is possible to address the need for new work place qualifications through an on-going desire to alter traditional approaches to work organisation, training policies and employee relations.

Summary of the Case-study in Relation to the General Framework

Problems of quality which were brought to the company's attention by a major export customer, led the company to rethink its management, organisational and technological systems. The introduction of new process technologies, accompanied by the division of the factory into distinct business units, provided opportunities to introduce team-work oriented work processes (see Figure 6, 1[1]).

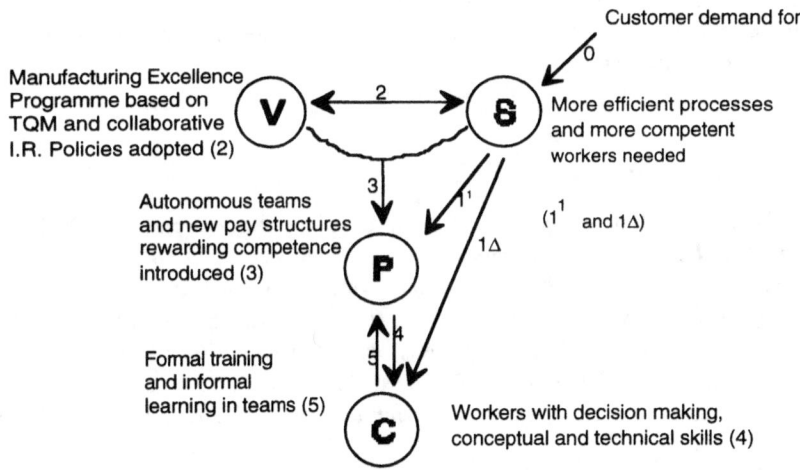

Figure 6. *A TQM driven change process*

The Manufacturing Excellence Programme adopted was based on Total Quality Management and Human Resources Management Strategies. Great attention was also paid to creating good employer-union relations, and as a results an adversarial industrial relations climate gave way to one based on mutual trust and cooperation (see Figure 2).

TQM necessitated work processes which challenged traditional horizontal and vertical task boundaries. Autonomous teams began to operate within the factory and Quality Action Teams, which included occupational grades at different levels, met regularly to assess needs and to ensure all aspects of production and maintenance were considered before purchasing new equipment (see Figure, 3).

New pay structures were introduced at operator level which encouraged the acquisition of skills. A new grade was introduced recognising new enhanced skills at operator level, and a new grading structures ensured that craft workers were rewarded for enhancing their own skill levels.

The integration of TQM and HRM management techniques combined to create an environment which supported learning.

The vertical integration of tasks manifested itself in sets of *new competencies* for two occupational groups, craft-level workers, and, operators (see Fig. 6, 4).

Craft-level workers
Judgement, communication, problem-solving, team-work skills integrated with higher levels of technical skills to assist the adaptation of new microprocessor based technology.

Operators
Communication, quality management, team-work skills for all operators. Some operators gained new higher level of technical skills related to new microprocessor based technology. At operator level, a modular training programme was introduced to raise technical skill levels. Experienced operators and craft workers received training in pedagogic skills (see Figure 5).

A modular training programme was also used to assist learning of cross-trade technical skills at craft-level while informal learning methods were utilised in acquiring higher level skills related to programming new machines.

References

Atkinson, J. (1992) "Welcome to what?", in *Work, Employment & Society*, 6, 309-310
Attwell G., (1992) *Developing the Common Core - A New Approach To The Comparison Of Qualifications In Europe*, Cardiff: Welsh Joint Education Committee
Batstone E., (1986) "New Forms of Work Organisation: The British Experience", in Grootings, P., Gustavsen, B. & Hethy, L. (eds) *New Forms of Work Organisation and their Social and Economic Environment*, Budapest: Statistical Publishing House
Batstone E. & Gourlay S., (1986) *Unions, Unemployment & Innovation*, Oxford, Basil Blackwell
Braverman H., (1974) *Labor and Monopoly Capital: The Degradation of Work in the Twentieth Century*, New York: Monthly Review Press
Collard R., (1989) *Total Quality: Success Through People*, London: Institute of Personnel Management
Daniel W.W. (1987) *Workplace Industrial Relations and Technial Change: Based on the DE/ESRC/ACAS Surveys*, London: Frances Pinter
Elger, T. (1990) "Technical innovation and work reorganisation in British manufacturing in the 1980s: continuity, intensification or transformation", in *Work, Employment & Society*, 4, special issue, 67-101
Guest D., (1987) 'Human resource management and industrial relations', *Journal of Management Studies*, 24, 503-21

Guest D., (1989) "Human resource management: its implications for industrial relations and trade unions", in J. Storey (ed) *New Perspectives on Human Resource Management*

Guest D., (1992) "HRM in the UK", in B.Towers (ed) *The Handbook of Human Resource Management*, Oxford: Blackwell

Hill S., (1991) "How Do You Manage a Flexible Firm ? The Total Quality Model", in *Work, Employment & Society*, Vol. 5, No. 3: 397-415

IDS (1986) "Flexibility at Work", in *Incomes Data Services Study*, No.360, London: Incomes Data Services

IDS (1988a) "Flexible Working", in *Income Data Services Study*, No.407, London: Incomes Data Services

IDS (1988b) "Teamworking", in *Income Data Services Study*, No.419, London: Incomes Data Services

IDS, (1990) "Flexibility at Work", in *Income Data Services Study*, No.454, London: Incomes Data Services

IDS (1992) "Skill-based Pay", in *Income Data Services Study*, No.500, London: Incomes Data Services

Industrial Relations Services (1992) "British Aerospace reaches out to the 'New World'", *Industrial Relations Review and Report Employment Trends*, No. 504: 11-15

IRS (1992) NVQs 3. "The controversy: more details", in *Industrial Relations Services*, Recruitment and Development Report No.26: 15-16

Jarvis V. and Prais S., (1989) "Two nations of shopkeepers: training for retailing in France and Britain", in *National Institute of Economic Review*, May

Jones B. and Scott P., (1988) "Occupational Structure and Vocational Training Provision In the Metalworking Industry in The United Kingdom", A report for CEDEFOP project on Comparability of Vocational Training Qualifications in European Community Member States, unpublished, University of Bath

Kelleher M., (1993) *Skill Shortages and Work reorganisation in British manufacturing*, Unpublished PhD Thesis, University of Bath

Kern H. and Schumann M., (1987) "Limits of the Division of Labour", in *Economic and Industrial Democracy*, vol 8, no 2: 151-170

Kinnie N., (1992) From IR to HR? Change and continuity in industrial relations- a longitudinal case, paper given to ERU Conference- The Challenge of Change: The Theory and Practice of Organisational Transformations, Cardiff Business School, September 1992

Lane C., (1988) 'Industrial Change in Europe: The Pursuit of Flexible Specialisation in Britain and West Germany', *Work Employment and Society*, Vol.2., No.2, June, pp141-168

Lane C., (1989) *Management and Labour in Europe: The Industrial Enterprise in Germany, Britain and France*, Aldershot: Edward Elgar

NCVQ (1992) *Manufacturing: Level 2 & Level 3*, London: National Council for Vocational Qualifications

NCVQ (1992a) *The NVQ Monitor*, London, National Council for Vocational Qualifications

Penn R., (1984) *Skilled Workers in the Class Structure*, Cambridge: Cambridge University Press

Penn R., (1990) *Class, Power and Technology*, Cambridge: Polity Press

Piore M. and Sabel C., (1984) *The Second Industrial Divide: Possibilities for Prosperity*, New York: Basic Books

Pollert, A. (1988) "The 'flexible firm': fixation or fact?", in *Work, Employment and Society*, 2: 281-316

Pollert, A. (ed.), (1990) *Farewell to Flexibility ?*, Oxford: Basil Blackwell

Prais S., (1991) "Vocational Qualifications in Britain and Europe: theory and practice", in *National Institute Economic Review*, May

Smith C., Child J., Rowlinson M., (1990) *Reshaping Work: The Cadbury Experience*, Cambridge: Cambridge University Press

Storey J. (ed) (1989) *New Perspectives on Human Resource Management*, London: Routledge

Storey J. (1992) *Developments in the Management of Human Resources*, Oxford: Blackwell

Wilkinson A., Allen P. and Snape E., (1991) "TQM and the Management of Labour", in *Employee Relations*, Vol. 13, No.1: 24-31

Notes

[1] The debate surrounding the concept of flexibility has not only been extensive but also acrimonious (see Pollert, 1988; 1990; Atkinson, 1992).

[2] I am grateful to the Science and Engineering Research Council for their financial support from 1989 to 1992. The original research for this project was towards a doctoral thesis at the University of Bath.

[3] I am grateful to Peter Cressey at the University of Bath for his comments on earlier drafts of this figure.

[4] Time-served craft workers are those who have served a recognised apprenticeship

[5] The EITB was one of the first industrial training boards in the United Kingdom to introduce modular training. It is now defunct as a result of the present government's preference for market-led training policies.

[6] This example has been taken from General National Vocational Qualifications - Manufacturing Level 2 & Level 3 (NVCQ, 1992).

[7] Although research was not conducted at the other major factory on the Bournville site, the continuing Tayloristic divisions of labour and their associated training and industrial relations approaches in that factory was mentioned by all of the respondents interviewed at the moulded factory.

Chapter Eleven

Many Small Companies under One Roof: The Production Island Principle at Felten & Guilleaume

Ludger Deitmer and
Uwe Köster

Introduction

The case study describes a comprehensive renewal process of nation-wide importance at a middle-sized North-German manufacturing company as it occurred during the eighties and continues to develop today. The central focus of this project was not only the conceptualisation and installation of new manufacturing technology, but to support the company in achieving greater efficiency through complete organisational renewal. The key element in this process was the qualification programme. A learning organisation was achieved in which functional learning took place leading to a growth in the self-esteem of employees about their own abilities and motivation. Through organisational renewal the company made further developments to the concept of Islands. These were introduced throughout production and administration.

The factory had to be redesigned, and the organisation reshaped towards a down-sized and de-layered hierarchy. The positive results obtained from this process, and the difficulties inherent in the process of change, have shown that such reorganisation measures must be well structured. The changes can be made attractive for the employees by offering them new award systems and a motivating workplace within the new organisational structure.

The conventional approach is heavily segmented by function: when a set of duties has been completed they are passed on to the next group. In the new concept these factors are replaced by decentralisation which ensures that power is shifted out from the centre and moves downwards. Power shifts to the "front line troops", which can generate the awareness of issues and create solutions necessary for company's survival into the next decade. This requires a wide range of competence on the part of management as management will be regarded as the in-house "change agents" and coaches. In this company such a team was available, involving a range of employees from production engineering officials to comprehensive training professionals working near the workplace.

This chapter will cover some basic principles of learning organisations. It will also present some guidelines for work-based learning programmes. Major obstacles in the process of change will be highlighted and also strategies to counteract them.

Felten & Guilleaume: A Medium-Sized Enterprise

The Nordenham plant of Felten & Guilleaume Energietechnik AG (a power engineering company) manufactures the following range of products:

- approximately 20 basic types of special electric motors (e.g. explosion-proof), in more than 5000 different models; batch sizes range from 1 to 5;
- a number of basic accessory types, including 2,500 different models, such as connecting elements for cables, power distribution equipment for apartment blocks; batch sizes range from 10-200 (100 on average);
- small switchgear, approximately 300 models, with batch sizes ranging from 5,000-2,000,000.

Today, Felten & Guilleaume consists of three "independent" factories producing electric motors, accessories and switchgears. The reorganisation process at Felten & Guilleaume has been completed. Between 60 and 70 partly autonomous assembly, production and administration islands have been established across all these three divisions. Metal part production, which deals with around 5000 items and 150 item-families, has been arranged into 10 Production Islands. These Islands are run as profit centres and may be described as small companies.

Weaknesses of the Old Factory Concept: Excess Information and Organisational Chaos

At the beginning of the 1980s, the Nordenham factory was making substantial losses, despite considerable investment in automation technology.

The studies conducted by the company (1) showed that the recession, which at that time was already beginning to be felt, was not to blame for this difficult situation. The market itself had undergone changes which the company's internal organisation had not been designed to cope. The move from a "seller's market" to a "buyer's market" meant that higher quality, greater product variability, and shorter delivery times were demanded from Felten & Guilleaume and its products.

The following economic and organisational weak points were identified in the studies:

- terms of delivery were not adequately met;
- there was insufficient flexibility with regard to types and models;
- there were problems relating to the quality of production, high wastage and performance guarantee costs;
- too much capital was tied up due to overstocking;
- there was insufficient motivation of staff;
- co-operation and communication was assessed to be inadequate;
- there was too much need for management and co-ordination;
- shop-floor personnel had little opportunity to develop their own skills;
- there was little trust of the management;
- there was a lack of confidence in personnel by management.

All these factors accounted for the plant's failure to cover its own operating costs. A structure was therefore needed that could cope better with changing market demands and make production profitable.

The previous organisational structure at Felten & Guilleaume was characterised by the following features:

Factory organisation was based on volume growth
Production was planned, controlled and monitored by numerous planning specialists, with the result that an increasing number of variation in products led to difficulties with planning times. A large number of people were working on an indirect level, so pre-planning was very extensive.

Factory organisation was based on the workshop principle
The various machines stood in separate groups and rooms for turning, milling, punching, etc. This resulted in a complex system for communication and co-operation which turned out to be very time-consuming, susceptible to faults and breakdowns. It was difficult to control in the face of frequent and rapid changes in orders.

Tasks were broken down into their constituent elements
Factory organisation was such that production in any one section did not bear any obvious relation to a completed product. The workers did not know the purpose of what they were producing. Any incoming order was split up by the planning department into the constituent activities involved in producing the desired result. These were then distributed to separate production areas scattered across the factory premises in such a way that each worker had only a very restricted and repetitive part of the overall task to perform.

The management system was based on the principle of planning, steering and control
The upgrading and updating of machinery and technology was seen as first priority. There was little trust in peoples' abilities, therefore the tight definition of working places as well as their control-system was given great importance. Middle-managers regarded themselves as "cops" not "coaches".

This kind of factory organisation made it very difficult for Felten & Guilleaume (Fig.1) to see its production processes in their entirety. This led in turn to a growth in the amount of planning, controlling and monitoring work carried out by the planning and coordination departments. At the production level, employees had little opportunity to make any decisions, to develop or to improve their qualifications. This kind of factory organisation was not motivating for shop-floor workers.

Other negative aspects of the old organisation according to the studies were as follows:

- cooperation was assessed as bad, there was a tendency towards greater individualism among shop-floor workers, this could be seen, for example, in their withdrawal into private activities, such as active involvement in clubs and associations, etc;

- little demand for theoretical knowledge at the production level; For example when breakdowns occurred or when maintenance work needed carrying out, specialists normally had to be called in;
- relations between shop-floor workers and their foremen or planning specialists were strained;
- talking amongst colleagues was barely possible on account of the individual workload;
- work at shop-floor level was judged to be monotonous;
- there was either no job rotation, or only very little as the organisation of production barely permitted it;
- the sequence in which orders are worked through could not be decided by the individual.

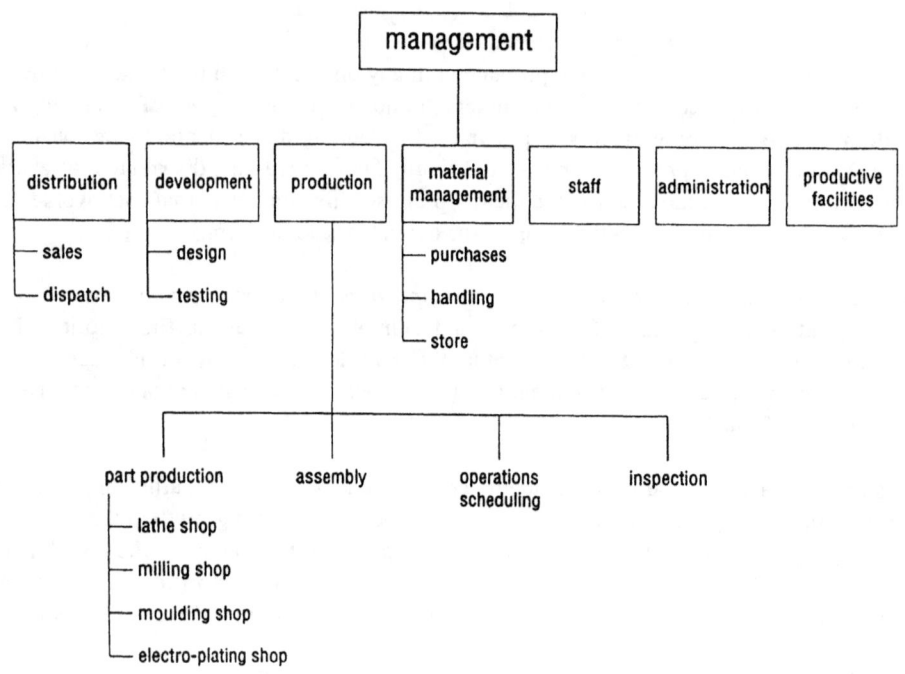

Figure 1.*Traditional departmentally-oriented organisational structure*

Aims and Basic Considerations for the New Company

The comprehensive analysis of Felten & Guilleaume's operations (Fig.2) quickly made all those involved realise that the renewal process at the factory could not be accomplished without radical changes in the company organisation and systems. The following objectives were central to change:

- Improving the effectiveness and efficiency of the company:
    - optimising the flow of information and material; reducing throughput time;
    - greater flexibility in the production process;
    - limiting the range of parts produced;
    - improving order-processing and delivery times;
    - reducing stocks and the amount of circulating capital;
    - reducing transport and energy costs.

- Improving the attractiveness of jobs (especially at the production and assembly levels):
    - investment in the training of staff to enable them to supervise themselves; and to acquire the knowledge required for more self-regulated factory production work;
    - more confidence in the self-regulating mechanism operating among groups of people;
    - increasing job satisfaction by providing jobs needing higher skill-profiles.

In devising a concept to meet these requirements, it became apparent that the objectives could only be achieved by a solution involving all departments within the company. Two alternative strategies were discussed:

- attempting to remedy the deficiencies through further automation, and by introducing flexible production cells and powerful computer aids;
- deciding in favour of comprehensive reorganisation, ignoring Taylorist principles and re-integrating knowledge into the production process. The whole concept would be carried out by a an "HRD-Human Resource Development Strategy" in which the qualifications of the staff plays an essential role.

In spite of the general euphoria over CIM prevalent at that time, i.e. the idea of achieving new production objectives through the use of fully automated technology, the decision was taken to concentrate on organisational renewal and further training. Various attempts at automation at Felten & Guilleaume during the 1970s had proved the ineffectiveness of these systems because of the greater and more complex demands of everyday production, and the considerable inflexibility caused by these systems. Finally, Felten & Guilleaume recognised that the workshop production principle with its rigid division of labour was the root cause of the problems that were making the factory unprofitable.

The reader should not misunderstood this decision. The CIM concepts at that time were quite complex, and their cost-intensive layout was more suited to the needs of large scale producers. Felten & Guilleaume recognised quite early that this concept did not suit their needs. They found out that the CIM factory model was based on a strong division of work. Nowadays more user-oriented CIM-systems are available on the market. They are based on standardised computer blocks and their Open Architecture offers the possibility for more integrated and flexible computer-aided and integrated production (CAIM).

The strategy for implementing the new organisational principle at Felten & Guilleaume was characterised by the following steps.

Preliminary Test Phase

The execution of the preliminary phase consisted of planning, installing and testing two model islands in the metal parts manufacturing section, with the aim of comparing the old and the new organisation. The idea of this step-by-step approach was to test the new Island concept and to show its practicability. It was intended to demonstrate to the factory personnel, especially the sceptical middle management, that the use of model islands would create a sustainable advantage for productivity and for human related aspects. The project team wanted to find the critical factors for the change-process.

Main Phase

At the beginning of the main phase of the project the Island principle was to be implemented throughout the factory, within production, sales, administration, and development and design:

- planning and installing the production islands:
    - arranging items into families;
    - forming processing families;
    - allocating the available machines to item and processing families;
    - combining item families and machines to form Production Islands;
    - designing factory and Island layout;
    - devising schedules appropriate to working in Islands, and training staff accordingly;
- backing up the production islands by introducing complementary structures within administration ("administration islands");
- introducing computer aids adapted to the new organisation;
- developing and implementing a programme for training staff.

Tests with model Islands at Felten & Guilleaume led to positive interim results as regards humanisation and the efficiency of the new work practice:

Production Personnel
The staff involved in production were granted much more scope for decision-making at the workplace. It was possible to have variation in the work. This allowed workers to switch between tasks involving different stress levels.

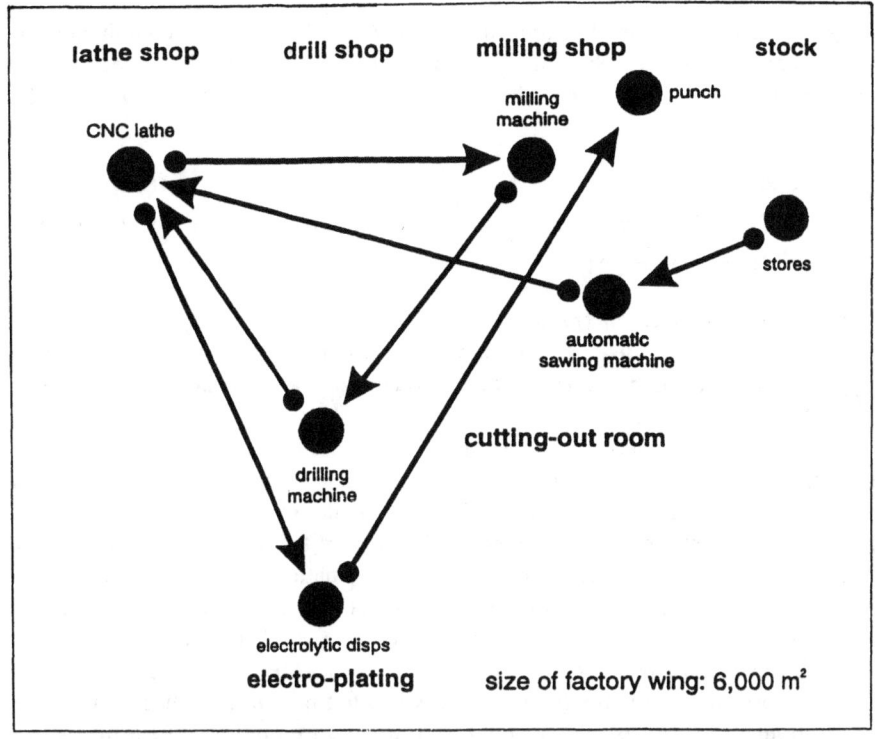
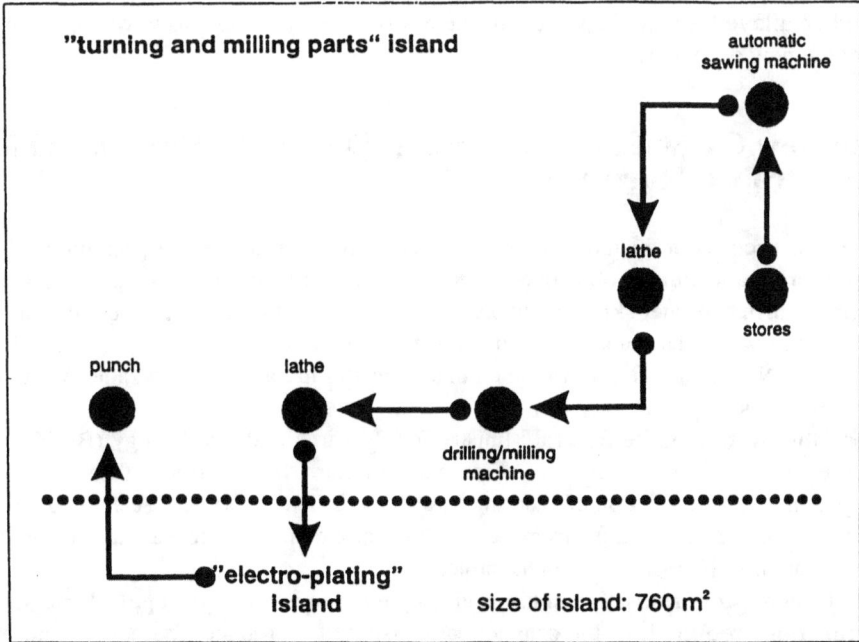

Figure 2. *Comparison between old and new systems for producing moulded cable-shoes*

Flow of Information
Through the simplification of information pathways, all data relevant to production are more easily accessed in situ. Support for written communication by direct face-to-face communication in the Islands contributes significantly to improved and confident decision-making.

Space Requirements
Reduction of interim storage, and the amount of transportation equipment needed, led to a reduction in space requirements.

Material Flow / Throughput Times
The material flow was disected and re-organised along simpler lines. A random sample analysis of new throughput times showed a reduction of between 20% and 50% throughout the new Island-based organisation.

In addition to the teaching of separate production teams (factory manager; work preparation; "Meister") about the organisational changes, and the active involvement of foremen and tool-setters in the design of the two model Islands, the actual island workers themselves (both skilled and unskilled workers) were taught about the organisation and operation of island production. But so far no systematic training measures based on an elaborated training concept were carried out. It soon became clear that there was a need for a conceptual framework for the training programme (which includes involving training experts) if the change-process was to be company-wide. Meanwhile the factory employees had the opportunity to see the Island in reality and to find out from those employed on the Islands about the changes which would later affect all employees. Fear of the unknown could be allayed, but at the same time there was growing anxiety as to whether one could meet the new demands.

The New Organisational Concept: Flatter Hierarchies and More Decentralised Structures

Given the success of the model islands (Fig.3) during the test phase, especially with regard to economic and human objectives (shorter throughput times; more scope for production work requiring greater skill and involvement; less stress through higher quality of work), the attempt was then made to implement the new organisational principle throughout the company. Nevertheless, innovation on this scale still involved considerable financial and personal risks.

In this situation, the Federal Ministry for Research and Technology (BMFT, Bonn) decided to become involved in some parts of the overall project through its R&D programme "Humanisation of Working Life" (now called "Work and Technology"). In the light of the experience gained from the test phase special importance was attached to training when planning the main phase of the project.

The consistent realisation of the island organisation involves the optimal integration of all functions required for the complete processing of a product. The new organisational structure including a human resource development approach, followed a branch-based concept. Each branch (at Nordenham these are: electric motors, accessories, and switchgear) deals on its own with all stages involved in processing orders. The island principle thus constitutes the basic pattern according to which the new organisation is shaped. Therefore each branch is comprised of a number of production and assembly Islands.

Islands can be seen as self-supporting steering units. Through the structural design of work the production goals can be better attained. The internal design can vary considerably. In series production the tasks performed by the island personnel are concentrated to a greater extent on process-related activities, whereas in single unit production the main emphasis is on product-related aspects. The latter type of Island requires high skills on the shop floor, autonomous order scheduling and in general much more intensive participation of the shop-floor personnel in the production process. Many human-related investment tasks from the management side have to be used. In-house qualification and organisational development plays an important activity in this concept. The first island type i.e. "series production type" has a stronger tendency towards machine-intensive investment and to shop-floor level specialisation. The production process is not so work-intensive; the workplace can decline because it can be automated. As explained above this island type did not feature at Felten & Guilleaume.

Thus not only had production islands to be installed, but the administration also required restructuring (Lingemann, H.F.; Theerkorn, U. 1987). The administration Islands for each branch are "development and design", "production", "logistics", "administration" and "sales". Here islands can take the shape of institutionalised, regular and co-ordinated meetings. According to the principle of placing everybody and everything within easy reach of each other, order managing clerk, material managing clerk and purchases work together in one room. They receive customer orders from the sales department, work out deadlines, provide material and arrange delivery. Problem solving occurs in discussion involving the people sitting around one table. Through such computer programs as sales information systems and production information systems, as well as basic and purchasing data the members have good access to information and can come more easily to an agreement.

For example when there is an incoming order with special customer needs, such as product-modification and strict delivery requirements, questions such as whether they can deliver in four weeks, will be clarified during one of the daily regular meetings. Equipped with computer support and telephone, stock questions, such as whether the production island has enough time to complete orders, as well as design will be resolved by dialogue with the island spokespersons.

Through the Felten & Guilleaume approach, administrative boundaries were removed by handling the administrative task, which includes designing, development, logistic and general administration, in a more communicative manner. Before the factory reform, described herein, took place an order was handled in a 'functional kind of way'. The order was processed from each administrative sub-department to the next separately. This caused long processing times as well as errors and misunderstanding. Nowadays more effective order-processing can take place through better planning at the production island level- by means of the above described coordinated meetings- together with the participation of all the relevant experts from the administrative departments and with representatives from the production departments.

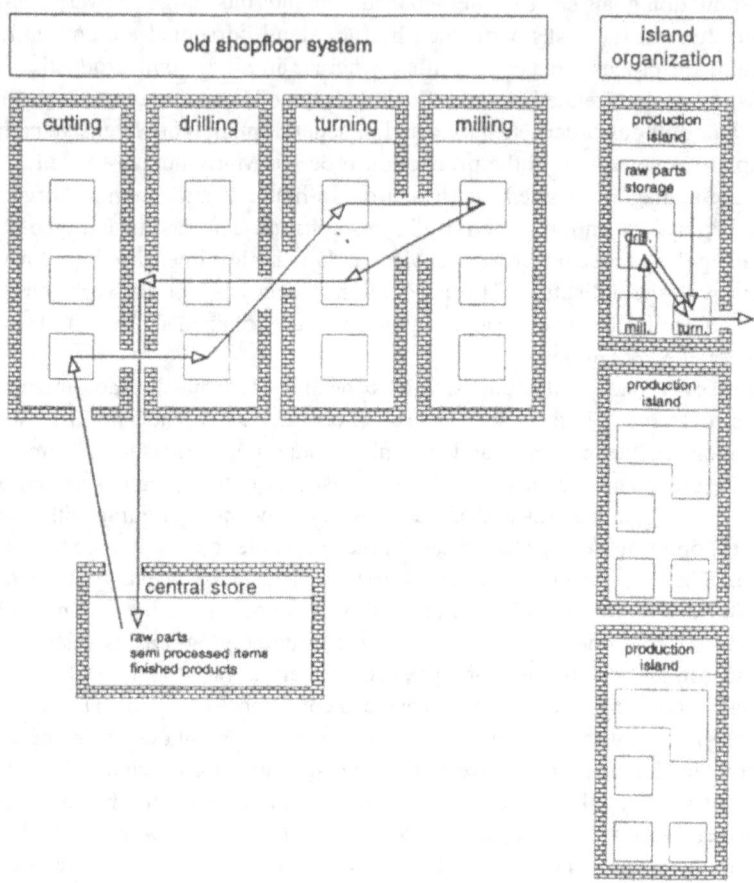

Figure 3. *The layout differences between the old and new system*

Thus the boundaries between administrative and productive tasks and responsibilities have been usefully weakened. A new balance between direct and indirect production levels was the result of this organisational development. While production islands take over more planning tasks, the administrative function does much less micro-planning and more long-term, strategic planning. For this method of production, overlapping knowledge is necessary: the administrative side must know more about the tasks of production as well as vice versa.

This total renewal of the production process affected the entire factory organisation and led to radical changes at production level. In the following, we discuss the new skill-profile that is now required among production workers.

New Roles and Responsibilities of Workers in the Production Islands

The tasks for which shop-floor workers in the production islands are responsible comprise of the planning and production of complete products. According to the principle of group technology, families of similar product elements are organised as far as possible through the spatial and organisational grouping of production facilities and skills within the islands. In contrast to the workplace situation before commencement of the project, the skilled worker now bears greater responsibility, being also responsible for planning, disposition and monitoring tasks in addition to the actual execution of the phases of the work. These tasks were removed from the planning level/department within the company and allocated instead to the production islands. The tight system of regulation and control in the factory organisation as it existed previously was dismantled, so that one can now speak of autonomous control within the Islands. The Islands generally comprise of 5-8 people with qualifications ranging from tool-setters (skilled workers who have received special training) to workers without special skills or training.

Production and administration Islands (Fig.4) are connected to each other by a bi-directional information flow, not by one-directional instructions. Preliminary planning occurs at regular intervals, involving both logistic and production group leaders. During these meetings two-week-long rough scheduling is done. The island leader has to clear these schedules with all the staff in the island before signing the schedules. Detailed planning is up to the island staff themselves. The production information system facilitates the scheduling of the island staff, giving an overview of delivery dates and priorities. Each Island has at its disposal the necessary stock of material as well as the tools and appliances required for the production of the particular items. Work-scheduling is not done in the Island. This includes programming the CNC-machines. Felten & Guilleaume seeks to enable the island teams to have direct access to design departments.

Considerable difficulties were initially experienced at Felten & Guilleaume when trying to achieve the objective of self-regulating and competent Islands, with independent planning and production within each island as if it were itself a small factory. Some employees were very deficient in certain skills and experience. They were not capable of taking over planning and monitoring functions within the islands with their existing skills and experience.

As long as such deficiencies continued to exist, some of the planning and disposition activity had to be carried out at the planning level within the company. A major barrier had to be overcome here in changing from the old way of doing things to the new island-based organisation. People at the planning level had previously understood their work to be producing guidelines, regulations and instructions. This task-allocation left those performing such orders with minimal scope for action. Those with the least room for manoeuvre were engaged directly in the mass production area. Their tasks were restricted to the receipt of production materials, production documents and orders from the foreman. All planning skills, including the installation and adjustment of the machines, were the responsibility of the foreman, departments elsewhere along the production chain, or in administration departments.

The New Motto: Talking to and Learning from Each Other: the Skills Profile in the Islands

The integration of planning and production meant that there was now a great need within the company for higher qualifications and preparation of employees for the new situation of working in islands. Whether or not the new organisational structure could survive on a permanent basis depended on the success of the training measures for island workers.

The introduction of group-work in the Islands was beneficial. Different qualification-levels of island staff promoted organisational development and learning processes essential for the new organisation (the principle of "talking to and learning from each other"), promoting the balancing out of the differences. Planning, disposition and work-preparation of task-elements were all brought back into the Island domain.

The employees on the shop-floor level took over the following tasks during operation in production islands:

- autonomous decision-making on order-scheduling within the two week period;
- micro-planning of the order of activities;
- optimising the production process through integrated order processing;
- management of material;
- part of the administrative work;
- CNC programming;
- quality assurance;
- maintenance;
- coordination with other Islands specifically with logistics.

These tasks were to be integrated successively as responsibilities of the Island according to the rising competencies available in the Island.

The work in each island has the character of a "holistic" task in which the principle of the entirety of planning, steering, production and control is enacted. The principle veers very much towards group-work. Instead of isolated work, group-related production takes place. The need for co-operation and consultation during the work-process has to be learned.

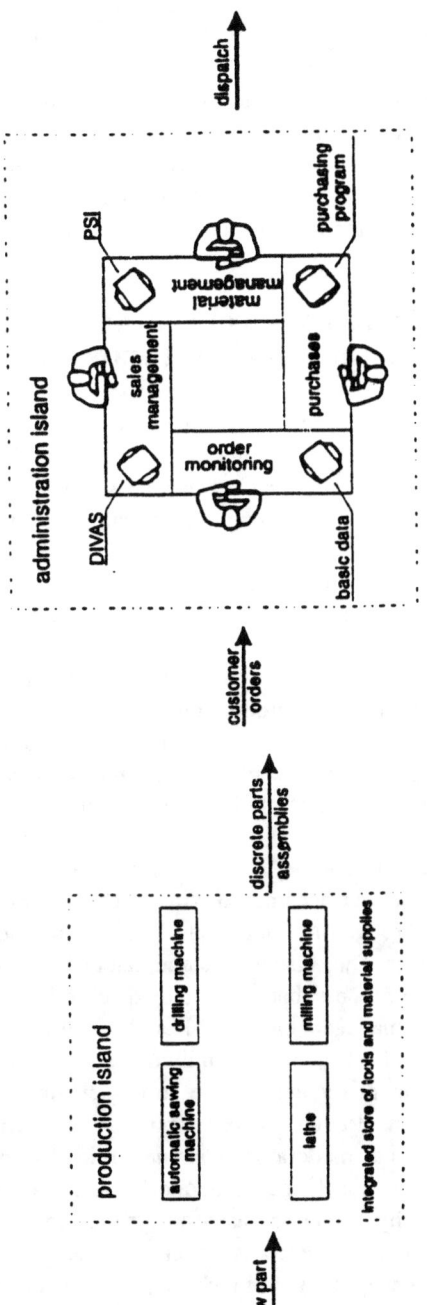

Figure 4. *Examples of a typical production island and an administrative island*

Regular participation in training measures was required before individual group members could expand their scope for action, from the simple execution of a single operation according to instructions issued by a foreman, to the self-regulated management of work-planning, production and monitoring in the manufacture of complete parts or subassemblies. The Human Resource Development Strategy, particularly in the form of specific in-company training and personnel development programmes, became the strategic factor determining whether the new market-oriented and management-oriented organisational structure, the creation of Islands in administration and production (Figure.5) could be successfully established in the factory on a lasting basis.

Middle Management Situation - from an Administrative Control Function Towards Moderation of The Innovation Process

The internal staff department (VTN) responsible for the establishment of the project made a central mistake in the starting phase. They did not integrate the middle management - here regarded as foremen, 'masters" etc. - into the change process because of the lack of close communication and dialogue with them. Through consultation and information about the project ideas, there was the opportunity to make them the sponsors of the project. This missing communication strategy created an indifferent and cynical position. Their point of view could also have been a negative influence upon the shop-floor employees.

When following the former production principle, middle management was an important intermediary between direct and indirect production. Through their leadership they carried out important co-ordination and kept the production process going. Between direct and indirect production areas they acted as a "buffer". However, changes in the market domain led to the increasing complexity of problem solving which middle management had to carry out. This resulted in an increase of uncertainty in decision making. It also led to conflicts with the shop floor.

It was in this conflict situation that the island project began to be established. Some middle-management representatives became convinced of the new philosophy. They understood quite quickly that through the delegation of trust to the shop floor they gained more room for their own activities. They also understood that their role was much more that of moderators of the production-process than holders of specific professional knowledge-holders. In other words, middle managers must enable and encourage workers on the shop floor to become independent and self-confident individuals in the work process. At this point the internal staff department recognised the strategic importance of the middle management. Through close consultation it became possible to "define" their new role: moving from a "master" towards a "moderator". This new role also implied the ability to coach other people. This role of "coach and moderator" was in contradiction to the old command-and-control philosophy, which is based on a rigid hierarchy and the implicit assumption that the purpose of management was "to tell other people what to do and make sure they did it". In the new concept they do much more rough scheduling: they help to schedule and to handle the processing of big orders. They were also responsible for the arrangement and coordination of innovation processes on the shop-floor level.

This new role also required a new qualification profile which imparts specific vocational and basic competencies. Therefore the company-wide qualification concept had to integrate middle-management and to qualify it also from a technical and social standpoint. Only after integrating this company level into the concept, could necessary support and dynamic development be gained. At Felten & Guilleaume some of the masters became promoters of the project goals.

Finally, not only top management supported the project right from the beginning, they also had to learn their lesson regarding the shift in the management style from that of direction towards co-operation.

How Were Shop Stewards to Behave in the Change Process?

The Felten & Guilleaume shop stewards were intensively involved in the on-going change process (IG-Metall 1989). At the beginning of the project they arranged a companywide contract, and agreed on the execution of the quality-of-working life project as follows:

- giving guarantees to the employees for improving the working places;
- all decisions between stewards and management have to be accepted by every partner;
- participation of all company levels in the process;
- the experience and results must be open to other companies.

As the project organisation diagram (Fig.5) shows it was agreed to set up a steering committee. The task of the committee was to control the execution of the project within an agreed framework which included some of the following themes:

- agreement on the company-specific qualification programme;
- discussion on the factory layout;
- feedback control on on-going changes in the work place.

As well as normal contradictions of industrial relations, the cooperative work offered the possibility of more open dialogue. With this structure both partners departed from the juridical framework based on the German Industrial Relations Act. The work of shop stewards changed from a more reactive form to a "co-management" role. This role showed a great civil courage on the part of the shop stewards. The position of the stewards was quoted as being a strong position. The management said: "We were very lucky to have such strong shop stewards in the company, we managed the conflicts during the change process much better." The shop stewards themselves were able to have access to consultancy from their Union. In this case it was the central department for automation and technology which gave them an up-to-date-information about the debate on different, valuable production concepts. This debate, including specific training courses on the role of shop-stewards in the rationalisation processes, made it much easier for them to reach decisions.

It can be said that the large acceptance among the employees at Felten & Guilleaume of the island concept and their successful participation in the shaping of the project, was very much supported through the active role of the works council.

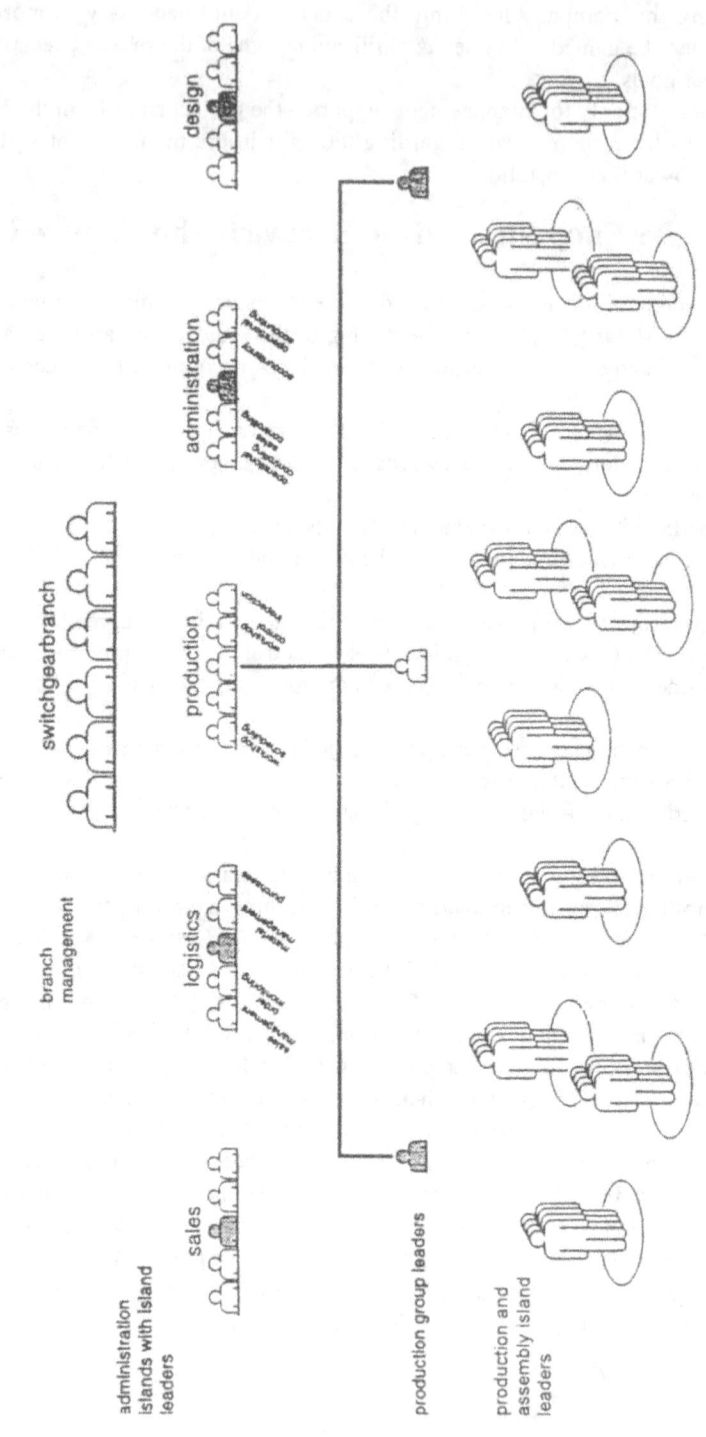

Figure 5. *The new organisational structure*

Technology Should Support - Not Replace

The decentralising of operations meant that the software applications in the computer-aided information systems also had to be structured according to the same principle. Because this process can only occur step by step, the CAD/CAM system installed at Felten & Guilleaume was based on an Open Systems architecture. This Open System could take into account the specific nature of processes within the separate islands, and provide effective support in executing them.

The interfaces within information and material flows that resulted from this division of labour were reduced to an absolute minimum through the introduction of Islands. Deterministic fine planning, in which all production orders had to be planned with considerable effort, now became superfluous. Planning was now the concern of the Islands, whose members now know when and how production orders are to be processed, with the objective of meeting the planned delivery dates and order volume.

Information is an essential ingredient if the island is to achieve this freedom and be able to make full use of the new scope it provides. Information which arises from discrete processes and is important for the subsequent organisation of production within the Island is now processed on the spot. This includes the generation of CNC programs. There is also the possibility of the islands doing such programming themselves. One of the requirements relating to the design of electronic data processing systems was that the production-specific density and complexity of information had to remain transparent to and changeable by the staff within an island. The separate islands had to have guaranteed access to all data relating to materials, processes and timing if they were to actively shape the organisation of work in their own areas.

A more open CAD/CAM system was developed during this project at Felten & Guilleaume, so that programming knowledge could be utilised within the islands for small batch sizes, as well as for optimising programs in use. Thus each production island can also be understood as a feedback instrument for the work of the development and design department.

In the further course of reorganisation at Felten & Guilleaume, especially the continuing trend towards smaller batch sizes and the production of product variants, programming is increasingly carried out within the Islands. The administration islands have access to the programs they require, namely:

- CAD systems (BRAVO, Applicon);
- central database containing all relevant data;
- information systems for calculations, ordering and order processing (FSI);
- CNC programming systems;
- CAD/CAM links;
- information system for purchasing department (DIVAS).

Felten & Guilleaume has demonstrated clearly that new directions in the design of computer systems can be taken in connection with the separation of functions and new forms of interaction between human and machine. Such computer systems are to be designed in such a way that they provide optimal support to, rather than acting as a replacement for skilled work in the Islands.

The Work-Oriented Training Programme

Considerable emphasis was placed from the start on the training programme (Koschnitzke and Köster, 1989). Suitable training is an important element in the overall reorganisation of the factory. The project team, which also included two teachers who worked as staff pedagogical experts, from local higher education schools, made particular use of experience gained in other companies.

The project was also concerned with the re-design of existing tasks and responsibilities within the organisation, an objective that was equal in importance to the planned restructuring in the technical-organisational field. Training was intended to supply the technical and social competence that employees needed within the changed organisation. Decisions relating to curriculum design had to take into account a number of conditions:

1. Because restructuring could only be implemented on a step-by-step basis, the training programme had to be very flexible in design.
2. Behavioural traits inherited from the previous organisation had to be taken into account in the design of training courses.
3. The direct dependence and interaction between the factory as a place of action and a place for learning had to be taken into account during the planning phase.
4. A training concept must integrate all training activities within the plant and ensure their usefulness for objectives that are themselves undergoing a dynamic process of change.
5. The participants in training courses must also be able to take an active role in shaping training, analogously to the new demands placed on them in the work process.
6. The problem of transfer requires the integration of trainers into the daily operation of the factory.

The objectives and function of training were derived from the objectives of the project itself, and can be described as follows:

- At the production level (production island) employees had to:
    - perform virtually all tasks arising in the island;
    - take over planning activities (planning of schedules, machine utilisation materials planning);
    - control functions (monitoring of production schedules, deployment of personnel, quality assurance).

- At administration level (administration island) employees had to:
    - concentrate at one integrated workplace combining several procedures previously subject to division of labour;
    - cooperate on an equal level with production islands (product-oriented).

Fundamental Aspects of the Training Programme

The content of the training programme were not confined to specific technical vocational training, but also included so-called "key qualifications", such as planning, decision-making and working in a team (Mertens 1974). The general objectives of the training programme were comprised of the following key elements:

- increasing work-based skills;
- increasing social competence - understood as new communicative and cooperative skills;
- increasing competence for action.

The two trainers planned and implemented the training concept and the actual training courses. This was necessary because the factory did not possess appropriate personnel who could be released for this task. Combining planning and execution corresponded to the guiding principle behind the project. The trainers had the task of implementing the training activities in coordination and cooperation with the project team, the works council and the factory management. They did not act in the capacity of external planners, but instead were integrated into the factory operations.

One general training objective was that employees should acquire the ability of coping with all tasks within an island independently and with assurance. Furthermore course participants should obtain an overview of their particular field, should acquire the ability to shape and act, and should improve their ability to cooperate and to successfully resolve conflicts that arise.

This last point showed the necessity, of developing the social competencies for self-regulative action within the new organisational concept. Not only was it important to develop practical and cognitive skills in a work-based context, it was equally important to improve "personality" and motivation. The table below of Required competence profiles (Figure 6) shows the meaning of a broad concept of competence development. The concept envisaged training at two locations:

- work-related learning in "learning circles" situated close to production;
- theoretical and practical training in the training centre at the factory.

Both elements were intended to mutually influence each other, and were organised accordingly as interlocking units. The work-based/related training elements in the "learning circles" constituted action-oriented training. The workers had to learn how to act in an innovative way in the production island. They had to learn how to make improvements during their work.

The theoretical training was necessary to broaden general competence-level on the shop floor. The project team found out that some unskilled people urgently needed specific knowledge in fields such as metalwork, CNC, quality guarantee, pneumatics, electric machine building, etc. The course included introductory basic learning elements such as mathematics and German in which especially some of the workers had great deficiencies. For example the period required for basic training Metal I took 320 hours; 80 hours were needed for general knowledge, German, geometry etc.; 120 hours for special elementary knowledge like the principle of a CNC lathe; 120 hours for special skills such as how to handle programs, and control CNC lathes.

Personal	Cognitive/methodical	Communicative
Readiness and ability to develop oneself	Independence and responsibility at work and for learning	Ability to learn and work in groups
Personal characteristic ability:	*Task-oriented ability:*	*Ability to communicate:*
e.g. - endurance - initiative - readiness to learn and achieve - competence in morals and aesthetics	e.g. - ability to work with abstraction - transferability - network thinking - capable of development - capable of solving problems - creative thinking	e.g. - ability to cooperate - ability to resolve conflict - ability to moderate - team ability

Figure 6. *Required competence profiles (Mertens 1974)*

A series of foundation courses (e.g. Metal I and II) was envisaged in the framework for the training programme covering basic areas, supplemented by special courses such as Fundamentals of CNC Programming or Introduction to CAD/CAM. The concept was also designed in such a way that technical and organisational skills were taught. The open curriculum was specifically designed to enable a modular programme structure, transparency, appropriateness for the target groups and the possibility of making changes as time went on. The participants were to have the opportunity to become involved in the design of course content.

This took into account the problem of transfer. The level and complexity of open curricula means that they can only be developed over many years according to the principle of "on-going reform". Realistic objectives are essential for success. From the very beginning, all those involved should be aware of the possible risks and the problems that need solving. The most important of these concern are:

1. The possibility of trainers and trainees being over-taxed.
   Are they both willing and able to accept open learning process, with all the risks it entails? Do most of the trainers possess the high degree of sensitivity for the situational needs in the respective course, and for the interests of the learners? Are trainers adequately prepared for taking into consideration general issues that affect the company? Are learners able to articulate their interests?
2. No teaching to take place that cannot be subjected to systematic evaluation.
3. Risk of insufficient learning with respect to knowledge, skills and abilities.

4. Risk of arbitrary or stereotyped regulation of the teaching process by the trainer as a result of the considerable freedom with which he can act and take decisions.

These risks should not in any case be underestimated in the effect they can have in actual practice. The team was confronted again and again by these problems in the various courses, although to differing extents. There is no ready-made solution that can be applied in all cases, but we would like to mention some principles that are useful in promoting more open dialogue and which contributed to the various participants becoming more aware of the concerns of others.

1. Clear presentation of objectives for the training measures, courses and the individual lessons.
2. Describing the significance and function of checks on learning.
3. Avoidance of "hidden pedagogics": describing the function of different training methods.
4. Integration of participants into didactic decisions.
5. Involvement of foremen and management with the content and organisation of courses.
6. Supporting the dialogue between participants and their supervisors at work about coursework and workplace problems that can arise as a result.
7. Constant reflection on the current status of the project.

The Learning Circle as an Instrument for Organisational Development

The learning circle functions as a work-place institution for group-oriented problem solving through collective learning. The learning circle involves the same people who are involved in the production island, and it takes place during the working time in the production island. The issues of these regular meetings concern technical as well as communicative/cooperative aspects. It is a platform for problem solving concerning work-related as well as personal aspects. The circle acts as an instrument for work-scheduling. It is moderated by an authorised moderator who is specially educated for this task.

The results of these group meetings are summarised in a short paper. The paper also circulated to the relevant middle management. Problem solving has to be completed in a limited time span (approximately 4 weeks) both for people in the Circle as well as the experts. Normally the group invites people (experts, managers) to discuss the problems.

Specific aims for the Circle members are:
- to be able to decide on relevant information;
- cooperative planning on schedules;
- defining organisational and competence-related needs;
- taking over responsibilities;
- decision regarding new personal needs.

There are no obligations for group participation. Firstly the education of moderators has to be part of the companies' training concept. Consequently the programme offers courses on "moderation of learning circles", later it is taken more and more as a regular principle for regulated action within the island. Every island by then has a fixed amount of hours free for their circle work. Middle management has the task of initiating the circles in its company as well as keeping them going. Management could only participate by invitation of the others, but could add their issues to the agenda of the meeting.

Participation in Needs Analysis

The needs analysis was concerned with two issues:
1. a precise analysis of training needs;
2. the description of target qualifications, i.e. the skill-profiles, that define the work situation of the future island worker.

The company had to find ways to generate substantial worker involvement in the planning, organisation and execution of training. Whereas participation had hitherto been confined to the internal organisation of courses, the issue within the project was how to enable worker participation prior to the training measures. This might seem somewhat exaggerated at first, but is in fact the logical integration of employee qualification into the training needs analysis. Only in this way can the demands of the work-place flow "unfiltered" into the planning of continuing training. If this is to succeed, the organisational structure of the company must satisfy several preconditions.

1. Employees must have access to an institutional level at which needs can be discussed and formulated (learning circle; quality circle)
2. The development of the organisational structure must include greater scope for action on the part of employees commensurate with higher qualifications
3. With fewer instructions and guidelines on positions of responsibility, greater decision-making competence in the production field must also show up qualification deficiencies
4. The pay system must reflect fairly the higher qualification levels of employees.

In practice, this participation in the determination of training needs took the form of discussions among employees about qualification deficiencies, either in the learning circles or in the weekly production meetings. The deficiencies can be in the occupational or in the social field. Once a certain requirement had been defined for production or administration, the relevant contact persons (in this case the trainers) were invited to the next learning circle meeting. Staff could then discuss with them appropriate measures for countering the identified deficiencies. In normal cases, either relevant decisions on new courses were made, or it was decided which courses had to be run again, e.g. because new employees had to be integrated into the production island as a result of staff fluctuation.

Within the following weeks, a rough sketch of the relevant continuing training scheme was produced for presentation to employees at the next possible opportunity. On the basis of this presentation, those interested in taking part entered their names in a circulated list. Circumstances in production were taken into account through talks with the production group leader or production manager. Finally, we received a list of participants in the course or courses from the area in question, and a suggestion when the course could start. Those colleagues who did not obtain a place were given an assurance that they, too, could take part in continuing training at the next possible opportunity.

Course Modular Concept: Organisation of Training and Methods

The courses provided function as discrete modules (Fig.7), or building blocks, each with a certificate of attendance. The course members can compile the continuing training programme that best meets their qualification requirements and interests from the range of training schemes on offer. This system was chosen because of the highly uneven structure of qualifications in production, where unskilled, semi-skilled and skilled workers work side-by-side. Design of training courses was based fundamentally on the learning abilities and previous experience of the participants, in such a way that knowledge already possessed was mobilised for the learning process. The participants exchanged experience in group-work and informed each other about their activities at work: reference was made here above all to other training experiences in an attempt to dismantle fears associated with learning. The principal method used was group-work (course size: 8-10 people). Practical skills were taught and practised in the teaching workshop nearby. Particular emphasis was laid on the acquisition of social skills. This meant that each unit included the development of self-confidence and social skills, in addition to the purely work-based content. Intensive recourse was made to the participation of those involved throughout the training period. The group's responsibility for the entire learning process included participation of the course members in course planning, in making conceptual changes, selecting training methods and utilisation of teaching media.

In all, courses lasted between 20 and 160 hours. The actual duration of a course depends mainly on the existing qualifications that participants have, so that more hours were planned for foreign employees, for example, and less for skilled workers. Courses were held at fortnightly intervals in the case of a 2-shift system (early and late shift), for 3 to 4 hours per week. In the case of 3-shift working, courses were held during the overlaps between individual shifts.

Start of the Implementation Phase

The first courses started in January 1985, with the main focus on metalwork. Based on the identified occupational and social requirements for coping with the tasks in the Island, planning resulted in a decision on a foundation course and a continuation course. Embedded within each foundation course is an introductory phase comprising the components:

- informing about the project;
- discussing problems at work in the factory;
- establishing mutual trust;
- dismantling existing fears associated with learning;
- enabling new experience to be gained through learning.

During this introductory phase the work-related components consisted mainly of general knowledge. The purpose here was to establish links with acquired knowledge, and in this way to ensure the foundations for work that followed.

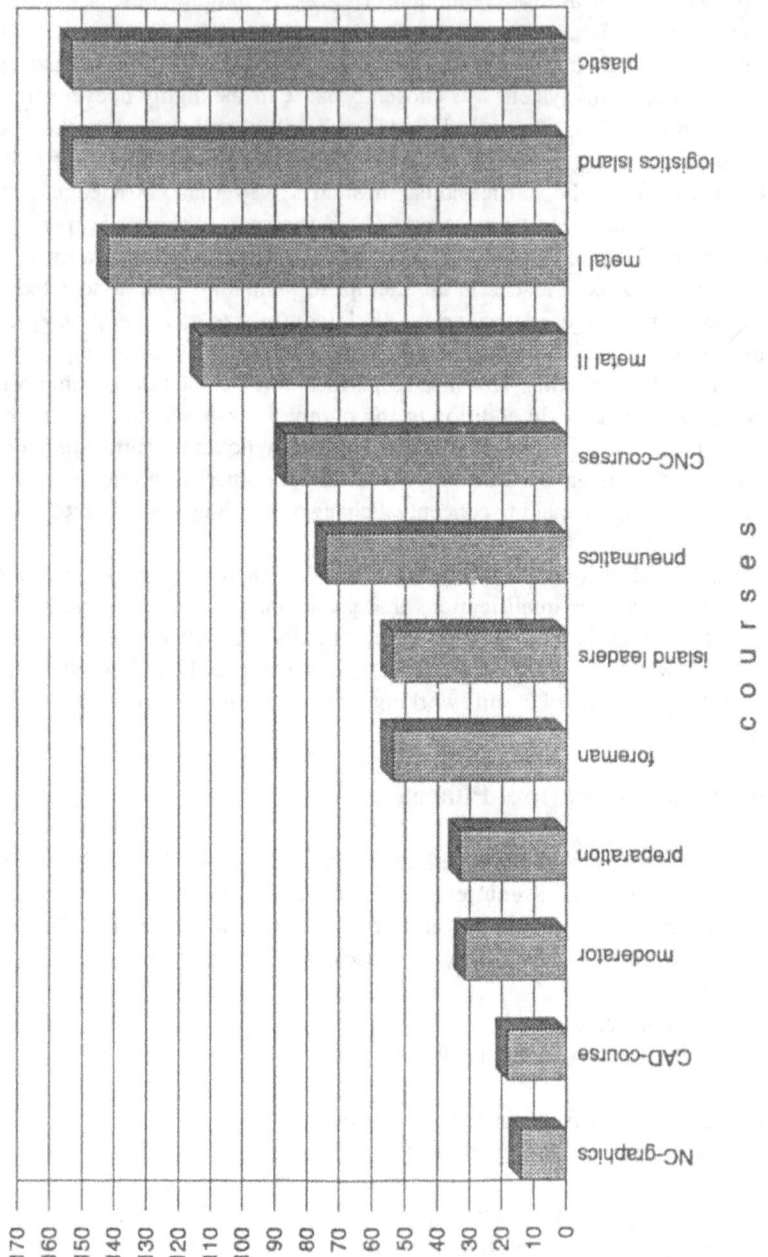

Figure 7. *Basic data on training Felten & Guilleaume 1985 - 1988*

In the main phase of the foundation courses, attention was concentrated on work-related topics. The choice of subject-matter was influenced by the tasks being performed in the island at that particular time. There was thus a clear link between training content and the current status of organisational development. It was recognised that the selected course content should also have application in practice. Guided learning was more pronounced at the beginning of the courses, but as the courses proceeded, a more interactive transfer of knowledge became increasingly significant. Besides work-related topics, interest also centred on new methods for acquiring and handling knowledge. In particular, experience was gained in self-governed and cooperative learning. In various projects, the participants themselves assumed responsibility for theoretical preparation and practical application of learning material. The trainers acted in a more consultative capacity here, providing advice with regard to problems or specialist questions when asked to do so, and less as purveyors of knowledge.

Coursework also involved, at all stages, in grappling with process-related problems encountered in the workshop. Dealing with such problems in the course provided an excellent opportunity for transferring acquired knowledge to the shop-floor level. This also gave rise constantly to ideas for corrections to course content. In the course of time, these process-related problems experienced in production became an increasingly important part of learning circle work, which was developing in parallel. This led to the learning circle increasingly formulating its own demands concerning the range of training courses on offer.

One important result of the project is the continuous co-operation of course participants with the supervisors . However, this is very difficult to realise in practice. Supervisors are primarily interested in results that comply with their view of things, and not in worker participation. This attitude is also understandable, especially if one considers the daily stress that already exists through 'normal' tasks at work. The acceptance of what are perceived as additional tasks can only be achieved in stages. But this acceptance is very important for the widespread recognition of in-company training. The experiences have shown that the support and involvement of management is also necessary to achieve this aim, not just at the end of training. Management must play a major role in supporting the development of training and in the integrating of in-company training into company structures, i.e. institutionalising it.

It was planned within the context of this project to do away with the old pay system by developing a new system that matched the organisational changes, a pay system in which individual qualification is a dynamic factor in the calculation of entitlement. In the process, qualification has become a new management instrument, and recognition of qualification is therefore essential for the smooth running of the company. Because the pay and qualification system acted as an important motivating factor for those taking advantage of training, previously existing barriers to promotion and improved wages could be broken down, especially in the industrial field. Management action also had a marked influence on the credibility of objectives, and thus on the broad acceptance among the work-force of the in-company training scheme and organisational development set in motion through the project.

The project application specifies six key qualifications that needed promoting through the planned training measures:
- ability and willingness to learn;

- capacity for creativity and innovation as regards processes and production;
- understanding new technologies;
- tolerance for the interests of others;
- self-confidence in asserting one's own interests;
- capacity and willingness to cooperate with others.

Impact on Employees and Factory Efficiency: Greater Productivity and Attractive Competence-Oriented Jobs Are Not a Contradiction

The introduction of group-work into the production islands had an impact on the workforce as follows:

Higher qualifications relating to the specific field of work
The expanded work fields that arose in the Islands demanded higher qualifications from employees. The broad-based training programme described above offered a range of in-company courses and continuing training modules, depending on the specific target group and group composition. In-company training measures, which were intimately linked to the organisational renewal of the company, were attended by a large proportion of the industrial workers directly involved in production, who went to one or more courses on offer. As a rule, successful completion of a course led to higher pay.

In addition to the expansion of competencies directly related to the individual work field, such as programming machines, assessing products or checking quality, general knowledge subjects (mathematics, German) could also be refreshed and improved. As well as the various foundation courses, there were seminars on forms of communication and cooperation of relevance to islands (courses in discussion management and team skills). Not only did these succeed in expanding occupational skills, they also improved the ability of employees to work in groups, i.e. their organisational competence could also be enlarged.

Whereas considerable persuasive skills were needed to entice the first 16 employees into courses, by 1989 there were waiting lists in all three production divisions at the Nordenham factory where employees had registered for courses to be held. The training measures have thus found broad acceptance among the work-force at Felten & Guilleaume.

Some individual employees from the various production islands have learned through training to carry out programming tasks of varying difficulty in the workshop directly or in a computer-aided workplace elsewhere in the factory. In the "drilling, turning and milling" Island, all CNC programming has been carried out by the island workers themselves since they received relevant training.

This supplied proof that specific measures for organisational renewal (Fig.8), supported by a training programme, are suitable means for reducing the time and money involved in planning and implementing innovation. Employees were able to be motivated to become much more involved in matters affecting the company.

Greater scope for action
The scope for action enjoyed by shop-floor workers went through a radical expansion during the project. All the separate tasks involved in the production of a part or sub-assembly are performed within the Island. For employees this meant that they no longer

Values and Mental Models

Before change

- cooperation and communication poor
- little trust in company
- less collective views
- minor changes on external demands
- update machinery and technology first
- planning, steering and control
- no needs analysis on production people
- lack of confidence in people

After change

- individual and group self-sufficiency
- round-table style communication
- more democratic dialogue
- constant change in external demands
- human resource development and technology
- arrangement by agreements

(Infra) Structures

Before change

- tight system with fixed processes
- explicit, complex rule system
- hierarchic
- little self-regulative action
- narrowly designed jobs
- lack of information and overview about current status of factory
- high indirect level
- direct production level well defined
- high pre-planning
- designing tight algorithm
- work-task broken down into subactivities

After change

- dealing more on its own
- integrated order processing
- more responsibilities
- self-regulation
- many small companies under one roof
- redesign of task and organisation
- smaller indirect level
- more collective approaches
- less pre-planning
- organisational/occupational structure supports the change

Learning processes and competencies

Before change

- missing knowledge in specific fields
- no learning-friendly environment
- ability to operate in well defined and stable environment
- self esteem missing
- working with closed models
- thinking in batch processing terms
- control instrument
- manager as cop

After change

- self-regulated learning
- new technical and social skills
- more demands from outside reinforce need for learning
- through communication to new organisational competencies
- new competencies on all levels
- manager as enablers
- manager as coach
- continuous learning activities
- systematic modular training

- **Shop floor system**
- **Management system**

Figure 8. *Before and after the change process at Felten & Guilleaume*

have to perform only single work steps the whole time, under pressure to observe certain regulations, but that they can plan, execute and monitor the production of the product themselves. The only data that are fixed externally are the model number, the quantity and the date for completion; otherwise, the island operates under autonomous control.

However, it must be said that the level of "autonomous control" is dependent on the skill-profiles of the island workers. If the available qualifications are not sufficient, then the tasks that the island was originally supposed to perform are then taken over by the next higher planning level in the company. In time, these islands will also succeed in operating autonomously, namely when the training measures take full effect. The speed with which the changes are carried out in the enterprise as a whole thus depends on the effectiveness and intensity of the training measures.

Communicative and cooperative behaviour in the factory was improved
Through the new structure of work within the factory, communication among and with the shop-floor workers in production was radically improved. Before the project began, workers in production did mainly piecework. This permitted communication only with the supervisor, from whom the piece-worker received his production orders. He could communicate with colleagues only during breaks. This resulted in a lack of information exchange at production level, which in turn caused high throughput times, lack of overview regarding the overall manufacturing process for a specific product. This then lead to considerable planning efforts in isolation from actual production.

The introduction of the island principle meant that communication within the factory could become more direct and open. It became obvious that this strategy could contribute significantly to the more efficient removal of all kinds of disturbances and faults. The learning circle helped to address all problems from the production field as they arose. Many production workers were thus given a chance for the first time in their working lives to discuss current problems with a colleague from the same section, especially problems within one work-step, and to devise solutions together.

One important effect identified during the project evaluation (intensive interviews before and after the project) concerned stress (HdA-Project, 1989). From the point of view of skilled workers, the feeling of stress has been greatly reduced since the introduction of production islands. Thanks to the variety of tasks performed in the islands, colleagues were able to work a job rotation system that meant alternating the demands placed on the individuals. Stress caused primarily by monotonous work and constant attention to the same task could thus be reduced.

Economic Effects

The project was very important for the company not only in personnel, but also in economic terms. The difficult economic situation described at the outset has meanwhile been improved considerably. The company is no longer 'in the red'. They have been able to increase turnover and have even recruited new staff in the meantime. The following figures demonstrate the economic success of the project:

- turnover increased by 25% over five years;

- costs reduced by 10%;
- savings in production space of approximately 40%;
- reduction of energy costs by approximately 15%;
- reduction of stocks by approximately 30%;
- release of tied-up capital - approximately 20%;
- reduction of throughput times by 60%;
- number of staff directly involved in production: increased by 7%;
- number of staff indirectly involved in production (especially planning/monitoring) reduced by 28%;
- reduction of wastage in metal parts production by approximately 71%;
- reduction of wastage in plastics production by approximately 73%.

The project resulted in a greatly improved cost-benefit ratio as well as enhanced product quality (Fig.9). An amortisation period of less than three years could thus be achieved. The economic improvements were not obtained at the expense of employees: on the contrary - employees directly involved in production have benefited most from these changes.

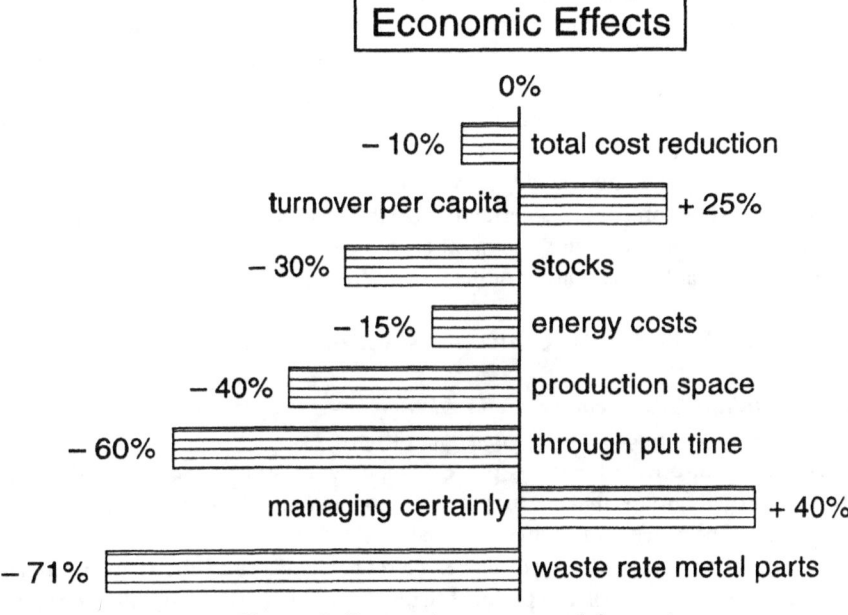

Figure 9. *Economic outcomes of the project*

Main Lessons from the Case Study

The case of the Felten & Guilleaume plant has acquired a certain degree of fame in the German-speaking countries. For the first time in Germany, a large-scale pilot scheme was implemented which involved the comprehensive introduction of production and administration islands into a medium-sized enterprise (less than 1000 staff), and with the financial support of the state through the Humanisation of Working life programme. Above all, by redistributing the planning and disposition tasks between production and administration, economic and social objectives could be achieved.

The approach taken by Felten & Guilleaume in their Nordenham factory achieved a high level of acceptance among employees. The more advanced the integration of the various status groups into the planning and implementation of the training activities, the easier it became to find solutions or compromises for the performance of their work. Of critical importance for acceptance among the work-force was the participation model involving direct integration into the planning and design of seminars by the work-force itself. This applies especially to workers at shop-floor level. All shop-floor staff who received training during the project were able to improve their position in the factory through specific improvements to their qualification levels. They are no longer confined in their thinking to a narrowly defined workplace, only capable of performing a limited range of tasks.

One critical comment that must be made is that the transfer of the experience and know-how acquired through the project into the 'normal' factory situation (i.e. without state grants) was accompanied by substantial problems. Even though all those involved had a very positive attitude to the approach that had been taken, little has actually happened since the project was completed in 1989. What followed was a phase in which the company "rested on its laurels": the implementation of such an approach at the everyday level can well lead to such stagnation after years of effort. However, the latest information from the factory is that this phase is being overcome. We are also glad to hear that the experience gained and the strategies developed during the project have become established criteria for new training measures. While these cannot be of the same order of magnitude as before, and understandably so, training activities are now being planned in response to recent developments. The approach that has already been tried out is thus becoming a 'normal' component of factory life, though with some delay.

Transfer to other companies is certainly possible, we believe, and indeed has already been carried out successfully in various other pilot projects. Some guiding rules can be established with regard to the transfer of the project concept.

Transfer of the Project Concept: Guiding Rules

1. *Change within a factory can be prepared, supported and assured in the long term by deploying the project group as an instrument in this process.*

Group and team-oriented learning processes are demonstrated excellently through the formation of project groups that are supported by top *and* middle management in initiating and maintaining the process of change. It is recommended that teams be formed under the leadership of an experienced project leader or representatives of the relevant divisions (possibly from line positions). The project schedule should envisage support from internal and external experts.

2. *The monitoring group should be established to safeguard the process of change with respect to labour law and the collective bargaining parties.*

The control group should comprise representatives of top management, the works council and the project group. Important decisions affecting the company as a whole should be taken in this body during the project and safeguarded through local collective bargaining agreements.

3. *The training programme is an instrument for preparing and implementing change.*
The company-specific training programme is designed to support change. Both technical and social competencies should be trained. One important training objective for employees should be the recognition that what is needed is 'life-long' learning.

4. *The principle of decentralised decision-making should be implemented on a systematic basis.*
Decision-making should be decentralised in order to ensure that as many employees as possible learn to take decisions independently (especially at production level). The ability to take decisions as a group should also be improved through appropriate measures.

5. *EDP and technology - computer-aided, integrated work systems.*
EDP should be understood as a tool for supporting "human resources". Through simulations, calculations and similar routines, technology should provide optimal support to people involved in the production process. "Low-tech" aids can also be taken into account to a greater extent. In addition, a standardised model for data and information should be developed for the entire factory, in which the tasks that occur in the various fields within the factory are classified and defined according to standard criteria. It should be possible for all staff to arrive at a clear and appropriate interpretation of data for the task in hand.

6. *Control over product variants by systematising product range.*
The product variety that the customer demands can be provided with a minimal number of parts and components. Production can be simplified enormously if this "building block" principle is applied to all products.

7. *Event-oriented production planning and control systems should support decentralised decision-making.*
Production planning and control must be restricted to basic data, e.g. the timely scheduling of design and development tasks and production orders with precise utilisation of capacity should provide optimal support for correct decision-making in the production islands.

8. *Step-by-step strategy.*
The change process should start in a company area where good visible results can be seen more easily. From there on, other areas should be integrated successively.

9. *Middle management involvement.*
Through close consultation and information, the middle management should be consequently involved into the project. Right from the start they should work within the project team to have an early and active start in defining their "future" role. Here are some aspects which were taken into account in designing the appropriate work-based learning programme for Felten & Guilleaume, and which can be used as guidelines for other companies.

10. *No limitation of qualification to technical issues*:
The organisational, planning and communicative competence elements should also be taken seriously.

11. *No one-off programmes.*
Qualification has to be understood as a permanent task which should be supported at difference places - in the training centre, at the workplace as well as outside the factory boundaries (technology training centres).

12. *No shock treatment.*
Introductory courses are aimed at reawakening ability and readiness to learn that often lie dormant. In this way, those who would otherwise resist learning new things, but who possess extensive experience with work and production, could be prepared for the new organisation.

13. *The training concept should be intimately linked to changes in the organisation of work.*
This created favourable conditions at Felten & Guilleaume for measuring the success of the learning programme in terms of the practical demands and the new scope for action in actual production. This had positive effects on the willingness of workers to participate in continuing training and to change behaviour.

14. *The learning concept should be task-oriented and open.*
In other words, the content of learning was related to the tasks and problems that arose through the organisational development process; the learning concept thus contained a dynamic component and was open for changing content.

15. *Immediate application of learning to practice.*
This was possible at Felten & Guilleaume because the wide range of continuing training measures was based directly on the requirements of the factory (organisational and technical changes); consistency with collective bargaining agreements was also maintained.

16. *Targeted expansion of qualification potentials.*
The system of graded modules and building blocks in continuing training was easy for unskilled workers to understand, so that each employee can pursue his or her own continuing training career within the company.

17. *Integration into the German vocational education system.*
Staff should have the opportunity to acquire formal qualifications (e.g. the "Meister" examination at the Chamber of Industry and Commerce; certificates for skilled workers), e.g. semi-skilled workers can improve their qualifications and become skilled workers with the requisite certificates, and skilled workers can improve their qualifications to a level where they can plan and perform their work independently and with a high degree of responsibility. Finally, there were some important aspects that could not be dealt with adequately at Felten & Guilleaume. However, these must be taken into account when planning and implementing change, because they can become major obstacles to progress.

18. *New management thinking and action is particularly necessary in middle management.*
The situation as experienced by middle management must be considered when organising training seminars. If "Meister" and planners are not integrated specifically into the strategy for change, projects of this kind are doomed to failure. Middle management must change its classical supervisory role to one of innovation and co-ordination. They are the persons who

do the broad scheduling by helping others to schedule. They are also responsible for the arrangement and coordination of innovation processes at the shop-floor level. They therefore need to acquire specific competencies which enable them to act as coordinators and to help out in difficult situations. Managers require specific training and guidance to prepare for their future role and tasks.

19. *Top management and works council must change their industrial relations policies to support the process of change:*

- Everyone within the factory must realise that the restructuring of the company is an ongoing and negotiated process the direction of which cannot be defined solely in terms of inherent necessities (e.g. economic).
- There must be constant efforts to achieve a consensus on aims and methods within the change process.
- The negotiation process must be open to the extent that active participation by the work-force itself is ensured. This demands considerable skill and sensitivity for social processes on the part of the project team and the control group.
- A basic agreement should be concluded in which each employee can recognise his or her future role in the factory.

These changes, as the example of Felten & Guilleaume shows, can result in higher productivity. This is not achieved through greater division of labour, but instead through qualified and holistic work that involves both mental and manual activities. Work becomes more attractive and an opportunity is created for both labour and capital to profit from it.

How the Case Study Fits into the Common Framework

Despite considerable investment in automation technology, Felten & Guilleaume continued to suffer substantial losses. Following a company review, a customer-centred focus was adopted. In order to respond to customers who were demanding individualised products, higher quality standards and shorter delivery times, the company initiated a radical change process. The human resource development strategy that underpinned this change process, meant that a massive worker-oriented learning and development programme was implemented (see Figure 10). The overall change programme received conceptual and financial backing from the German Federal Ministry for Research, becoming a pilot project in the 'Humanisation of Working Life Programme".

The new company structure meant a shift from a traditional Tayloristic approach to work organisation to one based on autonomous work groups, called "production islands". In each of these islands, "learning circles" were established as steering mechanisms for competence development. Initially the focus was on gaining workers' consensus on their learning needs as a basis for drawing up formal and informal competence development programmes. Expert learning consultants from outside the production area acted as mentors in the "learning circles". Because the learning programme was fully integrated with the organisational development programme, the changes at the level of structure and process complemented each other (see Figure 8).

Likewise the development of new competencies, such as autonomous decision making, team-work and "learning from each other", gave rise to a working atmosphere in which workers and management changed their perceptions of each other (see 3 in Fig. 10). Bottom-up change-influences became more prominent as workers' competencies and control functions increased.

Following a company review, a customer-centred focus was adopted. A massive development programme for workers was seen as the way to realise the renewed company (1^1, 1^2, 1^3)

The new company structure was based on a series of "production islands". "learning circles" were established in each of the islands. Changes at the level of process and structure complemented each other (2)

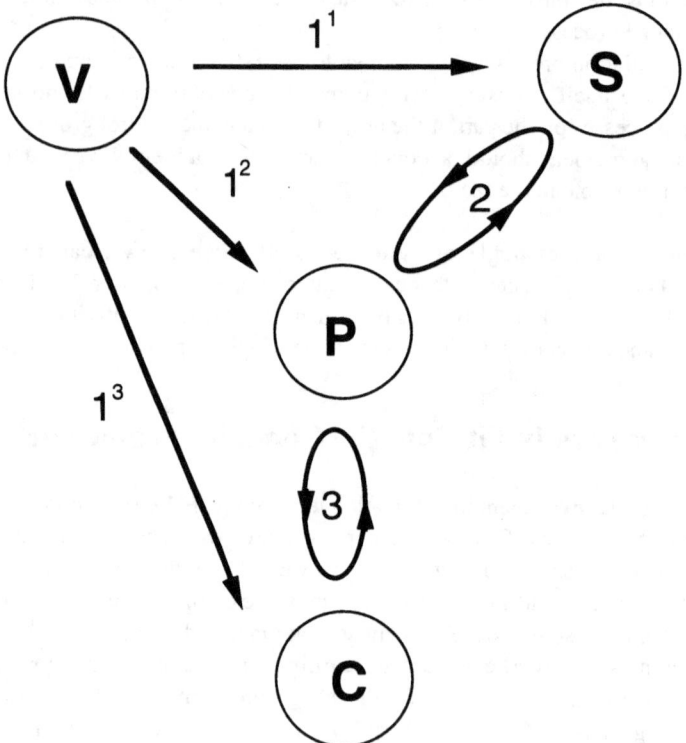

The development of workers competencies such as autonomous decision-making had an impact on how work processes were designated (3)

Figure 10. *A human resource based change process*

The final section of this chapter has examined a number of other issues in the evolution of the company change process. This was done in the overall context of drawing lessons from the case-study which could have relevance for other companies confronted with problems similar to Felten & Guilleaume.

Notes

(1) The analyses were carried out by an internal staff department ('change agent in the company') called VTN, with external scientific support, and provided the rationale for a comprehensive reorganisation project. This project was supported over various periods by the "Work and Technology" research and development programme sponsored by the Federal Minister for Research and Technology in Bonn (BMFT). This support was mainly provided between 1984 and 1989. The Project evaluation was done through a commercial consultant (Lingemann) and a work-scientist (Prof. Frieling). From there results were documented. A complete documentation of the results was produced in connection with this support (for a complete documentary see Theerkorn, U. et 1991).

References

Brödner, P. (1985), *Fabrik 2000, Alternative Entwicklungspfade in der Zukunft der Fabrik*. Berlin.

Das Dorf in der Fabrik in Wirtschaftswoche No. 15, 08.04.1988

Deitmer, L. and Heidegger, G. (1992), *Changes in Industrial Work, Technology and Education - How do they interlock?* in Veröffentlichungsreihe des ITB, FB 11, Universität Bremen.

Durcan, J., Oates, D. (1994), *The Manager as Coach - Developing your team for maximum performance*. London 1994.

Dybowski, G., Haase, P. and Rauner, F. (1993), *Berufliche Bildung und Betriebliche Organisationsentwicklung*. Bremen 1993.

HdA-Projekt - Abschlußbericht 1989.

IG-Metall, Abt. *Automation/Technologie Arbeitsorientierte Gestaltung von Arbeit & Technik bei Felten & Guilleaume, Nordenham*, Werkstattbereiche. Frankfurt, 1989.

Kernforschungszentrum Karlsruhe (PFT) Autonome Fertigungsinsel - Flexible Fertigungsstrukturen für die Einzel- und Kleinserienfertigung. Essen, 1984.

Kiehne, R. and Kohl, W. (1988), "Das Konzept der Gruppenarbeit in Fertigungsinseln bei Felten & Guilleaume", in Perspektive Gruppenarbeit, Köln.

Klingenberg, H. (1987), "Humanisation Pays - Practical Models", in Klingenberg, Heide and Kränzle, Hans-Peter, Production and Production Control, Vol.2, Eschborn.

Koschnitzke, T. and Köster, U. (1989), "Vorgehensweise und Praxisbeispiele zur qualitativen Personalbedarfs-und Personalentwicklungsplanung", in Dybowski, G. u.a. Strategien qualitativer Personal-und Bildungsplanung bei technisch-organizatorischen Innovationen, Frankfurt.

Leonard-Barton, D. (1994), "Das Lernende Unternehmen I Die Fabrik als Ort der Forschung", in Harvard Business Manager, 16. Jahrgang. Hamburg.

Lingemann, H.F. and Theerkorn, U. (1987) "Neue Organisationsformen im Büro Verwaltungsinseln", in <u>Arbeit im Büro-heute und morgen, IfaA</u>. Institut für angewandte Arbeitswissenschaft e.V. Köln.

Mertens, D. (1974), *Schlüsselqualifikationen*. In MiTTAB.

Stahl, T., Nyhan, B.and d'Aloja, P. *The Learning Organisation*. Brüssel 1993.

Theerkorn, et.al. <u>Ein Betrieb denkt um-Die dualistische Fabrikplanung</u>, Berlin 1991.

Theerkorn, Uwe "Gestaltung von Arbeit und Technik bei Felten & Guilleaume", in <u>Forum Menschgerechter Technikgestaltung</u> Nr. 8 vom 2.-3.7.1991, ZATU-Zentrum für Arbeit, Technik und Umwelt e.V.

Warnecke, H.J. (1988) "Grundlegende Gesetzmäßigkeiten in der Produktion". <u>Fertigungstechnisches Kolloquium</u>, Berlin.

Chapter Twelve

The Development of "Collective Intelligence" at Autoplastique

Marie-Claire Villeval

Introduction

A new production model is emerging, emphasising innovation, flexibility, economies of scope and quality. This emerging model requires new worker profiles in terms of core competencies as well as employee commitment. This commitment can only be obtained in a more co-operative environment by comparison with traditional Tayloristic organisations. It means that a maximum automation strategy is not necessarily the most effective one. The search for economic efficiency brings to the fore the renewal of organisational schemes and the participation of employees in the management of innovation. A firms' capacity for reactivity and anticipation is improved not only by a negotiated introduction of new technologies but mainly by a negotiated change in work organisation even in the absence of physical investment. The present case study[1] (a progressive French SME, manufacturing plastic components, Autoplastique) illustrates an organisational shift coming about as a result of its partnership with the major car manufacturers and economic competition. After a presentation of the organisational change and the new worker profile, which we shall analyse using the notion of "collective intelligence", the stress will be put on the way in which those competencies are produced. However, despite the increase in core competencies, this firm does not constitute a real learning organisation and the case study provides evidence showing why this is difficult to realise. This paper concludes with an examination of the favourable and unfavourable factors affecting the implementation of genuine learning organisation.

A New Organisation Based upon a New Worker Profile

A Focus on Flow and Flexibility, Linked to Partnership with Car Manufacturers

Autoplastique designs and manufactures high precision pieces and functional technical assemblies based on techno-polymers, by means of injection technologies. Seventy percent of the turnover is realised with the automotive industry (shut-off, depression and canister bleed valves, pneumatic actuators, safety valves for fuel, discharge gate for cylinder heat, surge caps for cooling circuit and so on). It takes place in an expanding market (substitution materials) but in a situation of hard world-wide competition. Autoplastique employs 301 employees, with widespread knowledge and know-how in plastics, moulds, mechanics and fluids. Its main means are R&D laboratory, design department, CAD, CAM, mould workshop, 70 automatic presses and assembly lines.

Threefold Challenges Faced by The Company

The Search for Competitiveness

The search for competitiveness takes place in a context of reduction of the number of suppliers by the car manufacturers. Considering the increasing world-wide competition and the globalisation of economy, these latter increase the pressure on their suppliers. Via audits, they assess their strengths and weaknesses and operate a stern selection among them. While diminishing their number, they develop new relationships with the remainders. Partnership, institutionalised through charters (development, innovation, quality insurance), reduces uncertainty both for customers and suppliers, but it requires a tightening of the productive management.

The Management of The Triptych "Cost / Time To Market / Quality"

This requires an organisation dealing both with quantity and flexibility, defining a "customer-oriented flexible mass-production": modernisation does not mean the withdrawal of mass production (14, 000 surge caps for pressurised circuits are delivered daily in JIT) but its reintegration in a global stake of quality, flexibility and reactivity. The imperative of cost reduction is all the more strategic since world-wide competition is said to require a yearly cut by 5% of the car sale price. The imperative of quality requires the development of Total Quality Management. Most customers control the quality aptitudes of the firm through periodical audits and independent bodies verify the quality loop. Autoplastique's target is to reach the international ISO 9001 standard, demonstrating a shift from an audit approach to a proactive planning by the company.

An Increased Capacity of Innovation is Needed for Diversity of The Product Range

Global competition requires car manufacturers to increase the JIT of product innovation. MIT studies (MIT, 1989; Dertouzos, Lester and Solow, 1989) have shown that the firm supplying the market first with new products benefits from higher price and higher profit opportunities than competitors. This capacity for innovation is improved within organisations which are able to promote cooperative links among their members. The participation of manufacturing employees as well as that of suppliers in the design process increases this capacity by shortening the product design process. The supplier not only provides goods but also supports the effectiveness of "functions", i.e. both a design, production, the maintenance capability and the delivery of complex sets of products.

The guidelines for the organisational change at Autoplastique were initiated by five senior managers (within a steering committee "cercle de pilotage"), in consultation with the works council (which informs the employees). The guidelines were based on the information provided by the company's groups leaders, disseminated through publications in the firm's newspaper. These are:

- the development of a JIT organisation;

- a refocusing on the central business;
- a redefinition of the division of labour.

The Development of a JIT Organisation

Autoplastique closed its two previous factories in mid-1990, and moved into a new plant entirely designed for and devoted to JIT. It enabled Autoplastique to place all its activities in the same place and simplify its organisational operations and transportation costs between the two factories. The number of departments as well as the staff of some departments were reduced (maintenance, quality, control, storage). The flows of materials and goods became more effective. The equipment was reallocated in order to increase the visibility of production flows (e.g. the presses were arranged in rows according to their power). The JIT organisation aims at minimising two kinds of slack periods.

Firstly, the organisation has to reduce surplus production in order to implement a demand-led production process. Five years ago, the orders were dealt with over a three months period and inventories represented two months of activity. Today, both the orders and the deliveries are carried out on a daily basis and the stocks represent a two week period of activity. The orders are directly dealt with by the line managers; and the separation of organisational function has led to the increase in information flow, on time and the flexibility of production. Kan Ban principles were introduced in 1989 to ease the management of the interfaces between moulding and assembly workshops; they now lead 75% of the production (except small irregular series). Kan Ban is the name given by Toyota to the first "Just in Time" production management system: it consists of a system of tokens used to assist the availability of manufacturing components at the right moment in order to reduce inventory size.

In the Ken Ban system, the customer initiates the production: "the orders are no longer separated from the production; on the contrary, they are partly initiated there. Moreover, the Tayloristic preparation/manufacturing sequence is reversed. Manufacturing controls the planning ... and quality control is reintroduced as a manufacturing activity ..." (Coriat, 1990: 100),

Secondly, the organisation has to increase the operating time of machines, by minimising the risk of break-down (preventive maintenance), by developing shift-work (non-stop production), and by replacing the operations from the non-operational machines to operational machines. Autoplastique Ltd tries to increase the reconvertibility of equipment while reducing its reconversion time. It uses SMED (Single Minute Exchange Die) in order to reduce the slack period between the exchange of moulds, and thereby increase flexibility. The efficiency of such a methodology is not simply a matter of technology (hydraulic bindings) but also a matter of organisation (there is no point knowing how to change rapidly a mould if the next task is not prepared during this time).

However, these two aspects may become contradictory: it is necessary to establish a compromise between a maximum use of machines and a secure programme of flexibility (the regular rate of usage of the equipment is limited to 80%).

A Refocusing on The Central Business, A Diversification within This Business and The Development of New Design Methods

The firm tried to increase the number of its customers by developing diverse products (plastic pieces for the medical industry or for electric industries for example). However, the realisation of the need for considerable investments in technical systems, made the company refocus on its central business (the automotive one) and to increase its diversification within the automotive business. The investments were function-centred: the development of CAD and the expert systems; creation of a network-based computer-aided production management system (the new investment consists of a radical change of this system in order to link it with the customers' system); and the development of automation (15 robots) in order to increase quality, security and reliability. These investments are accompanied by a re-organisation of the design function, providing a room for a networked "cooperation learning", Autoplastique recognised that network cooperation was impossible when the design schedule was imposed from above but that it was essential imperative if the company were to take part in the collaborative project. Working in partnership with car manufacturers enables the temporary transfer of the functions of design department towards those of the car manufacturers and thereby the extension of project-teams. This partnership is linked to the practice of concurrent engineering in big companies, whereby suppliers are associated with the process of product innovation in order to reduce the delay between the beginning of the design stage and the availability of the new product on the market.

Concurrent or simultaneous engineering intends to integrate the manufacturing constraints into the design process as soon as possible, in contrast with the traditional sequential approach. By using these new design methods, the product realisation process can be considerably shortened (concurrent engineering is not only a set of technical and computer-aided tools; it is also an organisational methodology and an organisational challenge). This change requires the development of new organisational and communication competencies of newly transferred technicians, otherwise they cannot act as effective members of project teams.

A Redefinition of The Division of Labour

The moulding workshop is now divided into four groups, managed by "group-leaders" as small companies. Within these groups, the reform is not complete since there are no autonomous work teams (even if the supervisors have a certain individual autonomy) and the division between setters and operators is still alive. Nevertheless, the division of labour has gone through a radical change.

For the blue-collar workers, the redefinition is twofold. The first aspect is a widening of responsibilities. The operator must guarantee the qualitative management of his production by auto-control procedures. He guarantees the quantitative management of his production by enabling a good flow of production and by periodically controlling the conformity of the actual production to the set targets in order to identify possible drifts; he fills in a production form itemising all the results and events occurring during the day. The traceability is ensured by the worker's signature on each batch. In the past organisational tasks such as control, production management, cleaning, "sign-work" (in which the development is planned through the direct typing on the computer of the product information by the operators themselves), were assigned to specific departments.

The second aspect is a widening of the scope of intervention. Even if the automation supervisors are required to control increasing number of machines than before because of the enlargement of their functions, all workers may have to accept a higher mobility of assignment. The operators move several times a day according to the orders. This requires a certain degree of multiskilling.

There are three levels of hierarchy. The number of team-leaders was initially reduced from six to two per workshop but they were rapidly replaced by a new level (four "group-leaders") because it was found impossible to reconcile a broad domain of intervention and an in-depth multi-functionality. This new level is not a discreet reintroduction of a Tayloristic hierarchy but an illustration of the occupation of a new line-manager.

A Major Stake: The Development of "Collective Intelligence" - The New Core Competencies

The new core competencies defined as: "let's move away from Descartes".
The technological complexity of labour increased especially for the setters, their role has become more strategic: more frequent changes of moulds leads to higher wear and tear and the higher risk of break-down, all the more problematic in a JIT organisation. For the operators, the operating modes did not change a lot. Globally, the growing complexity of labour derives from organisational changes rather than from technological evolution. The main source of change of the core competencies consists of the necessity to adapt to changes and to anticipate the next operations before the end of the previous ones, say stopping a Cartesian sequence of tasks for a new organisational culture. Previously, operators were asked to perfectly finish each task before beginning the next one. Now, as operators have overall responsibility for a function (including manufacturing, quality control, cleaning, production proceedings), they no longer have to proceed according to a sequential ordering of operations but they have to work more and more in a concurrent and simultaneous manner. The efficient performance of product quality, variability and flow is the very heart of the new core competencies. For the operators, this means:

- to develop a systemic conception of labour, integrating the customers' requirements, so there is a need to anticipate the consequences of one's actions on the other workers (frequent mobility eases this process);
- a role in the optimisation of the production process in both qualitative and quantitative terms, including the COQ (cost of quality);
- a greater responsibility of the use and diffusion of information, requiring higher capabilities in abstraction and communication. Both individual and collective responsibilities are increasing, as well as their traceability.

Core competencies of technicians are not just the technical expertise but also the ability to work in a team, to contribute to informal problem-solving groups (for example, if a setter does not succeed in solving a break-down, he may consult the other setters to find the best solution), to integrate economic data (the cost of a break-down, the cost of quality, etc.). Core competencies of group leaders are managerial, technical and communication; the group leader has to guarantee a peaceful social climate (the consequences of a strike in a JIT organisation are easy to imagine) and he must know how to assess competencies; he is in charge of setters' training; he is a technical expert (he has to intervene if the setters cannot solve a technical problem) and has to improve the technological system; he is also a manager: he plans labour, he is responsible for the cost of quality and the rate of usage of machines, he analyses the monthly results and the production rhythms in consultation with the workshop leader. By comparison with the previous team-leaders, he also undertakes some tasks of the Methods Department and increases his managerial and organisational competencies.

This evolution reveals *a change in competencies.* The technical skills of operators have not changed but one can stress the development of organisational and communication competencies. The operators have to manage the links between individual and collective action, the timing of this connected action, the good quality of the manufacturing flow and the individual and collective treatment of dysfunctionings. Thus coordination is more and more a nodal feature of a good organisation of work. The work and related competencies are becoming more complex (not in technical but in organisational terms), more extended and more abstract. This does not mean that employees were not able to master these competencies before but that they were not asked to utilise them.

I propose to summarise this evolution through the notion of *collective intelligence* (in French, "intelligence collective") development because this notion is dynamic, systemic and takes on strategic meaning in team work, on individual and collective bases (this notion is promoted by researchers in artificial intelligence but is used here in different sense). This notion covers two dimensions. On the one hand, it represents a sum of knowledge and know-how (tacit or formalised), a series of shared data and representations which reduce uncertainty and ease collective action; on the other hand, it integrates the employees' cognitive abilities, say their capacity to elaborate cognitive strategies in order to formalise a problem, to take a decision, to improve their knowledge and their information. It covers technical, organisational and communication competencies and expertise. Lastly, collective intelligence concerns both the individuals and the whole organisation and it requires both individual and collective learning. As a matter of fact, collective intelligence represents more than the simple sum of individual competencies, notably because it integrates a kind of corporate cultural knowledge, a relational rather than individualistic knowledge. The efficiency of the work organisation requires this collective intelligence to be a permanent axis of development as regards the imperatives of flexibility and reconvertibility and the accelerated rhythms of innovation.

Collective Intelligence and the Evolution of Cognitive Strategies

The Limits Of Substitution Strategy and the Adoption of a Formal Training Policy

For improving flexibility and reactivity, Autoplastique developed two strategies for the external labour market: an important dimension of temporary workers (monthly average: 66 workers; temporary work is a systematic hiring channel) and a substitution strategy. When the firm moved to the new location, the staff decreased because of people leaving, dismissals and early retirements (40); then followed an intense hiring policy (80 recruitments) based upon a skill profile "far beyond the immediate needs" for enabling reconvertibility (baccalaureate or exceptionally Bac + 2^2). However, this strategy proved to be inefficient: a SME cannot really compete on the labour market with bigger companies, more attractive in terms of wages and upgrading; there are skill shortages on the external market (more exactly, it is difficult to find holders of both diploma and experience); the commitment of the new workers is difficult to obtain if they feel downgraded and trapped in dead-end jobs.

Autoplastique's HRD strategy relies on the growth of further vocational training. The French system of further vocational training is built on a public regulation which imposes upon firms to fund training: 1.5% of the gross wage bill must be devoted to further vocational training but the average was 3.2% in 1992. Apart from this compulsory expenditure, firms keep a quasi-total autonomy concerning its content. Training policies of French firms are primarily segmented according to the size and the sector of the firms. Training policies of SMEs are poorly rooted. Yet Autoplastique devotes 4% of its gross wage bill to further vocational training: far beyond the average expense of its category size. Further vocational training is considered less and less either as an unproductive expenditure or as a "second chance" for the lowly educated workers but increasingly as a strategic weapon for innovation. The main evolution of Autoplastique's training policy are the following.

- The courses focus more and more on the management of production flows and quality. A further step could be a "generalisation" of training, redefining it around the identity of work teams, the product and the innovation
- The training periods were raised to 34 hours in 1991 (national average: 15 hours). The unskilled and skilled have a growing opportunity to benefit from courses and contrary to traditional trends, foremen/technicians benefit more from training than engineers (the respective opportunities were 42, 26, 35 and 12 hours in 1991).
- The training policy is designed over a longer time span than before: managers try to define a 3-year planned programme. The idea is to bring the planning time of training planning closer to the planning time of technical investment.

The Growth of Informal Learning

Despite the French institutional context favouring formal training (that is, training courses organised either on an in-house basis or by external bodies), the new organisation both requires and enables the development of informal learning. We agree with the hypothesis pointed out by Barbier (1992) that the working situation enables learning when "the work becomes the occasion for reflection and problem-solving". There is a strong linkage between the new skill profile and these informal learning patterns. However, one must be cautious: the former organisational modes did not exclude informal learning; it was on the one hand less easy to achieve because of the very nature of the division of labour and of the prevailing mode of coordination and hierarchy, and, on the other hand, the informal learning was viewed rather in a pejorative way, as a cheap substitute for training courses for unskilled or semi-skilled employees. Three core ideas characterise informal learning. Informal learning is a matter of cognitive learning on both the individual and collective bases, relying more on an empirical basis than formal training courses because they are directly linked to working situations. This learning is mainly a co-operative activity, is essential for a global management of innovation, flexibility, total quality, as well as for the improvement of the competencies of all workers, including the unskilled.

Four Reasons Put Forward to Explain the Growth of Informal Learning

- The new organisational pattern derives from the import of "recipes" (from best selling management books, other reading, visits to Japan, consulting groups' advice, etc.). The firm has to adapt them to its own organisation, taking into account its history, its equipment and its manpower. Informal training has a part to play in this appropriation process.
- The new organisation is increasingly a matter of "cognitive rationalisation" (Jacot Dir., 1993), linking productive action, information action and cognitive action for the growth of responsibility and autonomy. It requires management to recognise knowledge previously denied for wider diffusion. Informal learning has always existed but the new organisation favours its development and its visibility.
- Labour is increasingly collective but the teams remain heterogeneous (45% of the employees have been with the firm for less than three years). The combination between formal and informal training provides a flexible answer to differentiated needs, easing the cohesion of teams and the in-house reconversion of operators below the intermediate level of secondary education.
- The cost of informal training (difficult to measure) seems to be lower than the cost of formal courses, all the more since workers are both trainers and trainees. In a context of budget savings, firms require a higher control of return of investment in the field of training as well as in the technological area.

The Growth of the Informal Learning Pattern Goes Through five Broad Modalities

The Project-Teams and Transversal Groups
The project-teams and transversal groups favour participatory learning. Whatever their initial purpose (product innovation or quality certification at Autoplastique), temporary groups enable the diffusion and the acquisition of tacit or explicit knowledge, technological or collective knowledge. Concretely, it enables the company by means of debates or through discussions, to confront diverse knowledge, various expertise and experiences, and points of view and conflicts. Under some circumstances, the conflicting knowledge as well as the machine break-down may induce a learning opportunity.

Spontaneous problem-solving meetings in the workshops (for example, the setters meet together in order to solve the break-down of a machine when needed) favours this approach but the main target could be the implementation of enlarged problem-designing groups. The "AMDEC" methodology consists of meetings of designers and manufacturing managers and technicians, aiming at the analysis of the problems which could emerge all along the life of the product, in connection with the customers' requirements. The participation of employees in the process of decision-making is always an opportunity of learning. However, Autoplastique as well as many other firms still exclude the major part of manufacturing workers from the decision-making process, and participation mainly involves engineers, managers and the top grade technicians.

These group-based approaches bring together not only "knowledge dispensers" but also create a basis for an interactive learning process producing "collective knowledge" wider than the sum of individual knowledge.

The "one-to-one" learning with colleagues
The "one-to-one" learning with colleagues at the workplace constitutes another vector for informal training. It covers various modalities far beyond simple imitation. The newly recruited technicians for the design department work in the production departments for several months in order to familiarise themselves with the constraints and knowledge of the manufacturing system. Moreover, because of the frequent mobility within the workshop, the workers have to collaborate together in order to improve their performance. In some cases, this learning takes the shape of a "game", whereby an operator puts some defective pieces aside and, at the end of the shift, she asks her successor at the workplace to detect the defect. This on-the-job training for cooperation, multiskilling or rotation involves communication networks and mutual aid behaviours. It has existed before but is now double-sided (technological and organisational learning), and is perhaps more abstract (mainly for technicians and setters at Autoplastique).

The coach ("tuteur") finds a new legitimacy
At Autoplastique, this organised on-the-job learning takes two shapes. Within the framework of public education and employment policies ("contrats de qualification" and apprenticeships), young trainees learn their work with a coach who gives them technical, organisational, behavioural advice and knowledge in order to transfer the school-based theoretical knowledge into the manufacturing activity. It also helps the trainees to improve their knowledge by embedding them within the corporate cultural framework. In other cases, the training of a new worker is organised "on the job" by the previous job holder before retirement or moving to another job. This kind of learning process enables a direct transfer of skills. In other firms, this modality is used in direct connection with formal training: a craftsman helps the trainee in the transfer of new knowledge in between the periods of formal training sessions.

Experts, experienced workers ("hommes-ressources")
Experts, experienced workers ("hommes-ressources") and technicians from the Method Department train workers *in situ*, and write explanatory leaflets about the new means of production in the same way as the descriptive workplace forms or the exposition of defective pieces are useful for the learning process. The equipment suppliers or the main customers can also provide advice on the occasion of audit procedures.

Self-learning
Self-learning is encouraged through computer-aided learning, the reading of books (for example about the Kan Ban - "Just-in-Time" - methods or the Japanese lean production model), and the writing of work reports. However, this kind of learning concerns mainly technicians, setters and group leaders. Formal training courses are also a modality of informal learning: they give an opportunity to observe pedagogical methods as a trainee, and this pedagogical learning will be useful later when they act as trainers at the workplace.

Both formal training courses and informal learning are encouraged in the firm and are favoured by the organisational change which demands new competencies and new rules of behaviour. The division between "formal training courses mainly for technicians, highly skilled workers and managers, and informal learning for unskilled or semi-skilled workers" is now over. However, the link between the two kinds of learning, formal and informal, is not really managed, even if the informal learning is a means for prolonging *in situ* the effects of formal training courses. Moreover, as we shall see below, even if the informal learning is directly linked to the organisational shift, it does not regenerate automatically and indefinitely. It is imperative that the collective intelligence and the development of organisational competencies should become permanent features of the new organisation. However, many conditions must be met in order to reach such a goal.

Opportunities and difficulties in the implementation of Learning Organisations

Two main conditions are required for speaking about a genuine learning organisation ("organisation qualifiante"). A genuine learning organisation must be able to favour the development of collective intelligence and must enable employees to be actors in the processes of innovation, in order to fulfil the targets of the economic performance (flexibility, reliability, quality and innovation).

Autoplastique's experience is a success story in terms of economic results. For example, in 1983, the turn-over was FF 80 million with 241 employees; in 1991, the respective figures were FF 214 million and 288 employees; while the firm gained higher capacities in flexibility, reactivity and innovation. However, if the capacity to improve formal and informal learning, technical, behavioural and organisational competencies has been strategic within the new form of organisation for reaching such a result, this capacity is not sufficient to consider Autoplastique as a learning organisation. To make such a capacity routine, other conditions have to be met. As mentioned before, there are no autonomous teams in Autoplastique; the division between setters and operators (which reproduces a division of labour based on gender: women are mainly operators, men are mainly setters) is persistent; the manufacturing workers enter the innovation process at an advanced stage. The early involvement of employees in the design and to management of innovations (innovation of product, technology and organisation) is a pre-condition for the successful reproduction and the development of individual and collective learning. This is the reason why we define a genuine learning organisation by means of the two aforementioned major characteristics: the development of collective intelligence and the early association of employees in the design and implementation of innovations.

This example and the other case studies realised for the CEDEFOP[3] study leads to the identification of favourable and unfavourable factors for the development of interactive learning capabilities and the implementation of a learning organisation.

Conditions for Developing Long-Lasting Collective Intelligence

As shown by Maroy (1993), a change in the industrial management standard is compatible with the maintenance of organisational modes which do not have broad learning effects. It is the very heart of the organisation of production and work which is at stake here. One can stress interactions between the dynamics of organisational changes and the dynamics of learning. The new organisation favours the development of an interactive learning. The function of instructors ("monitrices") as distributors of learning is important but in-depth learning takes place with colleagues on a continuous basis at the workplace. It is not necessarily a binomial learning process. The learning process must contribute to make the development of the rules of the organisation. For example, one can assert that the involvement of the manufacturing workers in the very definition of the procedures within the framework of a quality certification approach is an opportunity both for a collective learning process and for a possible questioning of the organisational rules themselves.

The mutual enrichment and the durability of the learning opportunities in working situations (in some cases, the learning opportunity is limited to the period of the change itself) requires several conditions.

A Global Conception of Design and Delivery of Innovation and Learning
Training must be provided "Just-in-Time". Learning is fostered if training and information (for example about a new product before its industrialisation) anticipate the evolution, in helping employees to build new indicators and references on interactive bases. Conversely, if provided too soon, training is ineffective; for example, at Autoplastique, the quality control courses were provided before the building of the new plant; it was necessary to provide a new series of courses after the move to new plant because the quality control knowledge was forgotten. One can express this idea in another way: the firm has to build a "concurrent engineering of learning". Formal and informal training must be conceived in a strong connection with new work situations and new organisational requirements, both concerning the design of the content and for an effective interpenetration of the cognitive processes. More globally, that requires a connection between social and economic dimensions of innovation processes.

A Compromise Between Inequalities of Power and Inequalities of Knowledge
Employees are vested with unequal power and knowledge based upon traditional divisions of labour; but these divisions do not necessarily correspond to modern realities. In other words, interactive learning is favoured only if managers recognise the existence of workers' knowledge and if common references (in terms of innovation or quality) can be set up. It is now generally accepted that the organisational competencies are all the more developed throughout the organisation for meeting and sustaining economic targets. For example, at Autoplastique, blue-collar workers proposed to develop the Kan-Ban system in a place where it had not yet been adopted. This economic proposal was accepted because it was consistent with the managers' targets; but under the fold regime, this kind of proposal would probably not even have emerged. This raises the questions of the negotiated participation of workers and their commitment to achieving negotiated objectives. This may require a widening of their participation in the design of innovations. Discussing economic aims and innovation design could be both a moment of learning and a basis for commitment.

A Compromise between a "Right To Error" and "Zero Defect" Approaches
Interactive learning is fostered by the increasing autonomy of employees, the right to decision making, and the exercise of their free will. But this demands risk taking in a context of strong uncertainty. Learning through risk taking will be deeper if the worker's right to error has been recognised. The worker learns by moving forward by trial and error but this can contradict the JIT concept and the concept of "get it right first time" approach. Similarly, such events as machine breakdowns or dysfunctions must not be regarded only as defects in the organisation but investment in the learning and improvement opportunities.

At Autoplastique, the operators do not have to intervene in the maintenance of equipment. However, observing the action of maintenance workers sorting out a break-down enables them to develop their knowledge about the equipment itself to identify the signs of future problems and to describe them, easing the first diagnosis during preventive or curative maintenance.

A Compromise between Continuous Innovation and Stable Progression
Innovation requires new references, new standards and new markers. It puts the routinisation of work into question. The upheaval of routines initiates learning. But the change must not be too frequent, otherwise it may generate destabilisation of routines and cause excessive stress. The firm has to achieve a compromise between constant innovation and stable progression. Learning also requires repetition and memory: innovation processes are handicapped if the organisation and its members cannot memorise passed experiences and trials (that is particularly true concerning the design activities). The problem is not to eliminate routines (these are an indisputable aid for the collective action) and former dead-end experiences, but to ease the construction of "innovative routines" and inculcate positive attitudes towards change, integrating the lessons of former successful as well as dead-end experiences. On the other hand, a daily change of activities and workplaces also favours learning in acquiring new cognitive strategies and in enabling comparative and cumulative experiences. But here too, as shown by the CEDEFOP research, a compromise is needed between distance (the inventive differentiation) and proximity (the communication between employees).

A Compromise between the De-compartmentalisation of Functions within the Company and Respect for the Specific Knowledge of Employees.
On the one hand, the development of a partnership between customer and supplier enables them both to identify major sources of dysfunctioning and thereby improve the processes in a co-operative way via audits and temporary transfer of the design department. On the other hand, internal decompartmentalisation, achieved via project-teams, computerised networks and linear organisation of manufacturing, eases the cognitive processes in mixing various experiences and different kinds of knowledge. But these new forms of visibility and communication do not require a generalisation of multiskilling (probably a nonsense) leading to a kind of uniformity and interchangeability between employees; the strength of interactive learning is not to enable the appropriation of the knowledge of everybody by everybody but to enable the construction of cognitive strategies partly by identifying people with specific competencies. Thus the project-leader does not have to be an expert in all fields of knowledge but he has to know exactly who those experts are.

Forces Restraining the Implementation of the Learning Organisation

The Contradiction between the New Distribution of Knowledge and the Inertia of Power Representations and Structures

P. Zarifian (1993) shows that a learning organisation is characterised partly by the capability of workers to manage and to cope with two kinds of events: the day-to-day events (such as break-down or changes in the manufacturing orders) and innovations.

Firstly, a contradiction emerges between the will to mobilise employees' abilities and their exclusion or very late association to the process of product or equipment design. A learning organisation is a cooperative organisation based on the association between the world of the product (marketing and design departments) and the world of the process (manufacturing departments), between engineers and technicians with various types of skills and different languages. Promoting concurrent engineering and asking workers to cope with the innovation approach requires the association of manufacturing employees in the process of innovation at an early stage, i.e. before the adoption of major irreversible decisions. This revolution needs a major change in engineers' and technicians' understanding of the workers' knowledge. To associate belatedly the workers to the management of change deprives the firm of important opportunities of learning and improvement. This relates to the broader question of power relationships. Learning organisations require the association of three kinds of employees' representations in the project management, as pointed out by H. Rouilleault (1993): work teams representing various hierarchical levels; employee representatives, and formal and informal negotiation with trade unions. In a small firm such as Autoplastique, these conditions are not met. More generally, it presupposes a change in the attitudes of both employers and trade unions as regards bargaining on work organisation.

Secondly, some blue-collar workers are still impregnated with the Tayloristic approach to hierarchical relationships, even in organisations promoting a management by results rather than by procedures. For example, at Autoplastique, some workers, upgraded just before the move of the plant on the basis of their seniority and knowledge in the previous organisation, waited for the orders of foremen to organise their work; this behaviour becomes contradictory to the new organisation rules and it hinders learning.

Thirdly, the status of foremen is questionable: they have to cope with a conversion of their function; they have to become organisers, trainers, technical experts, administrators, rather than controllers. This conversion is neither always prepared nor clearly validated. There may be a conflict of logics between some foremen upgraded on the basis of the previous organisation requirements and rules, and other foremen, younger, more highly certified, with different systems of values and representations. At Autoplastique for example, the workshop leader manages this tension by making a compromise between the needs of JIT management and human resources management: occasionally he thus prefers to postpone the launching of a new range of production rather than entrusting some group leaders with this launching.

Possible Contradiction between Learning and Economic Management Criteria

Another major index is still used at Autoplastique for the assessment of productivity gains in addition to value analysis: the number of hours of automatic functioning related to the total number of functioning hours of the presses. This kind of indicator reveals a still prevailing "logic of substitution" of labour by capital. Yet, if the firm's competitiveness is now more and more based upon "extra-price" factors (quality, innovation), then it requires the production of new criteria of economic management. If the criteria of assessment are based on the reduction of labour costs (i.e. workforce considered as an adjustment variable and not as a performance variable), then learning opportunities during the working day and at the workplace are necessarily considered, implicitly if not explicitly, as unproductive. In other words, the development of learning organisations requires a parallel evolution of both criteria of economic assessment of the activity and the criteria of validation of organisational competencies of the workforce.

Contradiction between Interactive Learning and Strict Work Prescription

The achievement of pre-specified quality standards (ISO 9000 certification) generates a new kind of production and work prescription. This approach requires an in-depth codification of knowledge and job content. It may seem profitable to formalise tacit knowledge inasmuch as it enables reorganisation, theorisation and diffusion. For the employers, the process of the "de-privatisation" of tacit knowledge may prove more strategic since the efficiency of the new organisation depends partly on the commitment of employees. For employees, this formalisation may provide room for the validation of their knowledge. Similarly, the codification of job content contributes to the specification of the workers' field of responsibilities. However, several problems emerge. The certification procedures may lead to freezing the qualitative skills of employees in particular their "tacit knowledge" and, in that sense, is may impede the continuing learning process. The horizontal coordination emphasised in Japanese work organisation requires a transcendence of the boundaries of employees' skills. The certification process provides for the harmonising of employees skills, thereby reducing the gap between the tacit dimension of their knowledge. In this sense, the certification process can provide a basis for both learning and organisational improvement.

Contradiction between the Emphasis on Learning Potentialities of the New Organisation and the Lack of Validation Means

From the viewpoint of internal validation, commitment and learning can be reproduced only if they are validated through wages, classifications, upgrading opportunities or employment stability (in Autoplastique, 49% of the employees are still classified as unskilled workers). How does one recognise not only the exercised competencies but also the acquired competencies and the very elaboration of cognitive strategies? This requires the redefinition of career planning and a reflection about the nature of hierarchy in the learning organisations. The shortening of hierarchical levels, the development of transversal teams, and the will to promote interactions between employees with different knowledge, will impose rotating promotions, detached from the notion of control and perhaps detached the job itself. (Why, for example, should the function of project-leader be permanent?) Are the present classification systems compatible and flexible enough to enable this evolution ? The debate is wide open.

From the viewpoint of the external validation, the debate is also still open: some authors consider that informal learning contributes to the increase of the firm-based specificity of skills. For us, the raising of organisational competencies reach a real degree of transferability on the external labour market (to be used to work in a JIT organisation, to get a systemic approach of labour); for example, at Autoplastique, the production manager considers that work experience in a Kan Ban organisation as a positive attribute among the job applicants he has to select. Nevertheless, informal training never leads to a certificate and there is a lack of the means of validation for these skills (as well as in the representations and consciousness of the workers themselves). There is a contradiction between, on the one side, the interest of the employer to minimise the process of skill transferability, and, on the other side, the necessity to create cooperative working environments through the validation of employees' skills on both internal and external bases.

Contradiction between Learning Opportunities and Selectivity in the New Organisation
Firstly, in an internal labour market, seniority and experience were the main criteria for upgrading. But one can stress a kind of short-sightedness deriving from decisions of promotion taken just before the change and based upon the competencies deployed in the previous organisation, whereas the new organisation may require new kind of knowledge and cognitive abilities. Even if the new organisation is less selective, for example, in terms of access to training, a new kind of segmentation emerges in terms of generation.

There are winners and losers and two kinds of attitudes emerge as regards the new constraints. Some workers equate the new organisation to management by stress, whereas others identify it with stimulating management by change. Moreover, the division of status may hinder the learning processes: the willingness to learn is differentiated, depending on whether the labour contract is short-term or not, on whether temporary workers have opportunities for getting a permanent contract or not. Secondly, many researchers have emphasised the learning abilities of unskilled workers; the CEDEFOP study (Villeral, 1993) points out a number of learning opportunities in the new organisations. Does it mean that the learning organisation is a solution for decreasing the unemployment of the less-educated workers? At the moment, at the micro-level, the new organisations observed in the CEDEFOP study are based upon very selective recruitment policies.

How Autoplastique fits into the General Framework

Pressures from its customers (auto manufacturers) necessitated a close working relationship and agreement in relation to cost, timing (JIT) and quality. This required a new more flexible organisational structure. A semi-decentralised system was introduced (see Fig. 1, 0).

- Team based work processes, but not autonomous teams, were set up to implement the new structure. Learning and competence development mainly occurred as a result of *"informal learning"* processes such as: learning in a project team, learning from more experienced workers on a one to one basis by means of coaching, or a learning contract and so on (see Figure 1, 1).
- As a result workers developed social/communication competencies (i.e. the ability to share know-how, both giving and receiving) and cognitive competencies (e.g. problem-solving skills etc.). Employees were thus *"generating"* and *"sharing"* in what is termed "collective intelligence" (see Figure 1, 2).
- This led to the creation of "learning organisation" values but only to a limited degree, (see Figure 1, 3-VΔ) because there was a clash between the "open" employee-centred learning values/processes and the "closed" prescriptive management-centred "power" structures.

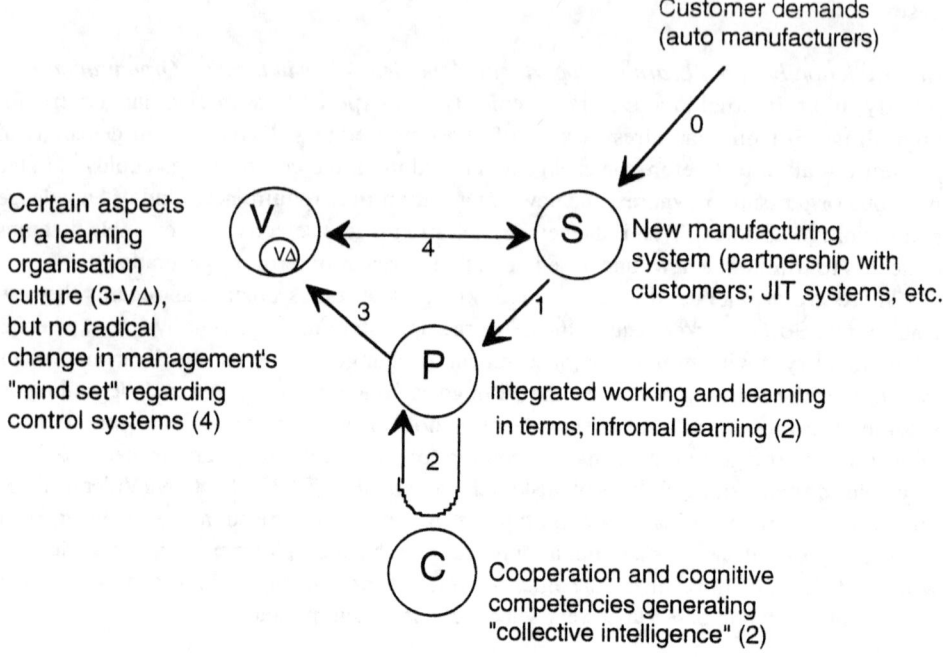

Figure 1. *Generating "collective intelligence"*

- This showed up an ambivalence in management's values and "mind set" concerning the control system to be installed and the role which they wanted workers to play in the company (see Figure 1, 4). In other words there had to be a trade off between the continued existence of a certain number of traditional authoritarian management and organisational practices, (including the prescriptive nature of some of the new management practices such as JIT) and participatory learning. This meant that a conflict existed between the manner in which "power" was still rather centralised while learning was decentralised. From this perspective one cannot claim that the company fulfils the criteria of a learning organisation.

References

Argyris, C. and Schön, D.A. (1978). *Organizational learning: a theory of action perspective*. Addison-Wesley Publishing Company.

Barbier, J.M., Dir. (1992). *Le développement de la fonction formative des situations de travail*. Paris, CNAM (pôle de recherche coordonné par le CRF du CNAM).

Baron, X. and Couvreur, E. (1992). Les grands projets, instruments du succès de la gestion des ressources humaines ? *Gérer et comprendre,* déc.

Bouabdallah, K., Villeval, M.C. (1993). *Changement organisationnel: une question d'apprentissage institutionnel ?* Dijon, Journées de l'AFSE, 26-27 May

Boyer, R. (1991). *New directions in management practices and work organisation.* Paris, CEPREMAP

Boyer, R. (1993). *The impact of flexible mass-production upon growth and unemployment.* Paris, CEPREMAP

Coriat, B. (1990). *L'atelier et le robot.* Paris, C. Bourgois

Dertouzos, M., Lester, R. and Solow, R., 1989. *Made in America.* Cambridge: MIT Press

Greenan, N., Guellec, D., Broussaudier, G. and Miotti, L. (1993). *Innovation organisationnelle, dynamisme technologique et performance des entreprises.* Document de travail G 9304 du Département Etudes Economiques d'Ensemble, INSEE

Jacot, J.H., Dir. (1993). *Formes anciennes, formes nouvelles d'organisation.* Lyon, PUL, forthcoming

Ginsbourger, F., Merle, V. and Vergnaud, G., 1992. *Formation et apprentissage des adultes peu qualifiés.* Paris: La Documentation Française

Hirata, H., Dir. (1993). *Autour du modèle japonais.* Paris: L'Harmattan

Maroy, C., Dir. (1993). *Changements socio-organisationnels et stratégies de formation des entreprises.* Louvain, Institut des Sciences du Travail

Midler, C. (1991). *Evolution des règles de gestion et processus d'apprentissage.* Paris: Colloque sur l'Economie des Conventions, CREA

MIT. (1989) The Working Papers of the MIT Commission on *Industrial Productivity,* vol.1, Cambridge, Mass. and London: The MIT Press

Rouilleault, H. (1993). "Changer le travail et faire évoluer les relations sociales", in Taddei, D. and Coriat, B. *Made in France,* Vol.2. Paris: Le Livre de Poche, forthcoming

Taddei, D. and Coriat, B. (1993). *Made in France. L'industrie française dans la compétition mondiale.* Paris: Le Livre de Poche

Zarifian, P. (1993). *Organisation qualifiante et flexibilité.* Noisy le Grand: CERTES, ronéo

Villeval, M.C. (1993). *La place de l'entreprise dans la production de la qualification, formation continue formelle et effets formateurs de l'organisation du travail,* Berlin: CEDEFOP, forthcoming

Notes

[1] The present paper is based on the results of a European research project realised for CEDEFOP about "the role of the enterprise in the process of skills acquisition - 'Formalised' continuing vocational training and the training effects of the organisation of labour" which the French part was coordinated by the author. The reference of the initial complete case study is the following : Villeval, M.C., 1992. "Partenariat, flux tendus et production des compétences - Une PME de la plasturgie". Lyon: ECT, 33p. The author takes full responsibility for the ideas expressed here.

[2] Baccalaureate corresponds to the completion of the second level education (it is the equivalent of A Level in the United Kingdom and of Abitur in Germany). Bac + 2

corresponds to the initial vocational training leading to technician certificates such as DUT or BTS.

[3] 9 case studies were realised in French firms which had changed their organisation, under the direction of L. Mallet (CEJEE), P. Méhaut (GREE) and the author.

Chapter Thirteen

A Learning Opportunity on the Shopfloor at AB Bygg och Transportekonomi

Christer Marking
Swedish Metalworkers' Union

Introduction

The introduction of flexible manufacturing leads to changes in work and skill requirements on the shop floor. This process of change is illustrated with the case study of a medium sized manufacturing company in Sweden, AB Bygg och Transportekonomi (ABT). The case of ABT shows how traditional divisions of work can hinder the attainment of economic benefits which could be gained with the introduction of the new technology. It also shows that the distribution of skills and competencies, necessary effectively to utilise this technology, is dependent on the approach management takes and the decisions it makes. For example, learning is determined by providing access to a range of problems and by the right, employees have to participate in problem solving within the organisation.

FMS at AB Bygg och Transportekonomi

AB Bygg och Transportekonomi

AB Bygg och Transportekonomi is a medium-sized manufacturing company situated in the mid-southern part of Sweden. ABT produces a broad range of lifters for the international market, from small manual fork-lifters to high-lifters for automated warehouses. The production has been concentrated in one place where the company had been steadily growing for many years.

The type of production varies greatly depending on the product, from custom-design to mass-production based on prognoses. These variations were absorbed in the assembly departments. At the time of this study the shop was functionally oriented and the production organisation was conventional. There was a formal control structure running through both a vertical division of work between blue-collar and white-collar workers and a horizontal division of work between blue-collar workers as well as between white-collar workers.

The problem

The process that led to the introduction of FMS-technology in ABT started when business was doing extremely well and the company's production resources were strained. Owing to the financial situation in the mother company, ABT was not allowed to expand its production site area and had a restricted investment budget.

The managing director gave the chief of the production engineering staff (CPS) the task to expand the production capacity within the restricted premises. At the time, in the mid-seventies, the introduction of production at night with reduced manning was under debate. The CPS was sent to Japan to seek a more feasible technology for making better use of space and time.

The solution

The CPS wanted to build a system which could deliver certain components just-in-time to the assembly line directly from the manufacturing department with reduced planning and unmanned production at night. The solution was based on a machining-centre with pallet loading.

The parts selected to be machined in the machine-centre were all made part of one component, a sub-assembly, that was used in a series of lifters. Thus, the supply of this component to the assembly-line could be made to closely match the demand from the line. The parts were fed to the machine by pallets to which they were fastened in fixtures.

The pallets were charged with parts in close vicinity to the machine-centre of the same operators that handled the centre. Pallets were stored in a vertical storage, handled by a high-lifting crane which handled the input and output to and from the centre. Alongside the vertical storage, which was double-sided, there were a number of NC- and CNC-machine-tools, all supported by the crane for the input and output of parts. The new machining-centre, with its pallets, had priority in the crane-control system which was integrated with the control system of the machining-centre.

The crane was manufactured by ABT and was part of ABT's lifter program. It was automated for the purpose of serving the machine-centre. The centre ran 24 hours a day. It was only manned during two shifts, with reduced manning during the second shift. The pallets were loaded primarily during the first shift, which started when the machine, having worked through what was loaded on the pallets during the day, began during the night.

The planning and the design of the system included a reassessment of the actual components that were chosen for the centre. Though the tool magazine was extensive, the number of tools needed exceeded the number available. Total redesign was not feasible due to the effect on the cost of spare parts.

The running in

The production engineer in charge of the technical side of the planning process made an in-depth study of the components and the parts programs. He went to Japan for tests, and to carry out simulations of the parts programs, etc. He was also in charge of the running-in process. To assist him, he had two operators: a female operator with skills in NC-machining and quality control work and a skilled worker who worked in the tool-room and also as an instructor. They formed a group that shared the same goal: to get the machine going. At the beginning, there were a number of problems, most of which they had to learn to resolve themselves. The team gained a lot of expertise in handling the debugging of the system. The production engineer gradually moved over to other tasks while the two operators brought in the various parts until all the planned parts ran smoothly.

New vertical relations

In the day-to-day running of the system, lots of problems occurred which the systems operators could not handle themselves; not because they were not able to but because they did not have authority to deal with the root of the problem. From time to time, the operators had to "borrow" the authority to make decision. Thereby, they developed close relations with people in the production planning departments, i.e. the scheduling department, the procurement department, the quality control department, the production engineering department, the works-study department, and the programming department etc. (see Figure 1).

In this concentrated little world, people got to know each-other in a way which would have been unthinkable earlier. Joint interests grew between people who belonged to personnel categories which normally had conflicting interests. This was a new experience for an environment where loyalty relations are normally horizontal, as is the case on the shop floor, and vertical loyalties are a problem, both in a sociological and psychological sense. As a person you have to handle double loyalties.

Previous "horizontal relations" between fellow workers were replaced by vertical relations which were more problem oriented than cooperative. The organisation which was well adapted to the needs of a functional shop, turned out to be rather inefficient for the new type of working-relations.

Supervisor without function

Normally, the supervisor would have handled the situation himself, for instance by making the appropriate contacts. In this case, the supervisor lacked the knowledge and the skills to either solve the problem or formulate adequate questions to get an answer which could help him solve it. His traditional authority, built on superior skill and access to the management, no longer had a functional base. The supervisor and the crew did not have a relation concerning work-matters but in other matters.

The disturbances and variations emanated not only from internal systems sources but also, and sometimes more often, had external systems origins which were not normally technical. For example, the cast iron that was used as raw material came originally from a foundry with very even quality. Cutting data was set according to the characteristics of that material. During a financial crisis in the mother company, ABT had to buy from a foundry affiliated to the mother company. It produced a different quality but also had problems with delivery times.

From time to time, the cast iron was rushed from the foundry and brought into the machine. Insufficiently aged as it was, its hardness ruined the thin bores, thereby creating stoppages which led to great problems, especially at night when nobody was there to start up the machine again.

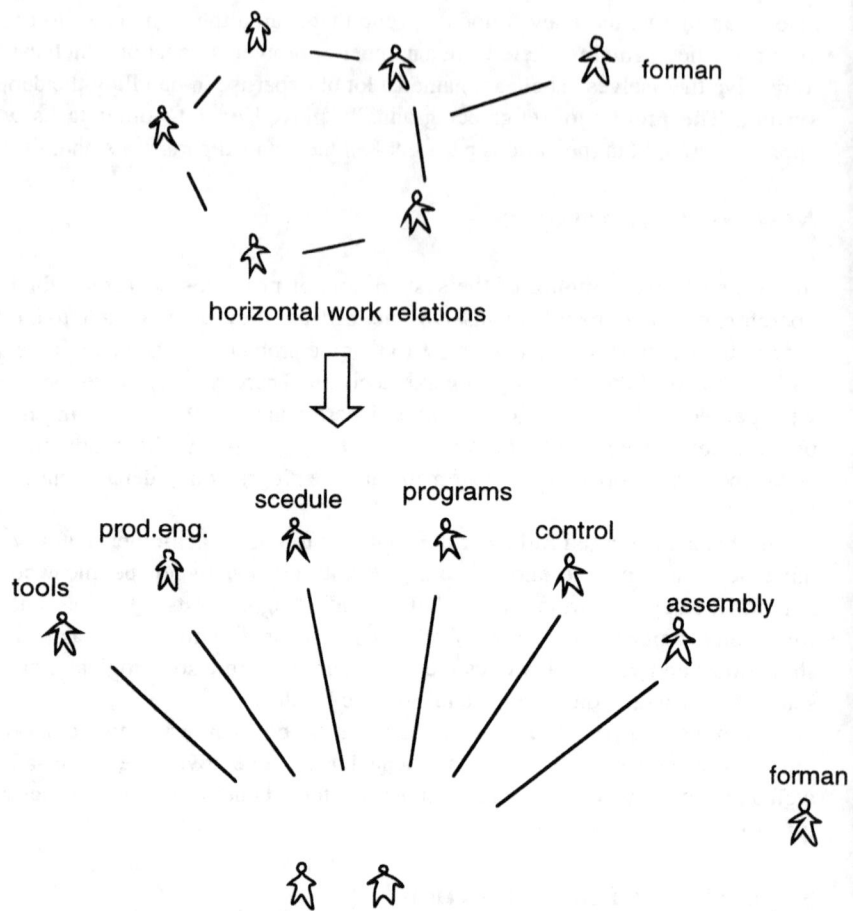

Figure 1. *Horizontal and vertical work organisations*

After a while, the crew took over the responsibility to order parts from the foundry. That made it possible for them to put pressure on the people at the foundry so that they actually supplied the FMS-cell with material that met the specifications and at right time.

New problems and new skills

Nobody in the company had adequate skills or competencies for handling the system that was installed. In the planning process, the work that the operator was assumed to do was very similar to that of the CNC-operators even if the complexity was higher, in terms of tools, part-programs, machine-configuration, crane-administration etc. The large variety of problems that emerged was unexpected, and the specific competencies needed to handle them could not have been foreseen. The emerging need to control a variety of prerequisites, internal and external, for the production process was learnt during the running-in and debugging period.

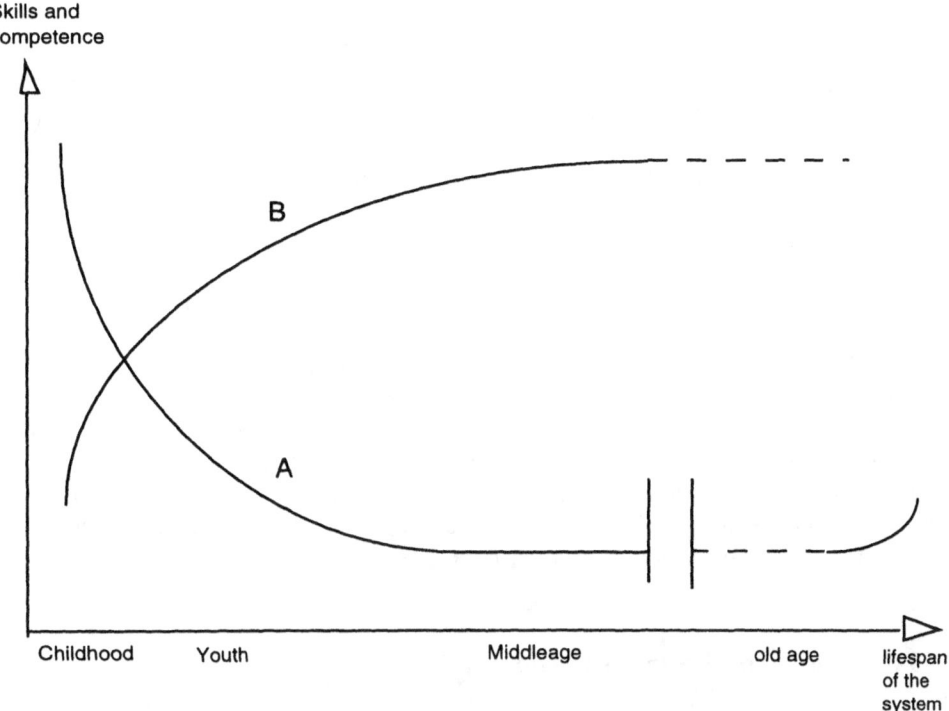

Curve A: Demand for skills and competence generated by the system during different periods of its life span
Curve B: The crews experience of its skills and competencies over the lifespan of the system

Figure 2. *Mismatch between acquired competence and demand for knowledge*

The operators developed their skills during this period of debugging and problem solving in the running-in period and in the first period of the production run.

Variations had to be taken care of before they became a problem. In close contact with the system, disturbances could be handled before they led to an automatic halt or severe quality-problems. Fixing the parts to be produced to the pallets had to be done in a way that corresponded to the "mode" of the working of the machine. Skilful operators could only allow small compensations for tool wear, hardness of material, etc. to obtain good quality.

However, the operators tried to reduce all sources of variation - compensations should really not be made in the steady-state. The result in terms of productivity was extremely good. In fact, this particular system had an uptime of an incredible 98% and reached even higher values temporarily, if regular maintenance is not included. The skill of assessing what actually took place in the system and anticipating the further development needed was crucial for keeping a high up-time and hence was very important to the economy of the system. Pre-planning and the ability to anticipate were key-competencies for running the system.

The reduction in the number of problems that occurred was therefore a result of pre-planning and the skill of interpreting the informational content of the noise that came from the system. Practice and knowledge made for the skill of detecting signals in the noise which indicated that something was going to be a problem. The crew was able to maintain a steady-state within certain limits. It was very seldom that the variations created problems that the crew could not handle. If they could not, there was nobody who could have done better. Periods when there were numerous problems arose when new parts were brought into the system. Then the skills of the crew were stretched and developed. During a smooth steady-state running, on the other hand, things were, to a great extent, much less demanding.

The system ran unmanned during nights. For the crew, this was a challenge but it was also a stress-factor. They tended to bring their job home with them. In the first instance, they had a problem leaving the workplace because of all the things that had to be checked and double-checked in order to keep the machine running. Then, when they were at home, they often called people who were working the late shifts, to ask them to check something. They found themselves frequently waking up in the middle of the night with the feeling they had remembered something they had forgotten.

Tendency to diminishing demands of skills

The more skilful the work team became in handling the sources of the problems and variations in the problems, the less they would have to do in steady-state running. Figure 2 illustrates how the need for problem solving in the system required a growth in the skills and competencies of the group. There was a growing mis-match between the two.

The group actually complained that the demands made of them in the steady-state were too low. They wanted to move into new areas to obtain a better control over the situation but they were not allowed to. You could say that their ambitions were not in keeping with the prevalent ideas about the division of work and the authority-structure in the organisation. Different dividing lines of the traditional organisation, however dysfunctional, prevailed.

Recruitment

The changes taking place raised questions about how people should be recruited and trained to run the system. Typically, people are recruited to replace some of the more experienced members of the work team. This probably takes place at a time when the demands for qualifications are rather low, i.e. at the lower part of the problem-curve in Figure 2. At this point, the opportunity to learn to handle all the problems that are latent in the system are scarce. When something happens, there will probably be a critical situation and more experienced staff will need to be brought in or the system will come to a halt.

The team actively brought in colleagues into their own work-organisation and created a learning situation whereby the newcomer could get gradually get acquainted with the different types of problems inherent in the installation. The work team had great difficulty in recruiting new operators to their group, even though they invited fellow workers to practise with them for a short time without formal commitments.

What is the work about?

Skills and competencies are normally socially acknowledged and valued. With the new integrated system, the skills and competencies needed for work are rather different from the ordinary trade-skills used on the shop floor. It was actually difficult for the people involved to describe what in fact had been learnt in the innovative process described above.

Some members of the work team found this problematic. When their friends or fellow workers asked them what they did, they were unable to describe their work in way that matched their feeling for it. It seemed much too simple when they talked about it. They knew that their work actually made the system very profitable but what they could tell was only bits and pieces, very anecdotal or case-oriented. Their knowledge was tacit.

The most experienced team members were disturbed that their fellow workers on the shop floor did not recognise the amount of work that went into the job they did. Some of the other workers were envious because they thought that the group had a relaxed and easy-way to earn a living. Others could not stand the seemingly idle work station that they thought the crew had. Almost no one could see or acknowledge the strain and the intensive attentiveness that was demanded from the group and they, in turn could not express it. For them that was one of the frustrating things about the new situation. It created a distance between them and their fellow workers. It created a situation where loyalties in the vertical organisation (cf. Figure 1) grow stronger than in the horizontal organisation, which actually had eroded due to the erosion in working relations.

After the first steps

The company gradually installed a number of automated flexible systems where some of the experiences from the first phase were picked up and developed further.

This first experience put ABT at the top of the list of companies at the fore-front of using the latest technology. By undertaking study-visits, case-studies and frequently participating in exhibitions and in lecture series, ABT made its concept known amongst people interested in automated flexible manufacturing both in Sweden and abroad.

Its production expanded even further and it became rational to invest in separate lines for the big volume products and then move into other technologies for parts production.

Ultimately this shed a new light on the procurement of parts. In-house manufacturing today in ABT is challenged by out-sourcing to, for example, Taiwanese subcontractors who are highly competitive in casting. The Swedish casting industry has almost been eradicated. Management has argued that if casted parts are bought from Taiwan, the parts might as well be finished there to save on transport, weight, and manufacturing costs. With this approach, there is a great risk that high in-house competence in cutting and in production-system design will be devalued.

Some Comments On The Case

Some aspects of the developments at ABT have been found in a number of other cases of similar development processes (Hautala 1986, Wobbe 1991). In the following section I will make some comments that point to general conclusions which could be drawn from the ABT case.

Change and the skills

Technological change in manufacturing has often to do with the mechanisation of earlier manual or mental tasks. Very often it is about the integration of processes that were earlier performed by separate machine-tools as, for example, with the integration of metal cutting by turning, milling, boring and grinding into machining centres.

The development of cutting materials has increased possible cutting speeds enormously. In order to make productive use of this possibility, the motor effect of the machine tools has increased and they are much more stable to cope with these effects. With the high speeds possible it is no longer feasible to control the cutting process manually. The control has to be computerised to create optimal cutting circumstances at each point in the process and in each type of cutting process. This change has led to important changes in the skills needed in manufacturing.

The skills and competencies that emerge from a specific work situation is dependent on the choices made in the technique and the organisation through which the production process is performed. Traditional skills typically evolve in relation to a specific cutting process, e.g. turning. It takes roughly seven years to become a skilled turner - a tradesman. To become a grinder takes even longer. Skills and competencies were developed in the interaction between the task, the workpiece, the cutting tool, the machine-tool and the control process performed by the machinist.

That skill will not necessarily develop with an integrated machine tool. The interaction is different and so is the learning process. But traditional skills are still needed because the basic cutting processes are the same: turning, drilling and boring, grinding and milling. The integration of different cutting processes into one machine centre moves the focus of the tasks from control of the tool to the control of the system. This requires a shift the knowledge and skill requirements.

A systems operator can acquire the skills that the design of the system and the organisational setting permits her or him to. In designing socio-technical systems, there is always a choice of work organisation. While the choice of technology is often restricted by what is available, the choice of work organisation is only restricted by the human mind and its traditions.

For any given technique, there are many ways to organise the work. If a technique is not provided, there are even more options. There is a multitude of development paths that could be explored to find solutions to a specific problem. The solutions chosen depend on the available technology. The solution is influenced by social factors. It is to a great part determined by the social conflicts. The design process is basically a construction of social realities, and it takes place in a social reality that sets out the dividing lines for choices to be made in the design process.

In order to get a better grip on the choices that are available concerning skills allocation and organisational structure, I have found it fruitful to categorise the tasks performed by the systems operators into three different categories.

The tasks

To handle the different organisational responses, the task of running the system could be described as consisting of three types. They refer to different aspects of the relation between the operator and the process. These categories relate to different mental regulatory levels used by the operator to handle the production process and will be simply called primary, secondary and tertiary tasks (for regulatory theory, cf. Norman 1988).

Primary tasks relate to the part of a task that is primarily concerned with moving the parts, for instance putting them into a machine, clamping them to a chuck or a pallet, and taking it away when processed etc. Typically, the primary task relates to the routine of bringing a part to the work table, processing it with the help of hand tools and taking it down again when it is ready, etc. Moving the parts and processing them is maybe the most obvious thing in a shop. Of course, primary tasks could be manually or mechanically performed. From a regulatory point of view, primary tasks are typically of a sensory-motor type, and take place in a repetitive steady-state situation.

Secondary tasks concern the control of tools. Secondary tasks evolve in relation to mechanisation. When we leave hand-tools and use machine tools, the guidance of the cutting edge has to be indirect. Control is mediated by different means, ranging from mechanical transmission of movements or intentions, to software programs that perform a sequence of mediated intentions in relation to the movement of the cutting edge. Secondary tasks involve a more rule-based type of problem solving which primary tasks do not normally do.

Tertiary tasks concern the handling of exceptional cases, the unforeseen variations, disturbances, etc. The problems arising from the use of new technology often have both a technical and an organisational origin. The process of problem solving, when handling these problems, is at a high regulatory level where creativity, intuition and knowledge is essential. Problems that occur regularly, once solved, are gradually handled at lower regulatory levels. Ultimately, they are incorporated in what could be called regular skills. This process is one of the crucial points in the organisational aspects of handling new technology - without the opportunity to be exposed to inherent problems, nobody could ever learn to handle a situation in a skilful way.

The rationale behind allocating the tasks into three different categories is that organisations tend to handle them not integrally, but separately. It is argued that the way in which these three aspects of the task is handled in the organisation determines not only up-time in the manufacturing system but also which skills and competencies that emerge in relation to the introduction of new technology.

Division of work - different modes in FMS-systems

Setting the borderlines of the system

From the point of view of skills, one crucial aspect in designing production systems is how to define the dividing lines of the system. What type of tasks should be done by the operators and what should be done by supervisors, production engineers, people at the planning department and even by people at the firm that has delivered the equipment to the system.

In a traditional organisation that is not a problem. Everybody can see the machine and there is an organisation to handle it. In an FMS system, the complexity is higher than is normally the case. The way in which the system is perceived determines what kind of skills could be developed on the shop floor, near to the system. Which problems should be solved there and which problems should be solved at higher levels in the organisation?

It might not be practical to consider the producer of cast iron as a part of the system, even if that producer greatly affects the system, but the decision-capacities needed to handle the environment of the system should probably be considered as being at the discretion of the system-operators. The way in which the system's borderlines are set, greatly affects the resources of the system and thereby, the actual functioning of the system. In order to illustrate this, a number of examples of work-partitioning from the perspectives of the three types of tasks discussed above are outlined as follows, where P, S and T stand for primary tasks, secondary tasks and tertiary tasks respectively. The geographical demarcations in the shop, used in the companies, are taken as a given. The examples are taken from ABT (Marking 1983a) and other cases reported in Marking (1983b) and Hautala (1986). A similar discussion can be found in Marking (1986).

S and T and vertically separated

Normally in this case-material, the technology brought into the companies was more or less new. The tertiary tasks were not foreseen and hence not planned for and the design therefore did not take them into account. Rather, they were considered to be due to poor design. In Figure 3, T is dotted owing to the fact that the competence for tertiary tasks is extremely hard to acquire outside the system. Of course, when it comes to repairs/maintenance, because specific skills are needed, the knowledge and skills required to act to prevent stoppages have to be developed and applied within the system. There is a time-space aspect of learning. Some skills can only be gained by being in close contact with the system.

The secondary tasks, such as programming, are often allocated outside the system in the design process. Skills concerning crucial aspects of the control of the system are thereby consciously allocated to non team members. The team will, if their autonomy is high, learn how to debug and reprogram the programs for individual parts, even if this is not expected or desired.

The design criterion in this case, however, is to assign low degrees of freedom to the group, in accordance with both management control strategies and existing skills allocations in the organisation. This typically results in a poor return on investment owing to excessive down-time, according to the experience of the case-companies.

Work-division within the border

A specialisation has developed between different persons in the team. Some handle the system from a cognitive and management point of view (S and T) and some handle the material flow, such as the loading and unloading of pallets (P) (see Figure 4).

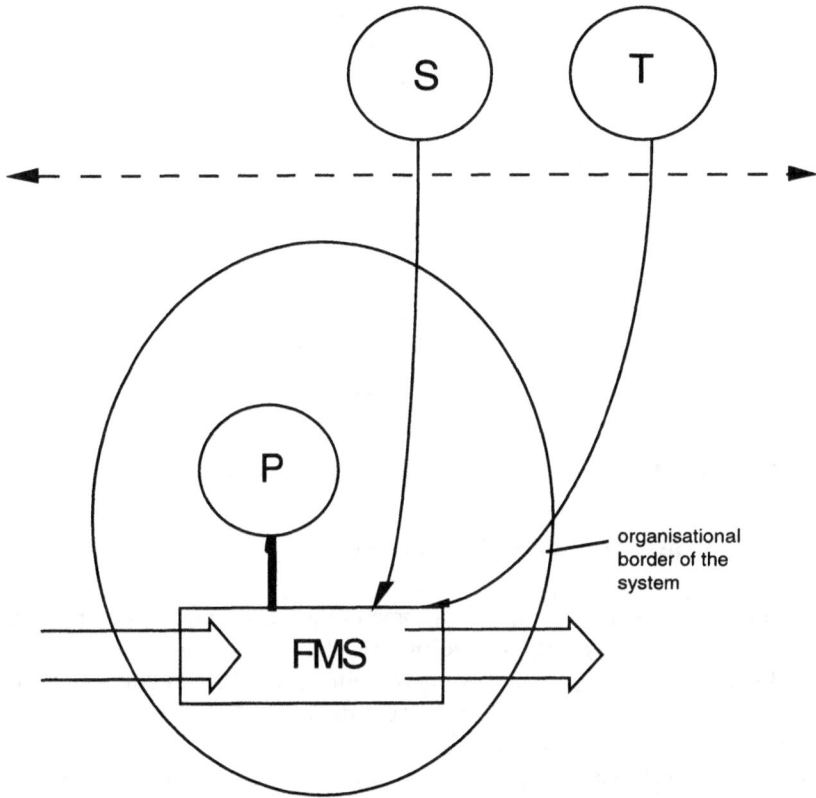

Figure 3. *Vertical division of work over the border of the system*

In systems which work in this way, the loading is physically separated from the machining centres which effectively takes away any possibility for these people to learn from problems occurring in the machines, and it shortcuts all feed-back loops. Unqualified personnel is typically brought into the system for the primary tasks and a two-level system is constructed with different reward systems and different locality-structures. This is the type of polarisation which actually generates disturbances, not least technical ones.

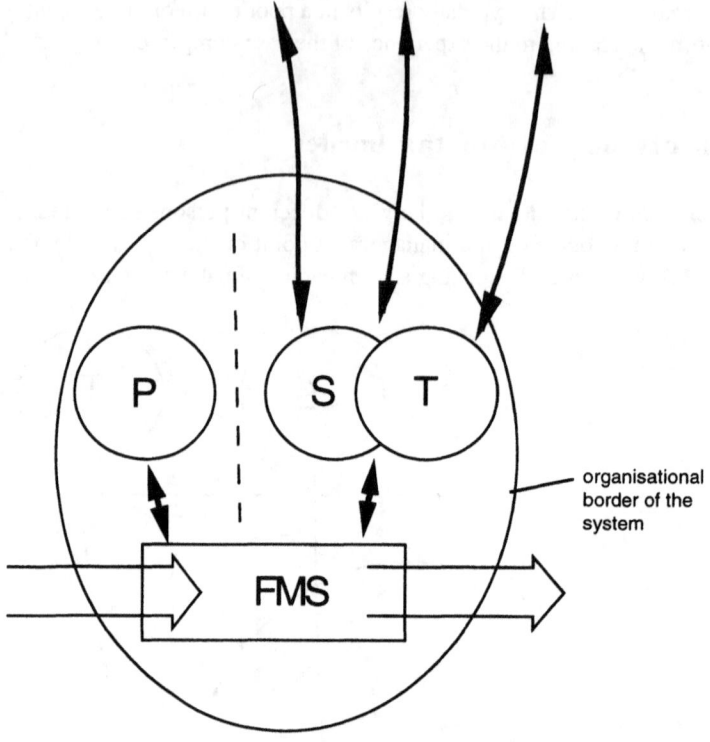

Figure 4. *Horizontal division of labour within the border of the system*

S and T horizontally aside the system

The model in Figure 5 has been applied in some of the case companies that believe the primary tasks to be the only ones needed in a steady-state. For a casual observer, the primary tasks is the only one you could actually see for yourself. Handling the down-time problems is typically an expert's job. The smooth running is taken for granted as that is what was paid for when the investment was made.

The problem is that these designs are in practice almost as big a failure as the ones involving a vertical parting of S and T.

Conclusions about division of work and skills-formation

The general conclusion to be drawn from this section is that the development of skills and competencies is contingent upon the design of the system demarcation and the organisational setting in which the system develops.

The integration of P, S and T in the system is provocative to a traditional organisation. It demands decision-making abilities or a degree of autonomy within the system that is not generally accepted in the line-organisation. The system demands a lot of attention from various specialists and also demands specific and new rules to be applied, for instance in the procurement of raw materials, tools, parts programs etc.

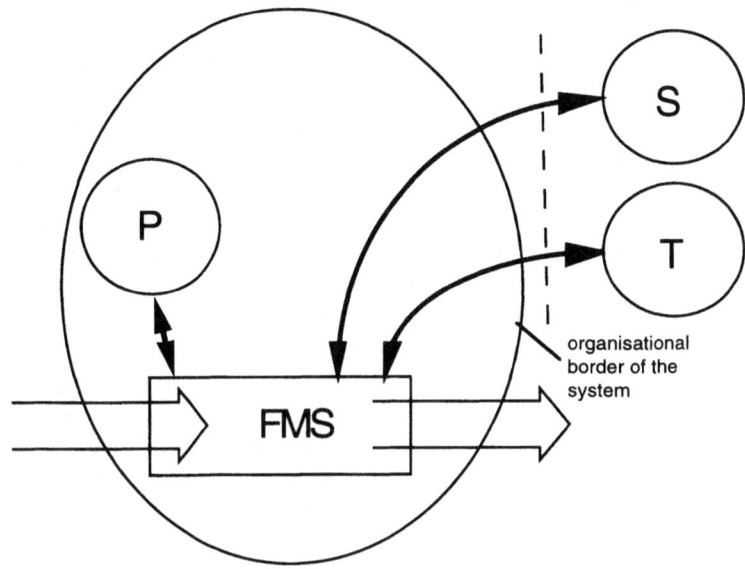

Figure 5. *Horizontal division of labour over the border of the system*

The problem-solving mechanism is not primarily skill-based, nor rule-based but to a high degree knowledge-based (Norman 1988, Rasmussen 1986) and that process has to be handled in the organisation. In order to do so, without making it obvious to the organisation that the existing division of work is dysfunctional in the new situation, the new technology was handled as a development project. The organisation was described as ad hoc and the possible threat the changes posed to the rest of the organisation was reduced thereby.

ntegrated technology demands integrated organisations

The situation depicted in Figure 1, of the vertical organisation, points to a systematic problem. If the number of FMS cells were to grow in a traditional organisation there would not be enough people to support them if they were to work as they did in ABT. The production organisation would have to be redesigned. Technology, together with demands for shorter lead times, reduced work in progress, increased quality, and created a push for new organisational designs. The demands for horizontal and vertical integration in the organisation converged. in ABT, more of engineering capacity has moved down to the shop level when new conditions for production have emerged.

The dilemma for production management

The changes in ABT have challenged the traditional aspects of the organisation. In a small part of the organisation, "surrounding" the new equipment, traditional technical and administrative control was, in some aspects, dysfunctional. Alternative control methods had to be applied.

The relations between management and workers are a matter of mutual dependencies. Each party tries to reduce its own dependency on the other party and to make the other more dependent. A changing balance also enhances the bargaining power of the gaining party. In ABT, the new technology made management dependent on a few skilful people who handled a huge investment at their discretion, particularly when it came to controlling the economics of that investment. Of course, management had a fall-back program in case of difficulties, but basically management had no control over the economic outcome. Management was entirely dependent on the group.

There were three strategies available to management for handling the organisational problems arising from new technology. One was to adapt the new technology to the traditional control structure and thereby accept a reduced return on the investment by under optimal use. The other was to accept that radical changes had to be made of the organisation, in order to make full use of the investment but at the same time take the risk that the change in control strategy may lead to a reduction in management's bargaining power. The third strategy was to treat the new system as an experimental concern and to let it live with new control structures within a temporary and ad hoc type of organisation. There would be a problem if the two types of control existed side by side. What was new had to be shielded by the creation of norms which would be legitimately applicable only to what was new. An ad hoc organisation was created with the purpose to handle the any perceived threat of the new system to the rest of the organisation.

Ad hoc organisations to relax tension

The third option, of an ad hoc organisation, was most frequent one followed amongst the cases studied, and could be clearly seen in ABT. It allowed high levels of skill to be allocated to the installation through a process of recruitment and autonomous development. The management style was flexible and supportive depending on the exclusive position of the system, i.e. how well it was shielded from the rest of the organisation. One could very say that a type of learning cell developed inside a more traditional organisation.

Control or autonomy?

Management's answer seems to be control by responsible autonomy. Here again the demarcation of the system is important. White collar workers have seen their position in the companies weakened. White-collar and blue-collar workers share more of the same problems today than before, which can be seen in the more frequent cooperation between their respective unions.

This means that control is performed in new ways over different groups of people and with different means. This is important when you discuss the design process. From this point of view, there is a great opportunity today to design efficient multi-skilled teams which could manage complex manufacturing systems.

Planning

Operative and tactical planning

Figure 6 suggests a design concept that should be viable for designing highly technical productions systems. P, S and T have to be integrated into the day-to-day work of the system. The operational planning of the production process has to be performed in the system in relation to its "customers". Tactical planning, developing the system as part of a whole production system in the company, development of customer relations etc., is more long term than operational planning and can be geographically separated from it but they are still mutually dependent.

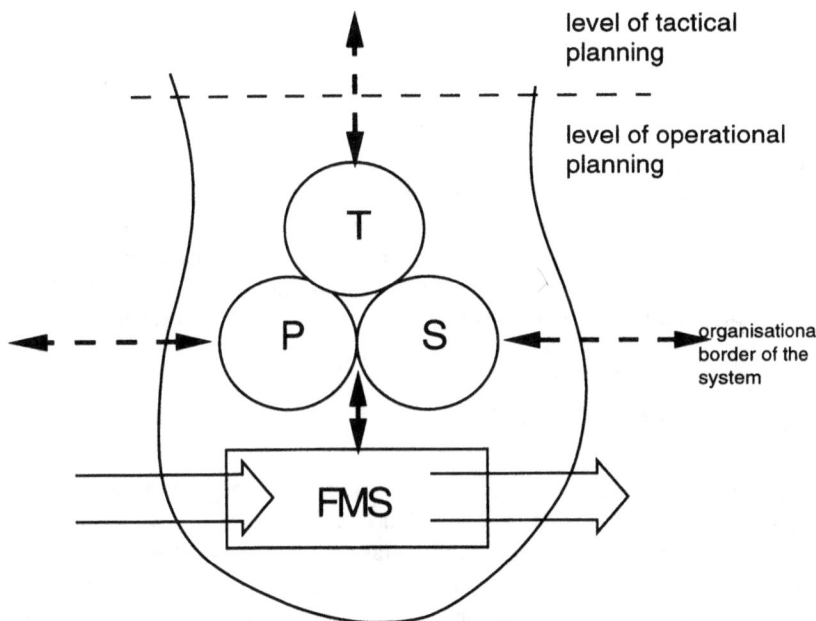

Figure 6. *Two levels of planning (tactical and operative planning) with mutual dependencies and integrated tasks.*

This type of design allows for a faster and deeper development of manufacturing skills in the workforce than the models that have been employed in almost all the case companies except ABT.

What emerges as patterns of qualifications is contingent upon the way in which the work and production organisation is developed. The idea that learning and the development of new skills is a crucial activity in productive systems has its base in a different perception of planning, where it has to be a mutual relationship between people working in different time-perspectives rather than a division of human capacities i.e. hand and brain.

Is there a tendency toward higher qualifications?

Tradition

In ABT, machining was not a core competence. Welding was the most valued skill and had been for many years. Other machining skills were paid less. The machinists were tended to be younger and left the company after a relatively short time for better paid work in other companies.

The development in machine-tools that took place during the 1970s vastly changed the characteristics of the shop. NC and CNC machine-tools were brought in but traditional trade hierarchies prevailed. The good thing was that the production engineers felt free to experiment in a way that was unheard of in companies where machine-skills were still prominent.

Organisation

Traditional Tayloristic organisations cannot cope with technology which demands immediate problem-solving and the presence of all "on-line" specialists at the shop floor level. Applying Tayloristic strategies to new technology is bound to render low productivity. ABT was basically Tayloristic but applied non-Tayloristic strategies to start up and run the system. In the other case-companies, various strategies were applied, some of which have been briefly covered above in the discussion about division of work and comparative levels of productivity.

Tradition prevails

Reshaping authority-structures in order to manage a second grade activity, which machining actually was in ABT, is not easily done. Management support was not there and the design of new systems was done on a relatively lower complexity level with an acceptance of a lower degree of up-time as a cost for the keeping up of traditional control structures. Control by responsible autonomy was all right as an ad hoc solution but was not accepted by management on a bigger scale.

General Conclusions

1. The development of skills concerning the control of the manufacturing process in the FMS-systems or cells, depends on:
    - how management conceives of the new system from the perspective of organisational control, i.e. how responsibilities and authorities are allocated in the organisation;

- how management handles the perceived threat of the new technology to the existing organisation.

2. The economics of the investment in new manufacturing technology, as with the FMS-cell at ABT, is dependent on the work-team's ability to handle the variations and disturbances that occur and hence, upon their skills and competence.

3. Flexible technology challenges traditional organisational structures if it is to be profitable. This challenge is due to:
   - the degree of autonomy needed at the shop floor-level to handle problems;
   - highlighting the dysfunctionalities of division of work in the production planning departments;
   - highlighting the dysfunctionalities of the traditional horizontal division of work.

4. The development of skills and competencies in connection with new technology are, to an extent, contingent on the uncertainties associated with its introduction. There is a tendency for the demand for skills to decline as organisations "learn" to cope with the technological challenges.

5. The new patterns of skills which emerge during horizontal and vertical organisational integration could quite simply be described as "reversed Taylorism", i.e. as the integration between hand and brain.

Analysis of ABT in the context of this study

Values, structures, processes and competencies

The company was rather traditional in the design of the production organisation. When the search-process in relation to a build up in capacity was initiated by the general manager, the prime restriction was on the production-area. There were no radical ideas about work organisation or skill-formation. The structure of the organisation was Tayloristic in many ways, except of course in functional supervision. Welding was the prime skill, and machining had a low status.

The concept of FMS and the idea of unattended night shifts was entirely new to the production engineers and others in the company. A group was formed consisting of an engineer and two operators. They actually handled the process of running-in the cell and thereby de-facto designed the work-practice and the work organisation around that cell. That also meant that the learning about this new technology primarily took place in a very restricted group with the location near the cell.

It all started in the process

The introduction of the new technology and the manufacturing process gave rise to new competencies. The group had a great influence on working-practices. Consequently, the FMS system demanded these new competencies be run effectively.

Structure had to adjust

The group needed a lot more autonomy than was ordinarily the case, or than was permitted in the production system. They had to handle a lot of problems which, in the hierarchy, belonged to somebody else. A traditional functional supervisory system might have been helpful in that situation. Something like it was informally erected because the team members had to have rather close contact with various preplanning departments in order to "borrow" their authority to solve problems.

This did not come easily in the traditional organisation. If it had been the rule rather than the exception, more informal handling of the problem solving process would never have been accepted in the management structure. As the installation itself was particularly exceptional it could be permitted as an ad hoc organisation within the more normal behaviour in the day-to-day running of the business.

Thus the structure had to adjust to the changed process and the changed competence in the group. The group members had superior knowledge about the functioning of the machine-system as a whole. Their competence was crucial for the efficient utilisation of the cell which represented a huge investment to the company. This fact made adjustments in the structure feasible.

Changing values

The change in values concerned the control structure. The new technology demanded that the team running it not only had responsibility of another dimension than what they normally would have had but they also had the right to make decisions in a vast area covering what would normally have been the task of other people in the planning department. This challenged the traditional way of perceiving the need for detailed control. This new phenomena was more like a partnership rather than a traditional control which eventually also affected the orientation of the people in the team. Not only did the values of management change but it also has an impact on the values of workers in relation to the overall workforce.

The management saw the change as a way of overcoming conflict between traditional working practices and new ways of organising profitable production. Management values reflected this change in the organisation and control of production. The management was also concerned with the perceived threat of this small-scale experience when applied to the whole organisation, because the large-scale change may not be amenable to traditional control. Thus from a control perspective, such a change was not feasible. What worked well on a small scale might get out of hand on a large scale. From the traditional value point of view, management had to restrict the impact of the new experience.

Breadth and depth of changes.

The process and the competencies represented a radical change. Since the change in the structure was radical and was handled as an ad hoc organisational experience, it did not have more than marginal impact on the overall organisation. Under the mechanism of dynamic conservatism, the old structures prevailed. The change in values was very important as part of a more global learning process. Although the change in values did not lead to major subsequent changes in this particular company, it did affect many people in other companies and in academia.

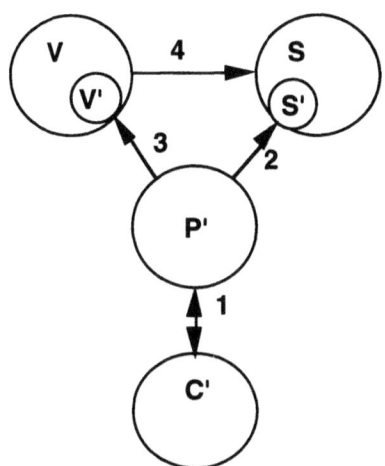

Figure 7. *Schematic figure over the change process.*

The changes in the competencies, the processes, the structures and the values were deeply radical but they did not have breadth and were unable to penetrate into other areas in the company. In fact you could say that the changes did not survive in the company in the long run. It is interesting to note, however, that the change in values which this company was a part of, is today penetrating the company from outside in the form of new ideas for the design of production system, and they are affecting the structures, processes and competencies from top-to-bottom.

In Figure 7 the meaning of the arrows 1-3 are clear. Arrow no 4 denotes that traditional values uphold traditional structures and marginalise the challenging change in P' and C'.

References

Hautala, O. & Marking, C. (1986).*Underlag för FMS-konferens* (memo), Stockholm: Svenska Metallindustriarbetareförbundet.
Marking, C. (1983a). *Fallstudier av produktionsteknisk förändring. AB Bygg och Transportekonomi.* Stockholm: Arbetslivscentrum.
Marking, C. (1983b). *Fallstudier av produktionsteknisk förändring. Saab-Scania AB* Stockholm: Arbetslivscentrum.
Marking, C. (1984). Mekaniserade system - utveckling eller utarmning. *Arbete, människa, miljö. 1984(1).* Stockholm.
Marking, C. (1986). *Arbeit und Arbeitsorganisation bei Automatisierung*, memo, Stockholm: Svenska Metallindustriarbetareförbundet.

Norman, D. M. (1988). *The Psychology of Everyday Things*. New York: Basic Books, Inc; publ. cit. from Ellström, P-E. *Lärande och arbetesorganisation* in Marking, C. (ed.) (1992) *Kompetens i Arbete* Stockholm: Publica.

Rasmussen, J. (1986). *Information processing and human.machine interaction*. Amsterdam: North-Holland

Warner, M. Wobbe, W. and Brödner, P. (1990) *New technology and manufacturing management. Strategic choice for flexible manufacturing systems*. Chichester: John Wily

Chapter Fourteen

The Evolution of Management Thinking on Production Systems at Clark-Hurth

M. F. Ghyssaert

Introduction

The Clark Hurth Components company, which is the object of this study, is situated in Bruges, in the northern part of Belgium, about 20 km inland from the coastal port of Zeebrugge.

The company was founded in 1968 under the name of Clark Components Europe, as the European distribution centre of the American multinational Clark Equipment Company. After a takeover and merger in 1990 with the company Hurth (which produces smaller transmission axles), Clark-Hurth received its present name.

At present, there are about eight types of torque converters and transmission in its product range. Because of its philosophy of flexibility and client-centred production, Bruges mostly designs adaptations of and specific accessories for its basic product. Because of the client-centred production and the specific nature of the final product, product planning has been centred on "just in time" orders. For the moment, production is taken up entirely with these orders.

In 1992, the company employed 636 people. The company does not employ female workers. The personnel of the company is very young - 70% of employees are younger than thirty-five.

Direct production is organised in four departments: the steel department, the heat treatment department, the main casting department and the assembly department. The focus of this study is the transformation process of the organisation and the job profile in the steel department between 1980 and 1992. In this department, steel and to a lesser degree aluminium raw pieces are subjected to the preliminary treatment and the metal machining operations (turning, milling, centring, drilling, tapping and in particular the different gear manufacturing operations). After the heat treatment the pieces are subjected to various finishing processes (esp. grinding) and after that they are ready for assembly.

How Work was Organised before the Change

In the 1970s, five types of torque converter and transmission units were manufactured on purpose-built automatons and NC-machines, which were programmed by experienced technicians and engineers from the production planning and programming department. This department was situated outside the production units.

The machine operators were to a large extent older employees without qualifications. The tasks of the machine operators remained very simple and were restricted to global visual control and to loading and unloading the pieces into and out of the machines. Highly qualified and experienced technicians were responsible for adjusting the machinery and for reporting technical malfunctions to the maintenance service; the foreman was in charge of the planning, and the quality control was carried out by an independent testing department.

Most of the equipment was arranged in groups of three or four machines. depending on type of technology (milling, turning, drilling, etc.). A machine group was operated by one worker in a continuous shift system (not during the week-end). In 1988, the steel department was composed of about 20 of these machine groups. In 1980, the company bought its first CNC systems, which were programmed, adjusted and operated just like the NC machinery in the production groups.

The Reasons for the Change

The growing competition and the deepening economic crisis of 1982-83, forced the company to develop a client-centred sales policy. Tailor-made deliveries resulted in a number of variations. The task of the preparatory department became more arduous and the quality control division lacked time and experience to make a proper quality evaluation and to develop adequate measuring procedures.

The diversification and realisation of the products also involved additional technical and administrative assignments for the assembly department. Over the entire production, the scrap volume (i.e. rejected components) and the modification of unserviceable pieces, increased considerably.

An Experiment with New Types of Production Groups

The management and the unions estimated that the source of the production problems were situated in the steel department, so the works council decided to set up automated (and not robotised) production groups in which multiskilled workers were to be employed.

In 1984, the company started the production of 250 different axles on a 50-metre long production line. It consisted of 22 machines and was operated by 11 workers in a continuous shift system. This production line had operations for finishing the components, such as turning, centring, drilling, tapping, milling and even gear-milling and pitching operations. In addition to these production groups and the so-called "production line", the company also installed a conveyer belt and a central warehouse. At the same time, production groups of four CNC turning lathes were set up.

In every production group, a certain number of similar components could be manufactured. The work reorganisation, based on the so-called "group technology", was targeted on saving time on machine preparation ready and reaching a more flexible production planning. By producing smaller batches, which is one of the basic concepts of the just-in-time principle, the company planned to shorten its production time and minimise its stock of semi-manufactured items.

Problems Arising in the New Production Groups

- Working in production groups caused problems to the machine operators: they couldn't handle the huge production variety due to the diminishing of the lot sizes, nor the many program adjustments which had to be executed during the supply of new components.
- The foreman was busy with the follow-up to the planning stage and was therefore not available to provide the necessary support. The communication between the operators and the planning officers was difficult because of the distance between their department and the production area. Program adjustments were done manually and off-line.
- By the end of 1984, eighteen months after the start of the production cells, half of the machine operators working in these cells had complained to the personnel department about the stressful working environment. Finally, the experienced operators asked permission to return to their former turning lathes and forget about the paperwork they had to deal within the new system.
- Only the young school leavers could handle this work situation and the unexpected technical problems it involved: they were the first to have received CNC training at school, and had combined theory with the newly organised 'school traineeships'.

The Technology Cell Solution

Because of the above-mentioned problems with the production groups and the reaction to them, the works council decided in 1985 to set up a work organisation in the steel department on the basis of smaller and less complicated technology cells consisting of two or three machines. In these cells, smaller series of 10 to 15 work pieces were manufactured on the basis of only one specific technology. The machines of these cells were provided with the necessary equipment to allow the workers to perform specific operations on each group of pieces.

In 1986, such cells were set up in the steel department. They were arranged laterally, in a so-called herringbone order, opposite an 80m-long automatic warehouse for the work pieces. A computer-controlled crane distributed the work pieces from the warehouse to the technology cells. The program for the warehouse has been developed by engineers from the company itself in cooperation with the company that delivered the crane.

The entire project was managed by a specially set up project group, which consisted of the production manager, the programmer, the planning officer and the trainer. The project group also examined the need for training and laid down the tasks of the foreman and the operators as described below. In 1986, the first cell was connected to the warehouse. The warehouse program was tested on this cell. The foreman was charged with the input of production assignments into the computer according to the production plan. During the programming process, special attention was given to user-friendliness and flexibility for the benefit of the foreman and the operator. The operator was given access to the planning data in order to enable him to consult the next orders without changing the planning sequence.

This allowed him to prepare the machine and the equipment for the next tasks. The operator could not however change the planning sequence; this task was assigned to the foreman only. After having finished an order, the operator was able to instruct the computer to dispatch the component series to the warehouse.

New Qualifications Profiles and Function

According to the project group, the operator of the technology cells had to be restored as a technical expert to his permanent work-station; he should have a multiskilled and more autonomous job:

- the operator must be able to introduce small program adjustments to the machine;
- the operator must measure the components immediately after the final operation and introduce the tool equipment corrections;
- the operator should be responsible for small preventive maintenance of the machine; before the more thorough maintenance or repairs, he has to prepare the work station (i.e. the machine and the surroundings) by cleaning up and executing preparatory dismantling;
- the operator should instruct the computer to dispatch the finished components to the warehouse; he must also know how to retrieve information about the next tasks from the computer.

Already from the start of the production groups, intensive action was taken for training the machine operators in order to familiarise them with the CNC systems and the programming techniques of the machinery.

Some machine operators could not cope with the new higher requirements. Because of the differentiation in the qualifications, the jobs of tuner-operator and tuner-monitor have were developed: the tuner-operator became an independent operator, able to introduce tool-corrections in the control systems according to the measurements of the work pieces; the tuner-monitor, an even more experienced operator, was able to adjust the program and the tool tuning of different machines.

Management Development

In order to meet the higher technical requirements for the personnel, the company started an intensive training in job analysis in 1986. Every engineer was obliged to follow this course. The foremen could participate on a voluntary basis: the course enabled them to notice organisational problems and to solve them in small groups.

The top executives tried to define a general training policy to meet the changed production requirements. In 1987, the executives attended a seminar at DEF International (Développement Ét Formation, a division of Association of Business Consultancy in Paris); the programme of the seminar was inspired by Tom Peters' book "In Search of Excellence" (Peters 1982) and focuses on five themes:

1. dynamic entrepreneurship;
2. practice-based organisation;

3. client-centredness;
4. stimulation of individual involvement;
5. implementation of the company values.

As a result, the directorate decided to follow a policy of continuous training, in which internal communication (workshops, company papers) played an important part to put the theoretical ideas into practice. The personnel manager trained 50 members of the middle management on the basis of the above-mentioned DEF themes.

As a result of this training, the executives realised the necessity of training the lower-level managers. In 1989, the company started an internal training project in effective management. These training activities took place between 1989 and 1992 and were spread over nine sessions. They were attended by 60 foremen and group leaders of administrative services.

Principles Underlying Management's New Strategy

The above training activities, together with the experiences with the project group mentioned above, led to a human resources strategy, that the management summarised as follows:

- simpler operations;
- better communication;
- integration of different functions;
- keeping the decision level as low as possible.

To solve technical and social problems related to the technology cells, the work preparation and planning department was integrated in the production area in a new work-group. An on-line connection was installed between the work preparation and planning department and the cells. This allowed the tuner-operator and the tuner-monitors to transmit the program adjustments in the CNC machines directly to the preparatory department.

The idea of work-groups as a new form of cooperation was well received by every department and by the social partners. From then on, the company has been creating a work group whenever new technology was introduced. Every work group consists of the trainer, two operators, the foreman, the planning officer and the quality inspector. It became a general rule that after the acquisition and before the delivery of a new machine or installation, the trainer, the planning officer and two operators were sent to the manufacturer for training. This training formula exerted a very positive influence on the motivation of the operators: they felt recognised in their technological experience and they discovered at the same time each other's technical and social problems.

Thanks to the introduction of the work-groups, it was easier for the trainer to localise the problems and to conceive more appropriate actions. On the other hand, the operators and foremen felt supported in their technical and social problems (e.g. their relation towards the planning officers).

In 1987, the quality and training policy of the company became definitive through the recruitment of the total quality manager and the manager for social relations. The latter, responsible for personnel training, was placed under the supervision of the personnel manager.

Development of Shop-Floor Workers

Owing to internal problems with production organisation, the management became aware of the need for training of the shop floor workers, who were directly related to the practice of the production process (the machine operators, tuners and foremen). In order to organise the training activities, it was necessary to modify the work organisation: the integration of the production planning and preparation department and the quality control department in the production area on the one hand, and the transfer of training from the production to the personnel department on the other hand. The growing competitive pressure on quality and price of the product and the facilities of the new computer-technologies (CNC, CAD/CAM, PLC) required a flexible and efficient production organisation: an "appropriate" use of the resources (human resources, machinery, energy and surroundings) had to lead to a 'proper' product.

In 1989, the supervisor trainer of the steel department and the instructors of the main casting and the assembly department were placed under the manager in social relations of the personnel department. This mutation was necessary to free the trainer from common production problems, which were allocated to the foremen and the tuner monitors. Through this the trainers could focus on realising the training policy.

For the development of this product organisation, the management has focused attention on human resources: flexibility and efficiency in an organisation is only possible if the personnel can handle the newly acquired software and hardware (planning, organisation, application, adjustments and previsions are still to be exerted by the personnel).

Both the internal training by the personnel manager (the DEF course for the middle management and the effective management course for the lower-grade managers and the foremen) and the external courses in job analysis and management for engineers and foremen, have always been focused on receptivity to "signals" (learning to see problems), handling these signals in a communicative environment (exchanging experiences in the work group), testing the actions by practical experience and learning from practice.

The Human Resources Strategy in Practice

1. A Simpler More Efficient Manufacturing Process

When designing its first transmission unit (1986-1988), the Bruges plant paid special attention to standardisation and simplification in the production of the components. This positively affected the cost price (because of the shorter production times and the simpler and low-priced machinery). With Computer Aided Design (CAD), other facilities were supplied. CAD however required new skills.

Experience shows it that the design mainly - for about 75% -determines the final cost price of a component. By simplifying the design, production can be organised through simpler, quality-guaranteeing production processes with lower-skilled personnel and more surveyable planning. For this reason the top management of the company decided in 1992 to authorise the setting up of a design group to the division of Clark-Hurth Components in Bruges.

2. Better Communication

For each technology cell, a work group was created which meets weekly and is presided over by the foreman. Every operator and adjuster of the cell has the opportunity to present his problems, for which a solution is sought. If necessary, the trainer can participate in the work group. In any case, the foreman reports to the trainer on the proceedings of the workgroup.

The foreman also holds an annual performance evaluation meeting with every employee. In this evaluation, the foreman does not assess the functionality of the individual in the work organisation. The work-group and the functionality evaluation are an important means for the foreman to understand the training needs for this group.

On the basis of the training demands, the social relations manager (personnel department) draws up an annual training plan and submits it for approval to the general manager. After approval, the personnel department keeps the evaluation of the trainees in the training file, which enables them to report to the general manager and the total quality manager.

3. Role of the Trainer in the Communication Process

The trainer plays an important role as a communication interface between the production area and the management, in the areas of human resources and production requirements.

The trainer discusses the needs for training needs with the social relations manager on the basis of his information from formal contacts with the work-groups and informal contacts with the machine operators and the tuners. He keeps himself informed about the qualification developments of individuals through personal contact (an "on the job" training conversation or a classical collective training) and by making enquiries during the training of machine operators.

The trainer uses this information as qualification needs to discuss the technical production problems which may arise during the production process, production planning and machine capacity, with the foremen and the planning officer.

Experience showed that the uniformity of the means of production was important: the installation of the same type of machines, control systems and tools, simplifies the production, and also the operations performed in the field. The training is simplified and the process of "self learning in the field" is given a better chance of success.

Technical problems that repeatedly appear, or have reached a critical stage, must immediately be reported to the production manager. If there is no solution available, the production manager orders the trainer to create and supervise a technical work group, composed of the planning officer, the foremen and the tuner operators. The trainer reports the results of the work group to the production manager. On the basis of this report, the production manager draws up an investment proposal for the works council. After approval by the social partners, the proposal is included in the annual budgeting plan.

4. Integration of the Different Functions

Until the introduction of the technology cells, the planning officer worked independently of the production environment. He was entirely responsible for the production process, because the programming and the planning were at that time strictly regulated. The technical evolution (the flexible dialogue-controls in CNC systems), the enhanced qualifications of the personnel (programming skills) and the client-centred market evolution resulted in flexible work-organisation in the technology cells. The planning officer handed over the more executive (programming) tasks to the shop floor, in order to be able to concentrate on his organisational and planning duties, such as the working of the project groups.

The Foreman was given the general responsibility for organising his technology cell. Because of the introduction of computerised planning, he acquired more facilities to develop the HRM in his cell; he was the prime contact for the trainer charged with outlining the personnel investment policy.

The tuner-monitor optimised the programs of the planning officer on the CNC machinery for the machine operators of the different cells. Within the scope of the production optimisation, he often had to consult the foreman and the preparatory department. He was also responsible for immediate technical support during the training period of new machine operators during their trial period.

The tuner-operator was responsible for the overall target level for every machine operator. As already mentioned above, he was responsible for controlling his machine, the program and the components; he had to follow up the production, keep his workshop in good repair and to report irregularities. His problems and suggestions were given a hearing in the work group, in which he took a permanent part.

In addition to his more executive tasks, the machine operator was also charged with controlling more operations thanks to the new facilities offered by the CNC control systems. In the new drilling centres, for instance, he could retrieve information about the productivity of the machine and the cutting time of the tools.

5. Keeping the Decision Level as Low as Possible

Because of the integration of functions, each individual at any level has acquired a 'self managing' position involving organisational, executive, controlling and decision-making duties. Thanks to the integration of the functions, the workers can acquire more experience, which allows them to be more independent in their jobs and participate expertly in the discussions in the work group. Their experience is appreciated by the management, which encourages a policy of increased staff participation and power of decision. On the other hand, everybody receives information on the actions of his environment. All these factors contribute to the self confidence and the motivation of each individual employee.

Summary

Clark-Hurth has experienced dramatic changes in the requirements for competition during the 1980s. The company has responded to these changes in several ways. The responses that are presented in this chapter illustrate a series of changes in management perspectives in relation to how to design production systems.

Each step brought with it substantial organisational learning and un-learning. There has been a shift in control structures in the company, going from a rather traditional direct control to a situation where the mutual dependency of management and workers gives room for skills development, more autonomy in the work roles of the workers and a production design more reliant on competencies at the shop floor level than on hierarchical control.

The company has subsequently developed new means to support the production, building on cooperation between trainers, production planners, formen and workers as the prime process. The new design of the production process provides opportunities for the long term development of enhanced competence in the production organisation in general and specifically among the workers.

Analysis of the Case Study according to the Common Framework: Values, Structures and Processes

Clark-Hurth was a rather conventional company with regard to the values the management held concerning how production should be organised, how control structures should be built and also concerning the ways in which the people in the shop floor and their competencies were perceived. The gradual changes have to be seen against this background. The changes that took place were at the outset management responses to a change as a prerequisite for combativeness in the marketplace (see Figure 1). The adoption of strategies

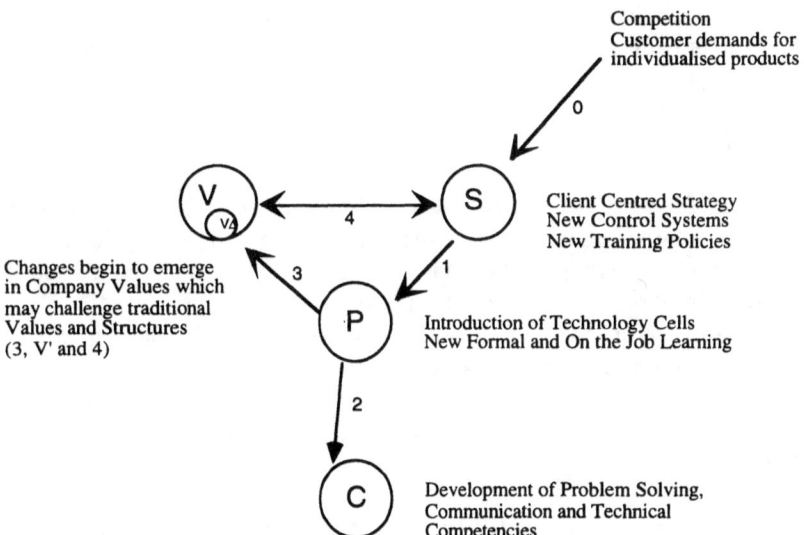

Figure 1. *Prerequisite for combativeness in the marketplace*

encompassed greater discretion and thus development of new work-roles and competencies among the workers, could be judged as an adaptation of more "modern" management strategies rather than a change in values of the management. That does not mean that management values did not change. It could be argued that the marginal change in control structures has led to an internalisation of the more enlightened parts of new management strategies.

Noting that the initial demand for change came as a result of external factors, we will focus on what took place inside the organisation.

It all started in the structures

Owing to the new client-centred strategy, much variation was required. The amount of information handling that was needed to cope with these variations grew exponentially. The old organisation could not handle them efficiently. The first solution was to reduce variations by production groups and group-technology. That did not solve the problem as the lot-sizes grew smaller and smaller. The information-load grew and the system collapsed.

The next step was the introduction of technology cells - whereby the variations were reduced to a level that could be handled. These cells gave the operators a slightly greater influence over the work process.

Management wanted the new strategy to be followed up by control measures, like new report responsibilities, new training policies, new incentive schemes, etc. (see Figure 1).

The Process had to develop

The new design created a need for new work practices. There was a gap in the competencies needed and those that the workers had developed in the old work structures. Thus formal and informal training programmes were implemented. Problem-solving and Communication competencies in particular became much more important (see Figure 1).

Changing Values

The development of new design-criteria was not a result of changing values, but rather a rethinking of the means for handling a very troublesome and necessary change of strategy. Maybe the result from the change period will be a change in mental models concerning the relationship between the different categories of employees.

The changes themselves do not fundamentally challenge traditional values but may like the Trojan Horse bring forth such a challenge (see Figure 1).

References

Clark-Hurth, *Doeltreffend leidinggeven* (Efficient management): Clark-Hurth course.
Nyhan, B. (1991). *Developing People's Ability to Learn.* European University Press: Brussels, 1991.
Peters, T.J. and Waterman, R.H. (1982). *In Search Of Excellence.* Harper &Row, New York.
Vlasselaer, M. (1992). *Activity Based Costing - a revolution in management accounting*; Vub-Ulb/Solvay Business Review , February-April 1992.

Chapter Fifteen

A HUMAN CENTRED FRAMEWORK Of LEARNING AS SOCIAL AND ORGANISATIONAL INNOVATION

Karamjit S. Gill

Introduction

Recently "skill-based", "human-centred" or "anthropocentric systems" (APS) approaches have formed the basis for the design of alternative forms of production systems which place a central emphasis on the importance of developing more humane work practices and organisational systems. New working innovations such as autonomous groups, quality circles and networking, not only highlight the inadequacy of hierarchical management structures, they also show the inadequacy of the divisive and exclusive nature of training and education structures for meeting the skill needs of the modern manufacturing industry.

The debate upon learning strategies such as multi-skilling, life-long learning, and the learning organisation, are part of the challenge of innovating new education frameworks. This chapter discusses the development of a human centred framework of learning as social innovation. The discussion is based upon issues arising from a number of studies on anthropocentric systems and technological innovations in the manufacturing sectors in Britain and Ireland. It also draws upon case studies of a network enterprise model and an exemplar of a tacit company.

Anthropocentric Production Systems (APS): a move towards new forms of organisational and working practices

The arrival of microelectronics technologies in recent times has raised a new "machine question". The technical phenomenon has not only removed the tool from the hand of the skilled craftsperson and inserted it into the machine, but has also separated human knowledge and experience from the head of the skilled operator, embodying it in the computer program, thereby controlling the process of design, planning and manufacture. On the one hand this has resulted in a higher level of technical knowledge and supportive computer power which is enabling effective intervention through the active redesign of alternative technical systems. On the other hand there have been increases in the rate of product and process innovation along with changes in market demand. These are providing an economic incentive to encourage the creation of more flexible and adaptive technical and organisational structures (Badham, AI & Soc. Vol. 5.4: 263-276).

A recent FAST (EC) research initiative on anthropocentric production systems is one of the most significant developments in shaping work, technology and organisational structures (Cooley, 1989; Charles et al, 1991; O'Siochru and Dillon, 1991). This shaping philosophy takes a holistic view of the production culture including organisational forms, working practices and work-based learning strategies. APS aims to enhance the level of human skill and participation in the production process, through the implementation of:

- new technologies that valorise and complement unique human attributes; and
- new organisational structures that increase the scope for participation and control by those engaged in the production process.

At a research level, APS takes two possible approaches. These are the human-oriented approach and the evolutionary approach. The first approach argues that APS is no more than a human-oriented modification to the production process and comprises coherent systems only in certain restricted circumstances. The second approach argues that APS is a new paradigm for the production process. The human-oriented approach emphasises the role of technological and organisational innovations in enhancing work experience, improving motivation and concentration, and generally harnessing untapped abilities and energies. Examples of this approach range from human factors in machine design, group technologies, through to the human resource management approach. However, the effectiveness of this approach depends upon a coherent and consistent strategy of human resource development being pursued by management at a corporate level. Such a corporatist strategy is possible in a country like Germany which has developed the necessary combination of autonomous processes and institutional forms, and also has a highly skilled workforce (O'Siochru and Dillon, 1991).

The evolutionary perspective of APS argues that the enhancement of human skills in production will constitute the new core paradigm for industrial development into the next century, taking advantage of opportunities opened up by the microchip revolution. For some researchers APS has a European cultural dimension. It could harness the inherent cultural diversity of Europe to create a permanent wave of creativity and innovation which, culturally as well as economically, would yield a global competitive edge for European industry - some what analogous to the "Japanese miracle" (Cooley, 1989). This European vision takes a historical view of evolution from the replacement of the tool to the machine, and recently the replacement of uniform Fordism by flexible post-Fordism impacted by the microelectronics revolution. The initial promise that new technologies of robotics and artificial intelligence would create an era of the automated factory is slowly fading away. The dream that technology is a solution to all problems and will give rise to a leisure society is now no longer sustainable.

It is now widely recognised that while the Fordist approach may have been undermined by the new flexibility offered by microelectronics, the replacing of workers by sophisticated machines causes its own problems. The automated factory creates its own rigidity and inflexibility when it is implemented under the old technocentric conditions. For example it results in a misalignment between human skill and machine capacity, and in many cases automation is inadequate in duplicating, replacing or transcending the skilled processes. Rosenbrock (1989) points out this misalignment between new technology and human skill results from the rationalisation of human activities. This leads to the creation of a work force which is rendered more passive as technology becomes more active. The tendency is to design increasingly complex technologies which are capable of handling a wide variety of tasks belonging to the human domain. Humans are left to handle trivial and single tasks which are too expensive to be handled by the machine. This situation gives rise to a "misalignment" between human abilities and the demands of some tasks.

The process of eliminating the misalignment between technology and human skill gives rise to a paradox. To use a complex machine to perform a trivial task is too expensive and hence there is a need to design a simple machine to perform the task cost-effectively. Where the task is too complex, the solution is to decompose the task into simple tasks which a machine can manage. In both these cases the concern is to use the machine more economically and to make full use of its abilities. There seems, however, to be no such concern shown for human skills and abilities.

APS is offered as an alternative to the Fordist approach as a "search for ways of designing work and technology which combine unique human capabilities with the performance of machines". Here APS is represented as a way of exploiting both the available technological and human resources. The limitation of this notion of resource exploitation is that those human attributes and knowledge which are unique and irreproducable may not be deemed economic in the production process, and may therefore be excluded from any learning or organisational innovation. There is also a concern that wholesale automation would destroy the skill base of society, undermining its ability to innovate and reproduce itself (Brödner, 1989).

To a certain extent the APS approach does deal with these concerns by adopting various forms of group technologies and collaborative and integrative organisational structures and working practices. One way to achieve this is through the integration of the work structure and the institution of a flat management hierarchy. That is, through a high horizontal integration of skills, initiative and decision making, using concepts of team work combined with the vertical delegation of planning and executive tasks to the shop floor and the institution of new patterns of participation (von Bandemer et al, 1989). Some innovations in this area are: extension of work cycles; modular production; integration of qualified indirect work (e.g. maintenance into manufacture); cooperation of team work; and quality circles. These innovations draw on a number of new directions in flexible manufacturing such as the British concepts of human-machine symbiosis (Rosenbrock 1989, Cooley 1987) and the Japanese concept of group work rather as opposed to individual work. The latter is based on high personnel flexibility, task integration, self regulation and the use of workers' knowledge, e.g. through quality circles. These innovations also draw upon the German concepts of the humanisation of work-life as well as the Scandinavian models of semi-autonomous work groups, which are particularly developed in the automotive industry (Eichener, 1991).

Within a broader vision of the industrial culture, The EC/FAST report (Cooley, 1989) argues that since the European manufacturing base is largely composed of SMEs, and is characterised by a highly skilled and flexible workforce, its future strength will depend upon the development of anthropocentric systems which build on skill, ingenuity and expertise of working people. It emphasises the need to develop infrastructures, educational forms, and means of production which accord with the cultural, geographical, economic and environmental realities of the European Community, and build upon the cultural richness and variety in Europe. The role of responsive education and life-long learning is seen as being central to this vision. It is also recognised that "developing the skill and competence necessary in the twenty-first Century will require nothing short of a cultural and industrial renaissance".

Technological Innovation And Skill

Technological innovation in the areas of flexible manufacturing systems, flexible specialisation and anthropocentric systems, requires a fundamental shift towards new forms of organisational and working structures. These in turn require new forms of skills, competencies and knowledge in order to make effective use of new technology. Central to these developments are new forms of education and training which transcend the current technical notions of skill and the elitist forms of university education. In spite of different industrial cultures, both Ireland and Britain have retained their narrow vision of skill and their elitist form of education. Theory and practice is reflected in the separation of skill and profession, and there is no proactive system of life-long learning within organisations. These issues are discussed by drawing upon studies undertaken by the EC in the area of anthropocentric production systems and on employment and training (FAST, APS Series, 1991). The discussion is complemented by case studies on innovation.

The clothing and textiles sector provides a critical case study for a flexible specialisation thesis associated with post-Fordism, with its new patterns of demand and market segmentation which reflect an increasing fashion consciousness, "post-modernist" emphasis on "style", and individualism (Wyatt, 1989). The clothing industry characterises production processes, technological innovation and organisational forms which illustrate the potential and limitation of adopting APS approaches. Traditionally the clothing industry has a typical Fordist culture with a rigid hierarchical work structure and a relatively inflexible assembly line to ensure maximum productivity. Productivity is maximised by splitting the work into extremely short, discrete operations using dedicated machinery. Maximum use of machine capacity is achieved by allocating machinists to specified positions in the assembly line, while placing a small number of multi-skilled "floating operators" at positions which may either not be catered for by the specialists or by the assembly line machinists. The result is that the specific efficiency of each operator becomes a critical factor in maintaining an optimum balance between the capacity of the assembly line system and maximum productivity. However, this type of balance is becoming more and more difficult to maintain due to changes in production demand for small batch production, short delivery times, and greater product variety.

O'Siochru and Dillon (1990) point out that technological innovations, such as the automation of certain machine operations, which use computer software for balancing the efficiency of the operator and the productivity of the machine, are still dealing with the old technocentric approach of production. Workplace innovations such as machine lay out, job design, flat management structures, planning, and levels of training still deal with the old emphasis of mass production. Lloyd (1988) points out that many of the small firms rely on low wages and have inexperienced management and low productivity. Although a few firms have followed the path of flexible specialisation, British firms in the main opt for numerical rather than functional flexibility through practices such as "core specialisation" and "peripheral casualisation".

Anthropocentric approaches, such as autonomous groups, offer working opportunities for supporting self development and enhancing work experiences. For example, the Danish experiments in autonomous group working (Banke et al, 1991) and flexible production in the clothing industry accept the participation of workers in planning production, and requires training not only in machining skills, but also in planning and supervisory functions. It is suggested that this type of innovation encourages both a higher degree of initiative and motivation as well as group responsibility for performance. In addition to improving job satisfaction, it also allows for greater flexibility at the work place and contributes to improved productivity.

The Irish clothing industry, on the other hand, has followed the path of incremental innovation and technical change rather than that of autonomous group production as in Scandinavia. The clothing industry in Ireland has to a large degree resisted the automation of lower skills, and technological innovations have largely been in the high skill areas of design, engineering and cutting. The use of CAD in design and the computerisation of production to meet batch and flexible production, however, requires higher levels of work and management skills. This highlights the deficiencies of strict hierarchical forms of work organisation, and the need for promoting forms of organisation which encourage "multi-skilling" and increasing delegation. Recently there have been signs in Ireland of a move toward innovations such as autonomous working groups. One such example is that of Aer Lingus which has implemented new work structures that will allow workers more control over the work progress and decision making (O'Siochru and Dillon, 1991).

A Need for New Organisational Forms

Recent developments in new forms of organisation such as team working, semi-autonomous work groups, quality circles, group technology, multi-skilling and organisational aspects of JIT, are associated with 'Japanisation' as is the earlier QWL (quality of working life) movement and the humanisation of work programmes in Europe. Despite the extensive discussion of new forms of organisation to reduce hierarchical levels, increase the transparency of decision making, and lessen the vertical and horizontal rigidities to increased integration, their application in Britain is limited and piecemeal. This is mainly due to the traditional managerial resistance to change, skill demarcation, and a general climate of "low trust" in industrial relations in the voluntaristic systems of British industrial relations. Employee involvement and authority, multi-skilling, and group forms of work organisation, form an important prerequisite for anthropocentric production systems and skill-based flexible production. Their implementation in Britain has been undercut by a combination of both the institutional and cultural features of the employment systems, in particular of low job security, and the system of industrial relations and narrow job related training.

This narrow view of job-related training is rooted in the job-related notion of skill used in Britain. As in any other country, the nature and level of skill in British industry reflects the nature of the industrial culture in Britain. This is evidenced by numerous cases documenting de-skilling through the new technology of the CNC machine and CAD systems. These cases reflect the managerial goal of using new technology to reduce the costs of direct labour, with just minimal interest in job design for the remaining workers. Since the managerial goal in British manufacturing has been to reduce costs, this has resulted in the reduction of jobs for unskilled workers, and the remaining jobs have been highly skilled ones. This is possibly resulting in higher skill profiles for the remaining British manufacturing workforce (Charles et al 1991).

The managerial concept of skill can be understood by considering the culture of British industry. British manufacturing is concentrated (by output and employment) in large organisations which are more likely to be bureaucratic with a rigid division of labour between departments and job categories. However, evidence from the small firm sector shows that the use of CNC indicates greater task ranges and the need for more skilled operators for a strategy of flexible and /or high quality production (Dodgson, 1989). The "low-trust" relationship between employees and employers, together with traditional rigid skill demarcations is a powerful inhibitor of flexible multi-skilling and work re-organisation. Jones (1988) notes that there is some evidence of horizontal job enlargement in small FMS cells but no evidence of moves towards autonomous work groups. The strategy of larger corporations seems to be that of automating the gaps between islands of FMS in the direction of system-integration and CIM. Charles et al (1991) comment that UK manufacturers are opting for "numerical" rather than "functional" flexibility via increased sub-contracting and casualisation of labour - relying on a part-time and temporary peripheral labour segment to increase enterprise flexibility. British manufacturing strategy appears to lack direction in terms of the new production concept. It is caught in the choice between the strategy of upgraded Fordism and variants of diversified quality production which rely heavily on employee involvement and highly skilled human capital.

From the APS study on Ireland (O'Siochru and Dillon, 1991), it is worth noting that the attitude of Irish and British management towards life-long learning is very similar and short-term. In the Irish industry as whole, firms are reluctant to provide training in more flexible and transferable skills because of a concern that employees so trained may leave, thereby taking benefits elsewhere. In these circumstances, industry as a whole loses out - since most firms recognise that they would benefit from a highly skilled workforce - although individual companies are each acting rationally in their own interests. Strict demarcation of employee tasks also acts as an impediment to broader training for more flexible production and employment. There is therefore a need to adopt a collective approach to further training at a strategic level in order to maximise industrial and individual gain.

British employers have remained traditional in their concerns with short-term returns on investment. The departmental budgeting and accounting controls encourage short-termism and thereby inhibit long-term innovations in integrated manufacturing and organisation systems. Although computer-aided production management systems are now recognised as a vital feature of advanced manufacturing, for example, MRP (material requirement planning), and JIT (Just-in-Time), their implementation has not made a significant headway in Britain. It may be that the British management culture of control and short-termism is not amenable to fundamental organisational changes of integration and collaboration required by MRP and JIT. Haywood and Bessant (1989) and Jones (1988) comment that the high failure of both FMS and production planning in the UK are attributable to a common cause: a predisposition to implement new technology whilst neglecting human and organisational issues. This technical approach to new technology has meant that FMS systems are frequently used inflexibly as a substitute for dedicated automation for high volume, standardised production, and that production planning systems are grafted onto traditional organisational structures and practices.

New Technology, Multi-skilling and Innovation

Bowan et al (1991) in their study on information technologies and the implications for skills, point out that multi-skilling is a general trend which applies right across the economy, from banking to telecommunications and manufacturing. In manufacturing, the trend towards multi-skilling is related to the trend towards mechatronics - systems which incorporate both mechanical and electronic elements. Unskilled work is often superseded by higher level work which requires more knowledge and technical skills. They comment on a number of studies on the impact of advanced manufacturing technology (AMT) upon engineering skills and qualification requirements. The study (cf. p.34) notes that of two engineering firms which installed CNC machine tools showed that it was employment and industrial relations policies, rather than the new technology, that determined changes in work practices, control and qualifications. It is suggested that firms developed totally divergent organisational practices to deal with the adoption of new technology. The study (cf. p.35) also notes that after the introduction of the flexible manufacturing system the work organisation was not technologically determined, but depended on an interplay of economic, technical and social factors. On discussing the move towards flexibility due to developments of CNC technology in Danish firms, Hofstede (1984) points out that flexibility is a result of traditional education and work practices that have resulted in the Danish work and production culture being defined by a high degree of individualism, the ability to accept change, and a preference for team responsibility among most workers. It is generally emphasised that the skill requirements for new technology are influenced by existing education, training policies and work cultures.

Bowan et al highlight the significance of the skill and work culture in the machine tool industry. The existence of a skilled labour force is a major factor influencing inward investment. American investment in the EC has tended to concentrate on countries with a tradition of machine tool production. Spain has been a focus of much attention while Ireland has been ignored. Semi-skilled tasks have been incorporated into automated machinery thus reducing labour cost advantages of countries such as Greece and Portugal. Efficient production - using and producing machine tools - on new capital equipment is reliant on skilled not cheap labour due to its capital intensive nature. Even the assembly of machine tools from Japanese kits in the UK is now carried out by skilled and experienced labour. Germany has so far refrained from either outward or inward investment in machine tool production and has concentrated its activity within its borders where plentiful skilled - if high cost- labour exists.

The CHERI report (1986) notes that as with other industries, the way in which technology affects organisation and skill requirements in the automobile industry is to a large degree a matter of choice. For example, Renault's move towards team working requires a different set of basic human resource skills, such as the ability to function in a group, rather than working individually. Where group work has been introduced it has normally required workers to become - if not multi-skilled - at least multi-functional.

New occupations such as 'systems controllers' have developed with the integration of quality control, maintenance, machine programming and the regulation of flow. The 'polyvalent' production worker (polyvalent in the sense that he can carry out maintenance operations in addition to his direct functions), is much sought after to maximise the utilisation of high cost automated machines. In general, new categories of workers such as "strassenfuhrer" in Volkswagen have presented problems for the regrouping of work functions around them. Management's attempt to introduce new occupations to deal with technological problems may affect the established social cohesion of the firm, and ultimately production. For example firms have to walk a careful line between promotion based on seniority - in which case those chosen may not be most the appropriately skilled workers in new technology - and promotion based on qualifications, in which case company loyalty may be seen to have no virtue. Fiat's engine assembly plant at Termoli in Italy has dealt with the probable technological impact on organisational change in a different way. Three broad social objectives have been introduced in the design and construction of the plant. These are: to reduce repetitive work, broaden the skill base of workers, and improve the working environment.

The CHERI study notes that there is a general move towards polyvalence for workers in automobile production. The introduction of new technology at Volkswagen resulted in a company decision to substitute worker competence for the traditional concept of skill. Qualifications sought from operatives are now similar to those for professional workers, for example the ability to communicate, plan and cooperate. It has been argued that although such qualifications are not directly related to the introduction of new technology, they are a prerequisite for it.

Bowan et al conclude (cf.p.69) that there is a move towards broader based skills in all production sectors. Generally craft based skills and unskilled jobs are being replaced by higher skills based on knowledge and technical skills. In printing, for example they note that the work of compositors has decreased and, in some sectors, is being eliminated. Editors and journalists are required to have extra skills and this reduces the need for clerical staff. Traditional demarcations of trade have been eroded and the distinction between unskilled and skilled work is blurred. They also point out that both the food processing and packaging industries and clothing and textile industries also reflect the convergence in the skill profiles of manufacturing operatives and management. Here too there has been a growing demand for computer specialists to program, monitor and maintain microprocessor based systems. These changes have resulted in structural and cultural problems in the readjustment of the existing workforce. Government programmes for support during the restructuring process, for example, financial support and retraining for displaced workers have gone some way towards easing these difficulties.

Learning Beyond the Technical Skill

New forms of work and organisation require new forms of skills, a widening of technical task competencies, interpersonal skills for team working, the capacity to self-learn through experience, and the capacity to think holistically. Skills are developed through national systems of education and training provisions and also through the development of the abilities of the existing workforce. Responsive forms of education and training can contribute to developing an initial competence for lifelong learning, that will facilitate in particular the horizontal mobility of persons between related areas of skill and at broadly similar levels; providing opportunities for adding new competencies, both "horizontally" in related areas at the same level and "vertically"; and providing opportunities for those at the lower skill and education levels to gain access to higher levels (Charles et al, O'Siochru and Dillon).

It is worth noting that in both Ireland and Britain, being an apprentice and a technician is generally looked down upon. Vocational training has tended to be very directly related to perceived short-term needs of industry, leading to a narrow approach. An emphatic distinction between training and education is reflected both in training and education programmes. People with professional skills and those with practical skills follow different career paths within enterprises. There is very little mobility of semi-skilled craft workers to skilled craft workers, and from skilled craft workers to professional and management levels.

Charles et al note that the features of the British education system reflects the elitist legacy of academic education, the divorce between theory and practice, and the low status of non-university technical training. Social science and organisational studies are insufficiently incorporated into the curriculum of technical and engineering courses and post-school vocational training initiatives have been inadequate in the context of a voluntaristic system of provision.

Current education and training systems in Ireland are rigid, restrictive, class based and produce people with a narrow outlook and narrow skills. There is a need for an education system which produces a highly skilled, educated and flexible population, possessing a broad understanding of social, economic, and industrial systems, and capable of innovative, even radical approaches to their work and life. Such an education system needs to make ample opportunities available for further education and career changes. The goal of an apprenticeship system should be to produce a 'competence platform' from which craft workers can take on new areas and develop existing skills further. Apprenticeship systems should have as their central aim the introduction of broad based skills, coupled with deep and extensive competencies in chosen specialist areas. The whole focus of human resource planning must change towards planning for uncertainty. The focus should be to reach a "competence platform" which is capable of creating, sustaining and attracting highly skilled jobs, and that can adapt to new circumstances as they evolve. Because of the British colonial heritage, Ireland until recently lacked an industrial culture. In this vacuum, conservatism thrived on all sides amongst employers, unions, and the government. Because of the lack of an old industrial culture, Ireland now has an opportunity to promote an industrial culture based on human centred and anthropocentric concepts and practices (O'Siochru and Dillon, 1991).

Innovation of Network Organisational Cultures

New ideas and experiments in multi-skilling, learning organisations, and life-long learning emphasise the development of new flexible and adaptable production cultures and working practices. The discussion above illustrates that industrial cultures such as those of Britain and Ireland have not been enthusiastic in adopting Scandinavian or German production models such as flexible manufacturing or autonomous groups. It has been suggested that this may be due to wider social and cultural factors such as the demarcation between education and training, hierarchical structures of social systems, elitist and exclusive practice of university education which form the foundation of the industrial culture. Two case studies, one of an Italian company, Benetton, and the other of a British SME, Snell and Wilcox (S&W), are presented below to illustrate innovations in new forms of production cultures which build upon their own regional craft and social traditions.

Benetton: social innovation of a network organisation

Benetton exemplifies new forms of network models of technological and organisational innovations which remain rooted in the social and cultural traditions of their regions, while successfully adapting to and learning from innovations emanating from other industrial cultures. Mitter (1992) suggests that the most successful application of the principle of JIT on European soil has been in the "third Italy" (the central and north-eastern regions of Italy) in the form of creating network models of production and organisation. The Japanese system, Just-in-Time (JIT), has inspired organisation innovation in Europe. The JIT system is essentially a customer oriented approach. Central to it is the "pull" principle whereby goods are manufactured only and precisely in response to changes in market demand. The pattern of technological change is more complex in this case than the usual automation approach. JIT is a total production design method which assures strict quality control and has zero defect policies. The success of JIT depends essentially on an effective contractual relationship between the parent company and their loyal subcontractors.

These network models, described either as "flexible specialisation" or as "models of productive decentralisation", consist of networks linking small factories (subcontractors) to large companies, whereby the small factories produce parts or whole products for the big retailing companies. This organisation model is attractive to conservative planners because it strives to achieve labour flexibility, and is attractive to socialist planners because it offers the decentralisation of economic power and opportunities for self employment.

Benetton in Italy can be regarded as the most successful example of this network model of firms. Nearly 70% of the total value added of the company comes from 300 or so small artisan firms. Belussi (1992) shows the unique way Benetton has used computer-aided technology to achieve an optimum combination of production and market strategies. A novel part of Benetton's innovation network lies in achieving mass production through decentralisation of production while retaining central control of the market. In other words, the "geographical spread of the moving assembly line". Information technology is playing a crucial role in integrating the JIT strategy of production with the JIT strategy of distribution, and in the case of Benetton, the information system allows the linking up of a network of wholesalers and retailers with a large constellation of producers.

However, this "third Italy" network model is situated in the Italian regional economic cultures, and is based on the historical traditions of regions like Veneto. Companies like Benetton are able to draw upon the tacit skills of women and men workers who are involved in the decentralised operations of assembling, ironing and finishing. Non-technological and entrepreneurial aspects linked to design, trademark and advertising have been just as important as computer-aided machines in accounting for the success of Italian clothing companies. The crucial entrepreneurial characteristics of the Italian network model reside in the family like organisation structure of small Italian firms, providing a framework for distributed working, experience based learning, and the tacit dimension of entrepreneurial skills. Benetton itself is a family firm, and its networking with subcontracting firms can be regarded as part of the extended family structure, with the tacit understanding that all firms pull together for the good of the parent company. Companies like Benetton provide a model of how to use computer technology to not only improve the quality of management, control, coordination and production on the main factory floor, but also to facilitate the decentralisation of skilled work to smaller units in and around Veneto. The network model such as that of Benetton itself creates a paradox. The paradox is that whereas the decentralisation of production erodes the rights and privileges of workers, it also enhances the prospect of self-employment especially for women. Belussi questions the validity of replicating the "third Italy" model elsewhere in Europe and beyond. Decentralisation of production which is also not accompanied by the decentralisation of skill leads to the exploitation of home workers as well as workers of the small subcontracting firms.

She argues that the evolutionary growth of a "small firm network" into a "big firm" leads to the emergence of new organisational "concentrate regimes". The success of network models such as Benetton's lies also in the nature of the industry itself. One of the characteristics specific to the fashion industry is the domination of small firms, due mainly to the volatility of demand, low entry barriers and a lack of economies of scale. The Benetton strategy has been aimed specifically at reducing the potential competitive advantage of small firms in expanding its market share. Benetton's dominance over the peripheral network of subcontracting firms thus comes through its technological leadership and its retailing power. The effects of Benetton's organisational revolution, matched with a high propensity to innovate, have deeply modified the pre-existing market structure.

Organisational innovation
Benetton signifies the essence of entrepreneurial innovation based upon the traditional family and social network cultures which still exist in many parts of Europe and the developing world. The historical development of Benetton provides an insight into how informal social and cultural networks can be used to build and sustain new forms of production structures and working cultures. It is significant to note that inspite of the technological innovations and global competition, Benetton remains a family firm, consisting of one sister, Giuliana, and three brothers, Luciano, Gilberto and Carlo Benetton. The division of labour amongst the family remains clear-cut: Luciano deals with marketing, Giuliana with the design function, Gilberto with administration and finance and Carlo is in charge of production. Benetton was formed in 1965 as a general partnership, under the name of "Maglificio di Ponzano Veneto fratelli Benetton (Group di Lavoro IRES 1984). Benetton's story began with Luciano Benetton and his sister Giuliana. Luciano was a shop assistant in a textile shop in Treviso and his sister was working in an artisanal knitwear-production factory. In 1957 they decided to work together. Giuliana had discovered she had a talent for designing and making knitwear; Luciano would collect orders and Giuliana would produce them at home. So the origin of Benetton's organisational structure lies with the ancient local "putting out" system, which was never fully superseded by the factory mode of production. The Benetton draws its network characteristics from the social system, and thus provides a creative industrial cultural model for innovations in new forms of working and living.

S&W: a case study on the making of a tacit learning company

Snell & Wilcox Ltd is a high tech SME situated in Hampshire in the UK. It designs and produces "high technology" vision processing equipment for use in TV studios in UK and elsewhere. The company belongs to a new generation of network based SMEs with its production, administration, and marketing distributed geographically over sites in various parts of the world. The group's core activities relate to production activities such as R&D, assembly and quality assurance, and peripheral activities, such as planning, procuring materials, job scheduling, monitoring inventories and production status, quality assurance record keeping, marketing, processing sales orders, invoices and shipping details, personnel and training, corporate financial reporting and other financial recording.

The corporate headquarters is situated in Richmond, London where the chairman and chief executive, and the director of corporate communications, along with their personal assistants and others, are involved with corporate financial matters, and marketing and advertising. The production functions of the company are distributed geographically over three sites in the UK. There is also a company in the USA, Snell & Wilcox Inc., which forms a customer support organisation comprised of a clerical officer, a marketing person, and a product support engineer. The group also has a number of company agents situated in France, Italy and Japan, and agents in other countries. At present overall, the group is comprised of some 155 people, there are some 60 people at the Waterlooville site of Snell & Wilcox. The latest products are manufactured at Waterlooville because Electrocraft at the Liss Mill site does not have surface-mount capability. However, if possible, production is generally carried out on the site at which an item was developed. A third production unit - CEL, has recently been taken over by Snell & Wilcox. CEL differs from Snell & Wilcox and Electrocraft in the main part of the assembly work (all circuit board and mechanical manufacture and assembly) is subcontracted out, but carry out the final assembly and test in-house. Administration has now moved to the new Durford Mill site, and will shortly be followed by most of the engineering, production and test except for some products in normal series production (i.e. not subject to modification).

It is a highly successful group in which the organisational culture is cultivated by team work, shared participation, tacit knowledge and flexibility. This entrepreneurial culture is sustained by a dedicated and high skilled workforce which derives its fulfilment and self development from working in a high-tech expanding industry. However, the company recognises that an information technology (IT) system which provides effective support for improving production performance and management skills has become vitally necessary to support future growth, expansion and to enhance flexibility. Like many other small or medium businesses (SMEs), the group is interested in integrating microelectronics technology to enhance its production, management and organisational functions especially for the effective transfer of information within the organisation.

Whereas many of the SMEs have gone under and others have barely survived during the recession, S&W has not only expanded but has also become one of the leading high tech television manufacturers in the world, and it is determined to maintain this position. This remarkable success, according to our research, has been mainly due to the tacit organisational and working culture of the company. "Tacit" here means the recognition of informal participation in key processes of the organisation. The company is organised in a number of autonomous production working sites. Each site works like an old style social family unit, committed and competitive, while at the same time sensitive to the welfare and potential growth and creativity of all its members. Overall management and administration is kept to a minimum, and policy making and decision making is very much like the Japanese Quality Circle. Agreements are reached through a series of informal and formal discussions and meetings. Once the process of consultation and decision making is complete, all members of the company become committed to achieving the agreement.

Information flow throughout the company, has so far been people centred and informal, creating a working culture of trust, faith, and hope. In essence, its success depends upon its distributed organisation structure, semi autonomous group working units, informal information flow, and Quality Circle type of decision making processes. Above all, it is the people, their commitments, their expertise and their creative adaptability which makes the company what it is today, and not just the products, services and the costs. Because of the informal and social nature of the working culture, there is very little need for separate training and learning units. People learn from and with each other so the knowledge is transferred and exchanged all the time both through work as well as through social gatherings and informal meetings. If one is looking for a case of work based learning in the human centred sense then S&W is the best practical example one could find in the UK. The human centred working and learning culture of its people has enabled the company to undertake strategic policy decisions to expand and diversify its production, create an ambitious marketing and service network world wide, and become a leading high-tech SME in its domain. It should be emphasised that the company's faith in its future lies in the rich experiential knowledge, group-oriented working practice, high technical skills, informal decision making processes, and above all the mutual commitment of its people to innovation, survival and a high level of competitivity at a global level. Apart from the social flow of information within the company, individuals as well as the company's autonomous units have built up their own informal links with individuals and groups world wide.

As the company expands, the challenge is how to sustain the tacit dimension of its work and learning culture while at the same time remaining competitive in the fast changing world of high technology television. The challenge is also how to enculture newly appointed staff to the family type commitment to the company without denting the individual's identity and interests. Through its own working and social networks which include outside consultants, designers, researchers, academics, and policy makers, the company is able to gain information and exchange knowledge of production and marketing strategies in the relevant high tech sectors. The combination of informal process and formal decision making practice enables the company to undertake long term planning and make strategic moves at appropriate moments. Snell and Wilcox exemplify the practice of the human centred approach for innovation and competitiveness.

This means that the integration of any new technology in the company would be based on the assumption that people are at the centre of the decision making processes, however fully supported it is by IT systems. This systems development approach relies upon a participatory design approach involving those who use the system in the development of the system, in order to take full account of the range of explicit, implicit, and tacit knowledge within the company. Furthermore IT systems development is likely to be more effective if coordinated with a corresponding organisational culture and working practices. The system must be human-centred in the way it gathers and processes information and in the way it interacts with users. If a system is developed that does not provide tools which enable users to work effectively, it will not be used, thus paralysing the business concerned. It is held that the adoption of a human-centred approach should ensure that this does not occur. It is important that with any IT system, an organisational framework is developed which aims to facilitate and support the changes in the modus operandi of SMEs and the environment required. The issues include (Thorpe and Donaldson, 1992):

1. Organisational forms for decision support systems with proactive users.
2. Re-integration of learning with work as skill-life cycles decrease and flexibility which relies on the continuous adjustment of skills at an individual and organisational level.
3. Qualification models for successful implementation in SMEs.

The results of the case study are based on both informal and formal interviews, and group discussion sessions. The study has revealed that Snell & Wilcox Ltd, as a group, provides an interesting organisational environment (within the British cultural context) for the development of an integrated working and learning framework using informal and formal communication facilities.

Benetton and S&W: Towards the idea a tacit industrial culture

The case studies illustrate innovations in group and network working cultures which are based on the traditional family network cultures and craft traditions of service. Both have developed working and organisational environments which are rooted in their own cultural traditions and at the same time act as effective players in the global competitive market. The Benetton network model is rooted in the Italian regional economic cultures, and is based on the historical traditions of regions like Veneto. The S&W group is rooted in the very British voluntaristic traditions and the Quaker work tradition. These companies represent models for new forms of network based industrial innovations which are built around the ideas of sustainability through co-development, collaborative learning and cooperative working. Fundamental to network based innovation is the idea of tacit knowledge and skill. Tacit knowledge here enshrines experiential knowledge, personal knowledge, intuition, creativity, and human judgement. It is the tacit dimension which provides a balance between the formal and the informal, a symbiosis between the human and the machine, and an interdependence between working life and living conditions.

Much of the knowledge of an organisation is of a tacit nature, and often it requires a "translation" or modification to local circumstances. Managerial and organisational skills are very important in terms of translation, modification and the diffusion process. This points to the critical importance of human resource development which recognises the significance of the tacit dimension of knowledge flows. Science and technologies (communication multimedia, distance learning, etc.) can be employed to support the transfer, exchange and dissemination of the "pooled" technological and practical knowledge. This requires the development of cooperative and collaborative learning and working environments for creating a tacit culture which can make effective use of the 'pooled' knowledge. The crucial issue here is how to encourage new modes and trajectories of development of SMEs which support the cultivation of the tacit dimension of organisational culture, adopt life-long learning strategies, and encourage sustainable innovation.

At a European level, Benetton and S&W may provide models of production and organisational innovation small entrepreneurial companies who may like to exploit their regional traditions of skill and craft. Countries like Greece, Portugal and Ireland with their pockets or in certain cases extensive base of century old practice of craft skills, may have an advantage over the more technologically advanced countries for cultivating work practices and organisational forms which are more relevant to their own cultures. There is no reason why small enterprises in these countries cannot learn from Benetton and S&W, and leap-frog over the Fordist stage and go directly to human centred approaches, using sophisticated micro-electronics based technologies; the idea being in line with the evolutionary approach of APS.

Human Skill: beyond cognition

In seeking to define common training policies for Europe, there may be a temptation to define common core competencies and skills which allow for the flow of workers and their skills within and across organisations. The need for common skills may also arise out of the policies of social and economic cohesion and consequent strategies of harmonisation of education and training. In addition to these social and economic factors, there may also be a strong information technology push to define education in terms of core competencies and skills which can be transferred and exchanged within and across European regions without the physical flow of learners or teachers. In the case of SMEs, an even stronger case for the electronic transfer of skills may be made because of the lack of in-house training infrastructures and costs of external consultants and trainers. While the case for inter-cultural, inter-social, and language skills, as well as the case for common scientific, technological and managerial competencies is overwhelming, the danger is that the technology push may lead to describing human performance in terms of common cognitive processes, specific dispositions and action and reaction strategies. This may then lead to describing firstly learning in terms of core competencies, and then competencies in terms of the forms and rules of cognitive science. Learning could then be described as an ordered and a rule based procedure which could be broken down into discrete steps and governed by a series of rules, a kind of managed learning process. This idea of managed learning however assumes that organisations function rationally and predictably, and that people can be regarded as cognitive agents, rather than as people socially situated and possessing knowledge and skills that are culturally conditioned and given value.

One of the emerging technological research areas which takes a broader view of skill than that of the narrow technical view of cognitive science, is the area of computer supported cooperative working (CSCW). Here the idea of distributed cognition is developed which regards technology as a cognitive artifact. Artifacts serve the purpose of coordination, communication, information representation, storage and retrieval, i.e. core cognitive capabilities. Understanding these core capabilities is the key to user-centred design for cooperative working. The issue of human communication is turned into the issue of human-machine interaction, thereby shifting the idea of social mediation to the idea of mediation by the machine. This idea of interaction leads to seeing technology, for example, as providing the flexible inter-connectivity to extend the range of informal social encounters between people in work communities, e.g. over distances: a whole "space" of "new encounters" is possible, i.e. the laying out of a taxonomy of space of social interactions (CSCW, 1991).

Although this radical shift from human mediation to technological mediation recognises the importance of social interaction, human social competencies are increasingly seen in terms of cognitive skills. The crucial point here is that technology not only impacts upon the work and labour process, it also affects the description and role of skills. This trend tends to marginalise the crucial role of the tacit knowledge which people possess through its focus on their cognitive skills. It is therefore not sufficient to just study the emerging patterns of qualification and learning as a reaction to the integration of technology in the workplace, but it is also essential to study the processes of designing technology itself and taking a proactive stance to retain a balance between tacit competencies and cognitive competencies. From this perspective, the design of technological systems must be based on participation with people who really know the work process that is to be redesigned, and on the tacit skills that workers have acquired through their long and diverse experiences of learning-by-doing. This need is not only for democratic reasons but is also for strong epistemological reasons. One of the crucial epistemological issues for systems design is what Wittgenstein called "language-games". Language games in the context of design is the expression of the practices of both the users and the designers, where the users are experienced in the language games of their work or use situations, and the designers are experienced in the language games of design (Gill, SP, 1992).

This cognitive science notion of skill not only separates learning from its social and cultural contexts, but also separates individual learning from learning with peers and within the community of learners. Cognitive science centres around the "representation hypothesis": that is, the assumption that cognition rests on the manipulation of symbolic representations that can be understood as referring to objects or properties in the world (Winograd & Flores, 1986). This representation view of cognition allows for human knowledge and skill to be separated from the social context, and thereby separates objective knowledge from the tacit. This view of skill is deeply rooted in the three dreams of rationalism: the dream of the exact language, the rational method and the idea of a united science (Toulmin, 1991). The "exact language" seeks to define competencies and skill in the same universal language so as to realise their transfer across language barriers; the rational method seeks to describe skill performance in individualistic and mechanistic terms; and the united science seeks to define skill in terms of the "one best way". Although these "noble dreams" rooted in seventeenth and eighteenth century rationalism may continue to excite us for a long period of time, they may prove to be a dangerous legacy for an increasing interdependent world. Cognitive science, in building upon these "dreams", continues to seek for the description of skill in explicit, certain and unambiguous forms. This scientific description of skill is regarded as infinitely more important than the process of learning by doing or by working with or gaining knowledge from people. Description is thereby over valued and is taken as an absolute, instead being subjected to controlled use in particular circumstances. "Description will always be arbitrary and context bound, the kind and degree of arbitrariness depends upon the purposes, communicative, instructional, etc., for which the description is being fashioned"(Thorpe, 1991). Core competence are therefore as much to do with social and cultural skills as they are to do with cognitive skills.

It is therefore essential that the description of core skills and competencies for differing working domains, professions and disciplines should also consider learning contexts which enable their transfer, exchange and sharing within and across these domains. Even within the same domain, practitioners find it impossible to fully describe skills and competencies gained through long experiences. People use common sense and intuition to perform their skills effectively in different circumstances. It is the tacit dimension, i.e. knowing, common sense and intuition etc. which makes for skills, and not well structured symbolic descriptions.

Traditionally, skills are associated with the recognised production of culturally defined artifacts and skilled action is determined by social and working life contexts. Skilled action or competence is part of the value system of the culture in which action takes place. Here action embodies wisdom, skill embodies practice, practice embodies knowledge, and they are all culturally situated. The action of a skilled performer (competence) cannot be understood simply in terms of a set of rational rules and a series of structured instructions. In other words an understanding of what counts as skill cannot be reduced to descriptions of actions taken by the skilled performer.

In the modern working life, skill is a combination of traditional and technological skill, and is generally associated with a specific technology and production process. It is tempting to hypothesise that since technology such as CAD is transferable over production processes, modern skill can also be transferred across production processes. This is based on an assumption that technological skills can be separated from the praxis in which skill is learnt and applied. This is very similar to the false assumption which has been prevalent in cognitive science that objective knowledge can be separated from the tacit knowledge, and hence knowledge (objective knowledge) can be transferred across application domains.

What is transferable is the content and explicit descriptions of the objective part of the describable knowledge, but not the objective knowledge itself. Knowledge belongs to the person or a group, and resides in the social context just as skill resides in a particular work context. The effective transfer of skill or knowledge can only take place when the person/group owning the skill or knowledge is also transferred to a similar working or social environment. That is why many organisations and companies rely on specialist knowledge and high tech skill transfer, upon their consultants, and hire specialists, recruiting graduates and postgraduates from different universities and disciplines (Senker, 1993). This enables the companies to not only gain new knowledge and skill but also create a working environment in which the transfer of tacit skill and tacit knowledge takes place through participation and human communication. This brings us to a human centred framework of learning which enshrines participation within the group and interlocution with the environment, and thereby enables skill and knowledge transfer.

Many cognitive psychologists and educationists presume that the work of a skilled person is to do with problem solving, and therefore the only core skills which matter are the problem solving skills. Skill acquisition here focuses on an explicit rendering of knowledge. It is devoid of any "reflective practice" which embodies capabilities such as "seeing as", which is a form of inarticulated perception. Professional activity involves both problem finding (problem creation) and problem solving activities, problem solving cannot be separated from the activity of problem finding Schön (1983). A human centred learning framework enables us to consider issues of skill and competence in a holistic manner, within a broader horizons of the tacit dimension and human competence.

Core Competencies: a dilemma of transfer

How can we describe the core competencies and skills that reflect the wide range of vocational, educational and cultural varieties. Cooley (1991) points to the different perspectives and practices of skill training in different regions of Europe. For example, Ireland has a fairly well structured training scheme operated through its training agency FAS. However, he notes that the transition from well qualified work on the shop floor to technical and managerial posts seem to be more difficult than in Germany. The German dual systems with the on-site practical experience and off-site or college based "vocational education" seem to constitute some of the best schemes in Europe. Denmark still has a tradition of engineers qualifying through practice as well as through university. Those qualifying through practice have a shop floor-type apprenticeship and can see many role models in their companies. Furthermore, the upward mobility of people on the shop floor means that most supervisors and factory managers in SMEs will have come through this route. Because of a developing manufacturing infrastructure, problems confronting Portuguese SMEs with respect to training and new technology were very similar to those experienced by parallel companies in Greece.

A notably different perspective of training has emerged in Britain during the 1980s resulting in the rapid decline in apprenticeship training. This decline involves the replacement of apprenticeships by "training schemes". Many of these schemes are centred around a narrow machine or systems specific competence and do not provide the breadth and depth of knowledge available through such apprentice schemes as in, say, West of Germany.

The idea of core social competencies and skills requires a considerable cultural shift of British management. Currently there are very uneven patterns of SMEs in Europe. Some of them are struggling to survive by using primitive equipment, and they lack the politics for skill updating. On the other hand there are dynamic and outgoing SMEs who realise the importance of having multi-skilled workers who need to be creative, proactive and interventionist. Work based learning or learning-by-doing should focus on competencies such as the ability to acquire new knowledge and transform it ; draw conclusions about the unknown from the known; be able to adopt a holistic and critical approach; organise and manage change; undertake problem formulation and planning; accept responsibility; and be involved in team working.

It should be noted that learning programmes which are appropriate to multinationals are most unlikely to suit the requirements of SMEs. It is also foolish to believe that technology for large companies when scaled down, somehow becomes suitable for small companies. Furthermore many large companies have scales of production which mean industrial forms, quality control procedures and highly integrated systems which are not suitable to small and flexible SMEs.

One possible way forward is the network approach of work based learning. A systems of small companies networked to large companies, higher education institutions and training agencies could provide a holistic framework for learning which provides a resource for proactive learning and knowledge transfer in real life settings, across working environments and professional disciplines. Just as the idea of "economy of scope" is beginning to make sense in the manufacturing world of high quality small batch production for large scale companies, it similarly makes sense for SMEs to link into "network economies of scope" which are comprised of mutually supportive networks of SMEs.

Within the human centred framework, core competencies are part and parcel of working life and living environments, the social competence is inseparable from the functional competence, and the objective knowledge is inseparable from the experiential and the personal knowledge. While the objective part of core competencies in the scientific, economic, and technological domains may be transferred through formal channels such as text books, journals, and electronic media, the tacit dimension (experiential knowledge and personal knowledge) can only be transferred through the exchange and flow of practitioners and expertise.

Learning technologies based on the narrow production-oriented thinking favour the legitimisation of the dominant technologies, in the sense that recognition is derived from a homogeneous and enclosed peer group. This occurs against a background where economy and management are dominant forces which give rise to and/or reinforce structures that force people into a position of dependence or shut them out of society. Core competencies in the dominant technological mould are conditioned by the requirements of technology rather than by the requirements of the individual or the human organisation. Although apparently transferable, the purposefulness of technical competencies is determined by the availability and accessibility of technology, and not through supporting human environments which are able to interpret, translate and transfer these competencies to meet the needs of the receiving organisation. Innovation in this context is controlled by technology rather than being supported and cultivated by the skills and competencies, expertise and tacit knowledge of people. This is the dilemma of the increasing dependency of "Electronic Fordism" of the 21st Century (Gill, 1993).

Apart from the dependency barrier of technology, the concept of core competencies and their transfer also face problems of transcending disciplinary and sectoral boundaries. For example, there are problems of interaction across disciplines and problems of communication across boundaries. Core competencies which are located in one discipline, such as skills particular to a specific technology or a production process may only be transferable to another domain if the same technology exists or the same production process exists in that domain. Other barriers and obstacles to making full use of the potential of core skills could be of a valuative, institutional and economic form. These forms may lead to core skills being defined in terms of the "best cognitive practice" and dominant technology, in order to minimise the interdisciplinary and sectoral barriers. The danger is that the value and potential of core skills necessary to overcome these barriers may be lost.

Learning As Social Innovation: towards a human centred framework

The discussion on anthropocentric production systems highlights the need for new forms of education and training which support lifelong learning and enhance human skill and competence. The section on multi-skilling illustrates how the impact of technological innovation in the manufacturing sector goes beyond the narrow issues of production. It has broader implications resulting from economic, cultural and political realities. Later sections on skill and cognition show the limitations of the cognitive science view of skill and the techno-centric view of working life for an understanding of skill. This makes a case for a human centred view of skill and learning for innovation. Making this case recognises the reality that companies in the UK and Ireland give a very low (if any) priority to self-development, life-long learning, and multi-skilling. They are not proactive in initiating or undertaking new innovations in anthropocentric working practices or organisations structures. Moreover, the university education and training systems in both the UK and Ireland are still elitist, hierarchical and exclusive. It is evident that the narrow, view of organisational culture and working practices within the British and Irish industries is rooted in the "machine-centred" view of knowledge and skill, cost benefit view of work, the Taylorist view of production, and a causal view of science and technology.

The "machine-centred" view of skill excludes social competencies and describes human competencies purely in terms of technical skills. It thereby leads to the implementation of training programmes which separate the social value of work from its technical function in the name of efficiency and cost effectiveness. This technical view of competence renders learning into a managed form of training. The danger of this narrow view is that competence may be described as skill devoid of uncertainty, and that training may be used as an instrument for eliminating human judgement and intuition. Furthermore, by rendering explicit the "secrets" of craft, we prepare the basis of a rule-based system. The disadvantage of this view of training is that it separates learning from people's own knowledge, skills and expertise. Consequently, it prevents learners from enjoying the experience and gaining dignity from transmitting their experiences to the future generations (Cooley, 1987). Moreover, the machine-centred view of skill does not allow any questions about the validity or sanity of a *system* which destroys initiative and rots brains", and thereby acts as a barrier to any fundamentally new thinking on work and its purpose (Schumacher, 1991). The consequences of this narrow view of industrial culture is that it inhibits educational and training innovations which could enable the transfer, exchange and sharing of skill, knowledge, and experiences within and across organisations and social systems.

The human centred perspective, on the other hand, provide a wider view of the industrial culture. This perspective celebrates human creativity, and skill, and facilitates a purposive view of work and living, and it regards work and living as complementary and interdependent activities. The worker is not just a producer and a consumer of products but is also a social citizen with interests and concerns for the creation of socially responsive working and living conditions. This view is shared by the alternative, "Buddhist view of economics" (Schumacher) in which humans have a chance to develop their faculties, overcome their ego-centredness by joining with other people in a common risk, and produce goods and services for a becoming existence. This view of economics emphasises the development, liberation, dignity, freedom, and fulfilment of the worker. It does not measure the standard of living by the amount of annual consumption.

From this wider view of human-centredness, the idea of life-long learning requires a change of perspective on work from a purely production and consumption ethos to the ethos of working and living. This requires a change in the notion of learning from the idea of technical competence and skill to the idea of social competence and tacit knowing. However, this developmental focus of learning requires the adoption of a human centred view of working and purposeful living in which work is measured in terms of production and reproduction of resources rather than solely in terms of consumption. Technology, from this human centred perspective, should be designed as a facilitating tool for social innovation and emancipation instead of as an instrument for technical change.

The notion of social innovation from the human centred perspective is concerned with the social and cultural shaping of science and technology for making the world a better place for living and working. Innovation is seen in terms of social welfare and economic codevelopment. The notion of learning as social innovation takes a developmental perspective of working and living with relationship to both the individual and the society. This human centred approach sees the citizen, not just as a producer and consumer of products, but also as a social and cultural being who is a consumer and producer of knowledge, a user and a social assessor of science and technology, and a proactive participant in society at the same time. It focuses on enriching the interrelationships of individuals within the community by building upon the fundamental social values of cooperation, collaboration, interdependence and harmony. These values enable the development of socio-economic, educational and welfare infrastructures and processes which build on social and cultural resources. This approach of innovation promotes notions of codevelopment, coexistence and valorisation of diversity.

A central challenge for learning as social innovation is to shape education and research cultures which are based on the notion that "education is about the transmission, exchange and enrichment of cultures" rather than about the transfer of technical skills alone. To shape learning organisations requires the cultivation of scope and emancipation in the emerging network society. The idea of social innovation builds upon social competencies and widens the learning horizon from the idea of acquiring cognitive competencies within the narrowness of technological innovation. Social innovation here means organising change rather than just managing change. It is about acquiring social competencies for working life and living conditions rather than about acquiring cognitive skills to cope with technology embedded organisational structures. It places an emphasis on the processes of change and not just the results of change, and it is about problem finding rather than just problem solving. The SEAKE Centre's project "PAROSI" (Gill, 1985, 1991) emphasised the notion of social innovation and evolved an approach for acquiring the necessary competencies to deal with the realities of complex socio-cultural and socio-economic domains. The learning environment provided a complex social environment in which participants were able to act as learners, as teachers, as experts and as social mediators at various levels of knowledge exchange. The knowledge and language skills acquired by the team were not just of benefit for the project duration but were also of benefit for future use in other learning and real life practical situations. Emphasis was placed on the knowledge, experiences, intuition, expectations and cultural backgrounds of learners. The project consisted of a human network of adult learners, tutors, education officers from the local education authority, volunteers from the local community as well as student volunteers from both the local universities, voluntary and full time tutors, professionals and community experts, as well as researchers from both the university and continuing education sectors. The project was based in the local community centre and was linked to local schools and further education centres. It involved 38 adult students and about 60 volunteer tutors in the form of a learning network. It was a "learning organisation without walls", and has since been regarded as an important experiment of 'learning as social innovation'. The project subsequently became a basis for the EC Social Fund pilot project on *New Technology, Numeracy and Life Skills for Adults* (1983-1985).

"PRELUDE" (Programme of Research and Liaison between Universities for Development) is an example of a learning network which extends the learning philosophy of "PAROSI" from a local level to an international level. PRELUDE (Thill, 1993) is concerned with the transfer of scientific and technological skills and expertise and their appropriation through the auspices of an associated network of individuals. The networks are particularly active in a range of countries in the South and are composed of "voluntary researchers from different backgrounds, disciplines and horizons". The network is action oriented and challenges the rationalist view of development. It seeks social structures and functions that operate in harmony over time. Thus "inventiveness and long term efficiency go through pro-active suggestions for alternatives" requiring much individual involvement.

It recognises that a world governed by economic issues, with competition, and short term views as the rule encourages a techno-science where there is global domination of the technological, economic and financial processes. Therefore orientation is required for long term sustainability. However the notion of sustainable development does not signify subjecting humanity to single law: judicial or economic. In relation to diversity of need, action research should seek individual autonomy, and freedom.

The concept of co-development changes the meaning of knowledge and skill transfer. "It is expertise and skills which are exchanged, and not established and institutional knowledge or technologies". The network approach enables complex, highly heterogeneous situations to be tackled in a systematic and global fashion by putting into perspective the different symbolic, economic, educational, ethical, social, political, organisational and ecological components and dimensions. "Far from replacing institutions, associated networks complement them; they give institutions back their capacity to institute, and in so doing displace acquired balances. This is a pathway which promotes new centres of creativity within institutions and thus increases their capacity to innovate" (Thill, 1993).

Learning Organisations and Social Innovation

In order for enterprises to undertake organisational innovation, it is necessary to develop learning environments which promote continuous self learning and self development, as well as motivation, team work, autonomy and responsibility. In this scenario of the learning organisation the focus is on group learning or working situations where people have different interests, needs, aspirations and assumptions. In finding a harmonious balance between individual and group learning, dialogue acts as catalyst of change. Cultural assumptions are part of peoples cultures. They are expressed in the form of relationships. Dialogue helps people to resolve conflicts and work out these relationships. It is not the content of opinions or assumptions which matters but the process of working out relationships. In dialogue we seek coherence and order which is purposeful. We seek coherence through participation, communication, and sharing. Participating in a dialogue means partaking of the whole and taking part in it; not merely the whole group, but the whole (Bohm, 1993). This holistic view of dialogue provides an important conceptual handle for developing learning organisations which involve the sharing and exchange of knowledge and experiences. Docherty (1991) gives a management perspective of learning and points out that the nature of the learning organisation is very dependent upon the organisational culture, for example a "closed administrative culture" gives low priority to personal involvement and self learning. A "change-oriented culture" promotes personal learning and is characterised by communication and delegation. He comments that the Japanese "Human Resource Intensive" strategy recruits personnel with high skill levels and invests highly in the individual. Compared to this, the Anglo Saxon countries focus on the "mobility" strategy which recruits personnel with high skill levels, but relies on the market and the individual to exhibit initiative and flexibility. Docherty compares international strategies for skill development. The Anglo Saxon market led strategy shows once again some limitations for creating organisational cultures which enable participation, dialogue and life long learning. He cites Peddler's observation that "the learning organisation is not an entity but a 'generative theory', mobilising energy to shape shared perception and the will to change, as well as leading to concrete actions". This notion of the learning organisation is an interesting concept for further development.

Human centred concepts such as transcendence, shaping, sustainability, renewal and human purpose extend the dialogical process between the individual and the group at a societal level. This perspective of human centredness thereby provide a wider societal framework for the learning organisation. Some of the key ideas for developing a learning network as a social innovations process are outlined below.

- to cultivate a social and cultural shaping of science and technology which is based on the notions of the "valorisation" of diversity and coexistence;
- the need for the idea of social citizenship which regards the citizen not just as a producer and a consumer but also an active participant in decision making, and a cultural shaper and social assessor of science and technology;
- the use of holistic approaches of human centred systems design within the broader societal contexts of working life and living environments;
- education needs to be viewed as transmission, exchange and enrichment of cultures rather than as just transfer of technical skill and competence;
- to adopt a multicultural perspectives of cohesion and developments, and holistic notions of sustainability and co-development.

Human Centred Concepts for Learning as Social innovation

Developmental perspective
This perspective builds upon the social and cultural knowledge and experience of the individual and the group in order to shape and organise change. It recognises the constraints of "linear thinking", and promotes social innovation based on the dialectical view point in order to understand the tensions and contradictions of the diversity of social and cultural patterns. "Dialectical interplay of 'being part of ' and 'transcending' is one of the most essential aspects of understanding culturally bounded differences of innovative processes. The focus on how this interplay is carried out in different cultures is central to the human-centred approach" (Gill, 1996).

The shaping perspective
The shaping perspective sees innovation from a broader social environmental perspective. It is a proactive and action oriented process which does not fit into the causal view of science or the mechanistic world view. The shaping perspective, with its is roots in the idea of mutual exchange, takes a holistic view in which participants involved in innovation are able

to cross their own language, cultural, professional and organisational boundaries in order to exchange knowledge and experiences.

Social sustainability
The focus of this perspective is the harmonious inter-relationships between the individual, society and the social environment. These relationship reflect the common faiths and diverse hopes as well contradictions and tensions of social and cultural environments. This dynamic connectivity is central to the process of social learning and renewal. It provides a social framework within which the individual remains as part of while transcending the social boundaries, and thus provides for continuous learning and social renewal. The challenge and scope for human centredness is to shape science and technology which uses the potential of social sustainability to cultivate the processes of social innovation.

Dialogue and human development
From the human centred perspective dialogue is concerned with the exchange of knowledge, experience and practice. At a social level, dialogue is about cross-cultural understanding, sharing of values, minimising of misunderstandings, and accepting conflicts. This perspective of dialogue continually renews the interdependence between personal knowledge, experiential knowledge and explicit knowledge. It thereby confirms the diversity of knowledges rooted in the social and cultural contexts of peoples and rejects the idea of just one form of objective (scientific) knowledge. This perspective of dialogue shifts the focus of development from primarily being economic to that of human development. This cultural view of development however raises a doubt about maintaining individual autonomy which has increasingly been defined in economic terms in Western industrialised societies. Human centredness, does overcome this doubt as it seeks to shift the notion of material centred autonomy to autonomy arising out the dynamic balance between the individual, society and nature. This social view of autonomy poses a central challenge for developing the processes of social innovation (Gill 1991,1993; Rasmussen 1993).

The foundational concept of human centredness is essentially a developmental and learning process. It seeks a social and cultural understanding of working life, technology and living environments From this wider societal perspective, it regards learning essentially as a process of social and cultural innovation.

Conclusions

The APS research promotes humane forms of organisational structures and working practices, and emphasises holistic forms education and training which cultivate human skill and competence required for the modern manufacturing industry. The human centred approach enshrines human purpose, participation and emancipation, and thereby provides a wider societal horizon for shaping learning. To shape learning from a wider societal perspective, however, requires the creation of new alliances between universities, enterprises and communities. Learning from this societal perspective can be seen as a process of social and organisational innovation rather than a practice of "exclusion" and "demarcation" of the traditional university education and industrial training. The projects, PAROSI and PRELUDE exemplify learning as a social innovation process, and share a vision of enterprise innovation with Benetton and S&W. These network models of enterprise and anthropocentric models of production provide a way forward for developing human centred frameworks of learning as social and organisational innovation.

References

Badham, R. (1991), "Technology, Work and Culture", *AI & Society*, Springer-Verlag, Vol. 5, No. 4.
Banke, P., Clematide, B., and Rasmussen L.B. (1991), *Prospects for anthropocentric systems in Denmark*, FOP 255, APS Series, MONITOR, CEC, Brussels.
Boman, P, Senker S, and Senker P (1991), *Skill Implications of Information Technologies for the European Community*, EEC Conference 17 and 18 October 1991, Report M-BR 10.
Belussi, F. (1992), "Benetton Italy: Beyond Fordism and Flexible Specialisation. The Evolution of the Network Model", in *Computer-aided Manufacturing and Women's Employment*, S. Mitter (ed.), Springer-Verlag.
Bohm, D. (1993), "For Truth and Dialogue", in *Resurgence*, Devon, January/February 1993.
Boman, P, Senker S, and Senker P (1991), *Skill Implications of Information Technologies for the European Community*, EEC Conference 17 and 18 October 1991, Report M-BR 10.
Brödner, P. (1989), "In Search of the Computer-Aided Craftsman", *AI & Society*, Vol.3, No.1.
Charles, T., Charles, R., and Roulstone, A. (1991) *Prospects for Anthropocentric Production Systems in Britain*, APS Research Series, Report FOP 252, FAST, European Commission.
CHERI (1986), New Technology and Human Resource Development in the Automobile Industry, *OECD/CHERI*, General Distribution.
Cooley, M. (1987), *Architect or Bee?: the human price of technology*, Hogarth Press: London 1987.
Cooley, M. (1989), *European Competitiveness in the 21st Century*, FAST, EEC, June, 1989.
Cooley, M. (1991), Project ARTISAN, Report: D1004/P7064, DELTA, European Commission
CSCW (1991), *Proceedings of the Second European Conference on Computer Supported Cooperative Working*, Bannon L. and Robinson M. and Schmidt, K. (Eds.), Amsterdam.
FAST (1991): Prospects for Anthropocentric Production Systems, APS Research Series, Reports FOP , FAST: European Commission.
Docherty, P. (1991), "The Utilisation of Information Technology: A management Perspective on a Learning Issues", in Nyhan (ed.), *Developing People's Ability to Learn*, European Interuniversity Press, Brussels
Dodgson, M. (ed.)(1989), Technology Strategy and the Firm, Longman.

Eichener, V. (1991), Organisations and Concepts in German Industry, APS Research Series, Report FOP 270, FAST, European Commission

Gill, K.S. (1985), Basic Education and New Technology, Final Report, EEC Social Fund, European Commission, June, 1985

Gill, K.S. (ed.)(1986), *Artificial Intelligence For Society*, John Wiley & Sons, Chichester, 1986

Gill, K.S. (1988), "Artificial intelligence and social action: education and training", in Göranzon B and Josefson T (eds., 1988), *Knowledge, Skill and Artificial Intelligence*, Springer-Verlag.

Gill, K.S. (1991), "Artificial Intelligence for Social Citizenship: Towards an anthropocentric technology", *Journal of Applied Artificial Intelligence*, Hemisphere, Vol. 5.1, 1991.

Gill, K.S. (1992), "Human Centredness: A 21st Century Paradigm for Industrial Cultures" in *Human Centred Systems in the Global Economy*, (ed.) Masuda Y., Springer-Verlag: London, 1992.

Gill, K.S. (1993), "Socially Sustainable Technology: an agenda for human promotion", *in le Nuove tecnologie per lepromozione umana*, (ed.), A. Ardigò, Angeli, Milano, 1993

Gill, S.P. (1992), *"Dialogue and Design for Computer-Base Technology"*, in *Human Centred Systems in the Global Economy*, (ed.) Masuda Y, Springer-Verlag, London, 1992

Göranzon, B. & Florin, M. (Eds.), *Artificial Intelligence, Culture and Language: on education and work*, Springer-Verlag, 1990

Haywood, B. & Bessant (1989), New Directions in Electronic Manufacture, IFS, UK

Hofstede, G. (1984), Cultures Consequences. International Differences in Work-Related Values, Beverly Hills.

Jones, B. (1988), "Work and Flexible Automation in Britain", in *Work, Employment and Society*, Vol. 2, No. 4.

Lloyd, C. (1988), "Restructuring in the West Midlands Clothing Industry", in *New Technology, Work and Employment*, Vol. 2, No. 4.

Noble, D. (1989), "Cockpit Cognition: Education, the Military, and Cognitive Engineering", *AI & Society*, Vol.3, No.4

Mitter, S. (ed., 1992), *Computer-aided Manufacturing and Women's Employment*, Springer-Verlag.

Nyhan, B. (ed., 1991), *Developing People's Ability to Learn*, European Interuniversity Press, Brussels.

O'Siochru, S., and Dillon, B. (1991), Prospects for Anthropocentric Production Systems in Ireland, APS Research Series, Report FOP 258, FAST, European Commission

Rasmussen, L.B. (1993), Human Centred Methods of Social and Technical Design, Working Paper, Technical University of Denmark, Lyngby.

Rosenbrock, H.H. (ed.), *Designing Human Centred Technology: A Cross Disciplinary Project in Computer Aided Manufacture*, Springer-Verlag, 1989.

Schumacher, E.F. (1991), "Buddhist Economics", in *The Best of Resurgence*, (ed.) Button, J., Green Books: Devon, 1991.

Schön, D. A. (1983), *The Reflective Practitioner*, Basic Books.

Senker, J. (1993), "The Contribution of Tacit Knowledge to Innovation", in *AI & Society*, Vol. 7.3.

Thorpe, J. and Donaldson, L. (1992), A Research Report on Snell & Wilcox, SEAKE Centre, University of Brighton, November 1992.

Thorpe, J. (1991), Learning, Experiences and Learners, Working Paper, SEAKE Centre University of Brighton.

Thill, G. (1993), "Relevance of Associated Networks for/in a Sustainable Information and Communication Society", 2nd EC-Japan Conference on The future of Industry in the Global Context, Essen, Germany, March 15-19, 1993.

Toulmin, S. (1991), "The Dream of the exact language", in Göranzon, B. and Florin, M. (eds.), *Dialogue and Technology*, Springer-Verlag, 1991.

von Bandemer, S., Henning, J. and Hilbert, J. (1991), Prospects for Anthropocentric Production Systems in Germany, APS Research Series, Report FOP 251, FAST: European Commission.

Winograd, T. and Flores, F. (1986), *Understanding Computers and Cognition: A New Foundation for Design*, Ablex: New Jersey, 1986.

Wyatt, G. (1989), New Technology and the Economic Organisation of the Clothing Industry, Technology Analysis and Strategic Management, Vol. 1 No 3

GPSR Compliance

The European Union's (EU) General Product Safety Regulation (GPSR) is a set of rules that requires consumer products to be safe and our obligations to ensure this.

If you have any concerns about our products, you can contact us on

ProductSafety@springernature.com

In case Publisher is established outside the EU, the EU authorized representative is:

Springer Nature Customer Service Center GmbH
Europaplatz 3
69115 Heidelberg, Germany